ACCOUNTING RESEARCH IN THE 1980s AND ITS FUTURE RELEVANCE

Edited and co-authored by:
Richard Mattessich
Arthur Anderson & Co.
Professor emeritus
University of British Columbia

With Contributions by:
R.K. Atiase, Stanley Baiman, Michael Gibbins, R.S. Kaplan, J.A. Ohlson, A.J. Richardson, D.B. Thornton, S. Tse, and John Wilson.

The Canadian Certified General Accountants' Research Foundation

La Fondation de recherche de l'Association des comptables généraux licenciés du Canada

Research Monograph Number 17

MONOGRAPHS PUBLISHED BY THE CANADIAN CGA RESEARCH FOUNDATION

No. 1: Historical Cost Accounting and its Rationality, by Yuji Ijiri

No. 2: Accounting for Local Governments in Canada: The State of the Art, by Arthur Beedle (Out of Print)

No. 3: Local Government Financial Management and Accounting: A Research Framework, by Katherine Graham (Out of Print)

No. 4: Accountants' Roles in Industrial Organizations and Access to Information, by Newman, Smart, Vertinsky and Kanetkar

No. 5: The Financial Reporting of Contingencies and Uncertainties: Theory and Practice, by Daniel Thornton

No. 6: Research in Audit Decision Making: Rationale, Evidence and Implications, by Robert Ashton (Out of Print)

No. 7: Modern Accounting Research: History, Survey and Guide, by Richard Mattessich

No. 8: International Conflict of Accounting Standards, by Kenneth Most

No. 9: La compatibilité en périodes de changements de prix, par Daniel Zéghal

No. 10: Risk Assessment in Accounting and Auditing, by Theodore Mock and Ilan Vertinsky

No. 11: The Serviceability of Financial Information: A Survey, by Raymond Chambers and Haim Falk

No. 12: Materiality: An Empirical Study of Actual Auditor Decisions, by Chris Robinson and Len Fertuck

No. 13: Product Differentiation in Auditing: Auditor Choice in the Market for Unseasoned New Issues, by Dan Simunic and Michael Stein

No. 14: Analytical Review Procedures and Processes in Auditing, by Stanley Biggs, Theodore Mock and Paul Watkins

No. 15: Le marché de la vérification au Canada, par Daniel Zéghal

No. 16: The Value of Communication in Agency Contracts: Theory and Experimental Evidence, by Joyce Berg, Lane Daley, Frank Gigler and Chandra Kanodia

No. 17: Accounting Research in the 1980s and its Future Relevance, by Richard Mattesich.

No. 18: Accounting for Options: No Longer an Option, by Wanda Wallace and Duane Smith.

No. 19: Experimental Tests of Auditing as a Credibility Generating Mechanism, by Nicholas Dopuch and Ron King.

Ordering information is available from:

The CCGA Research Foundation
Suite 740, 1176 West Georgia Street
Vancouver, B.C. Canada V6E 4A2
Telephone: (604) 669-3555
Facsimile: (604) 689-5845

ISBN 0-919521-08-8

The Canadian Certified General Accountants' Research Foundation was incorporated and registered as a charitable foundation on May 30, 1979. The creation of the foundation grew from the desire of members of the Certified General Accountants' Association of Canada to make a meaningful contribution to accounting research in Canada by sponsoring research which would advance the accounting community as a whole. It is our desire to encourage pure and applied research in the areas of auditing, accounting and finance.

This monograph is the seventeenth in a series to be published by The Canadian Certified General Accountants' Research Foundation as part of CGA-Canada's continuing research effort. Each monograph expresses the viewpoint of its authors, and has been neither approved nor disapproved by CGA-Canada. These mongraphs are intended to stimulate thought, discussion and debate on matters relating to accounting, auditing and finance. The foundation welcomes comments from readers.

Ernest J. Boudreau, FCGA
President
The Canadian Certified General
Accountants' Research Foundation
May 1991

To the memory of our mothers.

The care a discipline bestows on its past,
reflects the hope it puts in its future.

Contents

Preface

The 1980s were unparalleled by any other decade when it came to the diversification and volume of accounting research. The number of academic accounting journals trebled during this single decade,[1] and accounting literature expanded into many directions. The result has been not merely a great richness of contemporary research, but also a bewildering variety that is difficult to survey and penetrate—even by academics, all of whom nowadays are bound to specialize. More than ever before, there is a need to discern meaningful patterns in this kaleidoscope of research interests.

This Supplementary Volume to the reprint edition of *Modern Accounting Research: History, Survey, and Guide,* similar to the original volume, presents surveys and related articles on recent accounting research. The need for such an anthology and its updating hardly needs to be emphasized. Accounting research has proliferated enormously, and theory texts (in contrast to readings with detailed commentaries) need to be supplemented, as they can no longer give sufficient details of various research endeavours. My Commentary will assume a more dominant position, not limited to the articles presented in this anthology, but offering a general overview of important publications and trends in accounting research during the past decade or so. The Commentary, more than the number or range of articles, justifies the title *Accounting Research in the 1980s and its Future Relevance.* For this reason, and due to the small number of articles reprinted in this volume, I have chosen a single, comprehensive, and above all, general Commentary at the beginning of this anthology, instead of specific commentaries in front of each Part (as in the Main Volume). This Commentary (and its subdivisions) attempts to integrate significant accounting events and research directions during the 1980s with a short discussion of each of the six articles incorporated into this volume. Although such a survey is bound to be slanted by personal experience, I hope to have captured the most essential features of this decade. Furthermore, it is important for us accountants to reflect on whence we are coming and whither we are going.

This book consists of six parts: Part I contains the Commentary, consisting of eleven Sections (i to xi) and a Bibliography. In looking at contemporary accounting theory, I have focussed on major trends instead of concentrating on technical details. Thus, despite referring to many individual publications, I have tried to maintain enough distance to show the "forest" rather than individual "trees". Section (i) of this commentary offers "A Glance into the 'Real World'", its difficulties, and its present as well as potential impact on accounting. Section (ii) asks "Is Accounting History Becoming Fashionable" and shows that there is, indeed, a growing endeavour by accounting academics to fathom the evolutionary forces behind our discipline. Section (iii), supported by a survey-paper by Kaplan [1986], see Part II, concentrates on "The Criticism of Management Accounting" recently encountered in the literature, its methodological impact, and some reactions. Section (iv), supported by a survey paper by Richardson and Gibbins [1988], see Part III, offers a combined discussion of "Organizational and Behavioural Accounting", emphasizing various branches of recently emerging organizational accounting research. Section (v), supported by a survey-paper by Atiase and Tse [1986] and one by Ohlson [1990], see Part IV, deals with "Positive Theory and Financial Accounting", discusses the continuation of established trends and briefly refers to other publications by J.A. Ohlson, who made and contributed to some of the most original accounting papers of this decade. Section (vi), supported by an award-winning paper by Thornton [1986], see Part V, deals with such related topics as "Income Measurement, the Ups and Downs of Inflation Accounting, and Social Accountability". It tries to clarify some misunderstandings about inflation accounting, and offers references to various branches of "social accounting." Section (vii), supported by a survey-paper by Baiman [1990], see Part VI, discusses some aspects of "Agency-Contract Theory", particularly the relationships among agency theory, management accounting, super-agency-contract theory, ethics and other recent trends. The remaining sections are not complemented by any reprinted paper: Section (viii) deals with "Research in Auditing", and tries to give a concise survey of major publications and trends during the last decade; Section (ix) does something similar for "International Accounting Research"; and Section (x) shows that there exists a "Growing Concern about the Reality Behind Accounting, and Other Foundational Issues". It raises questions as to the reality behind such notions as "income", "owner's equity", etc., and whether accountants measure real phenomena. An Epilogue, Section (xi), and the Bibliography to Part I close the Commentary.[2]

Several specialized accounting areas are not treated in the Commentary, but short references are supplied on the following: tax accounting during the 1980s continued to be occupied with issues of deferrals and related allocation problems. This research is reflected predominantly in the *Journal of Accountancy*—e.g., Davidson, Rasch and Weil [1984], Robbins and Swyers [1984], Skekel and Fazzi [1984], Stepp [1985]—and (since 1989) in *The Journal of the American Taxation Association*, also since 1987 in the journal *Advances in Taxation*.

Pension Accounting gained increased attention during the 1980s, and interesting contributions can be found by Skinner [1980], Schipper and Weil [1982], Pesando and Clarke [1983], Landsman [1986], Francis and Reiter [1987], Kemp [1988] and others, as well as in the survey article by Stone [1982].

Oil and Gas Accounting made further strides in the 1980s, and continued to challenge the historical cost method as well as existing standards, e.g., Dhaliwal [1980], Collins, Rozeff and Dhaliwal [1981], Collins, Rozeff and Salatka [1982], Lilien and Pastena [1982], Larker and Revsine [1983], Dharan [1984], Lys [1984], Wolfson [1985], Butterworth and Falk [1986], Maglio [1986], and others; for example, see also the *Journal of Petroleum Accounting*.

And, last but not least, the increasing interest in research in Accounting Education ought to be mentioned. Such research was previously published in *The Accounting Review* (e.g., Amernic and Beechy [1984]), and other journals. Since early 1986, the major outlet for such research has been the AAA's specialized journal *Issues in Accounting Education*.

The original volume was designed to be "a guide for students, practitioners and academics alike". The favorable response it received seems to provide evidence that this anthology fulfilled those goals. But the response also indicated that, in addition, this book has become a valuable *reference work*— not least due to a comprehensive INDEX OF NAMES (of almost 1,000 persons and institutions, some of them with more than 50 entries), now enriched by another comprehensive INDEX OF NAMES in this Supplementary Volume.

The remaining Parts, II to VI, contain the six reprint-papers (Numbers 1 to 6) and a biographical update of authors and editor, as well as the Index of Names.[3] Due to constraints imposed upon this Supplementary Volume by the publisher, the number of papers has been limited. But I hope that the comprehensive Commentary compensates for these constraints, as it offers some 500 reference publications to supplement those readings. I may add at this point that I have avoided the royal "we" and consistently used the first person, except where referring not only to myself but to the reader or other persons.

My thanks go, first of all, to The Canadian Certified General Accountants' Research Foundation and its Research Committee for providing the major financial support, and to the Social Sciences and Humanities Research Council of Canada and the Faculty of Commerce and Business Administration of U.B.C. for their continuous support. Special thanks go to the contributors and their publishers who have given permission for reproduction of the original articles. Further thanks go to our secretaries, Ms. Corinne McDonald and Ms. Christine Yungen for typing the many drafts of the manuscript. I am most obliged to all of those who assisted or advised me in compiling this volume, above all to Mr. Jasbir Singh Dhaliwal, my research assistant, to Professor Dan Thornton, and to Professor Yoshiaki Koguchi, visiting scholar from Chuo University, for valuable advice. Finally, I am grateful to the staff of The Canadian CGA Research Foundation and its management: Lyle Handfield, Keith Scott, Dr. Derek Yee, an anonymous reviewer and copy editor, and the staff who assumed the responsibility for both the production of the Index of Names and the proofreading of the reprinted articles; above all, I should like to express special thanks to Stephen Spector for the great competence and enthusiasm with which he took care of this project during the last year.

R.M.
Vancouver, B.C.
March 1991

PART I: Editor's Commentary: A Decade Of Growth, Sophistication, And Impending Crisis

"Our age was cultivated thus at length,
but what we gained in skill we lost in strength."
John Dryden

(i) A Glance Into The "Real World"

The 1980s were a decade of mergers and transition, perhaps laying the ground for a crisis of still unknown dimensions. Environmental degradation and over-indebtedness, for example, are time bombs, and the question is merely "when will they go off?".[4] Momentous economic events have deeply affected the accounting profession: the bankruptcies of an inordinate number of American and Canadian banks; the 500 billion dollar deficit of the U.S. Savings and Loan industry, together with the alleged fraudulence involved; and the use of dubious accounting and financial practices to camouflage the magnitude of the problem, as well as waning trust towards public accountants in general.[5] It is symptomatic of an age which rewarded the spend-thrift that the "thrift institutions" were the ones wasting more money than any other "industrial" sector. This was reinforced by the increasing indebtedness of American industry, accelerated by friendly and not-so-friendly takeovers, many of which were (and still are) financed through leveraged buy-outs, in which "junk bonds" played a significant role. The disastrous economic consequences of such over-indebtedness have already begun to make themselves felt, and the accounting consequences will become even more obvious under the recent U.S. Statement of Financial Accounting Standards No.94 (SFAS 94) requiring the "Consolidation of all Majority-Owned Subsidiaries".

This situation is compounded by the aggressive international lending practices of major banks, leading to the unmanageable indebtedness (estimated in 1989 to be about US $1.3 trillion) of many Third World countries, as well as subsequent repercussions upon the entire international financial system. This is not to speak of the deliberate laundering of drug monies by many banks of "high repute", Wall Street insider-trading scandals, or the scandal of the Chicago commodity exchange.[6] That such corrosive practices could happen, at hitherto-unknown dimensions, indicates that our relatively expensive mechanism of financial control—which is ultimately what a good deal of accounting is all about—seems to be inadequate. If public accountants argue that it is not their task to discover fraudulence and financial incompetence, nor to anticipate possible bankruptcies, then surely there is a need for a different and more thorough social system of financial controls. And who else could manage such a system but accountants?[7] It is ironic, just when American academic accounting has become more sophisticated than ever before and has assumed international leadership, our "financial cybernetics" has proven to be most inadequate.

Perhaps even the best control system will fail, once the moral fibre of an entire continent has begun to tear. And it may be no coincidence that the *Report on the National Commission on Fraudulent Financial Reporting* received the 1989 AAA Wildman Medal Award. Of course, dubious accounting practices are not limited to the American continent; the excellent book by I. Griffiths [1986] *Creative Accounting*, for example, affords insight into misleading accounting practices in Great Britain. Even if these practices stem from broader social problems, there are many who lay at least some blame on the shoulders of our profession.[8]

Yet not all negative effects stem from the financial sector; the industrial, trade, and government sectors too, have contributed considerably. The decline in productivity and international competitiveness, the immense trade and government deficits, the unrelenting accumulation of public debts (over $3 trillion in the USA and over $350 billion in Canada by the beginning of 1990), have all had a direct impact on accounting. Although accountants cannot be held responsible for the myopic "casino mentality" of a good deal of North American industry, nor for the other evils of our time, in most of the areas mentioned above, the control which accounting is supposed to exercise was either deficient or ignored. And as to the productivity problem, several authors did indeed blame accounting, e.g., Drucker [1973/85], p. 69, Halberstam [1986], pp. 230-232, Johnson and Kaplan [1987], particularly Chapter 8, and Peters [1988], pp. 480-502. During the past decade, the "paper prophets" of industry learned a one-sided lesson from modern finance theory: they were too much concerned with paper profits, with making money for the short-run, rather than making "things" for the long haul. Although moving money around can facilitate the generation of social wealth, it is no substitute for its production. And directly at the doorstep of the academic community lies the alleged neglect of relevant managerial accounting research at the expense of financial and auditing research—a neglect that some experts associate with the loss of productivity and competitiveness of American and Canadian industry.[9]

Finally, the weakest of all financial control mechanisms seems to be that of government. While billions are still spent on the Strategic Defence Initiative ("Star Wars"), the bridges, sewers, and watermains from New York to Detroit and Los Angeles begin to crumble. Furthermore, the numerous defence contract frauds at the Pentagon, the scandals in the Department of Housing and Urban Development and the Federal Housing Administration, as well as the widely published erosion of ethical standards (in Ottawa no less than in Washington), are likely to be only the tip of a much larger iceberg. Above all, the auditing work and the resources available for it, as well as the pertinent ongoing research, are disproportionately small in relation to the gigantic sums received and spent by governments. Thus the honest work of many government accountants, internal auditors, auditor generals and others is often deprived of its effectiveness by lack of clout—for recent publications on governmental accounting and auditing see: Baber [1983], Berry and Harwood [1984], Ives [1987], Ditthofer [1988], and Lapsey [1988]. Finally, it should not be forgotten that accounting, during the last decade or so, has greatly contributed to the increasing "bureaucratization" of modern life. Some even hint at a malignant growth of accounting and finance: a CBC program (September 1989) claimed that, relative to its population, Canada had (in 1989) 20 times as many accountants (and 50 times as many lawyers) as Japan, a country that puts higher emphasis on the education of engineers. It is against this backdrop that our commentary should be read and understood.

On the bright side, it must first be noted that the most prominent elder statesman among accounting researchers, William A. Paton, Sr., celebrated his 100th birthday on July 19, 1989 (though meanwhile he has died); further, this decade saw an accountant, or to be precise, a "social accountant", awarded the Nobel Prize. In 1984 Professor Richard Stone, holder of the Chair in Applied Economics at Cambridge University (funded by a public accounting firm), received the Memorial Nobel Prize in Economics for achievements *primarily* in accounting research.[10] But since most accountants, regrettably and quite illogically, do not regard national income accounting as a branch of accounting, this important event did not receive any particular attention in the accounting community (for further references to social accounting see Section vi). Second, the practical accounting achievements of this decade were dominated, on the legislative side, by accounting for price-level changes (current value accounting) which, unfortunately, was only temporary; and on the technical side, by the widespread use of micro-computer spreadsheet accounting. Both these achievements go back to basic accounting research done decades ago, and the pertinent original contributions are now forgotten by many accountants. The major pioneering work of current value accounting was done in a series of prominent books by Schmidt (e.g., 1921, 1927, 1929/51) and four decades later in the well-known book by Edwards and Bell [1961]—for further details see Section (vi)—and the first article and first book on budget simulation and related foundations, as well as the pertinent use of spreadsheets can be found in Mattessich [1957, 1961, 1964/77 and 1964a/79]—for further remarks see Section (x). A third practical aspect, increasingly influencing research, is the expanding number and growth of multi-national corporations and, in consequence, the continuing internationalization of accounting.

The shortcomings of present-day accounting cannot be disregarded by academics, and ought to give rise to related research projects or revised course offerings (e.g., the establishment of seminars on ethics as related to accounting, auditing and financial practices). But academic accounting is a comprehensive, long-range, and *cultural activity*, which cannot be limited to satisfy momentary business needs. The major task of the accounting researcher is the creation of new insights into a wide range of accounting problems, as well as the construction of *purpose-oriented models* (under the constraints of *certain cost-benefit criteria*) which ultimately are put at the disposal of practitioners. The extent to which these insights affect the practicing accountant, and which of these models will actually be used, or how appropriately and wisely they will be used, is usually beyond the control and responsibility of the scholar.

Unfortunately we live at a time when almost everything is geared toward immediate gratification: politics, business, private lives, and social attitudes. Even economic research is embossed with Keynes' aphorism that "in the long-run we are all dead". But should we not aim for a wider horizon, and draw hope from the fact that history gives each of us the unique opportunity to live beyond the momentary experience, creating ties with the past as well as the future?

(ii) Is Accounting History Becoming Fashionable?

What have the major research trends of our discipline been during the last decade or so? One area that seems to have improved and gathered refreshed interest during this time may surprise the reader. It is *accounting history*, still not a particularly glamorous, yet nevertheless important subject.[11] On this continent, *The Accounting Historians Journal* (founded in 1974 by the Academy of Accounting Historians—see also their comprehensive list of Working Papers) has in recent years made considerable strides in improving its quality, and in Great Britain, the journal *Accounting, Business and Financial History* was founded recently. The International Conference of Accounting Historians (held every four years) seems to have increased in popularity, even among those accountants who are not predominantly historians. Furthermore, the historical publication series "Foundations of Accounting" (including 36 volumes, of which 23 titles are published for the first time) edited by Professor Richard P. Brief, and published by Garland Publishing, N.Y. has found a most favourable response—one of its earliest publications was Gaffikin and Aitken [1982] *The Development of Accounting Theory: Significant Contributors to Accounting Thought in the 20th Century.* And above all, *Relevance Lost—The Rise and Fall of Management Accounting* by Johnson and Kaplan [1987], the book which stirred most accountants in the late 1980s, is predominantly an historical work, despite its impact on present-day managerial accounting research.

The preceding monograph and this *Supplementary Volume* ultimately deal with the history of modern accounting. Furthermore, a need for more *localized* historical monographs and articles has made itself felt: e.g., Zeff's [1982] *The Accounting Postulates and Principles Controversy of the 1960s*, Kinney's [1986a] *Fifty Years of Statistical Auditing*, Moonitz' [1986] *History of Accounting at Berkeley*, and Mattessich's [1989/90] *Academic Accounting Research in Canada: Evolution, Achievements, and Institutional Environment*. In addition, there are journal surveys such as Dyckman's and Zeff's [1984] "Two Decades of the Journal of Accounting Research", Sundem's [1987] "Overview of Four Years of Submissions to THE ACCOUNTING REVIEW", and Falk's [1989] "Contemporary Accounting Research: The First Five Years". Finally, recent publications of the *Accounting Literature Index* by Heck, Derstine, and Huefner [1990], together with its software, as well as the *Database of Accounting Search Software* by Pacific Research Publications, are most valuable tools for any accounting academic and historian, and therefore deserve to be mentioned here—see also Brown *et al.* [1989].

Historical research is not unrelated to studies of *publication and citation analysis*, which—although still often unreliable (because of the narrow choice of the number of accounting journals, the neglect of accounting books, and many narrow assumptions and doubtful technical aspects; see also Epilogue)—seems to have gained some popularity in the accounting literature and, in time, might become a valuable support of historical studies: e.g., Brown and Gardner [1985a, 1985b], Brown, Gardner and Vasarhelyi [1987, 1989] and Gamble, Doherty and Hyman [1987]. Another boost to accounting history has come from the archeology of the Middle East. It is this relation which I should like to emphasize in connection with a series of publications by Professor Denise Schmandt-Besserat [1977, 1978, 1980, 1981a, 1981b, 1982, 1983, 1984, 1986a, 1986b, 1988] of the University of Texas at Austin,[12] which has afforded revolutionary insights (about the precursors of abstract counting and pictographic writing) reaching into the past 10,000 years. This research offers exciting evidence that *it was "accounting" which gave rise to writing as well as abstract counting*, and *not* the other way around, as traditionally believed and asserted even in recent accounting texts. This would make our discipline or its precursor a major impetus of culture and civilization, *an insight so revolutionary that it has not yet been grasped by most accountants and laymen.*

This first data processing and accountability system began around 8,000 B.C., using simple clay tokens of various shapes which represented different commodities (mainly agricultural products, but also units of labour and silver) in such a way that the shape of a token identified what we now call the pertinent account. To represent physical transfers of goods and services, clay tokens of different shapes were originally placed in perishable containers, to "record" a variety of transactions as well as the corresponding claims arising from them. From about 3,200 B.C. onwards, those perishable containers were often replaced by hollow clay receptacles (called *bullae* or "envelopes" by archaeologists) which were sealed after a scribe or priest had placed several clay tokens into them. These sealed receptacles fulfilled a dual function: they provided a list of assets as well as an indication of equity for the holder of the clay envelope against the person identified in the seal. An alternative system, often used as a supplement for recording manufactured goods and pertinent debts, were more complex, incised clay tokens. These were often perforated and filed on a string, which was provided with a clay seal similar to that of the receptacle.

However, within fifty years, a pressing disadvantage made itself felt: nothing but the memory of two or three persons served as a reminder of what hidden tokens any sealed clay receptacle might contain. People forgot, or left, or even died; as a result, the practice was changed so that tokens (before having been placed inside) were impressed onto the outside of the receptacle, and thus revealing at any time the total equity represented by the receptacle, as a kind of "IOU". Although this was not yet double entry "bookkeeping", it certainly was a kind of double entry record keeping. By putting symbols of the commodities or assets into the receptacle (Dr) after having impressed their negative images and equity (Cr) on the surface, a double entry as well as a dual function was achieved. But a century or so later, it was noticed that this relatively complex system could be greatly simplified and made more efficient by impressing standard clay tokens (and later cuneiform symbols) onto flat clay tablets instead of impressing them into hollow spheres of clay. Thus it was a data processing and accountability system out of which the invention of cuneiform writing arose.

This newly discovered origin of writing came as a surprise not only to archaeologists but to scholars in many fields, including accounting. But what is no less surprising is the fact that these discoveries so crucial for our discipline and its cultural historical significance for many years found little attention among accountants, in spite of the fact that articles on Schmandt-Besserat's insights and disclosures appeared in *TIME Magazine* (August 1, 1977), *Scientific American* [238/6, 1978] and other popular journals. Although a short paper by Professor G.A. Swanson [1984] and a page-insert (from *TIME*) of an introductory accounting textbook by Walgenbach, Dittrich and Hanson [1980, p. 6] drew the attention of accountants to this kind of archaeological research, no attempt was made until 1987 to offer a systematic accounting interpretation of these revolutionary disclosures.[13] I have tried to offer such an interpretation from an accounting as well as philosophic-semantic point of view in a series of papers—see Mattessich [1987/90, 1988b, 1989a/91, 1989b]. These papers not only recapitulate Schmandt-Besserat's research, but show that the ancient people of the Middle-East were the first to apply the input-output principle to a representational system. The input-output principle originates in the actual commodity transfer and the creation or cancellation of debt and ownership claims, and primarily belongs to **reality** (physical as well as social), but the major function of the token accounting system is

conceptual, serving the representation of reality by means of some conceptual device. Among other things, I tried to show that the token system was based on the same logical structure as modern double-entry bookkeeping, which reflects some physical and social dualities of actual events in the Dr/Cr duality of a representational system. And if the placing of hardened clay tokens into a clay receptacle (after having impressed them on the unburned and thus softer surface of the receptacle), constitutes a kind of double-entry, it is not merely because a positive entry and its negative imprint occurred, but because the functions which this double recording fulfills are basically the same as those accomplished by the debit and credit entries of modern bookkeeping. But the ultimate relevance of these articles for contemporary accounting research lies in the insight that not only one but two or even three distinct dualities have dominated accounting for thousands of years:

- The relationship of a physical transfer of goods connecting an input with an output;
- The debt relations connecting a debtor with a creditor; and
- The ownership relation connecting an object or asset with an owner.

Of these three empirical relations, only the first is physical, while the other two (which may be combined since they both constitute claims) pertain to social reality. This insight (that social relations like debt and ownership claims are equal partners with physical relations) is one which can resolve the current controversy as to whether there is a reality behind income and stockholders' equity, as disputed by Heath [1987], and whether there are real phenomena behind the major accounting measurements, as disputed by Sterling [1988]—for details see Section (x).

Yet, as we have seen, modern accounting history spans the entire gamut from prehistoric accounting to Fritz Schmidt, the pioneer of current cost accounting (for details see Section vi), and finally to the evolution of contemporary accounting theory—e.g., Gaffikin and Aitken [1982] and Gaffikin [1987, 1988]. It is in this vein that Demski [1985, p. 73] says: "We cannot understand, or economically evaluate, accounting without this sense of history" and "we must find a way to bring history into the debate". Above all, without an affinity for history and a sound knowledge of the history of ideas, we would lack criteria for distinguishing short-term novelties and sophisticated routine applications from penetrating ideas and research of lasting importance. Although history has temporary moods which penetrate time like the ripples of a pond, it nevertheless is the major tool for thoroughly understanding a subject and for separating the wheat from the chaff. Yet there are still many accountants who show little enthusiasm for accounting history. However, if this sub-area is not yet quite "in", the topic of our next section, managerial accounting, certainly is.

(iii) To Part II: The Criticism Of Management Accounting

If accounting research of the late 1980s were to be characterized by a single feature, it would have to be managerial accounting. Of course, the alleged neglect of management accounting research—perhaps because of the strong influence of modern finance theory and the consequent overemphasis on financial accounting and auditing research during the last two decades—refers mainly to its relevance and practice-orientation, because *analytical* managerial accounting research has progressed throughout the 1980s. Although Johnson's and Kaplan's [1987] *Relevance Lost* electrified the accounting community, and resulted in a strong and renewed interest in management accounting, it was not the only research focusing on this sensitive area. The time was ripe for reassessment, and other prominent publications emerged during those years: e.g., Kaplan's [1983] award-winning paper, as well as papers by Hayes [1983], Tiessen and Waterhouse [1983], Kaplan [1984], Armitage [1985], Otley [1985], Bromwich and Hopwood [1986], Atkinson [1987a, 1987b, 1987c] who received in 1989 the now re-named "Haim Falk CAAA Award for Distinguished Contribution to Accounting Thought", as well as Bruns and Kaplan [1987], Ferris and Livingstone [1987], Staubus [1987], and Zebda [1987]. But this "renaissance of management accounting" not only entails new slogans, such as "activity accounting", "strategic cost management", but also an unexpected shift in methodology.

During the last quarter of a century, analytical and behavioural research, together with statistical hypotheses testing, was *de rigueur* and dominated the scene, while the case method, previously pioneered by the Harvard Business School, fell increasingly out of fashion. But the resurgent interest in management accounting, which has intimate ties to Harvard Business School (Kaplan is a Harvard faculty member, and *Relevance Lost* was published by HBS Press), may reintroduce the clinical method and "field-based research" as major approaches to remedy this loss of relevance. To improve the productivity of American industry via management accounting is an urgent task, and clinical research is undoubtedly more suited to short-run solutions, while analytical and behavioural-statistical research can bear fruit only in the long-run. The latter areas require a patience that actual business, and even some academics, are less and less willing to grant to accounting theorists.

The "renaissance of management accounting" has so far been predominantly descriptive. It has criticized traditional overhead allocation procedures (e.g., the direct labour basis) and suggested new ones (e.g., set-up times), but it has not yet produced any better theory that, for example, would be general or flexible enough to embed all past, present and future allocation bases.

As pointed out, management accounting has not been entirely neglected during the past decades: apart from dealing with more traditional topics such as transfer pricing—e.g., Manes and Verrechia [1981-82] and Swieringa and Waterhouse [1982]—several researchers endeavouring to apply information economics and agency theory to accounting (Amershi, Atkinson, Butterworth, Demski, Feltham and others), have shown considerable interest in management accounting—cf. the book in honour and memory of John Butterworth, edited by Feltham, Amershi and Ziemba [1988]. Some of those papers were "preliminary" (i.e., at the working paper stage), and most of this research is by necessity based on simplified and thus unrealistic assumptions. Although rigorous and valuable, this literature is of purely theoretical interest and, at this stage, does not aspire to much practical validity.[14] In spite of several decades of analytical research in accounting, we tend to forget the most important double-edged lesson:

1. that concern with simplified and thus "unrealistic" models is not idle play but the foundation of every scientific undertaking, and

2. that these models must be related to, but never be equated with, reality which is much more complex, and is rarely if ever captured completely by the models.

The perennial disregard of the second part of this lesson leads to a lopsided sophistication, which is particularly dangerous when practical recommendations are made without considering all the underlying assumptions. This holds no less for the assumptions of statistical hypothesis testing on the empirical side—see for example my reference to Beaver and Landsman [1983] in Section (vi). Small wonder that many accountants (particularly those who associate accounting theory mainly with financial accounting) underrate the long-range relevance of analytical research to managerial accounting. Indeed, something much deeper is involved here:

it is the clash between the "simple-minded" and the "muddle-headed" scholars (to use a comparative expression coined by Bertrand Russell, who asserted that every scholar falls into one of these two categories[15]). While the first type of scholar is concerned with rigorous formalization, concentrating only on essential features, the second type wants to capture as many features as possible, but is forced to abandon the rigour of representing those features. Some of them even think that mathematics is a haven for those for whom the real world is too complicated. But science needs both types, as well as their mutual respect and cooperation; their antagonism can only be harmful.

The pertinent selection for Part II (corresponding to Section iii) is Kaplan's [1986] paper, reprinted here as paper Number 1, "The Role for Empirical Research in Management Accounting". Kaplan's article begins by demonstrating the scarcity of empirical research, and above all field related studies in management accounting during the period from 1926-1983. The article is partly based on research by Klemstine and Maher [1983]. The fact that fewer than five per cent of the pertinent papers during this period have been actual field studies is surprising indeed. Obviously, analytical researchers cannot be blamed for this. Rather, it raises such questions as: What did all those clinical researchers do (particularly during the 1950s and 1960s) when the case method and field research bloomed? And what did all those behavioural accountants do during the past two decades, when their empirical research area began to fully unfold? Is the competition of auditing and financial accounting (*vis-à-vis* management accounting) the only culprit, or do we have to search elsewhere for a complete explanation of this neglect?

But the major thrust of Kaplan's [1986] paper is programmatic and methodological (it also is rich with quotations from and references to the pertinent literature). Apart from his general methodological exposition and the Appendix (which is omitted in our reprint), he offers interesting methodological details specifically related to field-based research. He distinguishes between case studies (intensive examination of a single entity), field studies (cross-sectional case studies) and field experiments (used more extensively in other social sciences, and involving experimental manipulation of one or more variables and subsequent measurement of resulting effects). He also points to the following advantages of case studies:

- they constitute the basis for other research activity;
- they help by concentrating on the innovative and leading-edge companies or practices (instead of choosing merely representative samples); and
- they form an excellent teaching tool, conveying to students the much richer and more complex situations which can be offered outside the ordinary class room.

Finally, he claims that the move to field and process-tracing studies enables the development of analytical knowledge. In concluding this paper, the author reminds the reader of what he deems to be the "current lack of theories in management accounting", and emphasizes that the researchers' distaste for field studies in this area must be overcome.

This paper was complemented by Kaplan's subsequent [1987] presentation "The Continued Evolution of Management Accounting Design Principles for New Systems" at the 1987 Annual Meeting of the Canadian Academic Accounting Association (summarized in the pertinent *Proceedings*, p. 22] in which he expressed his belief that instead of patching up the existing cost system (which performs well for inventory valuation but poorly as a performance measure, as well as a product costing procedure) it would be advisable to design separate and specialized systems.[16] Kaplan also sketches his "emerging theory for effective design of performance measurement and product cost system", in which the traditional variance analysis and cost allocations are de-emphasized to secure improved timeliness. To this Atkinson, [1987c] responded with the suggestion of "a general purpose database reflecting the lowest common denominator requirement of each of these three systems". But Atkinson [1987a, 1987b] in his award-winning work *Intra-firm Cost and Resource Allocation* and his *Cost-Estimation in Management Accounting,* has gone beyond the programmatic stage, helping to prepare a theoretical basis as well as a series of interesting management case studies to remedy the present situation. It will be interesting to watch to what extent this new trend will be able to remedy the current dilemma of management accounting. Obviously, not all experts are enthusiastic about the clinical method,[17] and some even suspect it of being an "ideological weapon"—see, for example, Smith, Whipp, and Willmott [1988].

Another paper worth referring to is by Armitage and Langdon [1988] "Management Accounting: A Discipline in Transition". It could supplement Kaplan's article and, in spite of its conciseness, offers an excellent overview of the positive response to Johnson's and Kaplan's [1987] book, from a slightly different angle. Such a perspective is influenced by Armitage's *Linking Management Accounting Systems with Computer Technology* [1985], in which he argued that management accountants are being left behind, particularly from the point of view of management information systems design.

The Armitage and Langdon paper first gives a short survey of Johnson's and Kaplan's [1987] book, discusses the pertinent implications for accounting educators as well as researchers; and then—based on a 1986 AAA Convention address by Kaplan—distinguishes between the old *academic management accounting* [AMA] paradigm and the new *organization management accounting* [OMA] paradigm. While AMA, based on information economics and agency theory, is considered to produce highly stylized models, offering a significant contribution only under the assumptions of the traditional and simplistic AMA view of the managerial world, OMA is seen as serving the practical needs of firms, their values, goals and strategies. This refers to my previous juxtaposition between the *simple-minded* and the *muddle-headed* approach; it is for this very reason that I consider it dangerous to regard the distinction between AMA and OMA as constituting two competing paradigms. As emphasized above, both approaches (the simple-minded as well as the muddle-headed one) are indispensable, at least for any branch of science that aspires to a long-term future. Yet what we are witnessing in the recent literature is not only an understandable reaction to "academic management accounting", but a typical over-reaction to a trend well-established since the 1960s or so. To concentrate on only one would be "throwing out the baby with the bath water". Basic analytical research—as irrelevant and simplistic as it may seem at the moment, particularly for an applied science—must not be sacrificed in favour of the momentary practical needs that a science is also to fulfill. Even those promoting "organization management accounting" will realize that a one-sided, exclusively practice-oriented approach is neither feasible nor realistic. But to make their point, these authors might have felt obligated, perhaps subconsciously, to exaggerate their case.

Armitage's and Langdon's paper concludes by discussing the pertinent implications and the demands of the profession. The organizational emphasis of this paper recalls another related trend in management accounting. I refer to the type of research that traditionally received more attention in Great Britain, particularly in the journal *Accounting, Organizations and Society,* and which has been promulgated predominantly (though not exclusively) by British scholars such as Bromwich, David Cooper, Hopwood, Otley, Scapens, Tinker, and others. But this topic is reserved for the next section.

(iv) To Part III: Organizational And Behavioural Accounting

Just as finance arose from accounting some 30-odd years ago, and in some respects came to dominate accounting, so during the past decade or more, a similar trend has become noticeable in the relationship between the Management Information Systems area and accounting.[18] Indeed, accounting, not unlike philosophy, seems to have been a mother-hen, breeding new areas, some of which have already matured enough to become independent subjects. In our age of increasing specialization, such "cell divisions" and bifurcations are as natural and inevitable as is any growth process. Yet, such newly created and separate subjects have repercussions upon the mother-discipline. Some accountants who became MIS-experts behaved as if they were leaving a sinking ship. Others asserted that the time was not far off when accounting would be torn apart, with the spoils to be divided between the economics of finance on one hand and MIS on the other.

However, our concern in this Section is not with that part of MIS already established as an independent discipline, but rather with the residual that runs under the flag of organizational accounting. Since at least one twig of this branch is closely related to behavioural accounting, the current Section combines both. But to obtain proper insight into recent developments in this entire area, one might better distinguish the following three sub-areas:

1. Behavioural accounting (mainstream behavioural research, see Table 1), also called "experimental research"—see Libby [1989];
2. Organizational accounting (interpretive perspective, see Table 2);
3. Critical radicalism (critical perspective or Marxism, see Table 3).

While the first sub-area is dominated by traditional scientific methodology, and is frequently encountered on the American continent, the other sub-areas are based on quite different philosophical premises (cf. Tables 1 to 3), and are promulgated mainly by accountants trained in Great Britain, although exceptions do exist.

(iv-1) Behavioural Research

Behavioural research (see Libby's [1981] award-winning *Accounting and Human Information Processing: Theory and Applications* and Ashton's [1984] *The Evolution of Behavioral Accounting Research: An Overview*) was discussed in the Main Volume, and is here represented and extended through the second article reprinted as paper Number 2, "Behavioral Research on the Production and Use of Financial Information" by Richardson and Gibbins [1988] see also Table 1.[19] This article is not a complete survey, but brings up to date the previous presentations by Dyckman, Gibbins and Swieringa [1978/84], Kaplan [1978/84], as well as Gibbins and Hughes [1982/84]—see Part V of the Main Volume. Richardson's and Gibbins' article, written with the assistance of John Wilson, is primarily concerned with financial information, and emphasizes the distinction between the *observational plane* (reality) and the *theory plane* (conceptualization).[20] Apart from a concise discussion of the assumptions common to the literature reviewed (rationality, self-interest, limitation of cognitive capacity, and institutionalization of context), the authors categorize this literature on the basis of three interdependent "roles" or criteria, i.e. depending on whether a publication is primarily concerned with *financial disclosure* or *analysis* (interpretive process), or *information use* (decision making vs. stewardship).

After their review—which mainly explores management motivations and external forces acting on the firm (e.g., "the authorized public release of financial information and individual and group processes leading to that event")—the authors conclude with some critical remarks about the pertinent research publications. This echoes the critique that was previously put forth in the Main Volume: paucity of results of much behavioural research, lack of critical mass and fragmentary nature of this research activity, as well as inadequate exploration of the underlying (or presumed) theories. If I may here add my own criticism, it is that behavioural and empirical research in general are *not* sufficiently concerned with the testing of hypothesized means-end relationships and analytical theories. Although examples of close cooperation between empirical and analytical research do exist, such cooperation occurs too seldom.[21]

In the "disclosure area" the authors praise the diversity of the research perspectives and the crystallization of central issues (e.g., searching for the determinants of accounting policy choice); in the "analysis area" they look favourably upon the search for appropriate decision models and the overcoming or control of bounded rationality. And finally, in the "area of use", they emphasize the shift from the decision making to the stewardship task of accounting. The major trend seems to be away from grand theories, toward theories of the mid-range; but as we shall see in Section (x) some analytical methodological researchers continue their search for a unifying basis of accounting.

Table 1

Dominant Assumptions Of Mainstream Accounting*

A. Beliefs About Knowledge

- Theory is separate from observations that may be used to verify or falsify a theory.
- Hypothetico-deductive account of scientific explanation accepted.
- Quantitative methods of data analysis and collection which allow generalization favoured.

B. Beliefs About Physical and Social Reality

- Empirical reality is objective and external to the subject. Human beings are also characterized as passive objects; not seen as makers of social reality.
- Single goal of utility-maximization assumed for individuals and firms. Means-end rationality assumed.
- Societies and organizations are essentially stable; "dysfunctional" conflict may be managed through the design of appropriate accounting control.

C. Relationship Between Theory and Practice

- Accounting specifies means. not ends. Acceptance of extant institutional structures.

* Reproduced from Chua [1986], Table 2, page 611, with the permission of the editor of *The Accounting Review*

Libby [1989] points out that the major thrust of this area is towards improving decision making procedures in accounting, and particularly in auditing (see also Section viii), and that two of the necessary conditions to achieve this are evaluating current decision making and understanding its underlying determinants. While in the 1970s and early 1980s this research relied on the *lens model* and on *probability judgments,* new impetus came in the mid-1980s in the form of a change of direction: exploring the differences between the ill-structured decision making in accounting hierarchies, versus decision making as explored in psychology.

(iv-2) Organizational Accounting (Interpretive Perspective)

Organizational accounting (interpretive perspective) is the main trend represented in the British journal *Accounting, Organization and Society.* Its major proponents are Cooper [1983], Hopper and Powell [1985], Hopwood [1988], and others, many of whom follow the sociological work of Burrell and Morgan [1979] and the social philosophies of Schutz [1962-66, 1967], Foucault [1972, 1979, 1980] and others. This branch is more oriented toward managerial accounting than the behavioural research discussed above. It relies on a different set of assumptions which, according to Chua [1986], are those shown in our Table 2. The entire area of organizational accounting (i.e. the interpretive as well as the critical-radical perspective) has come to prominence only during the last decade or so, and some of its publications are still shrouded in verbosity and a haze which probably stems from sociology, particularly as practiced in Great Britain and Continental Europe. Some of the pertinent papers are critical, emphasizing the "ritualistic significance" of much of accounting—see Dent [1987]. Some recent books that might be counted to this area are Ashton's [1982] *Human Information Processing in Accounting,* the anthology by Cooper, Scapens, and Arnold [1983] *Management Accounting Research,* and MacIntosh's [1985] *The Social Software of Accounting Information Systems.*

Table 2

Dominant Assumptions Of The Interpretative Perspective*

A. Beliefs About Knowledge

- Scientific explanations of human intention sought. Their adequecy is assessed via the criteria of logical consistency, subjective interpretation, and agreements with actors' common-sense interpretation.
- Ethnographic work, case studies, and participation observation encouraged. Actors studied in their everyday world.

B. Beliefs About Physical and Social Reality

- Social reality is emergent, subjectively created, and objectified through human interaction.
- All actions have meaning and intention that are retrospectively endowed and that are grounded in social and historical practices.
- Social order assumed. Conflict mediated through common schemes of social meanings.

C. Relationship Between Theory and Practice

- Theory seeks only to explain action and to understand how social order is produced and reproduced.

* Reproduced from Chua [1986], Table 3, page 615, with the permission of the editor of *The Accounting Review*

A special version of interpretive organizational accounting has been promulgated and applied to accounting by Roberts and Scapens [1985], in "Accounting Systems and Systems of Accountability". This "structural dualism", as I call it, follows the social theories of Giddens [1976, 1979, 1981], putting special emphasis on the relationship between *subject* and *object,* and stressing the interdependence between system and its structure. Other articles worth mentioning, and dealing with organizational control and normative models, are by Flamholz, Das, and Tsui [1985] and Waller and Jiambalvo [1984] respectively. But much more vociferous is a small group of accountants who follow the Marxist tradition and are discussed in the next subsection.

Three other important papers in this area that would have been reproduced, if space permitted, are Hopwood's [1987] "The Archeology of Accounting Systems" and Swieringa's and Weick's [1987] "Management Accounting and Action", as well as Kren and Liao [1988] "The Role of Accounting Information in the Control of Organizations: A Review of the Evidence". The first of these papers, despite its misleading title (it has nothing to do with the archaeological studies discussed in Section ii), investigates accounting systems *changes* (with some references to the last 150 years or so) and their preconditions, "sorting through the sediments of organizational history, however recent, to reconstruct the ways in which the present emerged from the past" (Hopwood [1987], p. 230). The paper by Swieringa and Weick [1987] is geared towards the dynamic and motivational aspects of management accounting, and thus touches the organizational as well as behavioural aspects discussed in this Section. Above all, the paper shows that such notions and procedures as "return on investment", "cost-volume profit analysis" and "variance analysis" may induce a short-term vision among management. The third and last of these papers offers a fine survey of the pertinent literature, with some ties to agency theory.

(iv-3) The Critical-Radical Perspective.

The major representatives of this trend are Tinker, Merino, and Neimark [1982], Tinker [1984], Lehman and Tinker [1985], Chua [1986], and possibly Lowe, Puxty, and Laughlin [1983] as well as Cooper, Lowe, Puxty and Willmott [1985]. Their philosophic basis is to be found primarily in Habermas [e.g., 1971, 1974, 1978], Marcuse [e.g., 1941, 1968] and other Marxist writers. The dominant epistemological and ontological premises of this camp are concisely stated in Table 3. This group emphasizes that accounting is *not* a *neutral* instrument but actively involved in the social conflict and control between classes. They plead for accounting research as a social critique, and stress the inseparability of social, economic, and political interest. Chua [1986, p. 626], however, admits that in such research it is still debatable as to what constitutes an acceptable theory or explanation.

In the face of the difficulties (pointed out in Section i) in which American business and public accounting currently find themselves, and aggravated by the relentless onslaught against the environment, it is hardly surprising that critical voices find an increasing echo. To what extent moderate-objective views[22] and to what extent radical-subjective views will influence accounting research during the next decades, may well depend on the political climate which a social and ecological crisis would engender.

Table 3

Dominant Assumptions Of The Critical Perspective*

A. Beliefs About Knowledge

- Criteria for judging theories are temporal and context-bound. Historical, ethnographic research and case studies more commonly used.

B. Beliefs About Physical and Social Reality

- Human beings have inner potentialities which are alienated (prevented from full emergence) through restrictive mechanisms. Objects can only be understood through a study of their historical development and change within the totality of relations.
- Empirical reality is characterized by objective, real relations which are transformed and reproduced through subjective interpretation.
- Human intention, rationality, and agency are accepted, but this is critically analyzed given a belief in false consciousness and ideology.
- Fundamental conflict is endemic to society. Conflict arises because of injustice and ideology in the social, economic, and political domains which obscure the creative dimension in people.

C. Relationship Between Theory and Practice

- Theory has a critical imperative: the identification and removal of domination and ideological practices.

* Reproduced from Chua [1986], Table 4, page 622, with the permission of the editor of *The Accounting Review*

(v) To Part IV: Positive Theory and Financial Accounting

Apart from Johnson's and Kaplan's [1987] book, Watts' and Zimmerman's [1986] *Positive Accounting Theory* [PAT] is probably the work that received most attention during the second half of the past decade—just as did the award-winning book by Beaver [1981] *Financial Reporting: An Accounting Revolution* in the early part of the 1980s.[23] Although much of it is a restatement of previous ideas (such as the notion of "political costs")[24] by Watts and Zimmerman (see Part III of the Main Volume), it contains important programmatic ideas as to the circumstances that influence the choice of a method for financial accounting. This choice is to be based on revealed and induced preferences (cf. Demski's review article in *AOS* [1988]). But where and how can "prices" and "quantities" *for methods* be observed, and where are the criteria or conditions that make the pertinent cost-benefits consistent with such a choice? Indeed, this approach has not only been highly praised but also widely criticized by a broad range of authors, i.e., from adherents of mainstream accountants (some of whom mix praise with concern) such as Demski [1988], Wittington [1987], and Young [1987], and more skeptical authors like Ryan [1982], Peasnell and Williams [1986], Christenson [1983/84], Boland and Gordon [1990] and Sterling [1990], to the "critical radicals", Lowe, Puxty, and Laughlin [1983] and Tinker, Merino, and Neimark [1982],[25] whose opposition to "positive accounting research" has deeper ideological roots.

Sterling [1990] is one of the more articulate critics of positive accounting theory, and considers its fundamental questions (as to what accounting measurement ought to be) as "illegitimate". As to Watts and Zimmerman [1986, PAT], Sterling refers to the major problems with it, as follows:

> From that (DP) perspective [i.e. that of opponents of the "Chicago School"] the problem with PAT [Positive Accounting Theory] is that it has an unacceptably *narrow* definition of evidence, *restricts* the research methods employed, and *ignores* evidence that is not in accord with the tight priors of the researchers. The greater error, however, is not that W&Z make the decision on the restrictive-narrow side but that they do not realize (or at least acknowledge) that such a decision must be made. All of those strident claims that 'a priori' or 'normative' work must be *replaced* by 'empirical' or 'positive' research are shown to be misguided by this example. Obviously one cannot empirically decide what ought to count as empirical evidence because one does not know what ought to count as empirical evidence for that decision. And doing positive research would not help because all that would do is show that DP adherents [i.e. of the "Chicago School"] do not count self reports as evidence, which is wasted effort because we already know that from Reder's (and others') description. For W&Z and others in 'the positive tradition' to dismiss discussions about decisions about what ought to count as evidence by labelling them 'a priori' or 'normative' must mean that they have normatively decided *a priori* what ought to count as evidence without realizing that they have done so. [footnotes omitted]
>
> Sterling [1990], p. 106

Market based accounting research [MBAR] is another important sector, and to summarize the results, reached by the early 1980s, let me quote Dopuch's paraphrasing:

> Lev and Ohlson [1982] provide four general conclusions drawn from their evaluations. Paraphrased they are: (i) Whereas accounting earnings data convey useful (and perhaps timely) information, the marginal contribution of non-earnings data remains largely unknown. (ii) Early studies of discretionary changes in accounting techniques which appeared to indicate investor rationality are now being undermined by "discomfiting" findings suggesting investor "irrationality". (iii) Studies assessing the stock market reactions to accounting regulations have provided consistent results regarding at least the following three cases—replacement costs, oil and gas accounting and lines-of- business data. (iv) MBAR has contributed to the finance discipline in two contrasting ways: (a) it has forced its researchers to reconsider the underpinnings of the capital asset pricing model and market efficiency by providing evidence which is inconsistent with either or both; and (b) it has provided evidence linking fundamental (firm-based) variables to the systematic risk of common stocks ...
>
> Dopuch [1989b], pp. 21-22

In the mid-1980s, a certain pessimism arose about directly influencing policy decisions as had originally been hoped. But the three major academic journals still "published more capital market research in the last half of the 1980s than the first half", according to Bernard [1989, p. 2]. One may refer, for example, to studies of impact disclosure by McNichols [1988] and Atiase [1985], and a considerable number of studies in cross-sectional analysis, etc., such as those by Bernard [1987] and Christie [1987].

A further area examines the problems and consequences of *income smoothing*, summarized by Ronen and Sadan [1981]. Furthermore, lobbying activity (for "preferred standards") was more thoroughly examined. Abdel-khalik says in this connection:

> What is new in accounting research in recent years is attributing preferences for accounting regulation, methods, and accruals to the managers' desires to enhance their self-interest or the interest of specific individuals or groups.
>
> Abdel-khalik [1989], p. 16

He refers in this connection to the Watts and Zimmerman [1986] study of divergent lobbying interests by the client-managers, (the standard's effect on the firm's value on the client-manager bonus) on one side, and the auditors' position (resulting from the standard's effect on his clients' preferences and other factors), on the other side. In addition, he cites the study by Lilien and

Pastena [1982], which anticipated the above-mentioned results and also concluded that leverage, etc. determine factors like the initial choice. Another study, by Puro [1984], deals with the lobbying behaviour of auditors in response to six accounting standards.

Most of "financial accounting research" has continued during the 1980s in its established track, putting particular emphasis on:

- problems of standard setting and regulation, e.g., Abdel-khalik [1980], Stamp [1980], the CAAA award winning book by Skinner [1987], Gaa's [1988a] *Methodological Foundations of Standardsetting for Corporate Financial Reporting*, see also Benston [1981, 1982a, 1982b], and the proceedings edited by Basu and Milburn [1982];
- objectives, e.g., Dopuch and Sunder [1980];
- on measurement, e.g., Staubus [1985];
- uncertainty, e.g., Thornton's [1983] *The Financial Reporting of Contingencies and Uncertainties: Theory and Practice;*
- the capital market, e.g., Gonedes and Dopuch [1989];
- the problem of recognition (materiality), e.g., Sorter and Ingberman [1987];
- problems of "earnings versus cash flow", e.g., Lee [1984, 1985], Egginton [1985], Lawson [1985], Charitou [1988/89];
- problems of earnings forecasting, e.g., Collins and Hopwood [1980], Jensen [1983] and Brown, Foster and Noreen [1984]; and
- financial reporting in general, e.g., Abdel-khalik [1983] and the anthology by Lee and Parker [1984].

Furthermore, the search for "alternative methods of relating accounting signals to security price changes" has resulted in an increasing emphasis on *explaining* security prices (not only their changes) by means of fundamental variables of accounting and finance.[26] This *new cross-sectional valuation perspective* stands in contrast to the *standard "returns" model* of market based accounting research [MBAR] developed by Ball and Brown [1968], and honored by the 1986 "Seminal Contribution to Accounting Literature Award" of the AAA, and by Beaver [1968], honored by the 1989 "Seminal Contribution to Accounting Literature Award" of the AAA. The new perspective received a major impetus from the article by Lev and Ohlson [1982], and is surveyed in the article reprinted here as paper Number 3 by Atiase and Tse, "Stock Valuation Models and Accounting Information: A Review and Synthesis". Atiase and Tse first point out the *advantages* of this valuation approach (e.g., precise "timing" of disclosure date is no longer as crucial, a choice among *several* price observations is available, cumulative effects over longer periods are taken into consideration), as well as its *limitations* (e.g., difficulties in the empirical specification of the model and measuring its independent variables, instability of coefficients, as well as context specificity of the valuation approach). They then discuss the differences between alternative stock valuation models, all of which rely on dividend discounting, but vary in their deviation from the dividend flows, as well as in their attitude towards the risk factor. After a literature survey (supported by their Table I, summarizing major research efforts in this area), some unresolved issues are discussed: e.g., the *ad hoc* nature of the models, difficulty in estimating expected growth, and several econometric problems. Atiase and Tse [1986] conclude that due to context dependence, both approaches—cross-section valuation as well as the older return approach—have their place in market-based accounting research, and may even serve as mutual confirmation or "cross-validation". But it seems that "valuation analysis" may be preferable for determining the effects of income components on stock valuation and related issues such as the inclusion of "off-balance sheet items" (e.g., pension assets and liabilities).

Another excellent and more recent survey article of this area is Lev's [1990] paper "On the Usefulness of Earnings and Earnings Research: Lessons and Directions from Two Decades of Empirical Research" from which our Table 4 is taken (based on his Table 1: "Sample Research [1980-1988] on the Relationship Between Earnings and Stock Returns"). Not only does this table list articles (and some of their properties) from this field published during the 1980s, but Lev's paper offers evidence that "the extent of earnings usefulness is rather low", partly because of shortcomings in research, and partly because of investors' irrationality. Lev lays the blame primarily on deficiencies in accounting measurement and valuation principles, and occasionally on the data manipulation by management. Above all, he calls for a reorientation of accounting research in capital markets, and a shift toward research in valuation principles and related measurement methodology.

> Indeed, there is a surprising imbalance between the level of efforts and sophistication that goes into statistical methodology of the returns/earnings studies, and the cavalier approach toward reported earnings. While some deficiencies in earnings are obviously adjusted for by financial analysts and even the media (footnote omitted), most researchers (including the author) accept the reported numbers at face value. This, of course, precludes current research from providing information on possible improvement in the measurement of earnings and insight on how financial information is used by investors. Research on the quality of earnings, shifts the focus to accounting by calling for a systematic examination of the extent to which the specific principles underlying accounting measurements and valuations, as well as managerial manipulations, detract from the usefulness of earnings.
>
> Lev [1990], p. 23 (of MS)

Bernard [1989] p. 3, also emphasizes that "if we introduce as much accounting and economics into our tests as we now have statistics and finance, the next few years will be interesting indeed". I wholeheartedly agree with such statements, and may add that the emphasis on statistical tools in recent accounting research may also have led to a neglect of important foundational issues of our discipline. Briloff contributes the following remark: "I lament this condition by observing that at this exalted level presumptive first-rate accounting scholars are constrained to demonstrate their competence as second-rate financial analysts, applying a third-rate mathematical methodology, predicated on fourth-rate data, compiled by fifth-rate drones." Briloff [1990], p. 28.

Although financial accounting research has been closely related to *accounting policy research,* Dopuch [1989a] sees a continuing erosion of such "policy" publications during the last decade or so—with the exception of Lev's [1988] article—particularly in comparison to the beginning of the decade, when such original papers as Foster's [1980] "Accounting Policy Decisions and Capital Market Research" and Maher's [1981] "The Impact of Regulation on Controls: Firms' Response to the Foreign Corrupt Practice Act" were published and subsequently received the AAA/AICPA Accounting Literature Award. Dopuch indicates that this trend is due partly to the fact that the policy-making bodies "do not feel obligated to rely on academic research in assessing the pros and cons of past and pending regulations", and partly "due to the nature, scope and complexity of the FASB's recent and pending regulations" (for both quotes see Dopuch [1989a, p. 496]). But he also blames the editors of academic accounting journals. As typical examples of this trend away from policy issues, he mentions such recent publications as Thomson, Olsen, and Dietrich [1987], and Holthausen and Verrechia [1988].

Table 4
Sample of Research (1980-1988) on the Relationship Between Earnings and Stock Returns

Author Reference	Sample Period	Return Variable	Earnings Variable	Earnings Expectations	Additional Independent Variables	Cross section or Time-series	"Window"	R^2
1. Hageman *et al.* JAR (Autumn 1984)	1974-1976	Residual returns	Quarterly EPS	Last quarter EPS	None	C-S	5 days around announcement	0.05
2. Wilson, JAR (sup. 1986)	1981-1982	Residual returns	Earnings	Time-series predictions	Components of cash flows and accruals	C-S	2 days	0.02-0.05
3. Hughes and Ricks, AR (Jan. 1987)	1979-1984	Residual returns	Quarterly EPS	Analyst forecasts or previous EPS	Two Independent variables: analyst and mechanical forecast errors	C-S	2 days	0.02 for entire sample; when extreme forecast were dropped
4. Hopwood *et al.* JAR (Spring 1985)	1973-1978	Residual returns	EPS	Time-series model	Interim sales and expenses	C-S	1 quarter	EPS=0.04 Sales=0.01 Expenses=0.004
5. Beaver *et al.* JAE (March 1980)	1958-1976	% change in price	EPS	Last year's EPS	None	C-S	Fiscal year	0.07 for individual securities 0.55-0.95 for portfolios
6. Bowen *et al.* AR (October 1987)	1972-1981	Residual returns	Annual earnings	Last year's earnings	Cash flow components	C-S	12 months	0.04
7. Fried and Givolvy JAE (October 1982)	1969-1979	Residual returns	EPS	Analysts Forecasts or Time-series forecasts	None	C-S	4/1-3/31	R^2=0.33 for analyst forecast R^2=0.27 for time-series
8. Freeman, JAR (Spring 1983)	1963-1977	Residual returns	Change in profit to total assets minus industry change	–	Leads & lags of industry & price variables approximating current costs	C-S	Fiscal year	0.07 0.10
9a. Jacobsen, AER (June 1987)	1963-1982	Raw returns	$ROI = \frac{\text{Net Income}_t}{\text{Total Assets}_{t-1}}$	–	–	C-S	12/31-12/31	0.02
9b. Jacobsen, AER (June 1987)	1963-1982	Residual returns	Residual ROI	–	–	C-S	12/31-12/31	0.05
10. Lustgarten JAR (October 1982)	1976-1977	Residual returns	Earnings	Last year's earnings	Replacement costs & sales	C-S	10 months (-6 to +4 of fiscal year-end)	0.02-0.04 for earnings alone 0.05-0.09 for all three variables

Table 4
Continued

Author Reference	Sample Period	Return Variable	Earnings Variable	Earnings Expectations	Additional Independent Variables	Cross section or Time-series	"Window"	R^2
11. Beaver *et al.* JAE (July 1982)	1977-1978	Raw returns	Net Income	Last year's Income	Cash flows, or inflationary gains	C-S	12/31-12/31	0.14-0.15
12. Lipe, JAR (Sup. 1986)	1977-1980	Residual returns	EPS	Time-series	6 earnings components	C-S	4/1-3/31	0.15
13. Hoskin *et al.* JAR (Sup. 1986)	1979-1981	Residual returns	4th quarter earnings to market value	Analysts' forecast	A large number of additional disclosures	C-S	two days	0.12-0.15
14. Rayburn, JAR (Sup. 1986)	1963-1982	Residual returns	–	Time-series	Components of earnings and cash flows	C-S	annual	R^2 of annual regressions fluctutae from 0.002 to 0.2
15. Beaver *et al.*, JAE (July 1982) for Easman *et al.* sample	1973-1977	Raw returns	Net income	Last year's income	Inflationary gain	C-S	12/31-12/31	1973=0.04 1974=0.30 1975=0.05 1976=0.03 1977=0.23
16. Sepe AR (July 1982)	1974-1976	Residual returns	–	–	Various financial ratios, risk, and inflation-adjusted measures	C-S	Fiscal year	0.30
17. Ajinkya and Gift, JAR (Autumn 1984)	1970-1977	Residual returns	Management Forecasts	Analysts' foecasts	–	C-S	Months before forecast to March next year	0.05-0.17
18. Imhoff and Lobo JAR (Autumn 1984)	1977-1978	Residual returns	Revisions in IDES forecasts	Last forecast	–	C-S	Month of forecast revision	0.01
19. Magliolo, JAR (Sup. 1986)	1979-1983	Changes in market value of firm	–	–	Reserve recognition data for oil & gas co.	C-S	annual	0.10-0.062

A second contribution to Part IV is the article reprinted as paper Number 4, "A Synthesis of Security Valuation Theory and the Role of Dividends, Cash Flows, and Earnings" by J.A. Ohlson [1990]. Not only is this paper the most technical among those reprinted here, but for a better understanding of it, a broader knowledge of Ohlson's other writings is desirable. Since his recent, prolific output is among the most significant contributions of the 1980s, I will offer a broader survey of Ohlson's work before referring to the paper reprinted here.

In "The Social Value of Public Information in Production Economies", Ohlson [1988] examines the social or welfare value of public information, with particular attention to the question: what are the necessary and sufficient conditions for public information to have such value? This is one of the fundamental questions of accounting and information economics which affects accounting no less than economics and finance. Previous attempts to tackle this problem have led to contradictory results, but the problem was finally solved for *pure exchange economies* in a crucial paper by Hakansson, Kunkel, and Ohlson [1982]: see the Main Volume pp. 187-188. However, *production activities* were not included in this solution. The first attempt to include production was made by Kunkel [1982] but under very restrictive assumptions. Only the paper by Ohlson [1988] brought forth a general solution to this problem, i.e., covering production as well as exchange conditions. Ohlson [1988] also inquires as to whether information can induce *externalities* in exchange/production economies, and suggests that costless information may have a more constructive function in this combined situation than under pure exchange. For a more basic background to this research, see Ohlson's [1987a] book *The Theory of Financial Markets and Information.* But another reason for referring to this paper is Ohlson's emphasis on the notion of "stockholders' unanimity" (about changes in information, production, etc.). This notion plays an important role in the two other papers by Ohlson [1987b, 1989a] briefly referred to here. These papers lead to his "theory of clean surplus" which, in a way, constitutes a return to a more traditional basis, and thus might be of particular interest.[27]

In another paper by Ohlson [1987b], "On the Nature of Income Measurement: The Basic Results", he maintains that income measurement demands a connection to welfare without any other requirements such as shareholders' unanimity, which in turn is supposed to be a sufficient and necessary condition for asserting that "more income is better than less" (as Beaver and Demski [1979] seem to imply). This paper also indicates that Beaver's and Demski's *rejection* of the "measurement perspective of accounting" is mistaken; in other words, even if the conditions of perfect competition, complete markets, and stockholders' unanimity are *not* fulfilled, income measurement remains a meaningful and fundamental objective of accounting. Thus, accounting is more than Beaver's and Demski's "cost-effective communication procedure". But Ohlson pleads for a combination of this *informational aspect* with the previously mentioned *measurement aspect* of accounting, quite aside from notions such as complete and perfect markets.

This task requires a rigorous theory of accounting which Ohlson [1989a] begins to develop in the paper "Accounting Earnings, Book Value, and Dividends: The Theory of the Clean Surplus Equation—Part I". There he tries, on one hand, to exploit the traditional concept of the *clean surplus relation* (change in book value of owners' equity + dividends = earnings) for the purpose of security evaluation; on the other, he explains why this equation need not be a tautology, but can be explained in economic and empirical terms. Thus each of the three variables of the clean surplus equation is supposed to act as an independent information component, leading in the long run to an *equilibrium* in the empirical sense.[28] The analysis shows how the earnings process affects the valuation of the firm, and how the flow variables (e.g., earnings) reconcile with the change in stock variables (e.g., Owners' Equity). This theory regards *the balance sheet and its stock variables as basic,* while the flow variables are regarded as derivatives that serve to further explain the changes of stock variables under uncertainty. This may give an inkling of the major thrust of Ohlson's recent research, and hopefully will whet the appetite for further concern with the clean surplus theory and related research.

Indeed, further studies by Ohlson [1989b, 1989c], and particularly his 1990 article reprinted here, show the surprising result that without conditions other than "no arbitrage" (between securities), *only anticipated dividends* (but *neither* cash flows *nor* anticipated earnings!) can serve for valuation on an expected present value basis, and that only earnings make sense as a sufficient information source or *determinant* of a security's *pay-off* (instead of the security's price). Thus, the main conclusions of Ohlson's reprinted paper are:

- the basic theoretical insight derives from a powerful condition of no arbitrage: there is no basic valuation theory;
- only anticipated dividends can serve as a generically valid capitalization (present value) attribute of security;
- the notion of risk in general, and models such as the CAPM, occur only as special cases;
- the notion that one can capitalize cash flows rather than dividends requires additional (and relatively stringent) assumptions; and
- the existing theory of pure earnings under uncertainty lacks unity regarding its meaning and characteristics.

Hence Ohlson argues that *only a simple notion of "pure" earnings is economically relevant,* and sufficient to determine a securities pay-off (i.e., its price plus dividend).[29]

Ohlson [1989b], in another of his prolific contributions, shows that the renowned paper by Ball and Brown [1968] falls short of "an equilibrium model linking value and earnings through expectations (or information)", and even more importantly, that Ball's and Brown's notion of unexpected earnings "appears to have the status of a 'folklore concept' with limited economic content". Thus the *earnings change* variable (on which the concept of unexpected earnings is based) seems to be inferior to the *earnings level* variable—something apparently confirmed by the empirical findings of Easton and Harris [1989]. This again seems to call for increased emphasis on cross-sectional valuation studies instead of events studies.

The length of this Section is a reflection of the wide span of financial accounting. But in concluding, it must be pointed out that during the past two or three decades, a great reliance has been placed on modern finance theory, the orientation of which is overly geared toward short-run profit maximization. Unless this theory is capable of adopting a more holistic point of view, further reliance on finance theory might impede rather than promote the progress of financial accounting.[30]

(vi) To Part V: Income Measurement, the Ups and Downs of Inflation Accounting, and Social Accountability

"In the history of accounting thought there is no other subject that has been more controversial than the determination of earnings (income, profit, etc.) and the related problems of valuation and matching."
Brief [1983], p. 15

A recent paper by Solomons [1987], "The Twilight of Income Measurement: Twenty-five Years On", shows how he and other accountants had to revise their views about income determination during the past decade or more. While there was a time when it seemed that the importance of the income notion would decline, the reverse proved to be the case. Acquisition cost accounting has survived with flying colours, and even the practice of current value accounting reached a peak during the 1980s. And, as Solomons admits, "earnings seem to be as important to financial analysts and to academic researchers as they ever were, and recent tax changes bring taxable income somewhat closer to accounting income than previously, thereby increasing the importance of the income concept rather than diminishing it" (p. 1). Thus the *twilight* of income measurement (predicted by Solomons a quarter of a century ago) seems to be that of a *dawn* rather than a dusk. Solomons is now strongly in favour of current value accounting, and expresses his disappointment with the FASB's policy of inflation accounting, as well as with its short-sighted and unphilosophical approach towards the "conceptual framework".

But as far as inflation accounting (including current value accounting) is concerned, the academic community is now more divided than ever. Inflation accounting has had an uneven fate, full of surprises and unexpected turns. After World War I, there was great interest in it on this continent—e.g., Middleditch [1918], Paton [1918,1920]—as well as in Europe—e.g., Limperg in Holland, and Prion [1919], Mahlberg [1921, 1925], Schmalenbach [1922a, 1922b], Walb [1921], and above all, Schmidt [e.g., 1921, 1927, 1929/51][31] in Germany and Delavelle [1924] and others in France.[32] By the mid-1930s, when Sweeney [1936] published *Stabilized Accounting*, the interest was gone, and inflation accounting was more a curiosity than a viable research field. In the mid-1950s, Jones [1955, 1956] began a revival of interest in this subject, and Edwards' and Bell's [1961] influential book[33] changed apathy to enthusiasm. Current value accounting became the rage, and many publications followed: for example, such major books as Gynther [1966/78], Ross [1969], Rosen [1972], Revsine [1973], Basu and Hanna [1974], Moonitz [1973], Baxter [1975], Chambers [1980], Minemura [1980], Johnson and Peterson [1984], the proceedings edited by Sterling and Lemke [1982], as well as books by Frishkoff [1982], Enthoven [1982], Whittington [1983], Bloom and Debessay [1984], Tweedie and Whittington [1984], Zéghal [1984], Milburn [1982, 1988], Beechy [1989] and many others—including an attempt by the AICPA Research Department to make general price level accounting palatable to practitioners (see AICPA [1963]).

Inflation accounting seems to have generated more *books* than any other accounting topic, even in the 1980s. And yet, accountants are at present, after several years of legislated supplementary inflation accounting in the U.S. and U.K. as well as Canada,[34] in greater disarray than ever before about which steps to take next, and which approach would be most satisfactory. This is reflected in a paper by Hanna [1988], "Accounting for Changing Prices: Dead or Alive?". This article points out that compulsory supplementary accounting for price-level changes in the U.K. and U.S.A. has been abandoned, while in Canada it has been "voluntary". But if it was "voluntary", why was a pertinent Canadian *standard* introduced in Section 4510 of the *CICA Handbook?* One reason for the ambiguity in Canada seems to be found in the fact that this standard has not been backed up by corresponding *auditing* standards and has thus remained more or less unenforceable.

Of no less interest is Hanna's investigation as to why this "experiment" failed. He lists several reasons (e.g., fixation on manufacturing companies, piecemeal approach, inadequate guidance, complexity). Whether one agrees with all of them or not, they certainly require augmentation. The major reasons for this "failure" seem to me to be the abating of inflation during the second half of the 1980s, and the resistance of management toward inflation accounting because of additional accounting costs, and the revelation of additional information not only to the public but also to the competition, and as well as the insufficient education (not only of the public but of financial analysts and even accountants) concerning the subtleties of inflation accounting. As a result of this last item, professionals as well as the public were often unable to interpret the resulting figures. In other words, the patient did not take the medicine, partly because he already deemed himself to be cured, and partly because he had lost confidence in it, due to a lack of understanding as to the long-term benefits, as well as its working. But whether this "experiment" was a "fiasco", as Hanna calls it, or a partial success, depends on one's point of view. Although more firms than ever before seem to apply inflation accounting on a voluntary or internal basis, from the practical point of "healing the patient", the experiment was a set-back. Because apart from constantly *shifting* prices, inflation is on the increase again, and an unadjusted inflation rate of four to six per cent accumulates quickly, leading to gross distortions in the accounting system.

Moreover, from the academic and educational point of view, the experiment certainly was no fiasco. Never before have so many people been aware of and even familiar with inflation accounting, and never before has a relatively complex accounting model (developed *for specific purposes* by academics over more than six decades) temporarily been legislated in several countries.[35] Whether inflation accounting will be resurrected in practice seems to be mainly a *political* question—after all, the FASB decision to discontinue inflation accounting seems to have hinged on a single vote. But from a theoretical point of view, inflation accounting is not dead at all, and its various models will be further developed and made available to practitioners whenever they are ready for it.

Our choice for reprint was Thornton's [1986] article, reprinted here as paper Number 5, "Current Cost Disclosers and Nondisclosers: Theory and Canadian Evidence" which in 1987 won the first CAAA Award for Distinguished Contribution to Accounting Thought. This is a study of the Canadian situation, but may prove to be of interest to a much wider audience because of the results revealed as well as the methodology applied (see also his follow-up study, Thornton [1988a]). Thornton [1986] shows that (in 1983), of the 380 firms which met the *CICA Handbook* criteria, only 73 (i.e., 19.2 per cent) complied with Section 4510, the section of the *Handbook* which prescribed disclosure of supplementary information about the effects of changing prices. Thornton's [1986] study offers evidence that the firms' disclosure decisions were based partly on what they believed to be "cost/benefit considerations" and partly on the basis of their auditors' advice. The latter influence is related to the fact that firms audited by other than the Big Eight public accounting firms made virtually no effort to disclose price-level effects—though utility companies, due to their special political-economic situation, seem to constitute a separate group more strongly motivated to disclose such information. Thornton's [1986] paper discusses the legalistic differences between pertinent U.S. and Canadian "legislation", as well as some previous work. It hypothesizes that disclosure of "nonhistoric cost financial statements" is related to *five* factors (materiality, SEC listing, auditor, size, and industry), discusses in detail the empirical research (including data and statistical tests on sub-populations), and presents the results, outlined above, together with a conclusion on some limitations of this excellent study.

Benston [1986] in commenting on Thornton's [1986] paper (at a conference organized by *Contemporary Accounting Research*) points out that similar empirical studies done in the U.S. found "that the disclosures [of current values] did not affect the risk and market-adjusted share prices of the disclosing companies", and praises Thornton's paper as offering "a good example of how methodology can be described and applied effectively." Benston also hints at the important, yet unresolved issue of cost-benefit analysis in connection with current value/inflation accounting, and is furthermore concerned with related issues of hypothesis testing. Another commentator, Buzby [1986], is concerned with the extent to which Thornton's study helps us to understand "the reasons behind the disclosure versus nondisclosure" of current values. He recommends, on one hand, a slightly more cautious conclusion than the one drawn by Thornton, but on the other hand, suggests that "the CICA's concern with cost/benefit should encompass the population of investors and creditors who make use of external financial statements", which seems to go beyond Thornton's analysis but which is difficult to accomplish.

Finally, it must be pointed out that a group of financial accountants—most typically Beaver and Landsman [1983]—have undertaken research which, according to their interpretation, indicates that none of the inflation accounting models supplies information superior to the traditional historical cost model.[36] Apart from the fact that some other pertinent studies seem to contradict those results,[37] the major fallacy of this award-winning monograph by Beaver and Landsman [1983] lies in accepting the short-term pricing behaviour of investors as the decision criterion, instead of pursuing a long-term cost-benefit analysis (cf. Espahbodi and Hendrickson [1986] and Stark [1987]). If investors are unable to read those supplementary statements correctly (as previously suggested), it may merely mean that the additional or incremental information supplied is not properly absorbed in the investment decision-making process. It does *not* constitute reliable evidence that inflation accounting models fail to *supply* incremental information, because a major premise of information or communication theory is that *the information content of a message cannot depend on the subjective ability of individual recipients to decode this information*. Beaver's and Landsman's [1983] study, financed by the FASB, may well have influenced the one critical vote against continuation of changing price-level accounting legislation in the USA. If so, it was a triumph of lopsided sophistication over common sense.

As to the future, and the issues of *complexity* and *capital maintenance* (physical capital maintenance *versus* real financial capital maintenance), Hanna's [1988] above-mentioned paper requires some additional thoughts. On the engineering side, actual practice was capable of mastering systems of much greater complexity; thus I believe that on the financial side the relatively moderate complexity of inflation accounting models can be successfully handled, provided the participating parties have the will to re-implement them. As to the capital maintenance question, the two FASB inflation models, and particularly the ultimate three versions of the CICA inflation models were flexible enough to satisfy *real financial* as well as *physical capital maintenance* (the latter is confusingly called "productive capacity maintenance" by the CICA and others). But since each model satisfies a different information purpose, I cannot agree with Hanna [1988] to categorically prefer one over the other.

With some stretch of imagination, inflation accounting may be regarded as belonging to the area of *social accountability,* and thus both topics are mentioned here in Section (vi). As to a concise survey of social accounting, one may refer to a short article (from *CGA Magazine*), "An Explanation of Social Accounting" by Mathews [1987], which clarifies the different ways in which the term "social accounting" has been used and describes concisely its different branches. Above all, it describes what seems to have become its most popular branch, "social responsibility accounting".[38] Traditionally, national income accounting together with other macro-accounting systems have been summarized under the heading "social accounting". For an excellent survey of this particular branch, I refer the reader to a reprint of Stone's [1986] Nobel Memorial Lecture. During recent decades (particularly during the 1980s), such other branches as "social responsibility accounting", "total impact accounting", "social indicators accounting" and "societal accounting" became prominent under the increasing clamour for greater social and environmental responsibility of business corporations—see also Belkaoui's [1984] *Socio-Economic Accounting.*

(vii) To Part VI: Agency-Contract Theory

The application of agency-contract theory to accounting, and the closely connected information economics, also continued during the 1980s, and followed fairly well-established lines: i.e., researchers were occupied with what T.S. Kuhn [1962/70] called the puzzle-solving of ordinary science. Several surveys or similar articles in this area have appeared since the first edition of our Main Volume: for example, Thornton [1984/85], Namazi [1985], Gamble and O'Doherty [1987], Hyman and Walker [1988], Eisenhardt [1989], and Baiman [1990]. Moreover, the most recent of these surveys (Baiman [1990]) is an excellent up-dating of Baiman [1982/84], previously reprinted in our original anthology, and accordingly, we offer this "second look" at agency theory to our readers. Reprinted as Paper Number 6, "Agency Research in Managerial Accounting: A Second Look", surveys a good deal of recent agency literature, with some emphasis on managerial aspects, but perhaps less so than in his original article. Here, Baiman's major intention is to relate different sub-areas to each other, and in doing so he distinguishes between the following three approaches or "models":

- The *principal agency model,* which Baiman sees as providing a more rigorous and coherent framework for dealing with such traditional managerial issues as *motivational problems, transfer pricing,* and *cooperative solutions.*
- The *model of transaction cost economics,* which showed that *incomplete* contracts create opportunistic managerial behaviour, which in turn may distort investment decisions (the *governance* problem). This also provides an alternative or perhaps complementary explanation for the diverse forms of the contractual organization of firms (the traditional explanation lies in the existence of monopolistic forces).
- The *Rochester* model (positive theory of accounting—see Section v) which attempted to relate agency theory to issues of management control, as well as to the choice of financial accounting policy, particularly in efficient markets. A further contribution of this model or school lies in promoting empirical testing through identifying regularities in managerial behaviour and executive compensation.

Another section deals with *empirical tests of the agency paradigm.* There exist many more such tests for financial than for managerial accounting—particularly the indirect testing as to the extent managerial decisions are influenced by various compensation plans. But since the tests are indirect, a certain plan may possibly be adopted for other reasons than reducing agency costs. This difficulty in identifying the "decision horizons" and related problems has been investigated empirically. Among such studies is Wolfson's [1985] AICPA/AAA-award winning paper "Empirical Evidence of Incentive Problems and Their Mitigation in Oil and Gas Tax Shelter Programs", in which, on the basis of four contract types and two partnership types (general vs. limited), different trade-offs between tax effects and incentive effects are distinguished and studied. But other investigations (e.g., Hagerty and Siegel [1988] and Amershi and Butterworth [1988]), question whether all theoretical results of agency theory can be tested, particularly whether it is possible to distinguish between the different demands that an executive contract is expected to fulfill (e.g., to overcome moral hazards vs. pure risk sharing). Indeed, empirical accounting research itself is subject to many constraints, and it is difficult to directly measure the variables crucial for contracts in agency theory.

The remaining part of Baiman's [1990] work deals with recent developments. Some of the papers discussed are designed to counter the criticism raised against agency theory; for instance:

- the difficulty of *court enforcement*, e.g., Fudenberg and Tirole [1988];
- *contract incompleteness and complexity* (multiperiod settings), e.g., Green and Laffont [1988a, 1988b], Kreps [1984], Lambert [1983];
- *measurement problems* and *strategic aspects* of contract selection, e.g., Fershtman and Judd [1984, 1986]; and
- *partial equilibrium of the labour market*, e.g., Holmstrom and Ricart-Costa [1986].

Other papers are more oriented towards managerial problems such as:

- the *value of monitoring* (see several unpublished papers cited by Baiman);
- *income manipulation*, e.g., Healy [1985];
- *income smoothing*, e.g., Lambert [1984] and Dye [1988];
- *delegating the choice of monitoring systems*, e.g., Demski, Patell and Wolfson [1984];
- *cost allocation*, e.g., Baiman and Noel [1985];
- *the distinction between performance measures and reward measures*, see Banker and Datar [1989]; and
- *strategies for enhancing the contributions of agency theory*, see Marschak and Reichelstein [1987].

One might also mention the application of agency theory to the budgeting process, which would follow from research done by Baiman and Evans [1983], Young [1985], etc. Some further and important contributions to this agency theory, not mentioned by Baiman [1990], seem to be Hughes' [1984] *A Contract Perspective on Accounting Valuation*, the Canadian CGA Research Foundation monograph by Berg, *et al.* [1990] on *The Value of Communication in Agency Contracts: Theory and Experimental Evidence*, and such articles as Amershi [1986], Atkinson and Feltham [1982], Kanodia [1985], Blazenko and Scott [1986],[39] Butterworth and Falk [1986], P.J. Hughes [1986], Feltham [1984/89], Feltham and Hughes [1988], and Scott [1988]. The latter received the 1988 CAAA Award for Distinguished Contribution to Accounting Thought. Furthermore, there are the two anthologies by Pratt and Zeckenhauser [1985], and Feltham, Amershi, and Ziemba [1988], though neither of them are limited to accounting issues; and finally, a book on contract theory is in preparation by Sunder [1991].

A short paper by Demski [1985], one of the major pioneers of information economics in accounting, does not so much concentrate on agency problems, but offers instead a general view of accounting research. Demski pleads for the adoption of a broader, perhaps "more holistic",[40] view of accounting, in which different models should not be seen as competing with each other but rather as complementing each other (as, for example, in the *combination* of earnings and cash flow models). Demski also stresses the importance of history in accounting (as previously mentioned in Section ii), particularly when choosing between short- run and long-term points of view. The major significance of this article lies in the admission, by a thoroughly analytical researcher, that *there can be dangers in a purely rational point of view* when it is applied to the short-run or not seen in its full context. I could not wish for a better reinforcement of my own philosophy, expressed in Mattessich [1978].

Further surveys of agency theory are found by Hart and Holmstrom [1987], Holmstrom and Tirole [1987], and Morris [1987]. The latter is called "Signalling, Agency Theory and Accounting Policy Choice"; it is partly a survey and partly an attempt to show how signalling theory and agency theory complement each other. Since this viewpoint goes somewhat beyond the traditional treatment of agency theory, it is particularly recommended to readers interested in this area. What is peculiar in this paper is the attempt *to compare* (without any mathematics) *the axiomatic basis* of signalling theory with that of agency theory. Furthermore, the *schematic* demonstration (of its Figure 1) shows under what circumstances two theories are *consistent* with each other, when one *implies* the other, when they are *identical* to each other, or when one *contradicts* the other. An alternative comparison, which relies on the predictions and consequences of both theories, is rejected by the author. Morris presents, in a non-mathematical way, the necessary and sufficient conditions of both theories, and demonstrates that agency theory and signalling theory, although *neither* equivalent nor implying each other, do share the same necessary conditions. Furthermore, the sufficient conditions of both theories, though not equivalent, are consistent with each other; therefore the combination of both theories into a "super-theory"—which Morris [1987], perhaps incorrectly, calls a "meta-theory" (which would mean a theory in the meta- language)—is feasible. The Appendix of Morris' paper demonstrates graphically "that information asymmetry can lead to agency costs which are borne by the agent in above-average firms, but by the principal in below-average firms" (presupposing efficient markets for both labour and capital, which transfer these costs).

The incorporation of information economics, signalling theory, the contract approach, etc. into a kind of super agency-contract theory, and the extension of the latter to accounting, auditing, economics, ethics, and finance as well as to management-organization theory (for the latter see Eisenhardt [1989]) is a healthy sign, and indicates that agency-contract theory is likely to be more than a temporary fad in spite of some criticism—e.g., Kaplan [1984]. Agency-contract theory is often regarded as a purely analytical area, but during the second half of the 1980s a series of *empirical* agency-contract studies emerged and are listed (together with some details about approach, sample size, agency variables, etc.) in our Table 5 taken from Eisenhardt [1989].[41]

Agency theory has an unexpectedly broad spectrum of application—cf. Antle [1989]—and one of its newest areas of application seems to be ethics. Since problems of ethics have stirred the minds of accountants considerably during the 1980s, it may be opportune to refer to "The Economics of Ethics" by Noreen [1988]. The basic thrust of this paper lies in the idea that agency-contract theory offers an excellent *analytical* illustration that the ethical behaviour of contracting parties may save costs and lead to a more efficient operation (i.e., ethics serves as

Table 5
Summary of Agency Theory Studies [of Empirical Nature]

Author(s)	Research Stream	Sample	Agency Variables	Companion Theory	Dependent Variables	Results
Amihud & Lev (1981)	Positivist	309 *Fortune 500* firms	Manager vs. owner controlled	None	Conglomerate mergers & diversification	Support
Walking & Long (1984)	Positivist	105 U.S. firms	Management's equity & options	Shareholder welfare & other controls	Managerial resistance to takeover bid	Support
Anderson (1985)	Principal-Agent	159 sales districts in 13 electronics firms	Importance of nonselling activities, length of selling cycle, & difficulty evaluating sales performance	Transaction cost	Representative vs. corporate sales force	Mixed
Eisenhardt (1985)	Principal-Agent	54 retail stores	Information systems, cost of outcome measurement, & outcome uncertainty	Organizational control	Salary vs. commission	Support
Eccles (1985)	Principal-Agent	150 interviews in 13 chemical, electronics, heavy machinery, & machine component firms	Decentralization	Equity	Type of transfer price	Inductive model
Wolfson (1985)	Positivist	39 oil & gas limited partnerships	General partner's track record	Tax effects	Share price	Support
Argawal & Mandelber (1987)	Positivist	209 major corporations	Executive stock holdings	None	Acquisitions, divestitures, & debt/equity ratio	Support
Kosnik (1987)	Positivist	110 major corporations targeted for greenmail	Proportion of outside directors, equity held by outside directors, & outside directors with executive experience	Hegemony	Payment of greenmail (Yes/No)	Mixed
Eisenhardt (1986)	Principal-Agent	54 retail stores	Job programmability, span of control, & outcome uncertainty	Institutional	Salary vs. commission	Support
Conlon & Parks (1986)	Principal-Agent	40 dyads	Monitoring	Institutional	Performance-contingent compensation	Support
Barney (1988)	Positivist	32 Japanese electronics frms	Employee stock ownership	Size & growth control	Cost of equity	Support
Singh & Harianto (in press)	Positivist	84 *Fortune 500* firms	Managerial stock ownership & takeover threat	Managerialist	Golden parachute contracts	Support

Note: this set of studies was developed through contacting other agency researchers, scanning journals, and following up referenced articles. Although the list is not exhaustive, it includes many of the releveant studies. Reprinted from Eisenhardt (1989), pp. 66-67 the "behavioural lubricant of social and economic systems"). In other words, a certain minimum of ethical behaviour (not taken into consideration in traditional agency theory) is necessary for any economy to function. As Noreen [1988, p. 360] says, agency theory "can be used to provide a series of instructive parables that illustrate the adverse consequences on social and economic systems of unconstrained opportunistic behavior." Therefore, agency theory could become an impetus in the search for further remedies to induce ethical attitudes. The author explores the ways in which the selection rules for ethical behaviour can be attained. He refers to Adam Smith's "impartial spectator", to Harsanyi's [1976] "blind" rule setting, and Gaa's [1986, 1988a, 1988b] "rules for security markets". Noreen also considers religious and other behavioural norms as well as genetic control mechanisms. His article is programmatic, and does not exploit agency-contract theory in any depth, but one of his students, Chi [1989], has taken up this very challenge, and has begun to examine settings (and their consequences) of agency theory in which some agents behave according to established ethical norms, while others rely merely on the maximization of their own utility.

In concluding this Section, it must be pointed out that at the present stage, the fusion of information economics with agency theory and other related areas, as well as further developments towards an agency-contract super-theory, seem to be some of the major steps of accounting research in the 1980s. The major contribution of agency theory, as Demski sees it, lies in clarifying certain control situations in which information use is *endogenous* (enabling internally consistent models). This in turn leads to the *combining* of information from different sources; that is, taking into consideration *non-accounting* information no less than accounting information. But agency-contract theory will have to be further developed, and enriched by additional empirical confirmation, before a final verdict can be given.

(viii) Research In Auditing

The space limitations of this supplementary volume regrettably did not permit the inclusion of a separate article on the state of auditing—Scott's [1984] excellent survey might have been the appropriate choice. Indeed, during the late 1970s and 1980s, auditing research experienced a surprising expansion. Auditing has been an important part of accounting for a long time, and it is no coincidence that such a classic as *Montgomery's Auditing* is still being published (see Sullivan et al. [1985]).[42] But from a research point of view, auditing has, for decades, been a backwater until gradually statistical techniques, decision models, behavioural studies, and even philosophical considerations were applied to it. Although this trend had begun already in the 1960s, its full impact has been felt during the past two decades, as auditing has become an integral and even leading part of the accounting research programme. Therefore, even without a separate reprint paper in this supplement, a concise survey (based mainly on Scott [1984] and some recent material) in this commentary is well justified.

A major manifestation of the increasing importance of auditing research is the founding of a separate journal in 1981/82, *Auditing: A Journal of Practice and Theory* (apart from the *Journal of Accounting, Auditing, and Finance* which had already been started in 1977/78 but is *not* exclusively devoted to auditing). These two publication series, pertinent monographs, and numerous articles in other accounting journals (particularly in the *Journal of Accounting Research, The Accounting Review,* and *Contemporary Accounting Research* as well as *Advances in Accounting*[43]) will have to be consulted for actual research results, while readers looking for detailed surveys are referred to Kinney [1986a], Felix and Kinney [1982], as well as to Scott's [1984] comprehensive paper "The State of the Art of Academic Research in Auditing", a book by Cushing and Loebbecke [1986] and an award-winning text by Herbert [1986], *Auditing the Performance of Management*. In addition, there are two anthologies from Great Britain, and two from America: Hopwood, Bromwich and Shaw [1982], *Auditing Research: Issues and Opportunities*, Kinney [1986a], *Fifty Years of Statistical Auditing;* and more recently, one edited by Lee [1988], *The Evolution of Audit Thought and Practice*, and another edited by Abdel-khalik and Solomon [1988], *Research Opportunities in Auditing: The Second Decade.*[44]

Scott [1984] views auditing as "a social mechanism to enhance the process of contracting, thereby improving the operation of securities and managerial labour markets" (p. 153). At the 1990 Annual CAAA Meeting, he pointed out that auditing offers a special kind of information, which happens to be a particularly complex kind of commodity. He is also of the opinion that in an efficient market "the investor is *price-protected*", and that it is management which has a particular interest in hiring an auditor. Auditing pivots on the notion of *efficiency* and, more recently, on *effectiveness* and thus mainly on normative models. Statistical sampling enables the auditor to quantify his or her sampling risk, and might also help to enhance the consensus among auditors.

During the 1980s, two official publications, referring among other subjects to statistical auditing, became particularly prominent: the CICA's [1980a] *Extent of Audit Testing* and the AICPA's [1981] *Statement on Auditing Standards* (SAS No. 39) the latter as a follow-up to AICPA [1972-74]. These publications discuss such notions as attribute estimation, hypothesis testing (mainly to avoid the acceptance of erroneous auditing hypotheses or Type II errors), compliance tests, auditing strategies and analytical reviews (for details on the latter two see also the CAAA monograph by Boritz, Gaber and Lemon [1987], and the Canadian CGA Research Foundation monograph by Biggs, Mock and Watkins [1989] respectively).

Other prominent publications in statistical auditing of the 1980's are Beck [1980] dealing with regression estimators when using auxiliary populations (e.g., book values) instead of true populations (e.g., current values); Ijiri and Leitch [1980] investigating the multivariate statistical problem faced by auditors (due to errors in one account causing errors in another account) and offering remedial models; the Wildman award-winning study on a comparison of audit methodologies by Cushing and Loebbecke [1986]; Duke, Neter and Leitch [1982] presenting an empirical comparative study of the error probabilities of different statistical estimators; Hylas and Ashton [1982] offering evidence that *analytical reviews* are quite effective in disclosing correlation errors (see also Biggs, Mock and Watkins [1989]); and Leitch, Neter, Plante and Sinha [1982] pointing out that the multinomial model (previously suggested by two of these authors) is computationally infeasible when (in Dollar Unit Sampling studies, which have become increasingly popular) too many errors arise as a consequence of "perverse" populations. Other studies concerned with similar sampling procedures are those by Dworin and Grimlund [1983] and Grimlund [1982]. The latter extends previously developed models of the internal control/final balance interface. Mock and Turner [1981] document considerable discrepancies in sample sizes: for a single group of auditors, such discrepancy seems to be even larger for inter-firm comparisons, as Ashton and Brown [1980] indicate.

Apart from sampling theory, there exists a vast literature dealing with the auditing application of *Bayesian decision theory* and alternatives like the Brunswik lens model. For the latter, see Mock and Turner [1981], and for the relationship between *information economic* models and *human information processing* theories, see Libby [1981, Ch. 3], as well as Hilton [1980], which demonstrates the consistency of the lens model with the decision model. But the literature on heuristics and biases suggests that in the auditor's complex environment, decision theory may be neither positively nor normatively valid (see Scott [1984] p. 171). In the application of decision theory (as in that of sampling theory) to auditing, much of the original literature is found in the 1970s (and thus is not quoted here). But apart from several surveys of this literature (see for example Joyce and Libby [1982]), and the publications mentioned above, the following references point out some highlights.

A series of experiments and behavioural studies further extended the use of *heuristics* in decision theory which was developed in the 1970s and then applied to auditing (see Joyce and Biddle [1981a, 1981b], Kinney and Uecker [1982], as well as Biggs and Mock [1983]). The impact of "situational" and interacting forces, blurring the auditing results, received special attention in Gibbins and Wolf [1982a, 1982b]. Furthermore, the application of *protocol analysis* and similar devices for investigating auditing decision situations has found some attention in Biggs and Mock [1983], and Gibbins [1982], Schultz and Reckers [1981], Solomon [1982], as well as Trotman, Yetton, and Zimmer [1983], while Boritz [1983], as well as Hamilton and Wright [1982], studied the influence of accumulated experience on the auditor's judgment. Two CCGA Research Foundation monographs, one by Ashton [1983], *Research in Audit Decision Making: Rationale, Evidence, and Implications,* and the other by Mock and Vertinsky [1985], *Risk Assessment in Accounting and Auditing,* offer important new insights in this area. Of course, the application of decision theory to actual auditing practice will take some time, but interest by practitioners (perhaps to justify smaller audit sizes) is increasing, as noted by Godfrey and Neter [1984]. Finally, Scott suggests that:

> ... if, across the set of all auditors, the various decision biases cancel out, decision theory may be a reasonable model of behaviour at the level of the average auditor even if it is not a good descriptor at the level of the individual auditor.
>
> Scott [1984], p. 179

Auditing is a broad field with a strong social perspective, and is by no means limited to statistical considerations. Indeed, Biggs, Mock and Watkins [1989] indicate in their CCGA Research Foundation monograph on *Analytical Review Procedures and Processing in Auditing* that "auditor judgment, rather than statistical modelling, is predominant" (p. vii). Thus it is hardly surprising that auditing has drawn other developments into its orbit, such as the theories of organization, pricing and monopolistic competition, as well as agency theory. The dominant role of the few large international public accounting firms, and the possibility of monopolistic competition led Simunic [1980] to a careful investigation which, however, could not reject the hypothesis of competitive pricing in the audit industry and thus does not confirm suspected monopolistic tendencies.

The related aspects of the auditor's independence and the conflict arising from his or her management advisory service are different concerns, and were also examined by Simunic [1984] with the conclusion that such services may instead have a beneficial effect upon the client, particularly when the auditor can perform them more inexpensively than a separate consultant. Another study with similar conclusions for Canadian firms was presented in Zéghal's [1989] CCGA Research Foundation monograph *Le marché de la vérification au Canada.* A further empirical study concerning the market for various audit services can be found in another CCGA Research Foundation monograph by Simunic and Stein [1987] on *Product Differentiation in Auditing: Auditor Choice in the Market for Unseasoned New Issues.* The somewhat more traditional topic of *materiality* has been taken up in a third CCGA Research Foundation monograph, *Materiality: An Empirical Study of Actual Auditor Decisions* by Robinson and Fertuck [1985]. This monograph examines how auditors make material decisions in actual practice. Finally there is a research project underway by Gaa on *Auditors and Society: The Ethical Foundations of Public Accounting* (preliminary title). For an introduction to this area, see Gaa [1988b].

The application of *agency theory* to auditing is intimately connected with the extension of the former into the realm of *multiperson* decision theory. But in auditing, the concern is not merely the introduction of several principals or agents, but the need for a system verifying the earnings reported by management, and other messages to better attract equity investors to the firm: see Evans [1980], Atkinson and Feltham [1982], Antle [1982], and particularly Gjesdal [1981]. The latter introduces a simple version of a multiperiod model, and suggests how the audit function (with sharing rules between principal and agent) can formally be specified in agency theory.[45]

Many challenging problems in auditing, as well as border areas concerning agency-contract theory and other fields, still remain open. One of the most important border areas relates auditing to electronic data processing, and expert systems. Although this area of specialization belongs more properly to the now-separate MIS literature (see our remarks in Section iv), we refer the reader to such books as Davis and Weber [1983] *Auditing Advanced EDP Systems: A Survey of Practice and Development of a Theory,* and Vasarhelyi's [1989] anthology *Artificial Intelligence in Accounting and Auditing: The Use of Expert Systems.* Another specialization concerns the area of international aspects of auditing, which is briefly referred to in the next Section.

(ix) International Accounting Research

The growth and continuing spread of multinational corporations, as well as the globalization of capital markets, has led to a steadily increasing interest in international accounting. During the waning 1980s, this may well have been the fastest growing sub-area of our discipline; and it may be no coincidence that the 1989 Annual Meeting of the American Accounting Association was held under the topic of "International Accounting" and the chairmanship of Professor Gerhard Mueller, a major pioneer of this particular sub-area. Here, too, we encounter the founding (in 1987) of a specialized (annual) research outlet, *Advances in International Accounting,* in addition to the older *International Journal of Accounting Education and Research* (and the professional publication *The International Accountant*). Furthermore, the founding of the International Association on Accounting Education and Research, three years ago, and its information bulletin, *Cosmos Accountancy Chronicle,* must be mentioned here.

The pertinent literature is still dominated by textbooks and supplementary readings; and, as Samuels and Piper [1985] point out, with reference to the 1980/81 International Accounting and Auditing Standards Committee, "... the Committee is critical of the research in this field, regarding much of it as dull, lacking a framework of reference, with few theoretical treaties and little scientific rigor in the empirical studies" (p. 1). Half a decade later, however, the situation had improved somewhat and the conclusion is on a more positive note: "it would appear that it will not be long before the standard of research in international accounting will rise to the level of that in other areas of accounting" (Samuels and Piper [1985] p. 156). And award winning books like Choi and Mueller [1984], winners of the Wildman Medal for 1986, have come forth.

Articles in this field span a wide range, and Scott's and Troberg's [1980] monograph, *Eighty-eight International Accounting Problems in Rank Order of Importance,* lists the following seven categories: (1) exchange rates and translations; (2) accounting standards; (3) auditing; (4) inflation accounting; (5) performance evaluation; (6) information control systems; and (7) taxation.[46] Among noteworthy books, beyond textbooks and anthologies, there are: a slim volume from Great Britain by Samuels and Piper [1985], entitled *International Accounting: A Survey,* and two books by Belkaoui, *International Accounting* [1985a] and *The New Environment in International Accounting Issues and Practices* [1988], as well as a C CGA Research Foundation monograph by Most [1984], *International Conflict of Accounting Standards.* Such books and their bibliographies afford the reader an excellent spectrum of major articles on a wide variety of topics. For national differences in consolidation accounting, see Parker [1984]. There is also a fine survey paper by Binden and Gernon [1987] which would have been reprinted here, were it not for the constraints imposed upon this *Supplementary Volume.*

Regarding the special area of international *auditing* and its standards, the major publications of the 1980s are Campbell's [1985] anthology, *International Auditing: A Comparative Survey of Professional Requirements in Australia, Canada, France, West Germany, Japan, the Netherlands, the U.K. and the USA,* and Needles' [1985] anthology, *Comparative International Auditing Standards.*

(x) Growing Concern About The Reality Behind Accounting, And Other Foundational Issues

In previous Sections, the issue of how realistic or unrealistic accounting models are, has been repeatedly touched upon. This Section deals with a quite different set of reality issues. A perennial problem emerging in the accounting literature of the 1980s was the search for what some accountants call *proxies* or *surrogates* (see Ijiri [1967]), and what other scientists address as *indicators* and *observational variables.* The latter are either part of reality or, at least, much closer to reality than the *theoretical variables* which have to be connected with the former by *indicator* (or *surrogate*) *hypotheses.*[47] Such accounting publications as Patell [1979], Dyckman and Morse [1986, pp. 7, 81, 83, 89], and many others, are much concerned with the fact that many accounting variables are not directly observable.

Thus, a series of questions arises: Which accounting variables are nothing but concepts; which are theoretical variables indirectly related to reality; and which are observational variables directly backed by reality? Is it true that such notions as "income" and "owners' equity" are concepts without any reality behind them, as Heath [1987], for example, asserts? Or can we accept Sterling's [1988, p. 4] claim that "with rare exceptions accounting numerals do not represent phenomena, any phenomena"? Is it possible to assign reality status to *values* of economic objects and claims? Can these problems be solved only by treating them as "metaphors", as Thornton [1988b] seems to suggest? I have tried to answer these questions in Mattessich [1991], briefly discussed below. Other, more metaphysical questions of the "reality issue" are raised by Tomkins' and Groves' [1983] "The Everyday Accountant and Researching His Reality", which evoked a rich response by such authors as Abdel-khalik and Ajinka [1983], Morgan [1983], and Willmot [1983].

Two major foundational works published during the 1980s, Devine's [1985] five volume *Essays on Accounting Theory,* and Ijiri's [1989] *Momentum Accounting and Triple-Entry Bookkeeping: Exploring the Dynamic Structure of Accounting Measurements,* both have their roots in preceding decades. The articles in Devine's [1985] collection were written over a time span of twenty or thirty years, and they cover the three broad areas of theory construction, behavioural accounting (of which Devine could be regarded as one of the pioneers), and income theory. The broad panoramic and philosophical view of this comprehensive work makes it not only one of the most monumental accounting publications of the 1980s, but also offers an excellent picture of the major efforts of theory development during the last three decades or so.

While Devine's [1985] work mainly mirrors the past, the full appreciation and practical value of Ijiri's [1989] publication which, no less than Devine's, is the result of decades of contemplation is geared to the third millenium. Preparatory work to this book can be found in Ijiri [1966] and subsequent publications; but the vision of this highly original work is so far-reaching that it may well have to wait for another decade or more to be materialized in practice.[48] Although its basis is *triple-entry* bookkeeping, its core-idea is not merely an extension of double-entry, but one that exploits the terminology and structure of physics to describe the dynamics of accounting.

Using w for wealth, Δw for income, and t for time (duration), Ijiri [1989, p. 85] characterizes such newly introduced concepts and measures as follows:

momentum	=	dw/dt	=	$\dot{w}$	impulse	=	$\Delta\dot{w}$
action	=	$\Delta^2 w$	=	$\Delta^3 \int w\, dt$	force	=	$\ddot{w}$
benefit	=	$\int w\, dt$			utilization	=	$\Delta \int w\, dt$

But these terms, borrowed from mechanics, have to be somewhat stretched before they fit accounting. If, for example, wealth (in accounting) is taken to correspond to mass (in physics), the structural analogies would *not* hold. But Ijiri, either consciously or subconsciously, made the ingenious leap of accepting *wealth* as corresponding to "mass times distance", and lo and behold, accounting assumes a structure analogous to some physical relations. Thus, the *income momentum* (called "momentum" = growth-rate of wealth per time unit) corresponds to the linear momentum (mass times velocity = mass-distance per time), *force,* or better, *income force* (growth-rate of income momentum per time unit) then corresponds to physical force (mass times acceleration = growth rate of linear momentum), and *impulse,* or better, *income impulse* (increase in the income momentum growth rate) would somewhat correspond to the mechanical impulse (increase in momentum = force times time).

Such analogies between physics and accounting (as well as economics) might seem trivial to many accountants, but in the long-run, they may prove to be of greater foundational value than most academics might be inclined to believe at this stage. Indeed, I consider the formulation of those structural analogies the true harbingers of Ijiri's theory, more so than the "triple-entry" or his three new postulates of momentum reconciliation, conservation, and attribution (see Ijiri [1989], pp. 104-106).[49] There is another particularly interesting and notable feature: Ijiri *internalizes,* i.e., incorporates, managerial-behavioural features into the framework of accounting proper, while most recent theories have more or less disregarded or abandoned this framework. These other theories convert accounting into a kind of economics or finance, or a branch of the behavioural sciences, thus *externalizing* our discipline.

A further crucial foundational issue concerns the claim asserted by Post-Kuhnian and structuralist philosophy, that *a theory is an entire net of theory elements* (and thus is much more than an isolated axiomatic framework). I have tried to apply this thought to accounting research in Mattessich [1990a] "Paradigms, Research Traditions and Theory Nets of Accounting", demonstrating that current "accounting theory" can indeed be interpreted as consisting of three competing research traditions, each constituting a network of several "mini-theories" or theory elements.[50] In another paper, "Epistemological Aspects of Accounting" (Mattessich 1990c], I extended this approach. Here, the analysis is no longer limited to the *purely conceptual* dichotomy of "theoretical *versus* non-theoretical variables" (as used by the structuralists), but enriched by the dichotomy between "non-(or not-yet) observational variables vs. observational variables" as encountered on the *reality level*.

Although this section (like the preceding one) does not provide a separate reprint, I take this opportunity to refer *en passant* to a paper of mine for readers interested in this fundamental and, in the long-run, crucial reality problem and research area. In Mattessich [1991], "Social Reality and the Measurement of its Phenomena" (1991 Haim Falk Award for Distinguished Contribution to Accounting Thought), I deliberately avoid the metaphysical question about ultimate reality, but concentrate on the juxtaposition between *physical* and *social* reality, as well as the linguistic use of the word "real" as encountered in everyday business dealings. In doing so, it is relatively easy to demonstrate that owners' equity and income (as, for example, a specific increase in owners' equity) are real in the sense that they are property rights. The latter are backed up by a social and usually even legal reality—how would you react if somebody argued that the right to your home or other property is not real? Immense confusion (and not only a linguistic one) would arise, were we to put income and owners' equity into the same pot with such notions as the natural number "3", the constellation of the "Big Dipper" and others that are *nothing but concepts,* and hence not backed by any empirical level in the hierarchy of total reality.

A somewhat more difficult and even more important concern discussed in the same paper deals with the closely-related problem of estimating or "measuring" the values of income, owners' equity, assets, liabilities, etc. The measurement of social variables is usually much more complex than that of some physical variables. But this does not justify Sterling's [1988,1989] assertion that accountants rarely measure (or estimate) real phenomena; it merely means that we are confronted with a highly complex *methodological* issue, which has to be dealt with on a cost/benefit basis, and under consideration of formal or informal reliability estimates.

Beyond the reality problem, there are further *foundational* queries which have experienced some revival during the 1980s but they too are more on the periphery than in main-stream accounting. For example, the search for a precise and general formulation of the *basic accounting assumptions* has recently been resumed in several quarters, perhaps because of the inadequacy of the FASB's *conceptual framework.*[51] For details, see such publications as Tanaka's [1982] *The Structure of Accounting Language,* Deguchi's and Nakano's [1986] "Axiomatic Foundations of Vector Accounting", Willett's [1987, 1988] "An Axiomatic Theory of Accounting Measurement–Parts I and II", Nehmer's [1988] *Accounting Information Systems as Algebraic and First Order Axiomatic Models,* Salvary's [1989] *An Analytical Framework for Accounting Theory,* as well as Balzer's and Mattessich's [1991] "An Axiomatic Structure of Basic Accounting: Towards a Structuralist Reconstruction". The latter reflects my collaboration with one of the leading structuralist philosophers of science, who in team work with other structuralists,[52] has previously axiomatized theories of several empirical and mathematical disciplines (see, for example, Balzer, Moulines, and Sneed [1987]).

This should bring accounting axiomatization into line with attempts at structural reconstruction in other disciplines, and promote a uniform approach across various empirical disciplines. While one objective of such a structuralist reconstruction of accounting is the disclosure and description of different theory nets, the other objective must be compared to that of *microscopes* and *X-ray pictures.* Indeed, the meticulous reconstruction of any theory reveals logical details and structural relations never seen before—something that is bound to be beneficial in an age of progressive computerization. Just as previous axiomatization attempts have led to matrix accounting, budget simulation (e.g., Mattessich [1961] and [1964a/77]), and ultimately to the many best-selling microcomputer *spreadsheet programmes,* so these new efforts may one day aid in the construction of accounting expert systems and new computerized data processing systems.[53]

Related to this is another recent revival of previously-done pioneering work, and concerns matrix accounting: e.g., Leech's [1986], "The Theory and Development of a Matrix-Based Accounting System", Mepham's [1980] *Accounting Models,* Mepham's [1988] "Matrix-Based Accounting",[54] and most recently Babad's and Balanchandran's [1989] "Operational Matrix Accounting". In the face of modern computer and microcomputer technology, the success of current matrix (spreadsheet) accounting has hardly exhausted its potential. Indeed, of particular concern during the waning 1980s were various types of expert systems, their construction and potential application in accounting areas: e.g., Abdolmohammadi [1987], Borthick and West [1987], Michaelsen [1987, 1988], Steinbart [1987], and above all, Connell's [1987] survey article "Expert Systems in Accountancy: A Review of some Recent Applications". This paper reviews some twenty financially-oriented expert systems (many of them developed in Great Britain), but concludes that most of them are still in the research or prototype stage, and that there are many stumbling blocks to overcome.

(xi) Epilogue

> *In recent years the 'purity' of science is ever more closely guarded by a self-imposed inquisition called the peer review. This well-meaning but narrow-minded nanny of an institution ensures that scientists work according to conventional wisdom and not as curiosity or inspiration moves them.*
> James Lovelock [1988], The Ages of Gaia p. xiv

There can be little doubt that future accounting research, up to the end of this millennium and even beyond, will be profoundly influenced by the predominantly consolidating and "puzzle-solving" research of the 1980s, as well as by the more "revolutionizing" research of preceding decades.[55] But the difficult and crucial question is whether the course chosen during the 1980s will be changed, and if so in which direction. The following attempt to take up this question is not intended to offer predictions, but is rather a personal observation and critique with which some readers may well disagree.

Accounting research during the 1980s has experienced an unprecedented growth in volume as well as sophistication. There have been, for example, at least *seven* accounting *theory texts* (apart from "readings") available during the 1980s: Hendriksen [1965/70/77/82], Most [1977/82], Belkaoui [1981/85], Henderson and Peirson [1983], Wolk, Francis and Tearney [1984/88], and Kam [1986/89],[56] while there was only one (Hendriksen's) during the 1960s, to which a second (Most's) was added during the 1970s. The number of *academic* accounting journals (in the English language) has, in a single decade, exploded from 14 to more than 42.[57] This does not include many new "mixed" journals (e.g., the *Canadian Journal of Administrative Sciences,* which also contains accounting articles but is not included among the 42 journals). Those in the areas of MIS and finance ought to be added for a more comprehensive picture. This proliferation has several aspects. On the positive side, it has created healthy competition and fresh outlets for a rapidly growing research activity; but on the negative side, it has put great financial strain on the accounting and academic communities, and may have caused problems of communication, intolerance and wasteful rivalry between various "schools".

The latter is manifested by such trends as "positive accounting" which not only fails to recognize that academic accounting is, at best, an *applied* science, but even denounces the endeavors of traditional, normative accounting as an aberration (cf. Section v). This is exacerbated by the no less dangerous tendency of presenting analytical models and statistical hypotheses as though they were realistically valid, without *constantly* taking the many simplifying assumptions into due consideration (cf. Section iii). Such sentiments are echoed by Antle [1989], whose "concern arises when, instead of generating fluid, useful boundaries, our processes of simplification lead to rigid, dysfunctional ones. Rigid boundaries encourage the expenditure of resources to fortify them. Advocacy and paradigm wars displace productive scholarly efforts" (p. 109). All this widens the gap between theory and practice, and even worse, may lead to detrimental recommendations for practitioners and legislators. The following case may illustrate this situation by means of an example pertinent directly to this Commentary and the accounting trends during the 1980s.

A survey over an entire decade, as presented here, can hardly be done without personal bias something already emphasized in the Preface. But compare this open admission with *statistical* surveys of recent accounting research trends such as, for example, the one offered by Brown, Gardner, and Vasarhelyi [1989] in "Attributes of Articles Impacting Contemporary Accounting Literature" (see also the corresponding book [1989] by the same three authors). The mere fact that this paper is carried out by means of sophisticated techniques and supported by "rigorous" hypotheses, *F*-values, standard deviations, confidence intervals, etc., lends it the aura of something far superior, less subjective, and more reliable despite the fact that this study is limited to only six journals, and completely disregards citations in books. Meanwhile, its title leads one to believe that the article deals with most or all of *contemporary accounting literature*. Nevertheless, the results of this analysis are closely related to our topic and are worth mentioning here (provided the limited scope of this paper is kept in mind). Brown, Gardner and Vasarhelyi [1989, p. 794] admit that "publication counts provide an excellent historical perspective", but claim that such counts "are not useful for measuring how the influence of a particular discipline's attributes have varied over time". Thus they recommend "citation analysis", and come up with impressive statistics (for the decade from 1976 to 1986 and the six leading accounting journals), the most important results of which may be summarized as follows:

1. Financial accounting articles have had a greater impact than managerial and auditing articles (and the latter more than information systems papers); nevertheless the influence of financial and managerial accounting papers decreased during this period while that of auditing and information systems papers increased.

2. The "relative publications" in behavioural accounting and capital markets have increased, while those in mathematical programming and accounting theory have decreased.

3. U.S. related literature has dominated non-U.S. related papers.

4. No single accounting research method has dominated, but "internal logic", "primal archival" and "lab studies" have been applied more frequently than the other methods; nevertheless "secondary archival" and "field studies" have gained in influence during this period.

In addition to the practice of conveniently disregarding grossly restricting assumptions—be it in titles or in the application of results—there is the perilous trend of increasing rigidity, hinted at in the above quote from such a renowned and original thinker as Lovelock [1988, p. xiv]. In a similar vein is an unpublished paper by Cooper and Zeff [1986], reacting to Kinney's [1986b] "Empirical Accounting Research Design for Ph.D. Students", the quote from Lev [1990] in Section (v), and above all the following quote from Sterling:

> Instead of flitting from one fad to another, my recommendation is that we carefully assess proposed research programs *before* accepting or rejecting them. Those programs that are too undeveloped to be assessed should be set aside until they become sufficiently developed to permit assessment. In this way we will encourage innovation and new research directions but we will designate each novel research program a 'cottage industry' (as it is called in science) until it has proven itself. All will be free to work on any subject they like, to join the mainstream or create a new cottage industry, to establish a journal, and so forth, but judicious application of scientific standards will prevent any cottage industry form becoming the latest fad that dominates the journals, the agenda, the terminology, and so forth, to the virtual exclusion of all other research programs. Specifically, I recommend that we welcome PAT as a cottage industry and hope that it will surprise us someday by supplying us with some interesting, perhaps even significant, findings. But in no way should we accept it as the new fashion and condemn everything else as old-fashioned.
>
> Sterling [1990], pp. 132

It is true that during the 1980s academic accountants have engaged in many fads, some of which were inflated beyond reasonable proportions, and even dominated our discipline. Is not one of the worst abuses of rationality the failure to recognize its limitations? But something else is no less worrisome: many of the sophisticated and impressive structures that have recently been built may rest on shifting foundations. Many accounting researchers, in their youthful enthusiasm, were more interested in impressive facades and surface structures than in foundational issues such as, for example, those hinted at in Section (x). Methodological and epistemological studies could have helped to improve those foundations, but many of these were considered backwaters and were relegated to obscurity.[58] In a more specific way, Bell [1990, p. 62], expresses a similar sentiment by suggesting:

> ... that the current emphasis on subject matter and methodology in the literature, if it is to comprise an "accounting revolution", must find ways to treat the primary traditional problems involving recognition and measurement ("valuation" problems to some). These problems are still very much with us. Limiting ourselves to study of "what is" (purposely ignoring "what can be", and how we might "make it be") bypasses the central issues of accounting.
>
> Second, it is not only overly-restrictive *methodology* which is unduly narrowing accounting today. The question of *whom accounting is to serve* is being approached in too limiting a fashion by many "Stakeholders" beyond owners and would-be owners.

Academic accounting is a relatively young discipline, and its foundations are still riddled with problems. Although no one would expect researchers to devote all their energy to those foundational and normative issues, the neglect the latter have experienced during the 1980s seems to have been a bane that might gravely affect research in the 1990s, unless remedied. Otherwise, the impressive endeavors of past decades may crumble, as have other structures erected on unexplored ground. All this finds a resounding echo in quotations such as those of Subotnik [1988] and Mouck [1989]:

> The scientific ideals introduced into accounting by Chambers, Mattessich, Devine and Sterling in the 1960s have been adopted by subsequent academic accountants who are less familiar (or

> in many cases, totally unfamiliar) with philosophy of science. This has resulted in accounting research that is largely characterized by a scientistic attitude: 'On the whole, our working image of science can be reduced to a single narrowly positivistic principle: truth is to be found only through application of empirical methods.' [Subotnik, p. 97] In short, what started as a move toward scientific accounting research, has largely degenerated to scientism and dogmatism. Many of the most prominent accounting researchers have developed an attitude that theirs is the only legitimate form of research.
>
> Mouck [1989], pp. 96-97

Indeed, whenever reason has exceeded its boundaries, i.e., become parochial or atomistic instead of holistic, it has ended up in unreason and intolerance. One may also wonder whether mainstream accounting is not being eroded by the disregard of foundational research and a fragmentation that is likely to continue in the 1990s. But if one wishes to go back to serious foundational research, one first has to convince the major trustees, i.e., the editors of accounting journals and their referees, to keep a much more open mind, and to base their judgments not so much on what conforms, or is "in", or is momentarily popular, but on what is truly novel, genuine, and important in the long-run. Unfortunately, we find ourselves at a stage when most research and publication activity is so institutionalized, even bureaucratized, that many of our peers find it safer to prefer "*routine* research using sophisticated tools" over "more *original* research that happens to be technically less sophisticated". In our discipline, for example, editors of prominent accounting journals are becoming aware of this problem of "technical sophistication for its own sake" and other closely related issues, and are, we hope, struggling to remedy this perilous situation. May all those editors, referees, authors, and committees be reminded of the "paradox of originality": thoughts with genuine staying power are rarely readily accepted, they often barely survive the short-run.

There can be little doubt that in actual practice the 1980s *in general* had more glitter than depth, more facade than substance, more "myopia" than future vision. It was a decade that mortgaged the future and promised much more than it could fulfill. And the inevitable question arises: "did some of this trend rub off on accounting and its research activity?". Did some of us perhaps unconsciously adapt to the advertising maxim that "truth is what sells"? The 1990s might be a sobering and hopefully more honest decade; a time when crucial decisions can no longer be postponed, either by government and industry, or by academia; a time when the superiority of "cooperative societies" (like Japan) over the "adversarial societies" (with which we are faced) will continue to be manifested; a decade in which we will have to deal with painful but inescapable facts, enforcing momentous decisions in preparation for an even more challenging new millennium.

ENDNOTES

1. For details see Epilogue.
2. For another survey of the state of the art in accounting, see the papers presented at the 50th Jubilee (June 1989) at the University of Illinois in Urbana, to be published under the editorship of L.A. Tomassini and Thomas Frecka—see also Abdel-khalik [1989], Dopuch [1989b], and Libby [1989].
3. The "Summaries" of the papers reprinted were omitted, since all of these papers are summarized in the Commentary.

4. A dozen years ago, when the environmental situation was less grave, I drew attention to short-sighted technical and economic attitudes and, as a remedy, proposed a holistic approach in my book *Instrumental Reasoning and Systems Methodology* [Mattessich 1978]. Yet Reaganomics not only prevented any decisive measures, but greatly aggravated the situation.
5. For recent developments in Public Accounting and the shift from attest services to growing non-attest services see Armstrong and Vincent [1988].
6. As to insider trading, etc., and its relations to accounting, see Buchanan and Gaumnitz [1987] and King and O'Keefe [1986].
7. Some moderate efforts in this direction are already under way—cf. Hill and Weber [1988] and Shaub [1988].
8. Briloff's [1972] brilliant *Unaccountable Accounting* foreshadowed this tendency more than a decade ago: see also Brilloff [1981, 1986, 1990]; and Tinker's [1985] *Paper Prophets: A Social Critique of Accounting* which carries such criticism into the political arena.
9. Cf. Belkaoui [1989], *The Coming Crises in Accounting.*
10. In contrast, Wassili Leontief received the 1973 Nobel prize in economics for his input-output analysis which, although also concerned with macro-accounting, is primarily economic research. Another Nobel laureate in economics (1971), who earned his laurels in national income research, is Simon Kuznets, but while he *opposed* the application of the *accounting framework* to national income statistics, Richard Stone vigorously promoted it.
11. Primary archival studies have more than doubled their influence, according to the citational analysis (Table 2) of Brown, Gardner and Vasarheli [1989], but due to editorial constraints, there is no paper reprinted in our supplement for this area or for accounting history in general.
12. See also Lambert [1976], Jasim and Oats [1986] and Vallat [1986].
13. A paper by Douglas Garbutt [1984], in spite of its title "The Significance of Ancient Mesopotamia in Accounting History", goes only back to 2,500 B.C. and completely ignores the much more crucial development of accounting (in Mesopotamia and the entire Fertile Crescent) before this time, although by 1984 several of Schmandt-Besserat's articles had already been published. Even now, some writers of introductory accounting texts reiterate the obsolete adage that writing and (abstract) counting were a prerequisite for early accounting.
14. Cf. Dyckman [1988], pp. 117-122. For a similar reason, Atkinson and Kaplan [1989] excluded agency theory from the second edition of their *Advanced Management Accounting.*
15. Bertrand Russell regarded himself, for example, as a "simple-minded" scholar and Alfred N. Whitehead, his teacher-friend and collaborator, he regarded as a "muddle-headed" one.
16. Something similar has been emphasized repeatedly by myself during the last twenty-five years or so: "Different tools, whose appearances do not resemble each other and whose ranges of error are hardly comparable among themselves, are necessary for these similar yet so different tasks. This analogy applied to accounting is very crude and limp, but might give the reader an inkling of the kind of problem we are confronted with when speaking *of the desirability of many monopurpose accounting systems.*" Mattessich [1964a/77], p. 13; italics added.

17. For an immediate response to Kaplan's [1986] paper see Tomkins [1986]. For an excellent and somewhat skeptical discussion of the Johnson and Kaplan [1987] book, see Noreen [1987]; and for a rejection of much of the blame put on traditional management accounting education, see Reider and Saunders [1988].

18. Obviously, finance, on one side, and MIS, on the other side, both have a plurality of roots beyond accounting (e.g. economics and computer science respectively). The above remarks are not intended to deny this, but refer more to the changes in the departmental structure of business schools.

19. A similar article (going into further details) worth the attention of the reader is Gibbins' and Newton's [1987] "Behavioral Research, Reporting Standards, and the Usefulness of Information".

20. For further clarification of the relation between the observational and conceptual levels, see Mattessich [1990a, 1990b and 1991].

21. For an example of such cooperation see the empirical work on FIFO/LIFO research by Sunder [1968, 1975], Abdel-khalik [1985], R. Brown [1980], Hunt [1985], Johnson and Dhaliwal [1986] and the corresponding *analytical work* by Jung [1985], Amershi and Sunder [1987], and Hughes, Schwartz, and Thakor [1988] which offer a theoretical explanation why in the U.S. the LIFO method is usually rejected by "high-quality" firms (i.e., those least likely to go into bankruptcy) in spite of certain tax advantages—see also Dopuch and Pinkus [1988].

22. I am aware of the difficulty of attaining complete objectivity in the social sciences, and thus regard objectivity as a matter of degree.

23. Another important publication of this decade that deserves more widespread attention is the five volume work, *Essays in Accounting Theory* by Carl Devine [1985]. Although he received for it the AICPA/AAA Literature Award for Notable Contributions in Accounting, as well as the AAA Outstanding Accounting Educator Award, the work itself has not yet exercised the influence which its broad panoramic view merits.

24. For a review of positive theory research up to the early 1980s, see Kelly [1983]. One of the major results of positive research in the early 1980s seems to be the insight that the choosing of different accounting methods depends on *firm size* as well as *leverage*. As to more current research, which is less concerned with regulatory agencies, the critical issue pivots on the question: what are the theoretical underpinnings of this research? Cf. Dopuch [1989b], p. 25.

25. These last three articles mentioned above refer not to Watts' and Zimmerman's [1986] book but to previous works of similar thrust by these two authors (see Main Volume). As to this previous work and its criticism, Watts and Zimmerman [1990] offer a ten year perspective of "positive accounting theory" and attempt to reply to some, but by no means all, of the criticism brought forth.

26. The anthology by L.D. Brown [1987] is representative for this "established tract", but almost exclusively contains papers of the early 1980s and before—see also the review article by Mattessich [1988a]. For other "reviews" of empirical research in financial accounting, see Ball and Foster [1982] and Griffin [1982/87]; for the use of financial modelling in this area, see Verrechia [1982].

27. Such a "rueful return" to traditional concepts may remind the reader of the recent revival of the stewardship notion by agency theory—see Part IV of the Main Volume, particularly my

comments on page 175—and may impress upon Ohlson's clean surplus theory the stamp of a "revolution" in the original Copernican sense of the word as "revolving back" to a previous position.

28. Another, perhaps related, "empirical equilibrium" approach, but employing the notion of *Goodwill*, is suggested by Balzer and Mattessich [1991], see Section (x).

29. Taken from the "Abstract" of Ohlson [1990] which is *not* reprinted in this *Supplementary Volume.*

30. Although I am very appreciative of modern finance theory as a crucial intellectual development, I am highly critical of the neglect of many of its simplifying assumptions and limitations when applied to actual practice in the USA and Canada. To my mind, modern finance theory and its teaching is partly responsible for a series of unsound financial and economic practices. To give only three major examples:

    (1) the encouragement of short-run maximizing strategies by basing the evaluation of managers (on this continent) on stock prices, instead of sound long-term investment and other long-term economic criteria (as in Japan and Europe);

    (2) the growing substitution of debt equity for owners' equity, thereby not only shifting the tax-burden to non-corporate sectors, but encouraging over-indebtedness, enhancing the risk factors, and aggravating the business cycle; and

    (3) the invention (and legal acceptance) of leveraged buy-outs through junk-bonds. Although this often maximizes shareholders' as well as bond-holders' short-run earnings, recent events have shown that a considerable number of investors from both groups (insofar as they were affected by these high-rate bonds) have suffered long-run losses in excess of related previous short-term gains.

31. See also Clarke and Dean [1986] and Mattessich [1986].

32. For details, see Mattessich [1982, 1986]. The above commentary is not limited to publications of the 1980s, as far as inflation accounting is concerned, because the Main Volume deliberately abstained from a discussion of this important topic—see Main Volume, pp. 4-5 and 22.

33. See also Mattessich [1986] and Tippett and Whittington [1988].

34. See FASB [1979, 1981, 1984a, 1984b, 1984c], ICAEW [1980], and CICA [1980b, 1982b].

35. For the same reasons I believe that temporary legislation of inflation accounting was *not* a Pyrrhic victory as Thornton [1985, p. 129] might suggest.

36. "The major findings are simple and dramatic: (1) Once historical cost earnings are known, the Statement 33 earnings variables provide no additional explanatory power with respect to differences across firms in yearly stock price changes. (2) Even after any one of the Statement 33 earnings variables is known, knowledge of historical cost earnings still provides additional explanatory power. In this sense, historical cost earnings strictly dominate the Statement 33 earnings variables." Beaver and Landsman [1983], p. 10.

37. Cf. Baran, Lakonishok, and Ofer [1980], Friedman, Buchman, and Melicher [1980], Grossman, Kratchman and Welker [1981], Schaefer [1984], Samuelson and Murdoch [1985], Lakonishok and Ofer [1985], Bernard and Ruland [1987], Peasnell, Skeratt and Ward [1987], Swanson and Shriver [1987], Sami, Curatola, and Trapnell [1989], Espahbodi and Tehranian [1989], Hopwood and Schaefer [1989], and Lobo and Song [1989]; see also Watts and

Zimmerman [1980], Bublitz, Frecka and McKeon [1985], and Smith and Anderson [1985-86] for different conclusions.

38. See, for example, Benston [1981, 1982a, 1982b] and its criticism in Schreuder and Ramanathan [1984]. For a regional sample survey of social responsibility accounting see Gordon and Mathews [1987].

39. Amershi [1986], pp. 93-94, for example, writes about this research: "In the accounting literature, to the best of my knowledge, Blazenko and Scott [1986] seem to be first to have realized that a modified and extended Arrow-Debreu framework has the potential to be a powerful paradigm to explain the existence of regulatory institutions and a demand for regulation ... This is a breath of fresh air in a landscape polluted by ill-conceived and vacuous "economic consequences" argumentation about economic regulation that has no basis in logically well-structured equilibrium theory ... They have provided us with a rigorously developed general equilibrium model, no matter how crude, of the demand for auditing standards." Some may still argue that the Arrow-Debreu framework has no role for institutions, particularly accounting institutions.

40. Some of his statements remind me of views expressed in the systems approach defended decades ago by Churchman [1961, 1968a, 1968b], Mattessich [1978] and others.

41. Eisenhardt distinguishes between the *positivist approach* and the *principal-agent approach* to agency-contract theory.

42. For "Some Aspects of Auditing Evolution in Canada", see Murphy [1980].

43. This journal often has a separate section on Auditing—its 1989 issue even has a separate *Supplementary Volume* on this subject.

44. Some of their articles are older ones, such as Brown's [1962] classic on "Changing Audit Objectives and Techniques" and excerpts from Mautz' and Sharaf's [1961] no less renowned book *The Philosophy of Auditing*, as contained in Lee's anthology, but their bibliographies constitute a particularly valuable source of reference.

45. Previously Ng and Stoeckenius [1979] presented interesting thoughts on the auditing conditions under which management is willing to report truthfully.

46. For the further international area of "Harmonizing Accounting Education Worldwide", see Gorelik [1988].

47. The neo-positivists' concepts of "rules of correspondence" and "correspondence" between theoretical and observational variables fulfilled a similar purpose, but are now rejected by most philosophers of science as too naive and unsatisfactory, though Sterling [1989] seems to invoke this very concept. For further details, see Mattessich [1991].

48. However, Ijiri [1990] has developed a pertinent software package for the Macintosh™ II computer, taking adantage of color graphics and audio capabilities, and using WINGZ™ for spreadsheet, text and graphic interface, etc. This should greatly accelerate the adoption of Ijiri's new approach by academics as well as industry.

49. Ijiri's postulate of momentum conservation, for example, does not correspond to momentum conservation in physics, and has little to do with my own discussion of the section "Accounting and the Principle of Conservation and Symmetry" in a CAAA award-winning paper—cf. Mattessich [1989a], pp. 19-21.

50. The insight that *a theory* (in the comprehensive and proper sense) *is actually an entire network* of quasi theories (theory elements), is one of the major achievements of post-Kuhnian philosophy of science. For details see Mattessich [1990a], Balzer and Mattessich [1991], and Balzer, Moulines and Sneed [1987]. Therefore an application of Kuhn's theory to accounting and its history, without taking the post-Kuhnian developments into consideration, as recently found, for example, by Cushing [1989], is not quite up-to-date.
51. For a discussion of the proper function of a conceptual framework of accounting, see Peasnell [1982].
52. Epistemic "structuralism" is one of the leading post-Kuhnian trends, seeking to fill the gap which the demise of neo-positivism left in its wake.
53. Cf. Thornton [1985], p. 137: "Whether his [Mattessich's] predictions will come true or not is an empirical question for future to resolve. I would venture a guess that a reader of Mattessich's 'Budget Models and Simulation' [1961] could scarcely have imagined, twenty years later, the many practitioners (and even undergraduate students!) using microcomputers, and doing just what he advocated, with Lotus 1-2-3™."
54. Mepham [1988], p. 377, mentions that "Leech's (p. 330) notes that Mattessich considered the 'matrix formulation' in this way in 1957. Since 1957 the development of relational database systems has made the framework even more suitable."
55. I refer to Kuhn's [1962/70] distinction between those two basic research activities of "normal" versus "revolutionary" science. However, some accounting publications of the 1980s do go beyond "normal science" (as, for example, Johnson and Kaplan [1987] or Ijiri's [1982] *Triple-Entry Bookkeeping and Income Momentum*), but even the latter harks back to previous publications such as Ijiri [1966] and others.
56. To this may have to be added one text in French by Tremblay and Cormier [1989], *Théories et modèles comptables*, which came to my attention just when this *Supplementary Volume* went to print.
57. Cf. Zeff [1988], pp. 8-9, who lists 42 journals, but meanwhile further academic accounting journals have appeared, e.g., *Critical Perspectives on Accounting* (Academic Press, Harcourt Brace Jovanovich) and *Accounting, Business and Financial History* (Routledge, Great Britain).
58. As pointed out, the most prominent books on foundational research of the 1980's are probably the five volume essays by Devine [1985] and Ijiri's [1989] recent work on triple-entry bookkeeping. But, as previously mentioned, both books originated from their authors' work in former decades. One important foundational research that truly belongs to the 1980's is Gaa's [1988a] AAA monograph on the *Methodological Foundations of Standardsetting for Corporate Financial Reporting* (see Section v).

BIBLIOGRAPHY TO PART I

Abdel-khalik, A. R., *Government Regulation of Accounting*, Accounting Series, No. 11 (University Presses of Florida, 1980).

Abdel-khalik, A. R., *Financial Reporting by Private Companies: Analysis and Diagnosis* (Stanford, CON: FASB, 1983).

Abdel-khalik, A. R. and B. B. Ajinka, "An Evaluation of 'The Everyday Accountant and Researching his Reality," *Accounting, Organizations and Society* (Vol. 8/4, 1983), pp. 375-384.

Abdel-khalik, A. R., "The Effects of LIFO - Switching and Firm Ownership on Executives' Pay," *Journal of Accounting Research* (Autumn 1985), pp. 427-447.

Abdel-khalik, A. R. and Ira Solomon, eds., *Research Opportunities in Auditing The Second Decade* (Sarasota: AAA, 1988).

Adbel-khalik, A. R., "Non-Market Accounting Decisions and Research: Connecting the Old and the New" (preliminary draft), *University of Illinois at Urbana—Champaign, Accounting Ph.D. Program—Golden Jubilee Symposium*, 1989 (27 pp.)

Abdolmohammadi, M. J., "Decision Support and Expert Systems in Auditing: A Review and Research Direction," *Accounting and Business Research* (Spring 1987), pp. 173-185.

Ajinkya, B. B. and M. J. Gift, "Corporate Managers' Earnings Forecasts and Symmetrical Adjustments of Market Expectations," *Journal of Accounting Research* (Autumn 1984), 425-444.

American Institute of Certified Public Accountants, *Reporting Financial Effects of Price-Level Changes* (New York: AICPA, 1963).

American Institute of Certified Public Accountants, *An Auditors Approach to Statistical Sampling* (New York, NY: AICPA, Vols. 1-6, 1972-74).

American Institute of Certified Public Accountants, *Statement on Auditing Procedure, No. 54* (New York, NY: AICPA, 1972).

American Institute of Certified Public Accountants, *Statement on Auditing Standards, No. 1* Codification of Auditing Standards and Procedures (New York, NY: AICPA, 1973).

American Institute of Certified Public Accountants, *Statement on Auditing Standards, No. 39,* Audit Sampling (New York, NY: AICPA, 1981).

Amernic, J. H., and T. H. Beechy, "Accounting Student's Performance and Cognitive Complexity: Some Empirical Evidence", *The Accounting Review* (April 1984), pp. 300-313.

Amershi, A. H., "Information Economics and Auditing: A State-of-the-Art Survey," Paper presented at AAA Annual Meeting, San Diego, California (August 1982).

Amershi, A. H. and J. E. Butterworth, "Explorations in the Theory of Single and Multiple Agents Agencies," in *Economic Analysis of Information and Contracts* ed. by G. Feltham, A.H. Amershi, and W.T. Ziemba (Norwell, MA: Kluwer Academic Press, 1988), pp. 197-219.

Amershi, A. H. and S. Sunder, "Failure of Stock Prices to Discipline Managers in a Rational Expectations Economy," *Journal of Accounting Research* (Autumn 1987), pp. 177-195.

Amershi, A. H., "Discussion of Model of Standard Setting in Auditing," *Contemporary Accounting Research* (Fall 1986), pp. 93-101.

Amihud, Y., and B. Lev, "Risk Reduction as a Managerial Motive for Conglomerate Mergers," *Bell Journal of Economics* (Vol. 12, 1981), pp. 605-616.

Anderson, E., "The Salesperson as Outside Agent or Employee: A Transaction Cost Analysis," *Marketing Science* (Vol. 4, 1985), pp. 234-254.

Antle, Rick, "The Auditor as an Economic Agent," *Journal of Accounting Research* (Autumn 1982), Part II, pp. 503-27.

Antle, Rick, "Intellectual Boundaries in Accounting Research," *Accounting Horizons* (June 1989), pp. 103-109.

Argawal, A., and G. Mandelker, "Managerial Incentives and Corporate Investment and Financing Decisions," *Journal of Finance*, (Vol. 42, 1987), pp. 823-837.

Armitage, H. M., and W. E. Langdon, "Management Accounting: A Discipline in Transition," *CA Magazine* (January/February 1988), pp. 75-85.

Armitage, H. M., *Linking Management Accounting Systems with Computer Technology* (Hamilton, Ontario: The Society of Management Accountants of Canada, 1985).

Armstrong, M. B. and J. I. Vincent, "Public Accounting: A Profession at a Crossroads," *Accounting Horizons* (March 1988), pp. 94-98.

Arpan, J. S. and D. D. Al-Hashim, *International Dimensions of Accounting* (Boston, MA: Kent Publishing Co., 1984).

Ashton, R., "An Experimental Study of Internal Control Judgments," *Journal of Accounting Research* (Spring 1974), pp. 143-57.

Ashton, R., *Research in Audit Decision Making: Rational, Evidence, and Implications* (Vancouver, B.C.: Canadian Certified General Accountants' Research Foundation, 1983).

Ashton, R., and P. Brown, "Descriptive Modeling of Auditors' Internal Control Judgements: Replication and Extension," *Journal of Accounting Research* (Spring 1980), pp. 269-77.

Ashton, R. H., *Human Information Processing in Accounting* (Sarasota, Florida: American Accounting Association, 1982).

Ashton, R. H. (ed.), *The Evolution of Behavioral Accounting Research: An Overview* (New York: Garland Publishing Co., 1984).

Atiase, R. K., "Predisclosure Information, Firm Capitalization, and Security Price Behaviour Around Earnings Announcements," *Journal of Accounting Research* (Vol. 23, No. 1, 1985), pp. 21-36.

Atiase, R. K. and S. Tse, "Stock Valuation Models and Accounting Information: A Review and Synthesis," *Journal of Accounting Literature* (Vol. 5, 1986), pp. 1-33.

Atkinson, Anthony, *Intra-firm Cost and Resource Allocations: Theory and Practice* (Toronto, Ontario: The Canadian Academic Accounting Association, 1987a).

Atkinson, Anthony, *Cost Estimation in Management Accounting—Six Case Studies* (Hamilton, Ontario: The Society of Management Accountants of Canada, 1987b).

Atkinson, Anthony, "A Commentary on How Many Cost Systems do You Need?" *Proceedings, 1987 Annual Conference* (Toronto: Canadian Academic Accounting Association, 1987c), pp. 109-122.

Atkinson, Anthony and G. A. Feltham, "Agency Theory Research and Financial Accounting Standards," in Basu and Milburn (1982), pp. 260 ff.

Atkinson, A. and R. S. Kaplan, *Advanced Management Accounting*, 2nd ed., (Englewood Cliffs, N.J.: Prentice Hall Inc., 1989).

Babad, Y. M. and B. V. Balachandran, "Operational Matrix Accounting," *Contemporary Accounting Research* (Spring 1989), pp. 775-792.

Baber, W. R., "Toward Understanding the Role of Auditing in the Public Sector," *Journal of Accounting and Economics* (December 1983), pp. 213-228.

Baiman, Stanley, "Discussion of Auditing: Incentives and Truthful Reporting," *Journal of Accounting Research* (Supplement 1979), pp. 25-9.

Baiman, Stanley, Agency Research in Managerial Accounting: A Second Look," *Accounting, Organizations and Society* (Vol. 15, No. 4, 1990).

Baiman, S. and J. C. Noel, "Noncontrollable Costs and Responsibility Accounting," *Journal of Accounting Research* (Vol. 23, No. 2, 1985), pp. 486-501.

Baiman, S. and J. Evans III, "Pre-Decision Information and Participative Management Control Systems," *Journal of Accounting Research* (Autumn 1983), pp. 371-395.

Baiman, Stanley, "Agency Research in Managerial Accounting: A Survey,"*Journal of Accounting Literature*" (Spring 1982), pp. 154-213. Reprinted in Mattessich (1984), pp. 251-294.

Ball, R. J. and P. Brown, "An Empirical Evaluation of Accounting Income Numbers," *Journal of Accounting Research* (Autumn 1968), pp. 159-178.

Ball, R. J. and G. Foster, "Corporate Financial Reporting: A Methodological Review of Empirical Research," *Journal of Accounting Research* (Supplement 1982), pp. 161-234.

Balzer, W. and R. Mattessich, "An Axiomatic Basis of Accounting: a Structurist Reconstruction", *Theory and Decision*, 1991, Vol. 30, pp. 213-243

Balzer, W., C. U. Moulines, and J. D. Sneed, *An Architectonic for Science* (Dordrecht-Holland / Boston, Mass.: D. Reidel Publishing Co., 1987).

Banker, R. and S. Datar, "Sensitivity, Precision and Linear Aggregation of Signals for Performance Evaluation," *Journal of Accounting Research* (1989), pp. 21-39.

Baran, A., J. Lakonishok, and A. R. Ofer, "The Information Content of General Price Level Adjusted Earnings: Some Empirical Evidence," *The Accounting Review* (January 1980), pp. 22-35.

Barney, J., *Agency Theory, Employee Stock Ownership and a Firm's Cost of Equity Capital*. Unpublished working paper, Texas A&M University, College Station, 1988.

Basu, S. and J. R. Hanna, *Inflation Accounting: Alternatives, Implementation Issues and Some Empirical Evidence* (Hamilton, Ontario: Society of Management Accountants of Canada, 1974).

Basu, S. and A. J. Milburn (eds.), *Research to Support Standard Setting in Financial Accounting: A Canadian Perspective*, (Toronto, Ontario: Clarkson Gordon Foundation, 1982).

Baxter, W. T., *Accounting Values and Inflation* (New York: McGraw-Hill, Inc., 1975).

Beaver, W. H., "Information Content of Annual Earnings Announcements" *Journal of Accounting Research* (Suppliment to Vol. 6, 1968), pp. 67-92.

Beaver, W. H., *Financial Reporting: An Accounting Revolution* (Englewood Cliffs, N.J.: Prentice-Hall, Inc., 1981).

Beaver, W. H. and J. Demski, "On the Nature of Income Measurement," *The Accounting Review* (January 1979), pp. 38-46.

Beaver, W. H., P. A. Griffin, and W.R. Landsman, "The Incremental Information Content of Replacement Cost Earnings," *Journal of Accounting and Economics* (July 1982), 15-40.

Beaver, W. H., R. Lambert, and D. Morse, "The Information Content of Security Prices," *Journal of Accounting and Economics* (March 1980), pp. 3-28.

Beaver, W. H. and W. R. Landsman, *Incremental Information Content of Statement 33 Disclosures*; (Stamford, Conn.: Financial Accounting Standards Board, 1983).

Beck, P., "A Critical Analysis of the Regression Estimator in Audit Sampling," *Journal of Accounting Research* (Spring 1980), pp. 16-37.

Beechy, T. H., *Accounting for Changing Prices* (Boston/Toronto: Allyn and Bacon, Inc., 1989).

Belkaoui, Ahmed, *Socio-Economic Accounting* (Westport, CT: Auorum Books, 1984).

Belkaoui, Ahmed, *Accounting Theory* (San Diego, CA: Harcourt Brace Jovanovich, Publs., 1981, 2nd ed., 1985)

Belkaoui, Ahmed, *International Accounting: Issues and Solutions* (Westport,CT: Quorum Books, 1985a).

Belkaoui, Ahmed, *The New Environment in International Accounting—Issues and Practices* (New York: Quorum Books, 1988).

Belkaoui, Ahmed, *The Coming Crisis in Accounting* (New York: Quorum Books, 1989).

Bell, P. W., "Accounting as a Discipline for Study and Practice: What Content? In Whose Interest?" in *Accounting Development–Some Perspectives In Honour of Sven-Erik Johannson* (Stockholm: Stockholm School of Economics, 1990), pp. 45-71.

Benston, G. J., "Accounting for Corporate Governance and Social Accountability" in *Corporate Governance: Past and Present* (Bird and Falborn, 1981).

Benston, G. J., "Accounting and Corporate Accountability" *Accounting, Organizations and Society* (Vol. 7, No.2, 1982a), pp. 87-105.

Benston, G. J., "An Analysis of the Role of Accounting Standards for Enhancing Corporate Governance and Social Responsibility," *Journal of Accounting and Public Policy* (Vol. 1 No. 1, 1982b), pp. 5-17.

Benston, G. J., "The Benefits and Costs to Managers of Voluntary Accounting Disclosure—A Discussion of: 'Current Cost Disclosures and Non-disclosures: Canadian Evidence'," *Contemporary Accounting Research*, (Fall 1986), pp. 35-44.

Berg, J., L. Daley, F. Gigler and C. Kanodia, *The Value of Communication in Agency Contracts: Theory and Experimental Evidence* (Vancouver, B.C.: Canadian Certified General Accountants' Research Foundation, 1990).

Bernard, V. L., "Cross-Sectional Dependence and Problems in Inference in Market-Bases Accounting Research," *Journal of Accounting Research* (Vol. 25, No. 1, 1987), pp. 1-48.

Bernard, V. L., "Capital Markets Research in Accounting During the 1980's: A Critical Review" (preliminary draft), *University of Illinois at Urbana—Champaign Accounting Ph.D. Program—Golden Jubilee Symposium*, 1989.

Bernard, V. L., and R. G. Ruland, "Incremental Information Content of Historical Cost and Current Cost Income Numbers: Time-Series Analyses for 1962-1980," *The Accounting Review* (October 1987), pp. 707-722.

Berry, L. E. and G. B. Harwood, *Governmental and Nonprofit Accounting: A List of Readings* (Homewood, Illinois: R.D. Irwin, Inc., 1984).

Biggs, S. F. and T. Mock, "An Investigation of Auditor Decision Processes in the Evaluation of Internal Controls and Audit Scope Decisions," *Journal of Accounting Research* (Spring 1983), pp. 234-55.

Biggs, S. F., T. J. Mock, and P. R. Watkins, *Analytical Review Procedures and Processes in Auditing* (Vancouver, B.C.: Canadian Certified General Accountants' Research Foundation, 1989).

Bindon, K. R. and H. Gernon, "International Accounting Research," *Advances in Accounting* (Vol. 4, 1987), pp. 43-68.

Boland, L. A. and I. M. Gordon, "Criticizing Positive Accounting Theory", (Vancouver, B.C.: Working Paper, Simon Fraser University, 1990)

Blazenko, G. W. and W. R. Scott, "A Model of Standard Setting in Auditing," *Contemporary Accounting Research* (Fall 1986), pp. 68-82.

Bloom, R. and A. Debessay, *Inflation Accounting—Reporting of General and Specific Price Changes* (New York: Praeger Publishers, 1984).

Boritz, J. E., "The Effect of Information Presentation Methods on Audit Planning and Review Judgments," working paper (Accounting Group, University of Waterloo, November 1983).

Boritz, J. E., B. G. Gaber, W. M. Lemon, *An Experimental Study of Review of Preliminary Audit Strategy by External Auditors* (Toronto: Canadian Academic Accounting Association, 1987).

Borthick, A. F. and O. D. West, "Expert Systems—A New Tool for the Professional," *Accounting Horizons* (March 1987), pp. 9-16.

Bowen, R. M., D. Burgstahler, and L.A. Daley, "The Incremental Information Content of Accrual Versus Cash Flows," *The Accounting Review* (October 1987), 723-747.

Brief, R. P., "Valuation, Matching and Earnings: The Continuing Debate," *Selected Papers From the Charles Waldo Haskins Accounting History Seminars of Texas, 1983* ed. by J.F. Gaertner (San Antonio University), pp. 15-30.

Briloff, A. J., *Unaccountable Accounting* (New York: Harper & Row, 1972).

Briloff, A. J., *The Truth About Corporate Accounting* (New York: Harper & Row, 1981).

Briloff, A. J., "Standards Without Standards/Principles Without Principles/ Fairness Without Fairness," *Advances in Accounting* (Vol. 3, 1986), pp. 22-50.

Briloff, A. J., "Accountancy and Society, A Covenant Desacrated," *Critical Perspectives in Accounting* (Vol. 1, 1990), pp. 5-30.

Bromwich, M. and A. G. Hopwood, eds., *Research and Current Issues in Management Accounting* (London: Pittman Publishing Ltd., 1986).

Brown, L. D. (ed.), *The Modern Theory of Financial Reporting* (Flano, Texas: Business Publications, Inc., 1987).

Brown, L. D. and J. C. Gardner, "Using Citation Analysis to Assess the Impact of Journals and Articles on Contemporary Accounting Research," *Journal of Accounting Research* (Spring 1985a), pp. 84-109.

Brown, L. D. and J. C. Gardner, "Applying Citation Analysis to Evaluate the Research Contributions of Accounting Faculty and Doctoral Programs," *The Accounting Review* (April 1985b), pp. 262-277.

Brown, L. D., J. C. Gardner, and M. A. Vasarhelyi, "An Analysis of the Research Contributions of *Accounting, Organizations and Society*, 1976-1984," Accounting Organizations and Society (No. 2 1987), pp. 193-204.

Brown, L. D., J. C. Gardner, and M. A. Vasarhelyi, "Attributes of Articles Impacting Contemporary Accounting Literature," *Contemporary Accounting Research* (Spring 1989), pp. 793-815.

Brown, L. D. and Vasarhelyi, *Accounting Research Directory: A Biography of Accounting Literature*, (New York: Wiener Publishing Company, 1985).

Brown, P., G. Foster, and E. Noreen, *Security Analysts Multi-Year Earnings Forecasts and the Capital Market* (Sarasota, Florida: American Accounting Association, 1984).

Brown, R. G., "Changing Audit Objectives and Techniques," *Accounting Review* (October 1962), pp. 696-703.

Brown, R. M., "Short-range Market Reaction to Changes to LIFO Accounting Using Preliminary Earnings Announcement Dates," *Journal of Accounting Research* (Spring 1980), pp. 38-63.

Bruns, W. S. and R. S. Kaplan, eds., *Accounting and Management: Field Study Perspectives* (Boston, Massachusetts: Harvard Business School Press, 1987).

Bublitz, Bruce, T. J. Frecka, and J. C. McKeown, "Market Association Tests and FASB Statement No. 33 Disclosures—A Reexamination," *Journal of Accounting Research* (Supplement 1985), pp. 1-23.

Buchanan, Harold II, and B. R. Gaumnitz, "Accountants and 'Insider' Trading," *Accounting Horizons* (December 1987), pp. 7-12.

Burell, G. and G. Morgan, *Sociological Paradigms and Organizational Analysis, Elements of the Sociology of Corporate Life* (London: Heinemann Educational Books, Ltd., 1979).

Burke, R. C., *Decision Making in Complex Times: The Contribution of a Social Accounting Information System* (Hamilton, Ontario: The Society of Management Accountants of Canada, 1984).

Butterworth, J. E. and Haim Falk, *Financial Reporting—Theory and Application to the Oil and Gas Industry in Canada* (Hamilton, Ont.: The Society of Management Accountants of Canada, 1986).

Buzby, S. L., "Discussion of 'Current Cost Disclosures and Non-disclosures: Canadian Evidence'," *Contemporary Accounting Research* (Fall 1986), pp. 45-49.

Campbell, L. G. *International Auditing: A Comparative Survey of Professional Requirements in Australia, Canada, France, West Germany, Japan, the Netherlands, the U.K. and the U.S.A.* (New York: St. Martin's Press, 1985).

Canadian Institute of Chartered Accountants, *Extent of Audit Testing*, a research study (Toronto, Canada: CICA 1980a).

Canadian Institute of Chartered Accountants, *Exposure Draft, Current Value Accounting* (Toronto, Ontario: CICA 1980b).

Canadian Institute of Chartered Accountants, *Analytical Review*, a research study by D.G. Smith (Toronto, Canada: CICA 1982a).

Canadian Institute of Chartered Accountants, "Section 4510: Reporting the Effects of Changing Prices," *CICA Handbook* (Toronto, Ontario: CICA 1982b).

Chambers, R. J., *Price Variation and Inflation Accounting* (Sydney: McGraw-Hill Co., 1980).

Charitou, A., "Valuation and the Components of Earnings and Cash Flow: A Cross-Sectional Investigation," *Presentation at the 1988 Annual Conference* (Windsor, Ontario: University of Windsor, 1989).

Chi, S. K., *Ethics and Agency Theory* Ph.D. Dissertation (Seattle, WA: University of Washington, 1989).

Choi, F. D. S., and G. G. Mueller, *International Accounting* (Englewood-Cliffs, N.J.: Prentice-Hall, Inc., 1984).

Choi, F. D. S., and G. G. Mueller, editors, *Frontiers of International Accounting* (Ann Arbor, MI: UMI Research Press, 1985).

Christenson, Charles, "The Methodology of Positive Accounting," *The Accounting Review* (January 1983), pp. 1-22; reprinted in Mattessich (1984/89), pp. 131-149.

Christie, A. A., "On Cross-Sectional Analysis in Accounting Research," *Journal of Accounting and Economics* (Vol. 9, No. 3, 1987), pp. 231-258.

Chua, W. F., "Radical Developments in Accounting Thought," *The Accounting Review* (October 1986), pp. 601-632.

Churchman, C. W., *Prediction and Optimal Decision: Philosophical Issues of a Science of Values* (Englewood Cliffs, N.J.: Prentice-Hall, 1961).

Churchman, C. W., *The Systems Approach* (New York: Dell Publishing Co. 1968a).

Churchman, C. W., *A Challenge to Reason* (New York: McGraw-Hill, Inc., 1968b).

Clarke, F. L. and G. W. Dean, "Schmidt's Betriebswirtschaft Theory," *Abacus* (September 1986), pp. 65-102.

Collins, William and W. Hopwood, "A Multivariate Analysis of Annual Earnings Forecasts Generated from Quarterly Forecasts of Financial Analysts and Univariate Time-Series Models," *Journal of Accounting Research* (Autumn 1980), pp. 390-406.

Collins, D. W., M. S. Roszeff, and D. S. Dhaliwal, "The Economic Determinants of the Market Reaction to Proposed Mandatory Accounting Changes in the Oil and Gas Industry: A Cross Sectional Analysis," *Journal of Accounting and Economics* (March 1981), pp. 37-71.

Collins, D. W., M. S. Rozeff, and W. K. Salatka, "The SEC's Rejection of SFAS No. 19: Tests of Market Price Reversal," *The Accounting Review* (January 1982), pp. 1-17.

Conlon, E., and J. Parks, "The Effects of Monitoring and Tradition on Compensation Arrangements," in F. Hoy (ed.), *Best Papers Proceedings* (pp. 191-195) Anaheim, CA: Academy of Management, 1988.

Connell, N. A. D., "Expert Systems in Accountancy: A Review of Some Recent Applications," *Accounting and Business Research* (Summer 1987), pp. 221-234.

Cooper, David J., "Tidiness, Muddle and Things: Commonalities and Divergences in Two Approaches to Management Accounting Research," *Accounting, Organizations and Society* (No. 2/3, 1983), pp. 269-286.

Cooper, D. J., A. Lowe, A. E. Puxty and H. Willmott, "The Regulation of Social and Economic Relations in Advanced Capitalistic Societies: Towards a Conceptual Framework for a Cross

National Study of the Control of Accounting Policy and Practice," paper presented at the Interdisciplinary Perspectives in Accounting Conference (University of Manchester, July 8-10, 1985).

Cooper, D. J., R. Scapens and J. Arnold, eds., *Management Accounting Research and Practice* (London: The Institute of Cost and Management Accountants, 1983).

Cooper, W. W. and S. Zeff, "Kinney's Design for Research in Accounting," (Austin, Texas: Working Paper/University of Texas, 1986).

Cornick, D. L., *Auditing in the Electronic Environment: Theory, Practice and Literature* (Mt. Airy, MD: Lomon Books, 1981).

Cushing, B. E., "A Kuhnian Interpretation of the Historical Evolution of Accounting," *The Accounting Historians Journal* (Fall 1989), pp. 1-41.

Cushing, B. E. and J. K. Loebbecke, *Comparison of Audit Methodologies of Large Accounting Firms* (Sarasota, Florida: American Accounting Association, 1986).

Cyert, R. M. and Y. Ijiri, "Problems of Implementing the Trueblood Objectives Report," *Journal of Accounting Research* (Vol. 12, 1974 Supplement), pp. 29-42.

Datar, S., "A Multi-Period Model of Auditing," working paper (Graduate School of Business, Stanford University, March 1983).

Davidson, Sidney, S. F. Rasch, and R. L. Weil, "Behavior of the Deferred Tax Credit Account, 1973-82," *Journal of Accountancy* (October 1984), pp. 138-142.

Davis, G. B. and Ron Weber, *Auditing Advanced E.D.P. Systems: A Survey of Practice and Development of a Theory* (Altamonte Springs, FL: The Institute of Internal Auditors, 1983).

DeAngelo, L, "Auditor Independence, 'Low Balling,' and Disclosure Regulation," *Journal of Accounting and Economics* (August 1981), pp. 113-26.

DeAngelo, L, "Auditor Size and Audit Quality," *Journal of Accounting and Economics* (December 1981a), pp. 183-99.

DeAngelo, L. E., *The Auditor-Client Contractual Relationship: An Economic Analysis* (Ann Arbor, MI: UMI Research Press, 1981b).

Deguchi, H. and B. Nakano, "Axiomatic Foundations of Vector Accounting," *Systems Research* (Vol. 3, No. 1), 1986, pp. 31-39.

Delavelle, E., *La comptabilite en francs-or*, 2nd ed. (Paris: Novelle Librairie Nationale, 1924).

Demski, J. S., "Accounting Research: 1985," *Contemporary Accounting Research* (Fall 1985), pp. 69-75.

Demski, J. S., "Positive Accounting Theory: A Review," *Accounting, Organization and Society* (13/6, 1988), pp. 623-628.

Demski, J. S., J. M. Patell, and M. Wolfson, "Decentralized Choice of Monitoring Systems," *The Accounting Review* (January 1984), pp. 16-34.

Dent, J. F., "Organizational Research in Accounting: Perspectives, Issues and Commentary," (London, U.K.: manuscript/London School of Business, 1987) may have been published meanwhile.

Devine, Carl, *Essays in Accounting Theory*, 5 vols. (Sarasota, Florida: American Accounting Association, 1985).

Dhaliwal, Dan S., "The Effect of the Firm's Capital Structure on the Choice of Accounting Methods," *The Accounting Review* (January 1980), pp. 78-84.

Dharan, Bala G., "Expectation Models and Potential Information Content of Oil and Gas Reserve Value Disclosure," *The Accounting Review* (April 1984), pp. 199-217.

Ditthofer, Mortimer, "Research in Governmental Accounting and Auditing," Advances in International Accounting (Vol. 2, 1988), pp. 201-203.

Dopuch, Nicholas, "The Impact of Regulations on Financial Accounting Research," *Contemporary Accounting Research* (Spring 1989), pp. 494-500.

Dopuch, Nicholas, "The Auto- and Cross-Sectional Correlations of Accounting Research," (draft), *University of Illinois at Urbana—Champaign Accounting Ph.D. Program Golden Jubilee Symposium*, 1989b (43 pp.)

Dopuch, N. and M. Pincus, "Evidence on the Choice of Inventory Accounting Methods: LIFO Versus FIFO," *Journal of Accounting Research* (Spring 1988), pp. 28-59.

Dopuch, Nicholas, and Shyam Sunder, "FASB's Statements and Objectives and Elements of Financial Accounting: A Review," *The Accounting Review* (January 1980), pp. 1-21.

Drucker, Peter F., *Management—Tasks, Responsibilities, Practices* (New York: Harper & Row, Publishers, 1973 and 1985).

Duke, G., J. Neter and R. Leitch, "Power Characteristics of Test Statistics in the Auditing Environment: An Empirical Study," *Journal of Accounting Research* (Spring 1982), pp. 28-41.

Dworin, L. and R. Grimlund, "Dollar Unit Sampling for Accounts Receivable and Inventory," working paper (July 1983).

Dyckman, T. R., "The King's New Clothes?" *Accounting Horizons* (June 1988), pp. 115-122.

Dyckman, T. R., M. Gibbins, and R. J. Swieringa, "Experimental and Survey Research in Financial Accounting: A Review and Evaluation," *The Impact of Accounting Research on Practice and Disclosure*, edited by A. Rashad Abdel-Khalik and T.F. Keller (Durham, N.C.: Duke University Press 1974), pp. 48-105, 99-134. Reprinted in Mattessich (1984/89):, pp. 299-323.

Dyckman, T. R. and Dale Morse, *Efficient Capital Markets and Accounting: A Critical Analysis*, 2nd ed. (Englewood Cliffs, N.J.: Prentice-Hall, Inc., 1986).

Dyckman, T. R. and S. A. Zeff, "Two Decades of the Journal of Accounting Research," *Journal of Accounting Research* (Spring 1984), pp. 225-297.

Dye, R. A., "Earnings Management in an Overlapping Generations Model," *Journal of Accounting Research* (Vol. 26, No. 2, 1988), pp. 195-235.

Easton, P. and T. Harris, "Evidence of Accounting Earnings as an Index in Change in Value," (New York: Manuscript/Columbia University, 1989).

Eccles, R., "Transfer Pricing as a Problem of Agency," in J. Pratt and R. Zeckhauser (eds.), *Principals and Agents: The Structure of Business* (Boston: Harvard Business School Press, 1985) pp. 151-186.

Edwards, E. O. and P. W. Bell, *The Theory and Measurement of Business Income* (Berkeley, CA: University of California Press, 1961).

Egginton, D. A., "Cash Flow, Profit and Performance Measures for External Reporting: A Rejoinder," *Accounting and Business Research* (Spring 1985), pp. 109-112.

Eisenhardt, K., "Control: Organizational and Economic Approaches," *Management Science*, (Vol. 31, 1985), pp. 134-149.

Eisenhardt, K., "Agency and Institutional Explanations of Compensation in Retail Sales," *The Academy of Management Journal*, (Vol. 31, 1988), pp. 488-511.

Eisenhardt, Kathleen, "Agency Theory: An Assessment and Review," *The Academy of Management Review* (January 1989), pp. 57-74.

Enthoven, Adolf, *Current Value Accounting* (Dallas, TEX: University of Texas, 1982).

Espahbodi, R. and H. Hendrickson, "A Cost-Benefit Analysis of Accounting for Inflation," *Journal of Accounting and Public Policy* (Spring 1986), pp. 31-56.

Espahbodi, R. and H. Tehranian, "Stock Market Reactions to the Issuance of FAS 33 and its Preceding Exposure Draft," *Contemporary Accounting Research* (Spring 1989), pp. 575-591.

Evans, J., "Optimal Contracts with Costly Conditional Auditing," *Journal of Accounting Research* (Supplement 1980), pp. 108-28.

Falk, Haim, "Contemporary Accounting Research: The First Five Years," *Contemporary Accounting Research* (Spring 1989), pp. 816-826.

Felix, W. L. and W. R. Kinney, Jr., "Research in Auditor's Opinion Formulation Process: The State of the Art," *The Accounting Review* (April 1982), pp. 245-271.

Feltham, G. A., "Financial Accounting Research: Contributions of Information Economics and Agency Theory," in Mattessich (1984/89), pp. 179-207.

Feltham, G. A., A. H. Amershi, and W. T. Ziemba eds., *Economic Analysis of Information and Contracts—Essays in Honour of John E. Butterworth* (Boston, Massachusetts: Kluwer Academic Publishers, 1988).

Feltham, G. A. and J. S. Hughes, "Communication of Private Information in Capital Markets: Contingent Contracts and Verified Reports," in Feltham, Amershi, and Ziemba (1988).

Ferris, K. R., J. L. Livingstone, eds., *Management Planning and Control* (Columbus, Ohio: Century Publishing Co., 1987).

Fershtman, C. and K. Judd, "Equilibrium Incentives in Oligopoly," J.L. Kellogg Graduate School of Management, Northwestern University, 1984.

Fershtman, C. and K. Judd, "Strategic Incentive in Manipulation in Rivalrous Agency," Institute for Mathematical Studies in the Social Sciences, Stanford University, 1986.

Financial Accounting Standards Board, *Statement of Financial Accounting Standards No. 33*: "Financial Reporting of Changing Prices" (Stamford, CT: FASB, 1979).

Financial Accounting Standards Board, *Financial Reporting and Changing Prices* (Stamford, CT: FASB, 1981).

Financial Accounting Standards Board, *Status Report No. 159*: "Financial Reporting and Changing Prices," (Stamford, CT: FASB, 1984a) p.1.

Financial Accounting Standards Board, *Statement of Financial Accounting Standards No. 82*: "Financial Reporting and Changing Prices: Elimination of Certain Disclosures, and Amendment of FASB Statement No. 33" (Stamford, CT: FASB, 1984b).

Financial Accounting Standards Board, *Exposure Draft: Proposed Statement of Financial Accounting Standards—Financial Reporting and Changing Prices: Current Cost Information* (Stamford, CT: FASB, 1984c).

Flamholz, E. G., T. K. Das and A. S. Tsui, "Toward on Integrative Framework of Organizational Control," *Accounting, Organizations and Society* (Vol. 10, No. 1, 1985), pp. 35-50.

Foster, George, "Accounting Policy Decisions and Capital Market Research," *Journal of Accounting and Economics* (March 1980), pp. 29-62.

Foucault, M., *The Archeology of Knowledge* (London: Tavistock, 1972).

Foucault, M., *Discipline and Punish: The Birth of the Prison* (Harmondsworth: Penguin, 1979).

Foucault, M., *Power/Knowledge: Selected Interviews and Other Writings 1972-1977* edited by C. Gordon (The Harvester Press, 1980).

Francis, J. R. and S. A. Reiter, "Determinants of Corporate Pension Funding Strategy," *Journal of Accounting and Economics* (March 1987), pp. 35-39.

Freeman, R. N., "Alternative Measures of Profit Margin: An Empirical Study of the Potential Information Content of Current Cost Accounting," *Journal of Accounting Research* (Spring 1983), 42-64.

Fried, D. and D. Givoly, "Financial Analysts' Forecasts of Earnings: A Better Surrogate for Market Expectations," *Journal of Accounting and Economics* (October 1982), 85-108.

Friedman, L., T. Buchman, and R. Melicher, "The Information Content of Replacement Cost Valuation Data," *Review of Business and Economic Research* (Spring 1980), pp. 27-38.

Frishkoff, Paul, *Fincancial Reporting and Changing Prices: A Review of Empirical Research* (Stamford, CN: FASB, 1982).

Fudenberg, D. and J. Tirole, "Moral Hazard and Renegotiation in Agency Contracts," Department of Economics, Massachusetts Institute of Technology, 1988.

Gaa, J. C., "User Primacy in Financial Reporting Rulemaking: A Social Contract Approach," *The Accounting Review* (July 1986), pp. 435-454.

Gaa, J. C., *Methodology Foundations of Standard Setting for Corporate Financial Reporting* (Sarasota, FA: American Accounting Association, 1988a).

Gaa, J. C., "The Auditing Profession and Society: Prisoners of a Dilemma" *A Profession in Transition: The Ethical and Legal Responsibilities of Accountants*. Proceedings of the Third Annual *Research Symposium* Chicago: DePaul University, School of Accountancy, 1988b).

Gaa, J. C., *Auditors and Society: The Ethical Foundations of Public Accounting* (Vancouver, B.C.: Canadian Certified General Accountants' Research Foundation, in preparation for 1992).

Gaffikin, M. J. R., "The Methodology of Early Accounting Theorists," *Abacus* (Spring 1987), pp. 17-30.

Gaffikin, M. J. R., "Legacy of the Golden Age: Recent Developments in the Methodology of Accounting," *Abacus* (Spring 1988), pp. 16-36.

Gaffikin, M. J. R. and M. J. Aitken, *The Development of Accounting Theory: Significant Contributors to Accounting Thought in the 20th Century* (New York: Garland Publishing, Inc., 1982).

Gamble, G. O., B. O'Doherty, and L.M. Hyman, "The Development of Agency Thought: A Citation Analysis of the Literature," *The Accounting Historians Journal* (Spring 1987), pp. 7-26.

Garbutt, D., "The Significance of Ancient Mesopotamia in Accounting History," *Accounting Historians Journal* (Spring 1984), pp. 83-101.

Gaumnitz, B., T. Nunamaker, J. Surdick, and M. Thomas, "Auditor Consensus in Internal Control Evaluation and Audit Program Planning," *Journal of Accounting Research* (Autumn 1982), pp. 745-55.

Gibbins, Michael, "Human Inference, Heuristics and Auditors' Judgement Process," *CICA Auditing Symposium* (Laval University, Quebec City, Toronto: CICA 1977).

Gibbins, Michael, "Regression and Other Statistical Implications for Research on Judgment Using Intercorrelated Data Sources," *Journal of Accounting Research* (Spring 1982), pp. 121-138.

Gibbins, Michael and Patricia Hughes, "Behavioral Research and Financial Accounting Standards," *Usefulness to Investors and Creditors of Information Provided by Financial Reporting: A Review of Empirical Accounting* (1st ed.) edited by P.A. Griffin (Stanford, Connecticut: Financial Accounting Standards Board, 1982), Chpt. 6, pp. 99-134. Reprinted in Mattessich (1984/89), pp. 347-360.

Gibbins, Michael and J.D Newton, "Behavioral Research, Reporting Standards, and the Usefulness of Information," *Usefulness to Investors and Creditors of Information Provided by Financial Reporting* 2nd ed., edited by P.A. Griffin (Stanford, Connecticut: Financial Accounting Standards Board, 1987), pp. 85-114.

Gibbins, Michael and Frank M. Wolf, "Auditors' Subjective Decision Environment: The Case of a Normal External Audit," *The Accounting Review* (January 1982), pp. 105-124.

Giddens, H., *New Rules of Sociological Methods* (London, U.K.: Hutchinson, 1976).

Giddens, H., *Central Problems in Social Theory* (London, U.K.: Hutchinson, 1979).

Giddens, H., *A Contemporary Critique of Historical Materialism* (London, U.K.: Hutchinson, 1981).

Gjesdal, Froystein, "Accounting for Stewardship," *Journal of Accounting Research* (Vol. 19, No. 1, 1982), pp. 208-231.

Godfrey, J. and J. Neter, "Bayesian Bounds for Monetary Unit Sampling in Accounting and Auditing," *Journal of Accounting Research* (Vol. 22, No. 2, 1984), pp. 497-525.

Gonedes, N. J. and N. Dopuch, *Analysis of Financial Statements: Financial Accounting and the Capital Market*, (Sarasota, FA: American Accounting Association, 1989.)

Gordon, I. M. and M. R. Mathews, "Social Responsibility Accounting, A Survey of CGAs," *CGA Magazine* (June 1987), pp. 26-30.

Gorelik, George, "Harmonizing Accounting Education Worldwide,' *CGA Magazine* (July 1989), pp. 36-37.

Gray, S. J., editor, *International Accounting and Transactional Decisions* (London: Butterworths, 1983).

Green J. and J. Laffont, "Contract Renegotiation and the Underinvestment Effect," Harvard University, 1988a.

Green, J. and J. Laffont, "Renegotiation and the Form of Efficient Contracts," Harvard University, 1988b.

Griffin, P. A., *Usefulness to Investors and Creditors of Information Provided By Financial Reporting: A Review of Empirical Accounting Research* (Stamford, CON: FASB, 1982; 2nd ed. 1987).

Griffiths, Ian, *Creative Accounting* (London, U.K.: Sidgwick & Jackson, 1986).

Grimlund, R. A., "An Integration of Internal Control System and Account Balance Evidence," *Journal of Accounting Research* (Vol. 20, No. 2, 1982), pp. 316-342.

Grossman, S., S. Kratchman, and R. Welker, "Comment: The Effect of Replacement Cost Disclosures on Security Prices," *Journal of Accounting, Auditing and Finance* (Winter 1981), pp. 136-143.

Gynther, R. S., *Accounting for Price-Level Changes, Theory and Procedures* (Oxford, U.K.: Pergamon Press, 1966/reprinted 1978).

Habermas, Jürgen, *Toward a Rational Society* (London: Heinemann Educational Books Ltd., 1971).

Habermas, J., *Theory and Practice* (London: Heinemann Educational Books Ltd., 1974).

Habermas, J. *Knowledge and Human Interest*, 2nd edition (London: Heinemann Educational Books Ltd., 1978).

Hagerman, R. A., M. E. Zmijewksi, and R. Shah, "The Association Between the Magnitude of Quarterly Earnings Forecast Errors and Risk-Adjusted Stock Returns," *Journal of Accounting Research* (Autumn 1984), 526-540.

Hagerty, K. and D. Siegel, "On the Observational Equivalence of Managerial Contracts Under Conditions of Moral Hazard and Self-Selection," *Quarterly Journal of Economics* (May 1988), pp. 425-428.

Hakansson, N. H., J. G. Kunkel, and J. A. Ohlson, "Sufficient and Necessary Conditions for Information to Have Social Value in Pure Exchange," *Journal of Finance* (December 1982), pp. 1169-1181.

Halberstam, David, *The Reckoning* (New York: Avon Books, 1986).

Hamilton, R. E. and W. F. Wright, "Internal Control Judgments and Effects of Experience Replications and Extensions," *Journal of Accounting Research* (Vol. 20, No. 2, Part II, 1982), pp. 756-765.

Hanna, J. R., "Accounting for Changing Prices: Dead or Alive?" *CA Magazine* (May 1988), pp. 38-43.

Harsanyi, J. C., *Essays on Ethics, Social Behavior, and Scientific Explanation* (Dordrecht/Boston: D. Reidel Publishing Co., 1976).

Hart, O. and B. Holmstrom, "The Theory of Contracts," in *Advances in Economic Theory, 5th World Congress* ed. by T. Bewley (Cambridge, UK: Cambridge University Press, 1987).

Hayes, D. C., "Accounting for Accounting: A Story About Managerial Accounting," *Accounting, Organizations and Society* (1/2-3, 1983), pp. 241-250.

Healy, Paul, "The Effect of Bonus Schemes on Accounting Decisions," *Journal of Accounting and Economics* (Vol. 7, No. 1/3, 1985), pp. 85-107.

Heath, L. C., "Accounting Communication and the Pygmalion Syndrome," *Accounting Horizons* (March 1987), pp. 1-8.

Heck, J. L., R. P. Derstine, and R. J. Huefner, *Accounting Literature Index* (New York: McGraw-Hill Publ. Co., 1990).

Henderson, M. S., and G. Peirson, *Accounting Theory Its Nature and Development* (Melbourn: Longman Cheshire, Ltd. 1983).

Hendriksen, E. S., *Accounting Theory* (Homewood, IL: R.D. Irwin, Inc., 1965; 4th ed., 1982).

Herbert, Leo, *Auditing the Performance of Management* (New York: Van Nostrand Reinhold, 1987).

Hill, R. S. and J. V. Weber, "Commentary on Current Developments," *Accounting Horizons* (December 1988), pp. 117-120.

Hilton, R. W., "Integrating Normative and Descriptive Theories of Information Processing" *Journal of Accounting Research* (Vol. 18, No. 2, 1980), pp. 477-505.

Holmstrom, B. and J. Ricart-Costa, "Managerial Incentives and Capital Management," *Quarterly Journal of Economics* (November 1986), pp. 835-860.

Holmstrom, B. and P. Milgrom," Aggregation and Linearity in the Provision of Intertemporal Incentives," *Econometrica* (March 1987), pp. 303-328.

Holmstrom, B. ad J. Tirole, "The Theory of the Firm," in R. Schmalensee and R. Willig (eds.), *Handbook of Industrial Organization* (New Haven, N.J.: Yale University, 1987).

Holthausen, R. W. and R. E. Verrechia, "The Effect of Sequential Releases on the Variance of Price Changes in an Intertemporal Multi-Asset Market," *Journal of Accounting Research* (Spring 1988), pp. 82-106.

Holzer, Peter, editor, *International Accounting*, (New York: Harper & Row, 1984).

Hopper, T. and A. Powell, "Making Sense of Research into Organizational and Social Aspects of Management Accounting: A Review of its Underlying Assumptions," *Journal of Management Studies* (September 1985), pp. 429-465.

Hopper, T., J. Storey, and H. Willmott, "Accounting for Accounting: Towards the Development of a Dialectical View," *Accounting, Organizations and Society* (12/5, 1987), pp. 437-456.

Hopwood, A. G., "The Archeology of Accounting Systems," *Accounting, Organizations and Society* (12/3, 1987), pp. 207-234.

Hopwood, A. G., *Accounting From the Outside: The Collected Papers by Anthony G. Hopwood* (New York: Garland Publishers, 1988).

Hopwood, A. G., M. Bromwich, and J. Shaw, editors, *Auditing Research: Issues and Opportunities* (London: Pitman Books, 1982).

Hopwood, W. S. and J. S. McKeown, "The Incremental Information Content of Interim Expenses Over Interim Sales," *Journal of Accounting Research* (Spring 1985), 161-174.

Hopwood, W. and T. Schaefer, "Firm-Specific Responsiveness to Input Price Changes and the Incremental Information in Current Cost Income," *The Accounting Review* (April 1989), pp. 313-328.

Hopwood, A. G. and H. Schreuder, eds., *European Contributions to Accounting Research—The Achievements of the Last Decade* (Amsterdam: Free University Press, 1984).

Hoskin, R. E., J. S. Hughes, and W. E. Ricks, "Evidence on the Incremental Information Content of Additional Firm Disclosures Made Concurrently with Earnings," *Journal of Accounting Research* (Supplement 1986), 1-32.

Hughes, J. S., *A Contract Perspective on Accounting Valuation* (Sarasota, Florida: American Accounting Association, 1984).

Hughes, J. S. and W. E. Ricks, "Association Between Forecast Errors and Excess Returns Near to Earnings Announcements," *The Accounting Review* (January 1987), 158-175.

Hughes, P. J., "Signalling by Direct Disclosure Under Asymmetric Information," *Journal of Accounting Economics* (June 1986), pp. 119-142.

Hughes, P. J., E. S. Schwartz, and A. V. Thakor, "Capital Structure and the FIFO/LIFO Choice," Working Paper, Anderson Graduate School of Management, University of California, Los Angeles, June 1988.

Hunt, H., "Potential Determinants of Corporate Inventory Accounting Decisions," *Journal of Accounting Research* (Autumn 1985), pp. 448-467.

Hylas, R. and R. Ashton, "Audit Detection of Financial Statement Errors," *The Accounting Review* (October 1982), pp. 751-65.

Ijiri, Yuji, "Physical Measures and Multi-Dimensional Accounting" in *Research in Accounting Measurement* ed. by R.K. Jaedicke, Y. Ijiri, and O. Nielsen (Sarasota, FA: American Accounting Association, 1966).

Ijiri, Yuji, *The Foundations of Accounting Measures* (Englewood Cliffs, N.J.: Prentice-Hall, Inc., 1967).

Ijiri, Yuji, *Triple-Entry Bookkeeping and Income Momentum* (Sarasota, Florida: American Accounting Association, 1982).

Ijiri, Yuji, *Momentum Accounting and Triple-Entry Bookkeeping: Exploring the Dynamic Structure of Accounting Measurements* (Sarasota, FA: American Accounting Association, 1989).

Ijiri, Yuji, *The Evolution of Bookkeeping From Single- to Double- to Triple-Entry Systems* (Interactive Coursework: Graduate School of Industrial Administration, Carnegie-Mellon University, Pittsburgh, 1990).

Ijiri, Y. and R. Leitch, "Stein's Paradox and Audit Sampling," *Journal of Accounting Research* (Spring 1980), pp. 91-108.

Imhoff, E. A. and G. J. Lobo, "Information Content of Analysts' Composite Forecast Revisions," *Journal of Accounting Research* (Autumn 1984), 541-554.

Institute of Chartered Accountants of England and Wales, *Statement of Standard Accounting Practice No. 16: Current Cost Accounting* (London: ICAEW, 1980).

Ives, Martin, "Accountability and Governmental Financial Reporting," *Journal of Accountancy* (October 1987), pp. 130-134.

Jacobson, R., "The Validity of ROI as a Measure of Business Performance," *American Economic Review* (June 1987), 470-478.

Jasim, S. A. and Oates, J., "Early Tokens and Tablets in Mesopotamia: New Information from Tell Abada and Tell Brak," *World Archeology* (February 1986), pp. 348-362.

Jensen, R. E., *Review of Forecasts: Scaling and Analysis of Expert Judgements Regarding Cross-Impacts of Assumptions on Business Forecasts and Accounting Measures* (Sarasota, Florida: American Accounting Association, 1983).

Johnson, B. and D. Dhaliwal, "LIFO Abandonment," Working Paper, Kellogg Graduate School of Management, North Western University (April 1986).

Johnson, J. R., J. Leitch, and J. Neter, "Characteristics of Errors in Accounts Receivable and Inventory Audits," *The Accounting Review* (April 1981), pp. 270-93.

Johnson, H. T. and R. S. Kaplan, *Relevance Lost The Rise and Fall of Management Accounting* (Boston, Massachusetts: Harvard Business School Press, 1987).

Johnson, R. E. and P. T. Peterson, "Current Value Accounting for S&L's: A Needed Reform?" *Journal of Accountancy* (Vol. 157, No. 1, 1984), pp. 80-85.

Jones, R. C., *Price Level Changes and Financial Statements—Case Studies of Four Companies* (American Accounting Association: 1955).

Jones, R. C., *Effects of Price Level Changes on Business Income, Capital, and Taxes* (American Accounting Association, 1956).

Joyce, E. J., "Expert Judgment in Audit Program Planning," *Journal of Accounting Research* (Supplement 1976), pp. 29-60.

Joyce, E. J. and G. Biddle, "Anchoring an dAdjustment in Probabilistic Inference in Auditing," *Journal of Accounting Research* (Spring 1981a), pp. 120-45.

Joyce, E. J. and G. Biddle, "Are Auditors' Judgments Sufficiently Regressive?" *Journal of Accounting Research* (Autumn 1981b), pp. 323-49.

Joyce, E. J. and R. Libby, "Behavioral Research in Adult Decision Making," *Journal of Accounting Literature* (Spring 1982), pp. 103-23.

Jung, W., "Accounting Decisions Under Asymmetric Information," Ph.D. Dissertation, University of California, Los Angeles, 1985.

Kam, Vernon, *Accounting Theory* (New York, NY: John Wiley & Sons, 1986; 2nd ed. 1989).

Kanodia, Chandra S., "Stochastic Monitoring and Moral Hazard," *Journal of Accounting Research* (Vol. 23, No. 1, 1985), pp. 175-193.

Kaplan, R. S., "Measuring Manufacturing Performance: A New Challenge for Managerial Accounting Research," *The Accounting Review* (October 1983), pp. 686-705.

Kaplan, R. S., "The Information Content of Financial Accounting Numbers: A Survey of Empirical Evidence," *The Impact of Accounting Research on Practice and Disclosure*, edited by A. Rashad Abdel-Khalik and T.F. Keller (Durham, N.C.: Duke University Press, 1978), pp. 134-173; reprinted in Mattessich (1984/89), pp. 325-345.

Kaplan, R. S., "The Evolution of Management Accounting," *The Accounting Review* (July 1984), pp. 390-418.

Kaplan, R. S., "The Role of Empirical Research in Management Accounting," *Accounting, Organizations and Society* (1986 Vol. II, Nos. 4/5), pp. 429-452.

Kaplan, R. S., "The Continued Evolution of Management Accounting: Design Principles for New Systems," (summarized in) *Proceedings, 1987 Annual Conference* (Toronto: Canadian Academic Accounting Association, 1987), p.22.

Kelly, Lauren, "Positive Theory Research: A Review," *Journal of Accounting Literature* (Spring 1983), pp. 111-150.

Kemp, R. S., Jr., "Examination of the Relationship of Unfunded Vested Pension Liabilities and Selected Elements of Firm Value," *Advances in Accounting* (Vol. 5, 1988), pp. .

King, R. D. and T. B. O'Keefe, "Lobbying Activity and Insider Trading," *The Accounting Review* (January 1986), pp. 76-90.

Kinney, W. R., ed., *Fifty Years of Statistical Auditing* (New York: Garland Publishing Inc., 1986a).

Kinney, W. R., "Empirical Accounting Research Design for Ph.D. Students," *The Accounting Review* (April 1986b), pp. 338-350.

Kinney, W. R., and W. Uecker, "Mitigating the Consequences of Anchoring in Auditor Judgments," *The Accounting Review* (January 1982), pp. 55-69.

Klemstine, C. F. and M. W. Maher, *Management Accounting Research: 1926—1983* (Saratoga, Florida: American Accounting Association—Management Accounting Section, 1983).

Kosnik, R., "Greenmail: A Study in Board Performance in Corporate Governance," *Administrative Science Quarterly*, (Vol. 32, 1987), pp. 163-185.

Kren, Leslie and W. M. Liao, "The Role of Accounting Information in the Control of Organizations: A Review of the Evidence," *Journal of Accounting Literature* (Vol. 7, 1988), pp. 280-309.

Kreps, D., "Corporate Culture and Economic Theory," Graduate School of Business, Stanford University, 1984.

Kuhn, T. S., *The Structure of Scientific Revolutions*, (Chicago, Illinois: University of Chicago Press, 1962; 2nd ed. 1970).

Kunkel, J. G., "Sufficient Conditions for Public Information to Have Social Value in a Production and Exchange Economy," *Journal of Finance* (Vol. 37, 1982), pp. 1005-1013.

Lakonishok, J. and A. R. Ofer, "The Information Content of General Price Level Earnings: A Reply," *The Accounting Review* (October 1985), pp. 711-713.

Lambert, M., *La naissance de l'ecriture en pays de Sumer*, (Paris: Société des Antiquités Nationales, 1976).

Lambert, R. A., "Long-Term Contracting and Moral Hazard," *Bell Journal of Economics* (Autumn 1983), pp. 441-452.

Lambert, R. A., "Income Smoothing or Rational Economic Behavior," *Accounting Review* (October, 1984), pp. 604-618.

Landsman, Wayne, "An Empirical Investigation of Pension Fund Property Rights," *The Accounting Review* (October 1986), pp. 662-691.

Larker, D. F. and L. Revsine, "The Oil and Gas Accounting Controversy: An Analysis of Economic Consequences," *Accounting Review* (October 1983), pp. 706-732.

Lapsey, I., "Research in Public Sector Accounting: An Appraisal," *Accounting, Auditing and Accountability* (Vol. 1, 1988), pp. 21-33.

Laughlin, R. C., E. A. Lowe, and A. G. Puxty, "Towards a Value Neutral Positive Science of Accounting: A Commentary," *Journal of Business Finance and Accounting* (Winter 1982), pp. 567-571.

Lawson, G. H., "The Measurement of Corporate Performance on a Cash Flow Basis: A Reply to Mr. Egginton," *Accounting and Business Research* (Spring 1985), pp. 99-108.

Lee, T. A., "Cash Flows and Net Realizable Values: Further Evidence of the Intuitive Concepts," *Abacus* (December 1984), pp. 125-137.

Lee, T. A., "Cash Flow Accounting, Profit and Performance Measurement: A Response to a Challenge," *Accounting and Business Research* (Spring 1985), pp. 93-98.

Lee, T. A. (editor), *The Evolution of Audit Thought and Practice* (New York/London: Garland Publishing, Inc., 1988).

Lee, T. A. and R. H. Parker, eds., *The Evolution of Corporate Financial Reporting* (New York: Garland Press, 1984).

Leech, S. A., "The Theory and Development of a Matrix Based Accounting System," *Accounting and Business Research* (16/64, 1986), pp. 327-342.

Lehman, C. and A. M. Tinker, "A Semiotic Analysis of: 'The Great Moving Right Show' Featuring the Accounting Profession", Paper presented at the Interdisciplinary Perspectives in Accounting Conference (University of Manchester, July 8-10, 1985).

Leitch, R., J. Neter, R. Plante, and P. Sinha, "Modified Multinomial Bounds for Larger Numbers of Errors in Audits," *The Accounting Review* (April 1982), pp. 384-400.

Leslie, D., A. Teitlebaum, and R. Anderson, *Dollar-Unit Sampling* (Toronto: Copp Clark Pitman, 1979).

Lev, Baruch, "Toward a Theory of Equitable and Efficient Accounting Policy," *The Accounting Research* (January 1988), pp. 1-22.

Lev, Baruch, "On the Usefulness of Earnings and Earnings Research: Lessons and Directions from Two Decades of Empirical Research," *Journal of Accounting Research* (forthcoming 1990).

Lev, Baruch. and J.A. Ohlson, "Market-Based Empirical Research in Accounting: Review Interpretation and Extension," *Journal of Accounting Research, Supplement to Volume 20 (1982) Current Research Methodologies in Accounting: A Critical Evaluation*, pp. 249-322.

Lewis, B., "Expert Judgment in Auditing: An Expected Utility Approach," *Journal of Accounting Research* (Autumn 1980), pp. 594-602.

Libby, Robert, *Accounting and Human Information Processing: Theory and Applications* (Englewood Cliffs, N.J.: Prentice-Hall, Inc., 1981).

Libby, Robert, "Experimental Research in Accouting" (draft), *University of Illinois at Urbana - Champaign Accounting Ph.D. Program Golden Jubilee Symposium*, 1989 (5 pp.)

Lilien, S. and V. Pastena, "Determinants of Intramethod Choice in the Oil and Gas Industry," *Journal of Accounting and Economics* (December 1982), pp. 145-170.

Lipe, R. C., "The Information Contained in the Components of Earnings," *Journal of Accounting Research* (Supplement 1986), 37-64.

Lobo, G. J. and I. M. Song, "The Incremental Information in SFAS No. 33 Income Disclosure Over Historical Cost Income and Its Cash and Accrual Component," *The Accounting Review* (April 1989), pp. 329-343.

Lovelock, James, *The Ages of Gaia* (N.Y.: W.W. Norton & Co., Inc., 1988).

Lowe, E. A., G. A. Puxty and R. C. Laghlin, "Simple Theories for Complex Processes: Accounting Policy and the Market for Myopia," *Journal of Accounting and Public Policy* (Spring 1983), pp. 19-42.

Lustgarten, S., "The Impact of Replacement Cost Disclosure on Security Prices," *Journal of Accounting and Economics* (October 1982), 121-141.

Lys, Thomas, "Mandated Accounting Changes and Debt Covenants: The Case of Oil and Gas Accounting," *Journal of Accounting and Economics* (April 1984), pp. 39-65.

Macharzina, Klaus, "Recent Advances in European Accounting," *Advances in International Accounting* (Vol. 2, 1988), pp. 131-146.

MacIntosh, N. B., *The Social Software of Accounting and Information Systems* (New York: John Wiley & Sons, 1985).

McNichols, Maureen, "A Comparison of the Skewness of Stock Return Distributions at Earnings and Non-Earnings Announcement Dates," *Journal of Accounting and Economics* (Vol. 10, No. 3, 1988), pp. 239-372.

Magliolo, J., "Capital Market Analysis of Reserve Recognition Accounting," *Journal of Accounting Research* (Supplement 1986), 69-108.

Maher, M. W., "The Impact of Regulation on Controls: Firms' Response to the Foreign Corrupt Practices Act," *The Accounting Review* (October 1981), pp. 751-770.

Mahlberg, W., *Bilanztechnik und Bewertung bei Schwankender Währung*, 2nd edition, (Leipzig: 1922).

Mahlberg, W., *Der Tageswert in der Bilanz* (Leipzig: 1925).

Manes, R. and R. E. Verrechia, "A New Proposal for Setting Intra-Company Transfer Prices," *Accounting and Business Research* (Vol. 12, No. 46, 1981-82), pp. 97-104.

Marcuse, H., *Negations: Essays in Critical Theory* (Beacon Press, 1968).

Marcuse, H., *Reason and Revolution*, 2nd edition (London: Routledge & Kegan Paul, 1941).

Marschak, T. and S. Reichelstein, "Network Mechanism, Information Efficiency and Hierarchies," Stanford University, 1987.

Mathews, M. R., "An Explanation of Social Accounting," *CGA Magazine* (June 1987), pp. 30-32.

Mattessich, Richard, "Towards a General and Axiomatic Foundation of Accountancy, with an Introduction to the Matrix Formulation of Accounting Systems," *Accounting Research* (October, 1957), pp. 328-355.

Mattessich, Richard, "Budget Models and System Simulation," *The Accounting Review* (July 1961), pp. 384-397.

Mattessich, Richard, *Accounting and Analytical Methods* (Homewood, Illinois: R.D. Irwin, Inc., 1964/reprinted ed.: Houston, Texas: Scholars Book Co., 1977).

Mattessich, Richard, *Simulation of the Firm Through a Budget Computer Program* (Homewood, Illinois: R.D. Irwin, Inc., 1964b reprinted in "Reprints on Demand Series", Ann Arbor: Microfilms International, 1979).

Mattessich, Richard, "Methodological Preconditions and Problems of a General Theory of Accounting," *The Accounting Review*, (July 1972), pp. 469-487.

Mattessich, Richard, *Instrumental Reasoning and Systems Methodology* (Dordrecht/Boston: D. Reidel Co., 1978).

Mattessich, Richard, "Instrumental Aspects of Accounting", *Accounting for a Simplified Firm Owning Depreciable Assets*, ed. by R.R. Sterling and A.L. Thomas (Houston, Tex.: Scholars Book Co., 1979), pp. 335-351.

Mattessich, Richard, "On the Evolution of Inflation Accounting," *Economia Aziendale* (December 1982), pp. 349-381.

Mattessich, Richard, "Management Accounting: Past, Present, and Future" in *Management Accounting 1980*, ed. by H. Peter Holzer; Champaign, Ill.: University of Illinois, 1980; pp. 209-240. Reprinted in Mattessich (1984/89), pp. 395-414.

Mattessich, Richard. ed., *Modern Accounting Research: History, Survey, and Guide* (Vancouver, B.C.: Canadian Certified General Accountants' Research Foundation, 1984/1989).

Mattessich, Richard, "Fritz Schmidt (1882-1950) and His Pioneering Work of Current Value Accounting in Comparison to Edwards and Bell Theory," *Contemporary Accounting Research* (Spring 1986), pp. 157-177.

Mattessich, Richard, "Prehistoric Accounting and the Problem of Representation: On Archeological Evidence of the Middle East from 8000 B.C. to 3000 B.C.," *The Accounting Historians Journal* (Fall 1987), pp. 71-91. Reprinted in *The Closure of the Accounting Profession*, ed. by T.A. Lee (New York: Garland Press, 1990).

Mattessich, Richard, "Review Article: L.D. Brown's *The Modern Theory of Financial Reporting*," *Contemporary Accounting Research* (Spring 1988a), pp. 620-630.

Mattessich, Richard., "Wittgenstein and Archeological Evidence of Representation and Data Processing from 8000 B.C. to 3000 B.C." *Philosophy of Law, Politics and Society* ed. by Ota Weinberger and Peter Koller (Vienna: Hölder-Pichler-Tempsky, 1988b), pp. 254-263.

Mattessich, Richard., "Counting, Accounting and the Input-Output Principle: Recent Archeological Evidence Revising our View on the Evolution of Early Record Keeping," *Proceedings of the 1988 Annual Meeting of the Canadian Academic Accounting Association* ed. by J. Kantor (Windsor, Ontario: CAAA, 1989a), pp. 199-230; to be reprinted in *Collected Papers in Honour of Dean Paul Garner*, ed. by O.F. Graves (Mississippi: Monograph of the Academy of Accounting Historians, 1991), pp. 1-24.

Mattessich, Richard, "Accounting and the Input-Output Principle in the Prehistoric and Ancient World," *Abacus* (September 1989b), pp. 74-84.

Mattessich, Richard, *Academic Accounting Research in Canada: Evolution, Achievements and Institutional Environment* (Vancouver, B.C.: Faculty of Commerce & Business Administration/U.B.C., 1989/90) Abbr. version published (in Japanese) in *Wako Keizai* (Vol. 22, No 2, Feb., Winter 1989/90), pp. 77-145.

Mattessich, Richard, "Paradigms, Research Traditions, and Theory Nets of Accounting", in *Philosophical Dimensions of Accounting: Edward Stamp Memorial Volume* ed. by M.J. Mumford, K.V. Peasnell and C. Lyas (Lancaster, UK: International Centre for Research in Accounting, in press for 1990a, actual publication might be 1991).

Mattessich, Richard, "Epistemological Aspects of Accounting" *Praxiology* (Polish Academy of Sciences, reprinted in *Keiri Kenkyu*, (Autumn 1990b), pp. 3-30.

Mattessich, Richard, "Social Reality and the Measurement of its Phenomena," *Advances in Accounting*, (Vol. 9, 1991), pp. 3-17.

Mautz, R. K. and H. A. Sharaf, *The Philosophy of Auditing* (Madison, Wisc.: American Accounting Association, 1961).

Mepham, M. J., *Accounting Models* (Afferton-Stockton: Polytech Publishers Ltd., 1980).

Mepham, M. J., "Matrix-Based Accounting: A Comment," *Accounting and Business Research* (18/72, 1988), pp. 375-378.

Michaelsen, R. H., "An Expert System for Selecting Tax Shelters," *The Journal of the American Tax Association* (Fall 1987), pp. 7-21.

Michaelsen, R. H., "Development of an Expert Computer System to Assist in the Classification of Estate Tax Returns," *Accounting Horizons* (December 1988), pp. 63-70.

Middletich, L., "Should Accounting Reflect the Changing Value of the Dollar," *The Journal of Accountancy* (February 1918), pp. 114-120.

Milburn, J. A., *Maintenance of Capital: Financial versus Physical* (Houston, Texas Clarkson Gordon Foundation Symposium Scholars Book Co., 1982).

Milburn, J. A., *Incorporating the Time Value of Money Within Financial Accounting* (Toronto, Ontario: Canadian Institute of Chartered Accountants, 1988).

Minemura, Shinkichi, *Inflation Accounting* (Tokyo: Keio Tsushin Co., 1980).

Mock, T. J. and F. Turner, *Internal Accounting Control Evaluation and Auditor Judgment* (New York, NY: AICPA 1981).

Mock, T. J. and Ilan Vertinsky, *Risk Assessment in Accounting and Auditing* (Vancouver, B.C.: Canadian Certified General Accountants' Research Foundation, 1985).

Moonitz, Maurice, *Changing Prices and Financial Reporting* (Lancaster: ICRA, 1973).

Moonitz, Maurice, *History of Accounting at Berkeley* (Berkeley, California: Professional Accounting Program/U.C.-B., 1986).

Morgan, G., "Social Science and Accounting Research: A Commentary on Tomkins and Groves," *Accounting, Organizations and Society* (Vol. 8/4, 1983), pp. 385-388.

Morris, R. D., "Signalling, Agency Theory and Accounting Policy Choice," *Accounting and Business Research* (Vol. 18, 1987), pp. 47-56.

Most, K. S., *Accounting Theory* (Columbus, OH: Grid Publ., Inc., 1977; 2nd. ed. 1982/1986).

Most, K. S., *International Conflict of Accounting Standards: A Research Report* (Vancouver, B.C.: Canadian Certified General Accountants' Research Foundation, 1984).

Mouck, Tom, "The Irony of 'The Golden Age' of Accounting Methodology" *The Accounting Historians Journal* (Fall 1989), pp. 85-106.

Murphy, G. J., "Some Aspects of Auditing Evolution in Canada," *Accounting Historians Journal* (Vol. 7, No. 2, 1980), pp. 45-61.

Namazi, Mohammed, "Theoretical Developments of Principal-Agent Employment Contract in Accounting: The State of the Art," *JAL* (1985), pp. 113-163.

Needles, B. E. Jr., ed., *Comparative International Auditing Standards*, (Sarasota, FA: American Accounting Association, 1985).

Nehmer, R. A., *Accounting Information Systems as Algebras and First Order Axiomatic Models*, Ph.D. Dissertation (Urbana-Champaign: Dept. of Accounting, University of Illinois, 1988).

Ng, D., and J. Stoeckenius, "Auditing: Incentives and Truthful Reporting," *Journal of Accounting Research* (Supplement 1979), pp. 1-24.

Nobes, C. W. and R. H. Parker, editors, *Comparative International Accounting*, (Oxford, U.K.: Philip Allan Publishers 1981; 2nd edition 1985).

Noreen, Eric, "Commentary: H. Thomas Johnson and Robert S. Kaplan's Relevance Lost: The Rise and Fall of Management Accounting," *Accounting Horizons* (December 1987), pp. 110-116.

Noreen, Eric, "The Economics of Ethics," *Accounting, Organization and Society* (Vol. 13, No. 4, 1988), pp. 359-369.

Ohlson, J. A., "Price Earnings Ratios and Earnings Capitalization Under Uncertainty," *Journal of Accounting Research* (Spring 1983), pp. 141-154.

Ohlson, J. A., *The Theory of Financial Markets and Information* (N.Y.: North Holland, 1987a).

Ohlson, J. A., "On the Nature of Income Measurement: The Basic Results," *Contemporary Accounting Research* (Fall 1987b), pp. 1-15.

Ohlson, J. A., "The Social Value of Public Information in Production Economies," *Economic Analysis of Information and Contracts* ed. by G.A. Feltham and A.H. Amershi, and W.T. Ziemba (Boston, Massachusetts: Kluwer Academic Publishers, 1988), pp. 95-119.

Ohlson, J. A., "Accounting Earnings, Book Value and Dividends: The Theory of the Clean Surplus Equation—Part I," (New York: Manuscript/Columbia University, 1989a).

Ohlson, J. A., "The Theory and Earnings, and an Introduction to the Ball-Brown Analysis," (New York: Manuscript/Columbia University, 1989b).

Ohlson, J. A., "Ungarbled Earnings and Dividends: An Analysis and Extension of the Beaver, Lambert, and Morse Valuation Model," *Journal of Accounting and Economics*, (July 1989c), pp. 109-115.

Ohlson, J. A., "A Synthesis of Security Valuation Theory and the Role of Dividends, Cash Flows, and Earnings," *Contemporary Accounting Research* (Spring, 1990), pp. 648-676.

Otley, D. T., "Concepts of Control: The Contribution of Cybernetics and Systems Theory to Management Control," (Lancaster, U.K.: Manuscript/University of Lancaster, 1985).

Parker, R. H., "Explaining National Differences in Consolidation Accounting," in Lee and Parker (1984), pp. 124 ff.

Patell, J. M., "The API and the Design of Experiments," *Journal of Accounting Research* (Autumn 1979), pp. 528-549.

Paton, W. A., "The Significance and Treatment of Appreciation in the Accounts," *Michigan Academy of Science, Twentieth Century Annual Report*, ed. by G.H. Coons, (Ann Arbor, Michigan: 1918).

Paton, W. A., "Depreciation, Appreciation and Productive Capacity," *The Journal of Accountancy* (July 1920).

Peasnell, K. V., "The Function of a Conceptual Framework for Corporate Financial Reporting," *Accounting and Business Research* (Autumn 1982), pp. 243-256.

Peasnell, K. V., M. J. Mumford and D. J. Williams, "Ersatz Academics and Scholar-Saints: The Supply of Financial Accounting Research," *Abacus* (September 1986), pp. 121-135.

Peasnell, K. V., L. C. L. Skerratt and C. W. R. Ward, "The Share Price Impact of UK CCA Disclosures," *Accounting and Business Research* (Vol. 18, No. 69, 1987), pp. 3-16.

Pesando, J. E. and C. K. Clarke, "Economic Models of the Labor Market and Pension Accounting: An Exploratory Analysis," *The Accounting Review* (October 1983), pp. 733-748.

Peters, Tom, *Thriving on Chaos—Handbook for a Management Revolution* (New York: Alfred A. Knopf, 1988).

Pratt, J. W. and R. J. Zeckenhauser, eds., *Principals and Agents: The Structure of Business* (Boston: Harvard Business School Press, 1985).

Prion, W., *Inflation und Geldentwertung* (Berlin: 1919).

Puro, Marsha, "Auditing Firm Lobbying Before the Financial Accounting Standards Board: An Empirical Study," *Journal of Accounting Research* (Vol. 22, No. 2, 1984), pp. 624-646.

Rayburn, Judy., "The Association of Operation Cash Flow and Accruals with Security Firms," *Journal of Accounting Research* (Supplement 1986), 112-133.

Reider, B. and G. Saunders, "Management Accounting Education: A Defense of its Criticism," *Accounting Horizons* (December 1988), pp. 58-62.

Revsine, Lawrence, *Replacement Cost Accounting* (Englewood Cliffs, N.J.: Prentice-Hall, Inc., 1973).

Richardson, A. J. and M. Gibbins (with the assistance of John Wilson), "Behavioral Research on the Production and Use of Financial Information," *Accounting Research: A Critical Analysis* ed. by K. R. Ferris, (N.Y.: Century VII Publishing Co., 1988), pp. 15-45.

Robbins, B. P. and S. O. Swyers, "Accounting for Income Taxes: Predicting Timing Difference Reversals," *Journal of Accountancy* (September 1984), pp. 108-118.

Roberts, J. and Scapens, R., "Accounting Systems and Systems of Accountability—Understanding Accounting Practices in their Organizational Contexts," *Accounting, Organizations and Society* (Vol. 10, No. 4., 1985), pp. 443-456.

Robinson, Chris and Len Fertuck, *Materiality: An Empirical Study of Actual Auditor Decisions* (Vancouver, B.C.: Canadian Certified General Accountants' Research Foundation, 1985).

Ronen, J. and S. Sadan, *Smoothing Income Numbers: Objectives, Means and Implications* (Boston, MA: Addison-Wesley, 1981).

Rosen, L. S., *Current Value Accounting and Price Level Restatements* (Toronto, Ontario: Canadian Institute of Chartered Accountants, 1972).

Ross, Howard, *Financial Statements: A Crusade for Current Values* (Toronto: Sir Isaac Pitman & Sons, 1969).

Ryan, R. J., "Towards a Value-Neutral Positive Science of Accounting: A Comment," *Journal of Business Finance and Accounting* (Winter 1982), pp. 565-566.

Salvary, S. C. W., *An Analytical Framework for Accounting Theory* (Fayetteville: University of Arkansas, 1989).

Sami, H., A. P. Curatola, and J. E. Trapnell, "Evidence on the Predictive Ability of Inflation-Adjusted Earning Measures," *Contemporary Accounting Research* (Spring 1989), pp. 556-574.

Samuels, J. M. and A. G. Piper, *International Accounting: A Survey* (New York: St. Martin's Press, 1985).

Samuelson, B. A. and B. Murdoch, "The Information Content of General Price Level Adjusted Earnings: A Comment," *The Accounting Review* (October 1985), pp. 706-710.

Schaefer, T. F., "The Information Content of Current Cost Income Relative to Dividends and Historical Cost Income," *Journal of Accounting Research* (Autumn 1984), pp. 647-656.

Schipper, Kathrine, and R. L. Weil, "Alternative Accounting Treatments of Pensions," *The Accounting Review* (October 1982), pp. 806-824.

Schmalenbach, Eugen, *Goldmarkbilanzen* (Berlin: 1922a).

Schmalenbach, Eugen, *Scheingewinne* (Jena: 1922b).

Schmandt-Besserat, Denise, "An Archaic Recording System and the Origin of Writing," *Syro-Mesopotamian Studies* Vol. 1, No. 2 (1977), pp. 1-32.

Schmandt-Besserat, Denise, "The Earliest Precursor of Writing," *Scientific American* (238/6, 1978), pp. 50-59.

Schmandt-Besserat, Denise, "The Envelopes that Bear the First Writing," *Technology and Culture* Vol. 21, No. 3 (1980), pp. 357-385.

Schmandt-Besserat, Denise, "Decipherment of the Earliest Tablets," *Science* Vol. 211 (1981a), pp. 283-285.

Schmandt-Besserat, Denise, "From Tokens to Tablets: A Re-evaluation of the So-called 'Numerical Tablets'," *Visible Language* Vol. 15 (1981b), pp. 321-344.

Schmandt-Besserat, Denise, "The Emergence of Recording," *American Anthropologist* Vol. 84 (1982), pp. 871-878.

Schmandt-Besserat, Denise, "Tokens and Counting," *Biblical Archeologist* (Spring 1983), pp. 117-120.

Schmandt-Besserat, Denise, "Before Numerals," *Visible Language* Vol. 15, No. 1 (1984), pp. 48-59.

Schmandt-Besserat, Denise, "The Origins of Writing—An Archeologist's Perspective," *Written Communication* Vol. 3, No. 1 (January 1986a), pp. 31-45.

Schmandt-Besserat, Denise, "The Precursor to Numerals and Writing," *Archeology* (Nov/Dec. 1986b), pp. 32-38.

Schmandt-Besserat, Denise, "Accounting in Prehistory," *Proceeding, 5th World Congress of Accounting History* (Sydney, Australia: 1988).

Schmidt, Fritz, *die organische Bilanz im Rahmen der Wirtschaft* (Leipzig: G.A. Gloeckner, 1921).

Schmidt, Fritz, "Die Industriekonjunktur Ein Rechenfehler," *Zeitschrift für Betriebswirtschaft* (1927), pp. 1-29, 84-114, 165-199.

Schmidt, Fritz, *Die organische Tageswertbilanz* (Wiesbaden: Gabler Verlag, 1929/51).

Schreuder, Hein and K. V. Ramanathan, "Accounting and Corporate Accountability: An Extended Comment," *Accounting, Organizations and Society* (Vol. 9, No. 3-4, 1984), pp. 409-415.

Schultz, J. and P. Reckers, "The Impact of Group Processing on Selected Audit Disclosure Decisions," *Journal of Accounting Research* (Autumn 1982), pp. 482-501.

Schutz, A., *Collected Papers* Vols. I-III, edited and with an Introduction by N. Nathanson (Den Haag: Martinus Nijhoff, 1962-1966).

Schutz, A., *The Phenomenology of the Social World*, translated by G. Walsh and F. Lehnert (Evanston, IL: North Western University Press, 1967).

Scott, G. M. with Pontus Trobey, *Eighty-eight International Accounting Problems in Rank Order of Importance: A Delphi Evaluation* (Sarasota, FA., American Accounting Association, 1980).

Scott, W. R., "The State of the Art of Academic Research in Auditing," *Journal of Accounting Literature* (Spring 1984), pp. 153-200.

Scott, W. R., "Economic Effects of a Mandate Audit in a Contingent-Chains Production Economy," *Contemporary Accounting Research* (Spring 1988), pp. 354-388.

Sepe, James, "The Impact of the FASB's 1974 GPL Proposal on the Security Price Structure," *The Accounting Review* (July 1982), 467-485.

Shaub, M. K., "Reconstructing the Code of Professional Ethics: A Review of the Anderson Committee Report and Its Implications," *Accounting Horizons* (December 1988), pp. 89-97.

Simunic, Daniel, "The Pricing of Audit Services: Theory and Evidence," *Journal of Accounting Research* (Spring 1980), pp. 161-90.

Simunic, Daniel, "Auditing, Consulting and Auditor Independence," *Journal of Accounting Research*, (Autumn 1984), pp. 679-702

Simunic, Daniel and M. T. Stein, *Product Differentiation in Auditing: Auditor Choice in the Market for Unseasoned New Issues* (Vancouver, B.C.: Canadian Certified General Accountants' Research Foundation, 1987).

Singh, Habir and F. Harianto, "Management-Board Relationships, Takeover Risk and the adoption of Golden Parachutes: An Empirical Investigation," *Academy of Management Journal* (forthcoming 1991).

Skekel, Ted and C. Fazzi, "The Deferred Tax Liability: Do Capital Intensive Companies Pay It?" *Journal of Accountancy* (October 1984), pp. 142-150.

Skinner, R. M., *Pension Accounting: The Problem of Equating Payments Tomorrow with Expenses Today* (Toronto, Ontario: Clarkson Gordon, 1980).

Skinner, R. M., *Accounting Standards in Evolution* (Toronto, Ontario: Holt, Rinehard and Winston, 1987).

Smith, C., R. Whipp, and H. Willmott, "Case Study Research in Accounting: Methodological Breakthrough or Ideological Weapon?" *Advances in Public Interest Accounting* (1988), pp. 95 - 120.

Smith, L. D. and J. J. Anderson, "Inflation Accounting and Comparisons of Corporate Returns in Equity," *Accounting and Business Research* (Vol. 16, No. 62, 1985-87), pp. 107-116.

Solomon, Ira, "Probability Assessment by Individual Auditors and Audit Teams: An Empirical Investigation," *Journal of Accounting Research* (Autumn 1982), Part II, pp. 689-710.

Solomons, David, "The Twilight of Income Measurement: Twenty-five Years On," *The Accounting Historians Journal* (Spring 1987), pp. 1-6.

Sorter, George and M. Ingberman, "The Implicite Criteria for the Recognition, Quantification and Reporting of Accounting Events," *Journal of Accounting, Auditing and Finance* (Spring 1987), pp. 99-114.

Stamp, Edward, *Corporate Reporting: Its Future Evolution* (Toronto: Canadian Institute of Chartered Accountants, 1980).

Stark, A. W., "Comment—Some Thoughts on A Cost-Benefit Analysis of Accounting for Inflation," *Journal of Accounting and Public Policy* (Fall 1987), pp. 209-218.

Staubus, G. J., "An Induced Theory of Accounting Measurement," *The Accounting Review* (January 1985), pp. 53-75.

Staubus, G. J., "The Dark Ages of Cost Accounting: The Role of Miscues in the Literature," *The Accounting Historians Journal* (Fall 1987), pp. 1-18.

Steinbart, P. J., "Materiality: A Case Study Using Expert Systems," *The Accounting Review* (January 1987), pp. 97-116.

Stepp, J. O., "Deferred Taxes: The Discounting Controversy," *Journal of Accountancy* (November 1985), pp. 142-150.

Sterling, R. R., "Confessions of a Failed Empiricist," *Advances in Accounting*, (Vol. 6, 1988), pp. 3-35.

Sterling, R. R., "Teaching the Correspondence Concept," *Issues in Accounting Education* (Spring 1989), pp. 82-93.

Sterling, R. R., "Positive Accounting: An Assessment," *Abacus*, (Fall 1990), pp. 97-135.

Sterling, R. R. and K. W. Lemke (eds.), *Maintenance of Capital: Financial versus Physical* (Houston, Texas: Scholars Book Co., 1982).

Stone, M. S., "A Survey of Research on the Effects of Corporate Pension Plan Sponsorship: Implications for Accounting," *Journal of Accounting Literature* (Spring 1982), pp. 1-32.

Stone, Richard, "Social Accounting: The State of Play," *Scandinavian Journal of Economics* (88/3, 1986), pp. 453-472.

Subotnik, Dan, "Wisdom or Widgets: Whither the School of Business?" *Abacus* (Fall 1988), pp. 95-106.

Sullivan, J. D., R. A. Gnospelius, P. L. Deflies, and H. R. Jaenicke *Montgomery's Auditing*, 10th ed. (New York: Ronald Press/John Wiley & sons, 1985).

Sundem, G. L., "Overview of Four Years of Submissions to THE ACCOUNTING REVIEW", *The Accounting Review* (January 1987), pp. 191-202.

Sunder, Shyam, "Optimal Choice Between FIFO and LIFO," *Journal of Accounting Research* (Autumn 1968), pp. 277-300.

Sunder, Shyam, "Accounting Changes in Inventory Valuation," *The Accounting Review* (April 1975), pp.305-315.

Sunder, Shyam, *Economics of Accounting and Control in Organizations: Contract Theory* (Englewood Cliffs, N.J.: Prentice Hall, Inc., forthcoming 1991).

Swanson, E. P. and K. A. Shriver, "The Accounting-for-Changing Prices Experiment: A Valid Test of Usefulness?" *Accounting Horizons* (September 1987), pp. 69-77.

Swanson, G. A., "The 'Roots' of Accounting," *The Accounting Historians Journal* (Fall 1984), pp. 111-116.

Sweeney, H. W., *Stabilized Accounting* (New York: Harper and Brothers, 1936).

Swieringa, R. J. and J. H. Waterhouse, "Organizational Views of Transfer Pricing," *Accounting, Organizations and Society* (Vol. 7 No. 2, 1982), pp. 149-166.

Swieringa, R. J. and K. E. Weick, "Management Accounting and Action," *Accounting, Organizations and Society* (Vol. 12, No. 3, 1987), pp. 293-308.

Tanaka, Shigetsugu, *The Structure of Accounting Language* (Tokyo: Chuo University Press, 1982).

Thomson, R. B. II, C. Olsen, and J. R. Dietrich, "Attributes of News About Firms: An Analysis of Firm-Specific News Reported in the *Wall Street Journal Index*," *Journal of Accounting Research* (Autumn 1987), pp. 245-274.

Thornton, D. B., *The Financial Reporting of Contingencies and Uncertainties: Theory and Practice* (Vancouver, B.C.: Canadian Certified General Accountants' Research Foundation, 1983)

Thornton, D. B., "A Look at Agency Theory—Parts I and II," *CA Magazine* (November 1984), pp. 90-97, and (January 1985), pp. 93-100.

Thornton, D. B., "Review Article of *Modern Accounting Research: History, Survey, and Guide*, ed. by R. Mattessich," *Contemporary Accounting Research* (Fall 1985), pp. 124-142.

Thornton, D. B., "Current Cost Disclosers and Nondisclosers: Theory and Canadian Evidence," *Contemporary Accounting Research* (Fall 1986), pp. 1-34.

Thornton, D. B., "Capital Value in Use vs. Replacement Costs: Theory and Canadian Evidence," *Contemporary Accounting Research* (Fall 1988a), pp. 343-370.

Thornton, D. B., Theory and Metaphor in Accounting," *Accounting Horizons* (December 1988b), pp. 1-9.

Tiessen, P. and J. H. Waterhouse, "Towards a Descriptive Theory of Management Accounting," *Accounting, Organizations and Society* (Vol. 8, No. 2/3, 1983), pp. 251-267.

Tinker, A. M., "Theories of the State and the State of Accounting: Economic Reductionism and Political Voluntarism in Accounting Regulation Theory," *Journal of Accounting and Public Policy* (Spring 1984), pp. 55-74.

Tinker, A. M., *Paper Prophets: A Social Critique of Accounting* (New York: Praeger Special Studies, 1985).

Tinker, A. M., B. D. Merino, and M. D. Neimark, "The Normative Origins of Positive Theories: Ideology and Accounting Thought," *Accounting, Organizations and Society* (Vol. 2, 1982), pp. 167-200).

Tippett, M. and G. Whittington, "General Price-Level Adjustment: Some Properties of the Edwards and Bell Model," *Accounting and Business Research* (Winter 1988), pp. 65-78.

Tomkins, C. and R. Groves, "The Everyday Accountant and Researching His Reality," *Accounting, Organizations and Society* (Vol. 8/4, 1983), pp. 361-374.

Tomkins, C., "Commentary on R. S. Kaplan 'The Role for Empirical Research in Accounting'" *Accounting, Organizations and Society* (Vol. 11/4-5, 1986), pp. 453-456.

Tremblay, D. and D. Cormier, *Théories et modèles comptables voies de recherche* (Québec: Press de l'Université du Québec, 1989).

Trotman, K. T., P. W. Yetton, and I. R. Zimmer, "Individual and Group Judgments of Internal Control Systems," *Journal of Accounting Research* (Vol. 21, No. 1, 1983), pp. 286-292.

Tweedie, David and Geoffrey Whittington, *The Debate of Inflation Accounting* (Cambridge, UK: Cambridge University Press, 1984).

Underdown, B. and P. Taylor, *Accounting Theory and Policy Making* (London, UK: Heinemann, 1985).

Vallat, F., "The Most Ancient Script of Iran: The Current Situation," *World Archeology* (February 1986), pp. 335-347.

Vasarhelyi, M. A., ed., *Artificial Intelligence in Accounting and Auditing: The Use of Expert Systems* (New York: Marcus Wiener Publ. Inc., 1989).

Verrechia, R. E., "The Use of Mathematical Modelling in Financial Accounting," *Journal of Accounting Research* (Supplement 1982), pp. 1-42.

Walb, E., *Das Problem der Scheingewinne* (Freiburg: 1921).

Walgenbach, P. H., N. E. Dittrich, and E. T. Hanson, *Principles of Accounting*, 2nd ed. (New York: Harcourt, Brace, Jovanovich, Inc., 1980).

Walker, Martin, "The Information Economics Approach to Financial Reporting," *Accounting and Business Research* (Vol. 18, No. 70, 1988), pp. 170-182.

Walking, R. and M. Long, "Agency Theory, Managerial Welfare, and Takeover Bid Resistance," *The Rand Journal of Economics*, (Vol. 15, 1984), pp. 54-68.

Waller, W. and J. Jiambalvo, "The Use of Normative Models in Human Information Processing Research in Accounting," *Journal of Accounting Literature* (Spring 1984), pp. 201-226.

Watts, Ross and Jerold Zimmerman, "On the Irrelevance of Replacement Cost Disclosures for Security Prices," *Journal of Accounting and Economics* (August 1980), pp. 95-106.

Watts, R. L. and J. L. Zimmerman, *Positive Accounting Theory* (Englewood Cliffs, N.J.: Prentice-Hall, Inc., 1986).

Watts, R. L. and J. L. Zimmerman, "Positive Accounting: A Ten Year Perspective" *The Accounting Review* (January 1990). pp. 131-156.

Whittington, Geoffrey, *Inflation Accounting* (Cambridge, UK: Cambridge University Press, 1983).

Whittington, G., "Positive Accounting Theory: A Review Article," *Accounting and Business Research* (Autumn, 1987), pp. 327-336.

Willett, R. J. "An Axiomatic Theory of Accounting Measurement (Part I)," *Accounting and Business Research* (Spring 1987), pp. 155-171.

Willett, R. J., "An Axiomatic Theory of Accounting Measurement (Part II)," *Accounting and Business Research* (Winter 1988), pp. 79-91.

Williams J., Bruns, Jr., and Robert S. Kaplan, eds, *Accounting and Management Field Study Perspectives* (Boston, Massachusetts: Harvard Business School Press, 1987).

Willmot, H. C., "Paradigms for Accounting Research: Critical Reflections on Tomkins and Groves' 'Everyday Accountant and Researching His Reality': Further Thoughts," *Accounting, Organizations and Society* (Vol. 8/4, 1983), pp. 389-405.

Wilson, G. P., "The Relative Information Content of Accruals and Cash Flows: Combined Evidence of the Earnings Announcement and Annual Report Release Date," *Journal of Accounting Research* (Supplement 1986), 165-200.

Wolfson, M. A., "Empirical Evidence of Incentive Problems and Their Mitigation in Oil and Gas Tax Shelter Programs," in Pratt and Zeckenhauser (1985), pp. 101-125.

Wolk, H. I., J. R. Francis, and M. G. Tearney, *Accounting Theory: A Conceptual Approach* (Boston, MA: Kent Publ. Co., Inc., 1984; 2nd ed. 1988).

Young, M., "Participative Budgeting: The Effects of Risk Aversion and Asymmetric Information on Budgetary Slack," *Journal of Accounting Research* (Autumn 1985), pp. 817-828.

Young, David, "Review of R.L. Watts and J.L. Zimmerman's *Positive Accounting Theory*," *The Accounting Review* (January 1987), pp. 243-344.

Zebda, A., "The Choice of Management Accounting Normative Models: A Synthesis," *Advances in Accounting* (Vol. 5, 1987), pp. 73-98.

Zeff, S. A., (ed.), *The Accounting Postulates and Principles Controversy of the 1960's* (New York: Garland Publishing, Inc., 1982).

Zeff, S. A., "The Surge of Academic Journals in Accounting, Boon or Bane?" *Accounting Education News* (May 1988), pp. 8-9.

Zéghal, Daniel, *La comptabilité en periodes de changements de prix* (Vancouver, B.C.: Canadian Certified General Accountants' Research Foundation, 1984).

Zéghal, Daniel, *Le marché de la vérification au Canada* (Vancouver, B.C.: Canadian Certified General Accountants' Research Foundation, 1989).

Part II: The Criticism Of Management Accounting

Accounting, Organizations and Society, Vol. 11, No. 4/5, pp. 429-452, 1986; reprinted with permission.

The Role for Empirical Research in Management Accounting*

Robert S. Kaplan

*I have benefited from conversations with Chuck Christenson, who also supplied me with many valuable references for this paper. I also appreciate the comments of my colleagues at the Harvard Business School, the participants at the Stanford Summer Research Conference [July 1984], and at a seminar at the University of Texas, Austin.

> *People who have spent their lives observing nature are best qualified to make hypotheses as to the principles that bring great numbers of facts together*
> (Aristotle).

> *It seems to me that those sciences which are not born of experience ... and which do not end in known experience are vain and full of error*
> (Leonardo da Vinci).

Several years ago, a conference was held at UCLA on "Accounting in Its Organizational Context." Commenting on the lack of knowledge about how accounting functions in actual organizations, the authors of the first paper concluded:

> It would appear that the information-related behaviour of managers is an interest area for accounting research. Unfortunately, the most fruitful approach—field research—has not been a popular one with accounting researchers.
>
> Birnberg *et al* [1983], p. 126

Similarly, in his summary of the conference papers and discussion, Hopwood observed:

> The paucity of empirical studies of accounting in action was a major constraint on the conference deliberations. Repeatedly it had to be recognized how little was known of the accounting endeavor.
>
> Hopwood [1983], p. 302

The extremely limited number of studies of how accounting information is produced and used in organizations was likely surprising to the social scientists at the UCLA conference—psychologists, organizational behaviour researchers, and sociologists—who have extensive experience with studying actual phenomena in organizations. Unlike these other disciplines, accounting phenomena leave an extensive audit trail in the form of frequent cost accounting and management control reports. The outcomes of decisions and actions—such as production and sales, inventory levels, costs and profits, defects and yields, productivity measures, employee-related measures and new product introductions—are also available within many corporations. Thus, collecting accounting data and the consequences of managers' actions would seem easier than the direct participant observation, intervention policies, subjective evaluation, and other qualitative research methods that frequently characterize the data collection process for many social sciences (see for example, Van Maanen [1983]). Indeed as Hopwood observed:

> Our organizational colleagues had assumed that accounting researchers would be applied social scientists, committed to exploring the intricacies of accounting in practice. They had presumed that by now behavioural and organizational enquiries would have resulted in a mass of insights into the ways in which accounting was related to the fabric of organizational life ... The simple fact is that accounting research has tended to isolate from accounting in practice, if not accounting practice
>
> Hopwood [1983], p. 302

In two recent articles (Kaplan [1983, 1984a]), I too have expressed my concern with the lack of a field-based research strategy in management accounting. Major changes in the organization and technology of a firm's operations may be making the accounting and control systems of corporations obsolete (Kaplan [1984b]). Yet these phenomena will go unobserved and unstudied by accounting researchers unless they undertake studies in actual organizations. A major impediment to conducting field-based accounting research has been a concern that such research would be viewed as less elegant, less scientific and more time-consuming than the analytic, empirical, laboratory and survey research currently being done by accounting academics. Hopwood observed, about field-based research:

> ... all such investigations require the very commitment that is missing in accounting research to-date—a commitment to study, analyze and interpret accounting in the contexts in which it operates ... To-date the difficulty of access and the inexperience of accounting researchers have been important factors. More significant, however, may be those pressures of the academic reward structure which push for speedy and voluminous research, the very low legitimacy which somewhat paradoxically has been given to grounded empirical inquiry, and the marginal commitment which many academic accountants have to the research endeavor.
>
> Hopwood [1983], p. 303

In this paper, I will explore the legitimacy of empirical studies in management accounting and attempt to explicate the role they must play in developing a science of management accounting. The next section will summarize the past six decades of management accounting literature to document the scarcity of empirical research in this field. Thereafter consideration is give to the conduct of scientific research, especially the use of observation for studying organizational and management processes. On these bases, the vital role that empirical studies must play for developing theories in the social sciences is then discussed. The paper concludes with a discussion of some specific issues that arise when performing empirical studies in management accounting. While the objective of this paper is to explore the role for empirical research in management accounting, the message may also have relevance for other business school disciplines, including operations research, MIS, marketing, production and microeconomics. The detailed analysis for these disciplines, however, is left to specialists in the respective areas (see, for example, Teece & Winter [1984] for microeconomics, Graham [1984] for operations research, and Bonoma & Wong [1985] for marketing).

SURVEY OF MANAGEMENT ACCOUNTING RESEARCH

Klemstine & Maher [1983] classified management accounting papers that have appeared in the academic accounting journals, primarily *The Accounting Review*, *Journal of Accounting Research*, *Abacus*, *Accounting, Organizations and Society*, and AAA research studies. Of particular interest is their classification of papers by method of analysis that I have modified slightly for the purposes of this paper:

1. *A priori*—conceptual reasoning without an explicit model manipulation, experiment, or empirical analysis.

2. Modeling/Simulation.

3. Laboratory/Field Experiment—an experiment with students or practitioners on artificial data or in an artificial setting.

4. Survey—collection of data from actual organizations, not from direct observation; analysis performed in some studies.

5. Personal Observation—description of current practices in actual organizations.

6. Empirical—statistical analysis of data obtained from actual organizations.

7. Field Study—analysis of impact on accounting information on decisions, actions, or attitudes of managers in organizations.

A summary of management accounting literature by topical category and method of analysis appears in Table 1. A further summary, by method of analysis, is presented in Table 2. These tables provide a striking picture. Seven out of eight (87%) management accounting research papers have neither data from actual organizations nor are tested in actual organizations. Of the remaining papers, 5% (32) are summary descriptions of industry or country practice based on personal observation; two-thirds of these appeared before 1950, only one since 1970. Only 31 (less than 5%) papers are actual field studies and these tend to be concentrated in two areas: budgeting (12) and miscellaneous performance evaluation (11); no cost accounting or cost allocation field studies exist.

This analysis of the incidence of field studies in academic accounting journals understates somewhat the actual empirical base for teaching and research in management accounting. Many studies of actual practices have been conducted and published by professional organizations such as the National Association of Accountants (NAA), the Conference Board and the Financial Executives Institute. NAA, in particular, has attempted to document existing practice in cost accounting and many of the studies it sponsored in the 1950s undoubtedly influenced textbook writing from the 1960s to today.[1] The knowledge of management accounting practice for many academic accountants, particularly those of us who never served as cost analysts, cost accountants, or controllers in corporations, derives from the ideas contained in these textbooks. Thus, contemporary academic teaching and research is likely based on the summary descriptions of actual practice that were documented in the NAA studies of the 1950s. It is interesting, however, that few management accounting research papers reference any of these studies indicating that the influence of the studies has been filtered through such secondary sources as cost and management accounting textbooks.

TABLE 1:
Classification of management accounting research

		A priori	Modeling/ Simulation	Laboratory or Field Experi- ments	Survey	Personal Observa- tion	Empirical	Field Study
1.1	Fundamental concepts	53	1				2	
1.2	Information economics	5	16	5				
1.3	Firm and industry practices				3	15	1	
1.4	Human resource accounting	3	2	4				1
1.5	International comparisons				1	6		
1.6	Systems	14				1		1
1.7	Economics of internal organization	9	2				1	1
1.8	Miscellaneous	16				6		1
2.1	Direct/absorption costing	28	2		1			
2.2	Distribution costs	6			2	2		1
2.3	General product costs	19	1		4	1		
3.	Cost allocation	14	30					
4.	Cost estimation	8	4				1	
5.1	Cost-volume-profit	16	23					
5.2	Capital budgeting	25	7	1	1			
5.3	Decision making—behavioural	22	1	22				1
5.4	Decision making—general	23	14		1			1
6.1	Budgeting	2	4	11		1		12
6.2	Variance analysis and investigation	16	28	3			2	1
6.3	Transfer pricing	15	7		1			
6.4	Principal—agent		10					
6.5	Planning and Control—general	31	24	5	3		3	11
	Total	325	176	51	17	32	10	31

(Klemstine & Maher [1983])

TABLE 2:
Summary of research methods in management accounting

	Number	Percentage	Cumulative percentage
A priori	325	51.5%	52%
Modeling/Simulation	176	27.8	79
Lab/Field Experiments	51	7.6	87
Survey	17	2.6	90
Personal Observation	32	5.1	95
Empirical	10	0.8	96
Field Study	31	4.5	100
Total	642	100.0%	100%

This source notwithstanding, we can still conclude that the observations by Birnberg *et al*, [1983], and Hopwood [1983], quoted at the start of this paper, are well grounded in empirical evidence. The vast majority of management accounting papers are neither informed by data nor tested on data. This is a discouraging conclusion especially when contrasted with the activity in other social sciences. Herb Simon, in reflecting on progress in the behavioural and social sciences noted:

> In the social sciences, as in all science, the progress of our understanding is paced by the progress in our accumulation of a reliable and systematic body of factual knowledge ... Casual knowledge (does not) provide a satisfactory empirical foundation for general descriptive laws. Without systematic observation, including experimentation where that is possible, our samples will be badly biased, our observations will be severely filtered by our preconceptions, and the phenomena will be altogether too tangled and complex for satisfactory analysis.
>
> An important part of the history of the social sciences over the past 100 years, and of their prospects for the future, can be written in terms of advances in the tools for empirical observational in the growing bodies of data produced by those tools
>
> H.A. Simon [1980], p. 72

Unfortunately, management accounting cannot be included, with other social sciences, as having accumulated a reliable and systematic body of factual knowledge. Nor has it advanced its tools for acquiring empirical observations.

Is it possible that we can develop a systematic theory of management accounting without observation and measurement? Are the precedents or examples of fields where normative models and deductive reasoning are sufficient to develop a substantive body of knowledge? To answer such questions, we examine authoritative writings on scientific research to glean common aspects that are relevant to our topic. We are not attempting to critique these views or comment on their strengths and weaknesses. They are presented to illustrate what thoughtful observers believe is essential for scientific advances.

MODELS OF SCIENTIFIC INQUIRY

Many scholars have attempted to describe and to formalize the process of scientific inquiry. Some of these have been motivated primarily by research in the physical and natural sciences; other have attempted extensions to research in the social and managerial sciences. While differences among these various approaches may be obvious and profound to experts in the history and philosophy of science, a relatively uninformed, lay reader, such as myself, is struck more by the agreement on the basic scientific inquiry model than by the differences. In particular, the most striking finding is the contrast between the consistent view of scientific research and the actual research methods used in management accounting (and several other management and management-related disciplines). In this section, I will attempt to summarize the views offered on the scientific research process and contrast these views with the research record in management accounting presented in Tables 1 and 2.

No serious student of science is so presumptuous as to postulate the method for conducting scientific research. One can read in vain attempting to find a nicely ordered set of sequential steps that a researcher or an entire discipline should follow to perform legitimate scientific research. Nevertheless, at the risk of attempting what much wiser observers assiduously avoid, I believe there is general agreement on a broad set of activities that are necessary for a field to be characterized as scientific. I will attempt to identify and describe these activities, presenting them in a precedence ordering that can be easily misinterpreted. The precedence ordering derives from a rough view that activities described first must precede the initiation of subsequent activities. The ordering will be misunderstood if readers believe that the process is sequential, moving seriatim from one stage to the next. In fact, the process is characterized by continuous feedback and iteration with research findings at later stages generating a need for new research activities at earlier stages. Thus, the research process should be viewed at iterative, dynamic, even disorderly.

I will use a formulation of the research process developed by Roethlisberger [1977]. I have chosen Roethlisberger's organizing framework because, unlike perhaps better known scholars of the process of scientific inquiry, such as Popper, Kuhn, A. Kaplan, or J.L. Simon, who drew their experiences and examples from the natural and social sciences, Roethlisberger developed his thoughts from a profession lifetime as a clinical researcher of management processes. Roethlisberger formulated the process of scientific inquiry as a "Knowledge Enterprise"; (see Fig. 1).

Figure 1

The knowlege enterprise (Roethlisberger [1977], p. 393) (For the development of knowledge, read from the bottom up; for the practice of knowledge, read from the top down.)

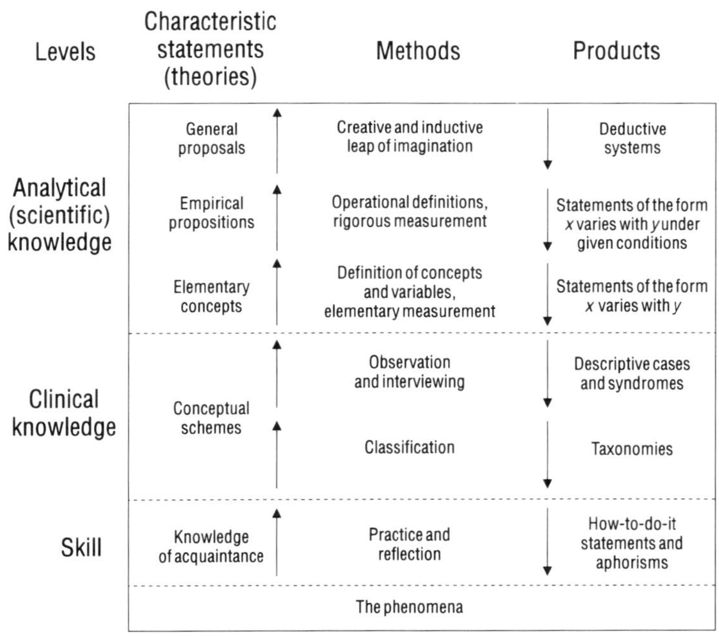

Skill

The Knowledge Enterprise starts with *skill*; the way by which man begins to improve his relations to his surroundings. Skillful practitioners, whether in management, medicine, or other professions, are not explicitly concerned with describing phenomena. Rather, they develop their skills to understand the phenomena with which they are dealing and thereby learn to manipulate them to their own advantage. Schön [1984] agrees with Roethlisberger that the study of skilled practitioners is of critical importance:

> We should be turning the puzzle of professional knowledge on its head, not seeking only to build up a science applicable to practice but also to reflect on the reflection-in-action already embedded in competent practice.

Description

Given the existence of skilled practitioners, management scientists can enter and attempt to develop systematic knowledge of the phenomena and the means by which skilled practitioners are coping. Such activists move us to the clinical knowledge stage of the Knowledge Enterprise, the stage which represents the start of scientific inquiry. Clinical research aims at description and its dominant research methods are observation and interviewing. At this stage, definitions are non-operational, measurements are not objective, and hypotheses are actually questions of the form, "What is going on here?"

J.L. Simon [1978] (pp. 44–46) concurs that the beginning of scientific inquiry in all disciplines is description:

> In the beginning, there is description. When one does not know anything at all about a problem, one must understand it in a general way before beginning to make specific inquiries about specific aspects of the subject. For example, the early explorer in a new land writes a general description of the appearance of the country, its geography, climate, people, flora, fauna, and much else ... The early explorer chooses to describe what he thinks to be important and interesting, without any rigid rules of scientific evidence.
>
> Descriptive research in the form of case studies is usually the jumping off point for the study of new areas in the social sciences. As Freud put it, "The true beginning of scientific actively consists ... in describing phenomena and (only) then in proceeding to group, classify and correlate them."
>
> ... a descriptive study does not have a set of clearly delineated dependent and independent variables. The absence of a limited number of well-defined variables distinguishes case-study descriptive research from other types of research.
>
> Students should not *automatically* shy away from descriptive research. Professors often tout studies off descriptive projects, however, because they are harder to do well and easier to do atrociously than are other types of research. Descriptive research does not reveal sloppy and brainless work as glaringly as do more "rigorous" types of research. For this reason, other types of research usually make better training exercises than does descriptive research.
>
> Path-breaking descriptive research, such as that of Freud, is especially difficult because one starts with empty hands—no guideposts, no standards, no yardsticks, no intellectual framework, no categories within which to classify what one sees ... (The researcher) must create his own classification and his own guideposts. He must decide what to look at and what to ignore, what to record and what not to record, which clues to follow up and which to drop, what is important and what is valueless. The early descriptive researcher has great freedom, but such great freedom can be terrifying.

As Simon notes, in the above quote, one of the major problems with advocating greater attention to clinical, descriptive research is that this activity is frequently afforded lesser status and value because it may not require the use of mathematics and inferential statistics. Such a danger was recognized well by Henderson [1970], pp. 108–109:

> Young men whose bent is intellectual often feel that the only studies worthy of their attention are those like mathematics and physics that deal with high abstractions, or those like

> philosophy that deal with noble sentiments, or those like politics that deal with great affairs. Such attitudes have logico-experimental foundation.
>
> Now the study of those features of the interactions between persons that occur very widely or generally in human affairs must evidently be concerned with very common or vulgar phenomena ... But obvious things are often important, familiarity is often a cause for overlooking things, nothing, as I have said, is trivial but feeling makes it so, common things are often the uniformities, and in order to make a successful analysis or synthesis it is necessary to take account of the necessary factors and to do so in the necessary way ... The fact that somebody thinks it vulgar or trivial or obvious is irrelevant, and unless he is a qualified investigator so also is his opinion that it is unimportant.

We have already noted (in the quote from H.A. Simon in the introductory section of this paper) the requirement that for scientific research, observation must be careful and systematic. This point is also emphasized by A. Kaplan [1964], p. 126:

> Scientific observation is deliberate search, carried out with care and forethought, as contrasted with the casual and largely passive perceptions of every day life.

In summary, careful observation and description are essential for scientific research.

Classification

One very important outcome from careful observation and description is a conceptual or classification scheme for the phenomena. J.L. Simon ([1978], pp. 46-49) defines well the classification process:

> Classification is the process of *sorting out* a collection of people or objects and of developing a set of *categories* among which you divide the collection. No sooner does the scientist see several different examples of a given phenomenon than she begins to say, "This one is like that one and both are different from the other bunch." Then she coins common names for those examples that are like one another. The sorting out may come first and the construction of categories (called "taxonomy") afterward, or the order can be reversed (*a priori* classification) ...
>
> Classification research is different form other types of research in that one does not usually go out and collect new data for a classification study. Rather one is likely to work with existing data, sorting it into a classification that makes sense of it. Therefore, classification research tends to follow after descriptive research in the sequence of scientific stages ...
>
> ... the classification scheme itself can be viewed as one massive variable or as a set of variables ... But the variable or variables are not "dependent" or "independent," at least until employed in other research.

A. Kaplan ([1964], p. 50) emphasized the important role of the classification stage in developing scientific theory:

> The important terms of science—semantics—give science its subject matter; they conceptualize phenomena. Things studied are classified and analyzed. Things are grouped together because they resemble one another; a natural grouping is one which allows the discovery of many more, and more important, resemblances than those originally recognized ... Every taxonomy is a provisional and implicit theory; as knowledge grows, concepts change; as concepts fit better, our knowledge grows.

One need only recall Darwin's activities during his travels around the world to understand the vital role that classification research can play in developing scientific theory.

An observant reader may have noticed that we discussed "Classification" after we discussed "Description" whereas, in Roethlisberger's Knowledge Enterprise, "Classification" appears below the "Description" stage of "Observation and Interviewing." In part, this reversal is due to the difficulty of establishing a precedence relation for two activities which continually feedback and cycle between each other. That is, careful description is invaluable for modifying a previously developed classification scheme, while a classification scheme is necessary for systematic observation. We can, however, distinguish between two types of Description activities, one which would typically occur before Classification and the other afterwards. The first type consists of the highly exploratory, almost aimless wanderings described by J.L. Simon by which the researcher becomes familiar with existing practice. The researcher is learning the rules of the game and how various people are performing in the game. It would be difficult to be careful, systematic and comprehensive at this stage since the researcher has little guidance on what to look for or what to record.

After obtaining familiarity with contemporary practice, the researcher can develop a classification or taxonomy of what appear to be the critical dimensions in the phenomena. Based on this taxonomy, the researcher can then undertake more careful and systematic observation. The classification scheme guides the researcher about what to look for and how to organize the observations found in the field. Thus, for fields in which some familiarity with the fundamental phenomena already exists, the classification scheme precedes, and provides the basis for, systematic observation and interviewing. This precedence is undoubtedly what Roethlisberger had in mind when he portrayed Classification occurring at a lower level of the Knowledge Enterprise than Description.[2]

Measurement

The next stage up the Knowledge Enterprise and the start of analytic knowledge occurs when the researcher becomes able to *measure* one or more aspects of the phenomenon being studied:

> Measurement research seeks to establish the *size* of a phenomenon on one or more of its dimensions ... Measurement differs from case-study description in these ways: Measurement research focuses on one or a few dimensions, and measures them systematically and in relatively great detail; case study gathers information on many dimensions of the phenomenon, with or without numerical description, and in a more *ad hoc* fashion. Deciding *what to measure* and how to draw the definitional boundary lines around the quantity to be measured—translating the theoretical (hypothetical) concept into empirical terms—is a crucial decision in measurement research.
>
> J.L. Simon [1978] p. 49

A. Kaplan ([1964], pp. 173-175) also comments on the desirability of measurement in social science research:

> Systematic study can be carried on in the social sciences as elsewhere by many devices which are less precise than strict quantitative measurement but nonetheless far better than unaided individual judgment ... There is a direct line of logical continuity from qualitative classification to the most rigorous forms of measurement, by way of intermediate devices of systematic ratings, ranking scales, multidimensional classifications, typologies, and simple quantitative indices.
>
> Nevertheless, when measurement is possible, it is a device for standardization, by which we are assured of equivalences among objects of diverse origin ... Also, it makes possible more subtle discriminations and corresponding more precise descriptions ... When descriptions give

> way to measurement, calculations replaces debate ... More important, measurement makes it possible to apply to inquiry available mathematical techniques for verification, prediction or explanation.
>
> A. Kaplan [1964], pp. 173-175

Discovering relationships

Our first set of scientific activities—observation, description, classification and measurement—attempt to reveal what phenomena *are*. The next stage of knowledge creation attempts to learn whether events are *related* to one another. We start to examine whether there is association between phenomena:

> An investigation into whether there is a relationship between two occurrences or variables is an attempt to find out whether two (or more) phenomena are part of the *same scheme of things*, that is, whether they are closely associated with each other in nature's cobweb ... If two particles are entrapped close to each other in a cobweb, and if one of them moves, the other will move in close agreement with it. But if the particles are much farther from each other, movement in one will not be as closely accompanied by movement in the other. Furthermore ... movement in particle A and in particle B can be related even if neither A nor B but rather C initiates the motion.
>
> J.L. Simon [1978], p. 53

While the most desirable state of affairs is to be able to infer cause and effect, relationships between or among variables can still be useful even without being able to determine causality. If the relationship is strong and consistent, we can use one variable (or phenomenon) to predict the occurrence of the second variable or phenomenon. Second, we can use one phenomenon to serve as a proxy measurement of the other, perhaps costlier to measure, phenomenon. Finally, we may be interested in the relationship between two proxy variables, such as the correlation between alternative stock market indices, or scores on different aptitude tests.

Vancil [1978] provides an interesting description of how a researcher with twenty years of clinical experience in management control issues moved one stage up the "Knowledge Enterprise" to obtain analytic knowledge (measurement and association) through an exploratory empirical study:

> I did not delineate a set of hypotheses to be tested by the data. Rather, I viewed my task as one of trying to invent new instruments which might measure some of the important dimensions that account for some of the differences in the ways that decentralized firms are managed ... I was seeking to discover relationships that I could rationalize and accept, and seeking to meld the set of such relationships into a cohesive pattern. Data reduction was almost mandatory, and I tried a variety of methods to create summary variables for the elementary concepts of authority, responsibility, and autonomy.
>
> Vancil [1978], p. 138

In summary, analytical knowledge starts with more precise definitions of concepts and variables. Then new methods for measuring these concepts are developed and, when successful, the researcher can attempt to discover correlations among variables of phenomena. Association can help us to discover certain uniformities in the phenomena, but the finds may be confounded with the circumstances under which they were obtained. Therefore, they cannot be generalized to other situations where the conditions may be different. For scientific explanation, we need to move toward explaining *how* variable x varies with variable y under certain given conditions.

This next stage, of producing empirical propositions, attempts to discover and verify hypotheses. Empirical propositions require operational definitions, rigorous measurement, experimental designs and sophisticated statistical procedures. Such propositions can be developed in the natural sciences and occasionally in the social sciences when investigating phenomena in which data are relatively easy to collect and analyze. The extensive research on capital market behaviour comes to mind as an excellent example of where we have been able to formulate and test empirical propositions. This development has been possible because of the ready and inexpensive availability of data bases on the information used by capital market participants as well as information on the exchange prices in these markets. For much research on social and managerial processes, however, such information and cardinal measurements may not be available. Consequently, formulating and testing empirical propositions in these fields could be extremely difficult. For such fields, our level of knowledge may therefore be restricted to knowledge about association and correlation; we may not be able to reach the Empirical and General Proposition levels of the Knowledge Enterprise.

Theory Building: General Propositions

The final stage of the Knowledge Enterprise, and one that may be exceptionally hard to achieve in the social/management sciences, is to obtain general propositions that explain the empirical propositions discovered and validated at the previous stage. The goal is to show how a variety of empirical generalizations follow logically from a small number of general propositions under certain conditions.

A. Kaplan [1964], p. 302, indicates that a theory is necessary:

> ... to make sense of what would otherwise be inscrutable or unmeaning empirical findings. A theory is more than a synopsis of the moves that have been played in the game of nature; it also sets forth some idea of the rules of the game, by which the moves become intelligible.

Henderson [1970], pp. 67-68, drew upon his medical background to describe the intimate interaction between observation and theory formation:

> ... *both* theory and practice are necessary conditions of understanding, and the method of Hippocrates is the only method that has ever succeeded widely and generally. The first element of that method is hard, persistent, intelligent, responsible, unremitting labour in the sick room, *not in the library* (emphasis added). ... The second element of that method is accurate observation of things and events, selection, guided by judgment born of familiarity and experience, of the salient and the recurrent phenomena, and their classification and methodical exploitation. The third element of that method is the judicious construction of a theory ... and the use thereof. All this may be summed up in a word: they physician must have, first, intimate, habitual, intuitive familiarity with things, secondly systematic knowledge of things, and thirdly, an effective way of thinking about things. His intuitive familiarity must embrace his systematic knowledge and his way of thinking as well as the things he studies ... Competent men of science are no more logico-experimental than other men when they step outside the field in which they have acquired intuitive familiarity with things.

There is general agreement that theory formation is much more than a synopsis or simple extrapolation of empirical propositions. Christenson [1976], pp. 640-641, critiques the views of some empiricists who believe that theoretical knowledge can accumulate with experience and observation:

> The picture suggested by this point of view is that of theoretical knowledge accumulating with experience. Like a drop of water added to a bucket, each new observation statement makes its own individual contribution to the sum total of theoretical knowledge.

Christenson argues, from the logico-experimental framework, that there can be:

> ... no generalization without theory. Theory is like the bucket, rather than like the water in the bucket. A person has to have a bucket before he can collect the water, and he has to have a theory—a framework for measurement—before he can collect "the facts." No matter how much water he collects, it will never accumulate to a bucket; no matter how many facts he collects, they will never accumulate to a theory.

In these remarks Christenson is emphasizing that we cannot wander around aimlessly looking for observations in the world. Even in the early stages of research, we must be guided by some conceptual or classification scheme. Thus, Darwin, with his theological background, was guided by the biblical model of creation of animal species. Initial studies in management accounting would be influenced by current classification schemes such as fixed vs variable costs, responsibility, controllability, traceability, decision influencing, risk sharing and incentive compatibility. Scientists in collecting observations will, implicitly or explicitly, subject their prior conceptual schemes to continual tests. When attempting to understand these observations, the scientist must, with a creative leap of imagination, construct a theory (the bucket) to organize and explain "the facts".

A Kaplan [1964], pp. 308-309, has described this process:

> Arriving at workable theories calls for the exercise of creative imagination, as has been emphasized by countless working scientists ... We may perhaps speak of "discovering" laws, but theories must be said to be "invented" or "constructed" ... The formation of a theory is not just the facts, of organizing and representing them ... A theory must somehow fit God's world, but in an important sense it creates a world of its own.

Popper [1959] has also emphasized the creative process of theory formation:

> Significant advances in knowledge occur when the inquirer goes beyond data; performs a conceptual leap of imagination to consider analogies, metaphors, models, myths as a way to explain the data. Such leaps are called conjectures. Conjectures are distinguished from myths in that tests can be devised for conjectures that could potentially falsify them. Conjectures gain in scientific stature the more they survive such tests.

Stephen Gould, in an essay in *The Panda's Thumb*, provided a vivid illustration of the importance of analogy and metaphor when constructing theories. It is well known that Darwin delayed for many years publishing his theory of natural selection and survival of the fittest. Only with the emergence of a rival, Wallace, was Darwin motivated to overcome his caution to produce The *Origin of Species*. Gould recounts that an important factor in Darwin's decision to finally go public was his reading of Adam Smith's *The Wealth of Nations*. The mechanism of the invisible hand in market economies and the optimality of an economically competitive system provided a close analogy to natural selection and competition in biology, and this correspondence increased Darwin's confidence in his own theory. This is an interesting instance of how a social science (economics) may actually have influenced the development of a natural science. (The anecdote may also serve to remind us that narrow training in a discipline does not encourage creative thinking and bold theory-building activities.)

Kuhn [1970a] agrees with Popper that theories must be invented to explain facts:

> Sir Karl (Popper) and I are united in opposition to a number of classical positivism's most characteristic theses. We both emphasize, for example, the intimate and inevitable entanglement of scientific observation with scientific theory; and we both insist that scientists may properly aim to invent theories that *explain* observed phenomena and that do so in terms of *real* objects ... Neither Sir Karl nor I is an inductivist. We do not believe that there are rules for inducing correct theories from facts, or even that theories, correct or incorrect, are induced at all. Instead we view them as imaginary posits, invented in one piece for application to nature.

Theory development, as characterized by A. Kaplan, Henderson, Christenson, Popper and Kuhn seems notably absent in management accounting. Upon reflection, this is not a surprising finding since all of the above authors stress the role of theory as a unifying framework to organize and explain observations. With virtually no observations (recall Tables 1 and 2), there has been little demand for an organizing, explanatory, refutable theory. Following Christenson's metaphor, without water we don't need a bucket. Yet we do observe that the great majority of management accounting research articles are "theoretical"; reasoning logically or deductively from a set of premises, stated either explicitly or implied by the author.

Theory And Mathematics

Many research papers in management accounting (and other disciplines such as economics, operations research, finance, and operations management) use mathematics extensively. Such papers are frequently referred to as "theoretical," perhaps to distinguish them from empirical papers which analyze data. While it is true that many theories are formulated and developed using mathematics, it is not true that every paper using mathematics and proving theorems is theoretical. This point has been made recently by Michael Jensen when indicating his reservations about mathematical representations of organization phenomena:

> Attempts to use (mathematics) at ... an early stage in the development of an area are often counterproductive because authors are led to assume the problem away or to define sterile "toy" problems that are mathematically tractable ... Mathematical is not the same as rigorous nor is it the same as analytical or theoretical.
>
> Jensen [1983], pp. 335-336

Mathematical models can only be considered theoretical when they are representing real phenomena. Models based on assumptions made for analytic convenience, rather than because they correspond closely to real-world phenomena, may be fine mathematics but they are not theoretical because they do not help to explain observations or empirical phenomena.

This distinction between mathematical models and theory may not be well understood; yet the distinction is extremely important. A. Kaplan deals extensively with this difference, especially the shortcomings of model building that is uninformed from observation. Rather than intersperse his observations here, however, I have excerpted the relevant sections in an Appendix to this paper and the interested reader can pick up the arguments there.

For our purposes, we can conclude with J.L. Simon's observation [1978], p. 217, on the value and limitations of deductive reasoning from well-specified and well-grounded models:

> If the premises are sound, deductive reasoning can be more accurate than empirical research. But often a scintillating chain of reasoning can be founded on incorrect premises.

Theory Testing And Falsification

Extensive literature exists on theory testing for the natural and social sciences. The writings of philosophers such as Popper, Kuhn, A. Kaplan and Feyerabend are centrally concerned with issues of falsification, normal science testing, crucial or nomological testing, and boundary testing (designed to identify the range of application of the posited theory). Given the lack of theory in management accounting, much less the lack of competing theories, a discussion on how to test theories in this field seems premature at this time. Perhaps, the theories we develop in management accounting will never be amenable to the crucial testing that characterizes natural science phenomena. That is, we will not have analogies of evolution replacing "creation" theories, continental drift/tectonic plate theory making obsolete previous geological theories, or quantum theory overthrowing Newtonian mechanics. Therefore, I prefer to have interested readers consult Kaplan [1964], Popper [1959], Kuhn [1970b], and Lakatos & Musgrave [1970] on theory testing and falsification and move on, in this paper, to a more detailed discussion of the role for clinical research and field studies for knowledge creation in management accounting.

CLINICAL VS ANALYTIC RESEARCH

Roethlisberger [1977], p. 390, observed that the clinical approach of acquiring knowledge by describing and classifying the activities of skilled practitioners, is frequently by-passed by researchers because clinical research is considered less elegant than deductive research:

> Going from the bottom up involves sweat, tears, toil, a great deal of imagination, and little deductive logic. However, one goes from the top to the lower levels by pure logic. So the tree, when looked at from the bottom up, is indeed less elegant than when looked at from the top down.

Roethlisberger [1977], p. 392, also warns of the dangers of attempting to use the tools and methods of one level to obtain knowledge that can only be obtained by working at a different level. Examples of such mistakes are:

> The clinician who plasters descriptions of situations with diagnostic concepts and thinks that he is thereby explaining them; the conceptual logician who thinks the he is explaining phenomena by tying concepts into neat logical bundles; the correlation seeker who thinks his significant correlations explain something; the causal hypothesis seeker who thinks he has the tools for getting hold or propositions ... ; the general proposition maker who is so enamored with scientific explanations that he ceases to understand the phenomena with which he deals.

Mitroff *et al.* [1974] have also criticized conventional forms of scientific activity, particularly in the managerial sciences, both for not starting from the reality of actual problem situations, and for not returning to reality for testing proposed solutions in actual settings. Instead, researchers using either a formal deductive approach (with axioms, models, and theorem proving) or a formal inductive approach (with well-specified rules for data gathering and hypothesis testing) alternate between ever more complex model building and model solution activities without either questioning initial starting assumptions or attempting to implement and test their solutions. In terms of the Knowledge Enterprise of Fig. 1, conventional scientific researchers in the managerial sciences seem to cycle within the upper reaches of the tree never getting near the phenomena they are attempting to understand or influence.

These views have also been articulated by Schön [1984] in describing the dilemma between rigor and relevance in all professional schools:

> Rigorous profession practice is conceived as essentially technical. Its rigor depends on the use of describable, testable, replicable techniques derived from scientific research, based on knowledge that is objective, consensual, cumulative, and convergent.

Unfortunately, as Schön observes:

> In the varied typography of professional practice, there is a high, hard ground which overlooks a swamp. On the high ground, manageable problems lend themselves to solution through the use of research-based theory and technique. In the swampy lowlands, problems are messy and confusing and incapable of technical solution. The irony of this situation is that the problems of the high ground tend to be relatively unimportant to individuals or to society at large, however great their technical interest may be, while in the swamp lie the problems of greatest human concern. The practitioner is confronted with a choice. Shall he remain on the high ground where he can solve relatively unimportant problems according to his standards or rigor, or shall he descend to the swamp of important problems and nonrigorous inquiry?
>
> Some researchers have continued to develop formal models for use in problems of high complexity and uncertainty, quite undeterred by the troubles incurred whenever a serious attempt is made to put such models into practice. They pursue an agenda driven by evolving questions of modeling theory and techniques, increasingly divergent from the context of actual practice ... A professional who really tried to confine his practice to the rigorous applications of research-based techniques would find not only that he could not work on the most important problems but that he could not practice in the real world at all.

Thomas & Tymon [1982] describe five problems that arise when researchers of management processes, driven by their desire to use "rigorous" research methods, appropriate only for the higher branches of the Knowledge Tree, attempt to study phenomena for which little clinical knowledge or awareness of practitioner skills exist. First the models or data will not be representative of the phenomena in an organizational setting. Because of a bias toward internal validity, the researcher will use research methods, such as controlled laboratory experiments, that constrain the data and phenomena so severely that the conclusions have limited external validity in actual organization settings.[3]

Second, in the choice of goals, the researcher may choose dependent variables that diverge considerably from practitioner concerns; variables that arise from the researcher's own values or *a priori* notions of managerial goals. Third, the researcher may focus on independent (causal) variables that the practitioner may be unable to manipulate. Fourth, the isolated researcher may find it difficult to produce a theory which meets or exceeds the complexity of common sense theory already used by a practitioner. That is, as researchers attempt to move from their deductive systems down the right-hand side of the knowledge tree to affect practice, they may find it difficult for their recommendations to improve upon the rules-of-thumb and considerable abilities of the skilled practitioner. Fifth, phenomena in organizations may change faster than scientists can come to grips with. Thus, many managerial scientists will find themselves working on problems that existed decades ago but not the critical problems facing managers of contemporary or future organizations.

In summary, the scientific inquiry of management processes must start and end with clinical research; observing skilled practitioners in actual organizations and observing how proposed improvements to practice actually affect real organizations. The methods used for clinical research will be less formal and less rigorous than those used at subsequent stages of the knowledge creation process. But accurate descriptions of the environment in which practitioners operate (the ecological context of decision-making) and the active involvement of practitioners with the research process are just as necessary, if not more so, than our traditional deductive and inductive research activities. It is in this area where empirical studies can play a decisive role.

EMPIRICAL RESEARCH METHODS

One can envision three types of research programs being carried out by systematic observation in cooperative organizations: case studies, field studies, and field experiments.[4] *Case studies* are characterized by the intense examination of a single entity. The case study provides a rich description of an actual situation such as management or organizational setting. The original case study, of course, is the detailed record arising from a physician's clinical examination. Case study data are frequently collected by multiple means. These include qualitative methods, such as personal interviews, personal observation and qualitative descriptions of a company, its markets, products, competitors, technology, systems, etc. But quantitative data sources, such as financial data, market performance data, and quantities of equipment personnel, materials and products should also be incorporated. The case study would also describe the context in which a management system operates and in which managers' decisions and actions occur. In general, however, no attempt is made by the researcher to manipulate or control for independent variables within the organization. Thus, for the most part, case studies tend to be used more for hypothesis-generation than for hypothesis-testing (an exception will be noted below). The principal benefit from a case study is to develop an in-depth description and understanding of a particular managerial problem. The primary drawback is that conclusions from case studies can be subject to numerous interpretations because of the possibility of confounding factors in the entity being studied and the methods by which case study data are collected, aggregated, and analyzed.

Field studies can be viewed as cross-sectional case studies. That is, the researcher would measure independent, dependent, and possible confounding variables in as an unobtrusive a way as possible across a number organizations. The research would be nonexperimental; based on extensive visits and data collection organizations, the researcher would attempt to develop classification schemes for phenomena, perhaps measure association by correlating variables across organizations, and even tentatively produce a theory to explain the observed phenomena. Recent excellent examples include Garvin's [1983] study comparing the quality of U.S. and Japanese air-conditioning companies, and Donaldson's [1984] study of the financial policies of twelve U.S. corporations. Field studies require long times for completion because of the need to obtain extensive and detailed information from many organizations. Time periods of three to four years would be typical, or even minimal, for the study of an interesting management phenomenon.

Field experiments involve the experimental manipulation of one or more variables within an actual organization and the subsequent measurement of the impact of the manipulation on one or more dependent variables. Field experiments where the researcher has some control over the type and domain of the manipulation seem less likely for studying management phenomena; they have been used more in other social sciences interested in studying the effects of government programs such as Head Start (education) and the negative income tax (welfare). It would be unusual for profit seeking (or even most non-profit) organizations to agree to a major change in their internal accounting and performance measurement systems in order to advance our understanding of management accounting phenomena.

But a fortunate researcher may become involved with an organization which, for its own reasons, undertakes a major change in its measurement and reporting system. With such an occurrence, the researcher would then be in a position to document the impact of the change. Such a study would be especially valuable if the researcher had previously performed a case study in the organization so that an extensive description of the former system already existed. With this strategy, a researcher could embark on a program of field research by performing an initial series of case studies. These would establish the researcher's credentials and reputation in the cooperating organizations. Then, should some of these organizations institute changes in their internal accounting systems, the researcher could return to study the impact of these changes.

The advantage of such a longitudinal study, which we may call a "process-tracing" study, is that confounding variables, which vary across organizations, do not arise when studying individual organizations over time. The disadvantage is that in such a nonexperimental longitudinal study, the change in the accounting system can occur simultaneous with or even be caused by more fundamental changes in the organization's strategy, technology and competitive environment. In this case, the researcher may find it difficult to distinguish impacts caused by changes in the management accounting system from changes also occurring in the firm's organization, strategy, technology and markets.

These three types of field-based research studies can be used across the spectrum of the knowledge enterprise; from description and classification through theory formulation and testing. Bonoma and Wong [1985] have devised a four-stage model to describe how field-based studies can be used throughout the research process:

1. "*Drift*. Explore and clarify the nature of the project's scope; learn the issues and hypotheses (accepted wisdom) in the field."

In the drift stage, the researcher writes case studies, attempting (a) to learn the concepts, locale, and jargon of the phenomenon as it is practiced in the field, and (b) to integrate the existing literature, prior concepts of the phenomenon, and what is observed in practice. The researcher must be open to new concepts and possibilities; management contexts are observed, informed practitioners are interviewed with an open-ended, flexible agenda in an attempt to glean the state-of-art of practitioner knowledge. Each case constructed at this stage can both be studied as an interesting problem in its own right and to stimulate further thought on possible general rules and classification schemes.

2. "*Design*. Collect observations at field sites to complete cells in a classification scheme."

The drift stage can evolve into design when the researcher develops a complete classification scheme and perhaps develops a tentative model or theory to explain the variety of observations collected to date. For example, if one discovers that cost accounting schemes vary by the organization of production operations (ranging from general purpose job order shops, through batch assembly and process operations), and by product type (frequent vs infrequent changes in product characteristics), then we will probably wish to have at least one or two observations for each combination of classifying variables.

3. "*Prediction*. Test tentative theories or models in new field sites."

At the prediction/test stage, the researcher has a model and a classification scheme that enable predictions to be made about the phenomena being studied. The researcher can then develop new cases at different sites from those used to develop the conceptual model. In effect, these new sites serve as a test or "hold out" sample for the researcher, but they can also serve to extend the theory to industries or settings that have not been examined in the prior two stages. These extensions permit an exploration of whether industry or setting-specific variables are relevant.

4. "*Disconfirmation.* Boundary experiments at extreme cases to determine the limits of the conceptual model."

The fourth stage attempts to test the emerging theory in extreme situations, where the generalizations from the theory might be expected to break down. For example, one might look at much smaller or newly emerging organizations, or explore service rather than manufacturing entities.

It may be implausible for us to expect theories of management processes ever to reach the stage of those in the natural sciences where a small number of experiments can disprove or overthrow a theory. Because of the complexity and ambiguity of social/managerial phenomena, it seems more likely that we will continue to have competing theories co-existing, as a function of researchers' varying perceptions of the critical issues in the phenomena they observe. Probably the best we can hope for is to develop theories that are applicable in different domains and circumstances. The purpose, therefore, of this fourth stage of case study research is to determine and delineate the domain of applicability of theories developed to explain phenomena observed in prior field research.

In summary the Bonoma-Wong proposal attempts to capture the full range of scientific activities by a sequence of field research projects. These projects are developed for: (1) Description; (2) Classification; (3) Theory Development and Limited Testing; and (4) Testing Limits of Theory.

Other social science researchers have also described the role of field research not just for their obvious roles in description and classification activities, but for their role in hypothesis and theory formation activities. Mohr [1985] describes conditions where detailed case study analysis, especially in a "before-after" design (a "process-tracing" study), can be more effective for theory building than traditional large sample research methods. For investigating the impact of an intervention (e.g. a change in production methods or a change in accounting procedures), a detailed process-tracing study, with a careful understanding of the underlying process, can provide a high level of internal validity. For associational research, Mohr believes:

> When the aim is understanding or explanation, there is a tradeoff between case-study research with (detailed diagnosis and process tracing) and large-sample research, typically rendered in correlations and regressions. The former emphasizes understanding *how and why* X and Y are related, on the average, across many subjects.

George & McKeown [1985] also argue that case studies, especially process-tracing, detailed within-case analysis, can provide valuable evidence, beyond that obtained from traditional "quasi-experimental" methods:

> The case study method differs from quasi-experimental approaches in its heavy reliance on *within-case* analysis as a way of evaluating claims about causal processes ...
>
> A second distinction between quasi-experimental and case study approaches lies in their treatment of the distinction between theory formation and theory testing. The conventional quasi-experimental position is founded on a clear-cut distinction between these two activities. Theory formation is a subject which is normally ruled "out of bounds"—statistical analysis,

> for example, is about testing hypotheses not about generating them. By contrast, *the case study techniques often entail viewing hypothesis formation as an objective of the study*. In case studies, a clear demarcation between hypothesis formation and hypothesis testing often is absent, because the research process often involved iterative cycling in which hypotheses are successively "fitted" to observations. Problems with the fit then lead to revision of the hypotheses and may also incite searches for additional data.

Yin [1981a, 1981b] also disputes the common stereotype that case study research:

1. should be used only at the exploratory stage,
2. leads to unconfirmable conclusions, and
3. is a research method of last resort.

Yin [1981b] argues that case studies are especially relevant for studying knowledge utilization because it is characterized by:

- a series of decisions that occur over a long period of time, with no clear beginning or end points;
- outcomes whose direct and indirect implications are too complex for single factor theories;
- a large number of relevant participants; and
- situations that are special in terms of (organizational) context, historical moment in time, and other key elements.

> ... if one is desirous of answering "how" and "why" questions instead of or in addition to questions of frequency, case studies are the more appropriate strategy.

Thus, were researchers in management accounting to undertake field research, they could draw upon the experiences and knowledge acquired by other social science researchers to guide their efforts. In particular, the study of knowledge utilization described by Yin seems especially relevant for studying the use of management accounting information in organizations.

SUMMARY AND CONCLUSIONS

We have surveyed and quoted, in previous sections, from many observers of the scientific research process. Despite the differing backgrounds and points of view of these observers, one can hardly avoid noticing that all agree on the need for scientific activity to start with observation and description of phenomena. Given the paucity of detailed, systematic observation and description in the management accounting literature, it seems compelling that we must initiate activities to overcome this serious defect.

Cost accounting and management control procedures function in complex organizational settings. Therefore, our initial effort to observe and describe management accounting practices must capture the richness of the organizational environment. Initially case studies would seem to provide the ideal vehicle for communicating these deep, rich slices of organizational life. The multiple data sources used to prepare case studies permit a variety of factors to be captured in the descriptive material. Clearly, the field researcher will need to understand more than just cost accounting issues. The phenomena being accounted for—production, marketing, R & D, administrative activities—must be described in some detail and patterns of reporting relationships, decision making, and control must also be captured if we are to understand the context within which the accounting system is functioning.

A continual stream of excellent, descriptive case studies can provide at least three significant benefits for management accounting academics. First, the case studies provide the basis for other forms of research activities. They will be the crucial building blocks for classifying cost accounting and management control practices. Our current schemes were derived 80 or more years ago; it would be useful to determine their validity and usefulness for contemporary organizations. The case studies will also provide a firmer basis for our modeling, theory-building, and hypothesis-formation activities, activities that today occur in the absence of data and observations. As a consequence, we tend to work on problems already in the literature or found in the literature of other disciplines, rather than on problems that emerge from the decision and control activities of managers in actual organizations.

A second benefit from descriptive case studies arises from the discipline they provide to seek out interesting organizations or interesting practices. Unlike the natural sciences where the underlying phenomena seem quite stationary (it is unlikely that gravitational constants, the speed of light, or the structure of the benzene molecule have varied during the past several hundred million years), organization and management phenomena must continually adapt to changing circumstances. The factors critical to the success of global corporations in 1985 can be very different from the success factors for Adam Smith's pin factories, 1850 textile mills, 1880 steel plants and 1920 automobile companies. In order that academic research does not fall too far behind changes in the competitive environment and the new procedures being introduced by innovative organizations, researchers need to be informed about contemporary practice and the evolving skill of the best practitioners. Because of these changes in the phenomena of interest, there is ever more of a need for continual observation and description in management-related disciplines than in the natural sciences (where, of course, observation and measurement are long established and accepted research practices).

When selecting organizations for study, the researcher should not be interested in obtaining a randomly selected or "representative" set of hypotheses. In other words, field studies in a theory testing mode can serve not only to document the existence or non-existence of practices but also to confirm *how* and *why* certain practices have, or have not, been implemented. Therefore, they provide a rich research method for the study of management accounting issues.

Given the potential for field research to illuminate the field of management accounting, one might reasonably wonder why a strong tradition for this research method does not already exist. The omission undoubtedly arises from an impression that field research activities lack legitimacy as scientific research; that scientific activity consists of either deductive reasoning, model-building and theorem proving, or the statistical analysis of large data bases. With this "model" of scientific activity, there is no role for rich description or for testing in relatively few organizations. The goal of this paper has been to document the role that observation, description and classification must play as the precursor for informed theory creation and model-building and the potential for testing theories about accounting in organizations by studying the accounting system of actual organizations. Stating the case somewhat stronger, it now seems implausible that research in a field can claim to be "scientific" when its models and theories are neither inspired from nor tested by actual observations.

There are a host of subsidiary reasons that also serve to inhibit clinical research activity. Among the inhibiting factors are that the research takes longer to accomplish, it requires additional resources for traveling to organizations, it may be difficult to gain access to cooperating organizations, the standards to distinguish "good" from "bad" field research are not yet established, and prestigious journals do not typically publish field studies.[5] Also, the necessary research skills for interviewing practitioners, gleaning information from operating organizations, and observing and listening carefully to learn about the key success factors in corporations are skills not typically taught in doctoral programs. But, these real concerns need not be decisive if it can be generally agreed that empirical research is essential to the future development of management accounting. If a commitment can be made to value the output of field research and field researchers, we can overcome all the other obstacles that may currently be serving to inhibit empirical research.

One additional concern, however, may be more difficult to deal with. At present research on many interesting financial accounting questions can be performed by researchers in their offices, at their computer terminals, and in their libraries. The availability of stock price data, periodic financial statements, and important news releases on computer data bases plus access to documents such as annual reports, proxy statements, lending agreements and prospectuses in libraries makes it possible for financial accounting researchers to conduct a full range of scientific activities without engaging in costly and time-consuming field studies. Therefore, if we advocate that management accounting research must start and eventually end with observations from actual organizations whereas financial accounting research can be performed without leaving universities, we could well be encouraging a further shift from managerial to financial accounting research.

Some differences between the way research can be conducted in financial and management accounting may be inevitable. A corollary of a proposition quoted by A. Kaplan in the Appendix, "Nature does not recognize mathematical difficulties", is that "Nature does not guarantee that research in all disciplines requires the same amount of time and effort". Even conceding such differences, however, prices and demand for accounting researchers may adjust to compensate, at least in part, for shifts in the supply of academics willing to do research in financial vs management accounting. Also, financial accounting researchers may soon discover the value of clinical research to supplement and perhaps substitute for their statistical analyses. As these researchers move beyond associational studies of capital market processes and attempt to understand managerial behaviour (how managers choose their accounting procedures, how they disclose information relevant to the firm, why disclosures are made at different times, and how accounting data are used to compensate senior executives, to name just a few topics currently occupying the attention of financial accounting researchers), they may eventually realize that these "how" and "why" questions are best answered by speaking directly with executives and collecting data within the organizations making these decisions rather than by attempting to induce causality from reduced form regression models with low explanatory power. Thus clinical research methods, once accepted and underway, may actually spread from managerial to financial accounting.

To conclude, field research seemingly provides the only mechanism by which management accounting can become a scientific field of inquiry. There is no disagreement among scholars of the scientific inquiry process that formal, systematic observation must be part of any science:

> It is in the empirical component that science is differentiated from fantasy. An inner coherence, even strict self-consistency, may mark a delusional system as well as a scientific one.
>
> A. Kaplan [1964], p. 34

Because management accounting practices can only be described and understood within the context of actual, ongoing organizations, the domain of empirical work in management accounting must be in these organizations.

The current lack of theories in management accounting also can likely be traced to our failure to observe, firsthand, how management accounting functions in organizations. Recall Henderson's [1970] observation that effective medical research starts with

> ... hard, persistent, intelligent, responsible, unremitting labor in the sick room, not in the library.

Daft, in a provocative essay on the "craft" of research on organizations, also emphasizes the role for on-site observation by researchers:

> The difficulty that many authors have developing interesting and insightful theories about organization(s) probably is explained by the lack of experience with organizations. G.R. Grice admonished his students who were trying to understand animal learning: "No matter how many assistants you may hire, always handle your own rat"
>
> Daft [1983], p. 543

For too long now, management accounting researchers' attitude to empirical research has had all the enthusiasm of most people for handling their own rats. This distaste for conducting research within organizations must be overcome if we are to gain the intuition, familiarity and experience that are necessary for management accounting research to progress.

ENDNOTES

1. I am grateful to Germain Boer for suggesting to me the importance of these field surveys on academic thought.
2. I am grateful to Urton Anderson for helping me to understand this point.
3. Note that the absence of external validity for laboratory experiments is a major difference between research in the natural sciences and research on management processes. Physical phenomena observed in the laboratory will be representative of phenomena occurring outside laboratories also. But experiments on students or even practitioners in artificial laboratory settings will give virtually no insight into the practice of management in its complex organizational setting.
4. The definitions and descriptions of these three methods have been adapted from Stone [1978], ch. 7. I have deliberately omitted three other types of empirical research methods described by Stone, laboratory experiments, surveys, and simulation, because I believe their external validity to be far too low for understanding management accounting phenomena. Chapter 7 in Stone [1978] contains an excellent discussion of the strengths and weaknesses of all these empirical research methods.
5. The issue of standards for field research and the lack of such research in academic journals is aggravated by having most management-related field research published in the *Harvard Business Review* or monographs (e.g. Garvin [1983]; Donaldson [1984]), whose intended audience is experienced practitioners, not other academics.

BIBLIOGRAPHY

Antle, R. & A. J. Smith, "An Empirical Investigation into the Relative Performance Evaluation of Corporate Executives", Graduate School of Business, University of Chicago Working Paper (November 1983).

Birnberg, J. G., L. Turopolec & S. M. Young, "The Organizational Context of Accounting", *Accounting, Organizations, and Society* [1983] pp. 111-129.

Bonoma, T. V. & K. B. Wong, "A Case Study in Case Research", *Journal of Marketing Research* (May 1985) pp. 199-208.

Christenson, C., "Proposals for a Program of Empirical Research into the Properties of Triangles", *Decision Sciences* (October 1976) pp. 631-648.

Cook, T. D. & D. T. Campbell, *Quasi-Experimentation: Design and Analysis Issues for Field Settings* (Chicago: Rand McNally, 1979).

Daft, R. L., "Learning the Craft of Organizational Research", *Academy of Management Review* (1983) pp. 539-546.

Donaldson, G., *Managing Corporate Wealth* (Praeger, 1984).

Garvin, D. A., "Quality on the Line", *Harvard Business Review* (September-October 1983), pp. 64-75.

George, A. L. & T. J. McKeown, "Case Studies and Theories of Organizational Decision-Making", in Coulam, R. F. and Smith, R.A., (eds) *Advances in Information Processing in Organizations*, Vol. 2 (JAI Press, 1985).

Glaser, B. G. & A. L. Strauss, *The Discovery of Grounded Theory: Strategies for Qualitative Research* (Chicago: Aldine, 1967).

Graham, R. J., "Anthropology and OR: The Place of Observation in Management Science Process", *Journal of Operational Research* (1984).

Henderson, L. J., *On the Social System* (Chicago: University of Chicago Press, 1970).

Hertenstein, J. H., "Innovation in Management Control: A Comparative Study of Inflation Adjusted Accounting Systems in Diversified Firms", Unpublished DBA Dissertation, Harvard Business School, 1984.

Hopwood, A. G., "On Trying to Study Accounting in the Contexts in which it Operates", *Accounting, Organizations and Society* (1983) pp. 287-305.

Jensen, M.C., "Organization Theory and Methodology", *The Accounting Review* (April 1983) pp. 319-339.

Kaplan, A., *The Conduct of Inquiry: Methodology for Behavioural Research* (Scranton, PA: Chandler, 1964).

Kaplan, R. S., "Measuring Manufacturing Performance: A New Challenge for Management Accounting Research", *The Accounting Review* (October 1983) pp. 686-705.

Kaplan, R. S., "The Evolution of Management Accounting", *The Accounting Review* (July 1984a) pp. 390-418.

Kaplan, R. S., "Accounting Lag: The Obsolescence of Cost Accounting Systems", Harvard Business School Working Paper, March 1984b.

Klemstine, C. F. & M. W. Maher, *Management Accounting Research: 1926-1983*, (American Accounting Association: Management Accounting Section, 1983).

Kuhn, T. S., "Logic Discovery or Psychology of Research", in Lakatos, I. and Musgrave, A. (eds) *Criticism and the Growth of Knowledge* pp. 1-23 (London: Cambridge University Press, 1970a).

Kuhn, T. S., *Structure of Scientific Revolutions* (Chicago: University of Chicago Press, 1970b).

Lakatos, I. & A. Musgrave, *Criticism and the Growth of Knowledge* (London: Cambridge University Press, 1970).

Miller, D. & P. H. Friesen, "Archetypes of Organizational Transition", *Administrative Science Quarterly* (1980) pp. 268-299.

Miller, D. & P. H. Friesen, "The Longitudinal Analysis of Organizations: A Methodological Perspective", *Management Science* (September 1982) pp. 1013-1034.

Mitroff, I., F. Betz, L. R. Pondy & F. Sagasti, "On Managing Science in the Systems Age: Two Schemas for the Study of Science as a Whole Systems Phenomenon", *Interfaces* (May 1974) pp. 46-58.

Mohr, L. G., "The Reliability of the Case Study as a Source of Information", in Coulam, R.F. and Smith, R.A. (eds) *Advances in Information Processing in Organizations*, Vol. 2 (JAI Press, 1985).

Popper, K. R., *The Logic of Scientific Discovery* (New York: Basic Books, 1959).

Roethlisberger, F. J., *The Elusive Phenomena* (Cambridge: Harvard University Press, 1977).

Schön, D. A., "The Crisis of Professional Knowledge and the Pursuit of an Epistemology of Practice", Harvard Business School 75th Anniversary Solloquium on Teaching by the Case Method (1984).

Simon, H. A., "The Behavioural and Social Sciences", *Science* (July 1980) pp. 72-78.

Simon, J. L., *Basic Research Methods in Social Science: The Art of Empirical Investigation* 2nd ed. (New York: Random House, 1978).

Stone, E., *Research Methods in Organizational Behaviour* (Santa Monica, CA: Goodyear Publishing, 1978).

Teece, D. J., & S. G. Winter, "The Limits of Neoclassical Theory in Management Education", *American Economic Review* (May 1984), pp. 116-121.

Thomas, K. W. & W. G. Tymon Jr., "Necessary Properties of Relevant Research: Lessons from Recent Criticism of the Organizational Sciences", *Academy of Management Review* (1982), pp. 345-352.

Van Maanen, J., *Qualitative Methodology* (Beverly Hills, CA: Sage, 1983).

Vancil, R. R., *Decentralization: Managerial Ambiguity by Design* (Homewood, IL: Dow Jones-Irwin, 1978).

Yin, R. K., "The Case Study Crisis: Some Answers", *Administrative Science Quarterly* (March 1981a) pp. 58-66.

Yin, R. K., "The Case Study as a Serious Research Strategy", *Knowledge: Creation, Diffusion, Utilization* (September 1981b) pp. 97-114.

Part III: Organizational And Behavioural Accounting

Behavioral Accounting Research: A Critical Approach edited by Kenneth R. Ferris, (1988), pp. 15-45; reprinted with permission.

Behavioral Research on the Production and Use of Financial Information*

A.J. Richardson and M. Gibbins with the assistance of John Wilson

*The authors would like to acknowledge the comments of Paul Dorsey, Jim Newton, and John Waterhouse on earlier drafts of this chapter.

In this Chapter we review behavioral research concerned with the production and use of financial information. There is a vast and disjointed body of literature in this field, and, in order to review this literature systematically, we have developed a model of the processes of interest based on our perceptions of the assumptions which underlie most research studies and the range of issues which have been addressed. The model focuses on the roles which people undertake to accomplish these processes, individual variations in role behaviors, the pressures which affect them, and the network of roles through which information flows. The literature review which follows examines the current state of knowledge with respect to each component of the model.

Our review is also critical. We attempt to identify the strengths and weaknesses of extant research and to suggest areas for further research. The critical intent of this review obliges us to explicitly state the standards which we have applied to the field. Chapter 14 is concerned with methodology and we defer to that chapter on standards of research method. Our review, however, is based on a particular epistemology which creates certain expectations about the relationship between theories of information production and use, and the underlying reality which those theories attempt to capture.

We perceive theory and reality as two loosely coupled planes of activity (see AAA [1971] p. 58). The lower or observation plane is the day-to-day reality of financial disclosure and information use involving a complex set of actors and information channels. This plane is constantly shifting as the composition of actors, both individual and institutional, changes and as the technology of information transfer and analysis evolves. The upper or theory plane, the focus of this chapter, is the cumulative body of theory, models, and empirical findings which attempt to capture something of the reality of information disclosure and use. The theory plane is also in transition as new empirical findings emerge and theoretical insights, frequently from other disciplines, are introduced to direct research and interpret empirical results.

In contrast to the natural sciences where the observation plane, representing phenomena based on natural laws, is relatively stable, it is unlikely that the content of the upper plane will ever achieve a high degree of congruence with the constantly shifting lower plane. The criterion for theory acceptance in accounting, and other social sciences, is, therefore, one of utility rather than strict correspondence to reality (see Mattessich [1964] for an extended discussion). Given this epistemology, we are prepared to accept a wide diversity of theoretical perspectives and to grant the validity of each perspective as a contribution to our understanding of the production and use of financial information.

A MODEL OF THE PRODUCTION AND USE OF FINANCIAL INFORMATION

We have identified four assumptions, which, we assert, are implicit in the majority of studies we review. First, all processes involved in the production and use of financial information are intendedly rational. On the basis of this assumption, we presume that actors are making choices among alternatives in order to achieve some goal or objective. It is entirely possible, however, that ex post the process will not appear as rational and orderly as this implies. Second, all parties are motivated by self-interest. This is a weak assumption, and possibly tautological, which allows us to impute goals where none are stated and to develop models from which to explore the processes of interest. Third, all actors have limited cognitive capacity. This assumption draws attention to the devices used to overcome these limitations, ranging from rules and standards at an organizational level to heuristics in individual decision making. Finally, all interactions occur within, and are conditional upon, specific institutional contexts. This assumption precludes the possibility of general theories of information production and use; hence, we expect to find "theories of the midrange" which deal with particular aspects of the processes of interest.

We theorize, based on our review of the literature, that the production and use of financial information occurs through individuals fulfilling institutionally embedded roles. The use of role theory as a basis for organizing a review of behavioral research in accounting is particularly appropriate given the reliance of this research on theories drawn from a range of social sciences. As Rommetveit [1955, p. 31] suggests, the role is "the theoretical point of articulation between psychology and sociology," being "the largest possible research unit within the former discipline and the smallest possible within the latter."

Three roles are of particular importance: the disclosure, analysis, and information use roles. By *disclosure* we mean the authorized public release of financial information and individual and group processes leading to that event. By *analysis* we mean an interpretative (cognitive) process by which the significance of financial information to particular users or uses is determined by a particular individual. The analysis role, therefore, is embedded in a larger context which we refer to as the use of financial information. We have adopted the term "use" rather than the more traditional "decision making" as the end-point of this sequence in recognition of the broad range of activities which rely on financial information (e.g., Burchell *et al.* [1980]). By *use*, then, we mean the use of financial information to support any political, social, or economic process including,

FIGURE 2.1 A role model of the production and use of financial information.

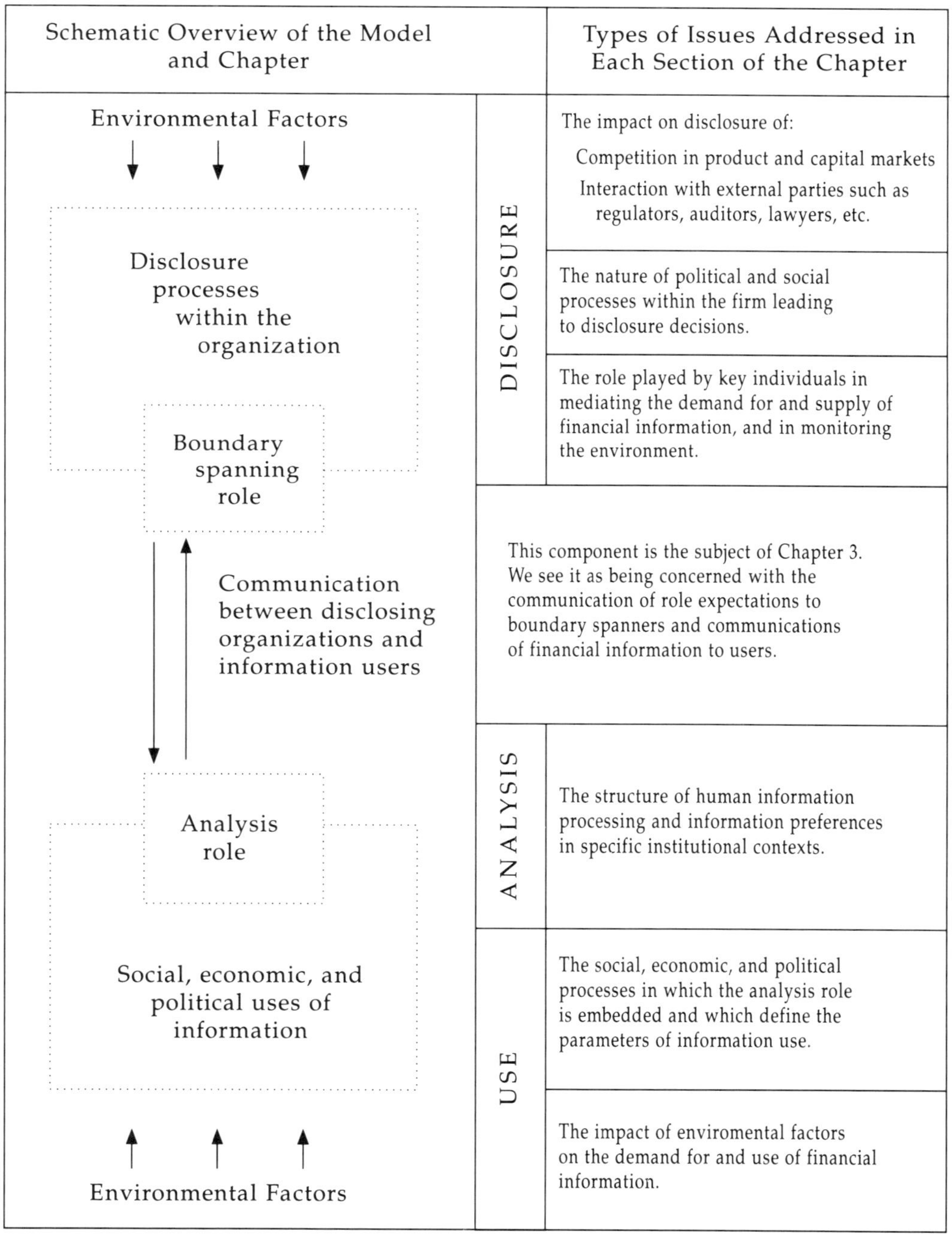

but not limited to, financial decision making, bargaining, and evaluation. Our model is summarized schematically in Figure 2.1.

On the observation plane, these roles may not be clearly differentiated—company managements present analyses of their results as well as simply disclosing them, analysis and use are complexly interwoven, and disclosure may be made strategically based on beliefs about the uses made of that information—but it is useful to separate them as a means of organizing the literature. Each role is subject to a range of pressures to behave in certain ways, for example, incentive schemes and authority relations. In addition, the role incumbent brings idiosyncratic variation to the role due to his/her personality, risk preferences, and cognitive capacity (among other factors). The role behaviors which emerge from this complex interaction of factors are directed to a network of individuals facing their own sets of individual and environmental pressures. It must be noted that communication is a central aspect of our model. Role expectations must be communicated between users and disclosers and the information produced must be communicated to users. The literature concerned directly with communication will be the focus of Chapter 3 and will receive limited attention here.

Our model draws particular attention to the context in which individuals perform their roles. Most of the individuals filling these roles are members of organizations. These organizations will have established bureaucratic controls and incentive systems designed to bring about particular types of behavior. In addition, external institutions such as tax authorities, securities commissions, unions, suppliers, and so on may create pressures for the production or use of particular types of information. The position of these roles within organizations also implies that role behaviors may involve joint actions with others in the organization and that the role, considered functionally, may be divided among a number of individuals. We believe that these contextual variables are important factors shaping individual behavior.

Overall, the role model of financial information production and use which we are suggesting as a means of organizing and evaluating the literature is a complex equilibrium model of behavior. It assumes that the roles we are examining are reciprocally interdependent. Information production is affected by user demands and reactions which, in turn, are dependent on the information produced. It also assumes that both information producers and users are behaving within an institutional environment, containing, for example, such things as regulations and social and cultural norms, which affects the way in which these roles will be fulfilled. In this context, models which rely on strict economic or instrumental rationality are unlikely to capture the process of balancing role expectations while facing ambiguity, conflict, and stress. The outcome is unlikely to reflect simple imperatives of any kind, whether economic, psychological, or social.

Our discussion of the field draws selectively on about 300 empirical studies which we identified related to the behavioral aspects of the production and use of financial information. Although space limitations preclude providing a complete bibliography of this literature, Table 2.1 attempts to convey a sense of the historical development and content of the field. In this table, each of the studies we identified have been classified by time period, methodology, and aspect of the process to which they relate. The table demonstrates the rapid growth of this field, initially focusing on disclosure and analysis issues, but more recently turning to consider the use of financial information. The table also demonstrates the growth in the use of experimental methodologies through the 1970s and the expansion in field studies (broadly defined) over the

TABLE 2.1 Schematic Overview of the Field
Legend:
E=Experiment I=Interview
S=Survey+Questionnaire FS=Field Study

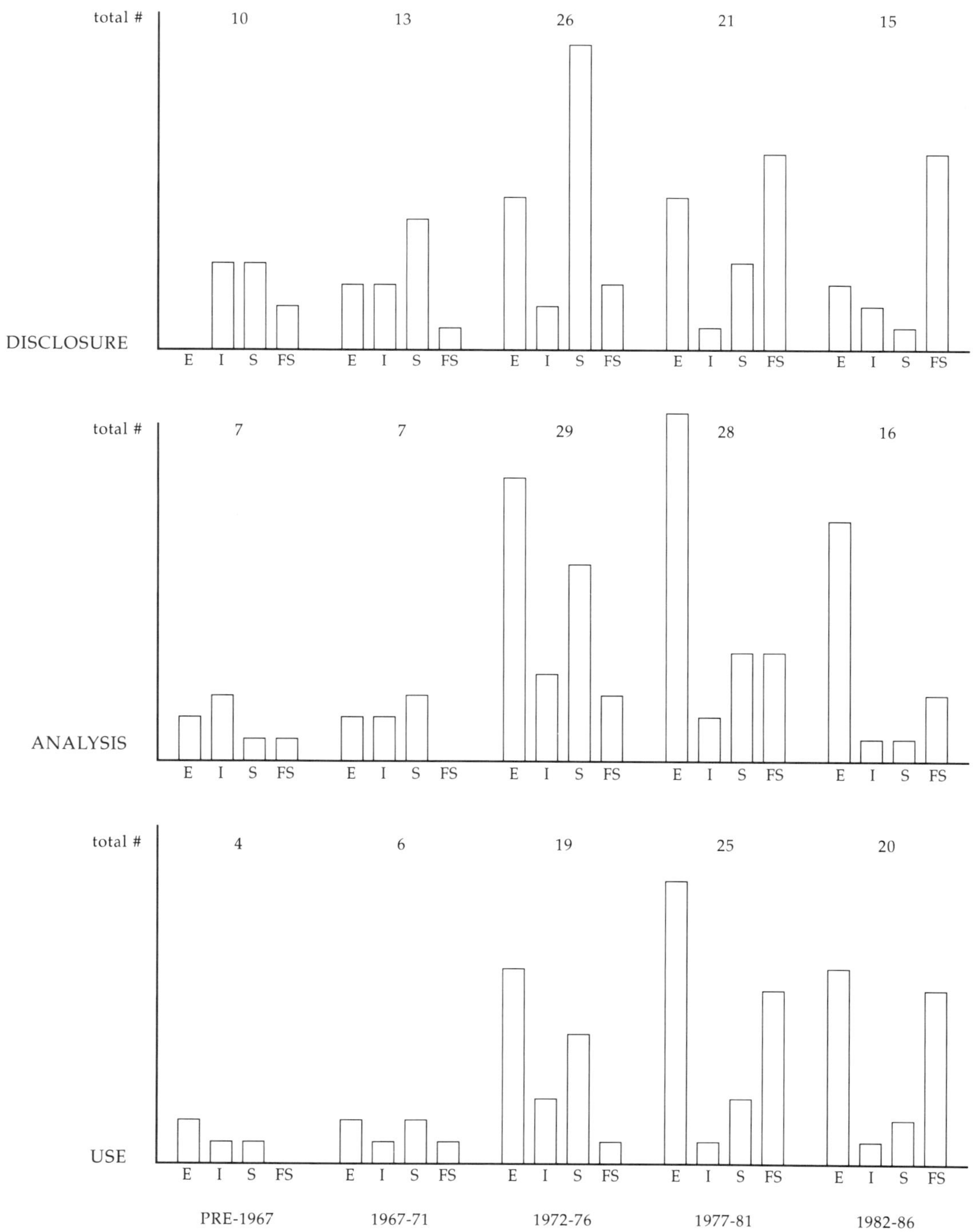

last few years. The significance of these changes is commented on generally below but substantive discussion of methodological issues is left to Chapter 14.

REVIEW OF THE LITERATURE

FINANCIAL DISCLOSURE

Financial information is generated by and about the economic activity of the firm. The disclosure of that information to outsiders is typically the responsibility of senior managers within the firm. Our focus, therefore, is on the needs and opportunities for disclosure which face the manager in this role, the processes which must occur to fulfil this role, factors affecting variations in role behavior, and, finally, the consequences of this role for managers and their firms.

The form and content of financial disclosures are of concern to a wide variety of regulatory bodies and users. The expectations for disclosure which are generated vary from country to country (Gray, [1980]; Scott and Troberg [1980]), and, in spite of the growing internationalization of accounting (Brennan [1979]), local norms must be respected. There is, however, considerable room for individual variation within these norms. Auditors facing the same set of facts may recommend different accounting treatments (McDonald [1968]; Sterling and Radosevich, [1969]; Sterling [1969]; Sterling, Tollefson and Flaherty [1972]), and there is unlikely to be unanimity among users on the appropriate disclosures (e.g., surveys on the usefulness of price level and current-value-accounting by: AICPA [1958]; Backer [1970, 1973]; Brenner [1970]; Estes [1968]; Garner [1972]; Hanna [1972, 1974]; Horngren [1955]; Rosen [1972]).

Within the broad limits set by cultural and regulatory norms, and the narrower limits imposed by existing standards and the auditor's interpretation of standards, therefore, management must ultimately choose the form and content of information disclosed. It has been suggested that firms may follow the lead of innovators such that disclosure practices diffuse among a group of firms linked by some common interest (Comiskey and Groves [1971]; Copeland and Shank [1971]; Piaker and Dalberth [1973]; Shank and Copeland [1973]). The conditions under which firms would decide to innovate with disclosure practices have not been investigated. (Harrison and McKinnon [1986] provide an analytic framework which might be useful in exploring this issue.) Alternatively, forms may follow the opinions of authoritative bodies (securities commissions, standard-setting bodies) even though no firm standard exists (Rakes and Shenkir [1972]; Ritts [1974]). This relationship, however, is not one-way. Managers and others also lobby standard setters to bring about standards which favor their interests (Moonitz [1974]; Horngren [1973]; Watts and Zimmerman [1978, 1979]).

The suggestion that management may follow the lead of innovators or opinion leaders in the choice of accounting policies need not imply that these acts are "economically rational." Although management self-interest may be affected by not following industry trends in disclosure, or by being caught on the wrong side of a future disclosure standard, these studies are also consistent with an "institutional" perspective (Meyer [1986]). Institutionalization theory suggests that some activities are undertaken simply because they have been legitimated as appropriate to certain companies and regardless of the instrumental consequences. Findings that financial statements are of little value in investment decision making are consistent with this perspective (Epstein [1975]; but see Most and Chang [1979]). This perspective challenges the implicit assumptions of the core body of literature in the field that the production and use of financial information is goal-directed and intendedly rational. The alternative assumptions implicit in this perspective have not yet received empirical examination.

The theories mentioned in the last two paragraphs focus on the nature of the disclosure as the determinant of reporting practice. An alternate approach is to focus on characteristics of firms such as their "corporate personality" (Sorter *et al.* [1964, 1966]). These articles assume that there is some consensus among senior officers of a company on the image the company would like to project. In any situation where a choice on the level or form of disclosure must be made, this consensus will be the determining factor.

A common basis for consensus among managers is self-interest. It has been suggested that managers attempt to "smooth" income where managerial compensation is tied to accounting numbers or, with additional assumptions about market efficiency, stock prices (Barnea, Ronen, and Sadan [1976]; Copeland [1968]; Copeland and LiCastro [1968]; Dopuch and Drake [1966]; Gagnon [1967]; Gordon [1964]; Gordon, Horowitz, and Meyers [1966]; and Ronen and Sadan [1981]; Koch [1981] presents some experimental evidence). Smoothing may be accomplished through the choice of accounting policies or, of greater consequence, through investment and production decisions.

These types of concerns have developed into a large body of literature, known as "positive accounting" (Watts and Zimmerman [1986]), which attempts to identify the external forces to which management is responding in their choice of accounting technique. This literature identifies a broad range of users and uses of financial information, and suggests that management must choose a "portfolio" of disclosures (Zmijewski and Hagerman [1981]) to balance competing demands on the firm. Thomas [1986] has suggested the need for a contingency theory of corporate reporting which ties reporting preferences to characteristics of the organization and its environment. This is regarded as an addition to the direct income effects which are the central concern of positive theories but which, typically, capture very little of the variance in reporting practices.

Most of the work on the disclosure role has been undertaken at an aggregate level. This will be contrasted with the emphasis of work on the analysis role below. There has been little effort to investigate the processes leading up to disclosures or the consequences of the disclosure role for incumbents. The relationship between the auditor and management has received some attention. Firth [1980], for example, examined users' and preparers' perceptions of auditor independence and of the effects of nonindependence on the usefulness of audited financial information. Predictably, nonindependence was perceived as impairing the usefulness of information for investment and lending decisions but there were differences of opinion among groups on the types of situations which might impair independence. Gibbins and Wolf [1982] suggest a high degree of client/auditor interdependence which could dilute the effectiveness of the audit in limiting managements' ability to influence accounting results. Thornton [1984] presents evidence on the impact of auditor recommendations on the disclosure of current cost information.

The relationship between auditors and management is only one aspect of the process underlying financial disclosures. If the firm is viewed as a political coalition (March and Simon [1958]), then negotiations among senior officers may affect disclosures. For example, the disclosure of financial information may improve access to capital markets but impair union negotiations, leading to differences of opinion among personnel and financial managers. This perspective suggests that the "corporate personality" may be a political compromise within the firm, or an authoritative pronouncement by a powerful individual or coalition, which can be subject to empirical investigation. Disclosure may also involve other external actors such as lawyers and underwriters. These aspects of the observation plane have yet to be described or modeled.

The consequences of the disclosure role for the firm and individuals have also received scant attention. Prakash and Rappaport [1977] argued that managers may be affected by the information which they are required to communicate, a phenomenon they refer to as "information inductance." This receives indirect support in surveys by Casey and Sandretto [1981] and Schwarzbach and Swanson [1981] which indicate that current cost data, although rarely generated by management prior to standards requiring its production, is beginning to be used by a few managers for decision making. Shank, Dillard, and Murdoch [1980] interviewed managers about their responses to the FASB's Statement No. 8 on foreign currency translation and found that, in spite of an apparent lack of reaction by stock markets to the standard, managers undertook action in the foreign currency area that would increase expected costs and risk levels in order to preserve "desired" relationships in accounting numbers. Johnson and Kaplan [1986] suggest, more generally, that procedures developed for external reporting purposes may be used for internal decision making, often with negative consequences for the firm. Weick [1983] and Libby [1983] raise the question of whether or not the requirement to prepare financial reports creates stress and, if so, whether this affects the performance to which those reports relate. These papers raise provocative questions about the effects of standards and mandatory financial reporting on the firm (cf. Demski [1973]; American Accounting Association [1977]; Dopuch and Sunder [1980]) but no conclusions can yet be drawn.

ANALYSIS

A broad range of financial information is released by companies through a variety of media and to a variety of external actors. The choice of media, characteristics of the information, and other aspects of the communication of financial information are the subject of Chapter 3. Our focus is on those actors who must interpret this information. Specifically, we review research concerned with information preferences, the effects of different types of information on the judgment process, the structure of human information processing, and individual variations in the analysis of information.

There is a long line of research which has been concerned with the preferences of individuals for financial information. These studies have either asked subjects to express preferences (Bradish [1965]; Ecton [1969]; Opinion Research Corporation [1974]; Cerf [1961]) or have examined their use of information and inferred preferences from their behavior (Horngren [1955, 1956, 1957]). The purpose of these studies has typically been to address the question of whether or not individuals analyzing financial information were satisfied with existing disclosures. Overall, the results suggest that disclosure is adequate, although there are great variations among companies, and there is little consensus on what additional disclosures would be useful. This finding is also consistent over time; for example, similar results were reported by Roper [1948] and Sanders [1948], even though the level of disclosure has increased markedly. There is no evidence that the increasing levels of disclosure have overwhelmed analysts' ability to use that information (Dyckman, Gibbins, and Swieringa [1978]). These observations suggest that individuals develop analytic strategies consistent with the information set available at a given time. This inference, in turn, raises questions of how and why the information set changes if users are continuously satisfied with the information set within which they operate. A transaction-based approach (e.g. Williamson [1975]; Johnson [1982]; Johnson and Kaplan [1986]) may provide a useful framework with which to address this issue.

The use of surveys and interviews to determine information preferences may not, in fact, provide useful data on individuals' use of information. In general, people seem to have little insight into their own decision processes (e.g., Gray [1979]; Nisbett and Wilson [1977]) although exceptions have been noted in simple experimental situations among auditors (Ashton [1974]; Schultz and Gustavson [1978]; Savich [1977]) and among student subjects (Wright [1977a, 1979]). There have also been attempts to study information use experimentally. These articles demonstrate discrepancies between actual decision processes and normative decision models. For example, people may react to redundant or irrelevant information, or use information inconsistently (Ashton [1982]). People also appear to revise probabilities less than Bayesian theory would suggest is appropriate (Shafer [1978]; Joyce and Biddle [1981]). Eger and Dickhaut [1982], however, suggest that some results are due to the method of eliciting probabilities. Finally, there is also evidence that individuals may not adjust their use of information when the procedures producing that information change (the "functional fixation" hypothesis: Ashton [1976]; Libby [1976b], Swieringa *et al.* [1979]; Marchant [1979]; Birnberg and Wilner [1986] provide a critique of this literature).

In recent work, alternative decision models based on "bounded rationality" (Simon [1979]) or utility functions which are not symmetric over gains and loses (Kahneman and Tversky [1979]) have been suggested as more appropriate models of decision making. One fruitful approach has been to examine the "rules of thumb" or heuristics that people develop to cope with complex cognitive tasks (Pattillo [1976]; Hofstedt and Hughes [1977]; Dyckman *et al.*, [1978]; Firth [1979]; Moriarity and Barron [1979]; Libby [1981]). For example, people may judge the frequency of events by the ease with which they can draw cases from memory, which biases judgments in favor of "vivid" events, or in making estimates people will anchor on any arbitrary number which is suggested and make adjustments from that point. The extent to which heuristics such as these are actually used and the means by which they are chosen and developed by individuals has not received attention (Gibbins and Newton [1986]). Biddle and Joyce [1981] and Kinney and Uecker [1979] have taken a step in this direction by examining the task characteristics likely to result in the use of heuristics.

There have also been attempts to determine whether or not there are differences in personality or "cognitive style" (e.g., the preference for aggregate versus disaggregate information) which affect decision-making behavior (Driver and Mock [1975]; Savich [1977], McGhee, Shields, and Birnberg [1978]; Benbasat and Dexter [1979]; Lusk [1979]; Pratt [1980]). These studies have failed to demonstrate a strong link between information use and cognitive style, and, with few exceptions (e.g., Gul [1984]), there is little activity in this area.

There have also been various "policy-capturing" (Libby and Lewis [1982]) studies which have examined the weighting of information cues and the degree of concensus among "judges." For example, a series of studies have focused on the ability of individuals to predict business failure based on financial information (Libby [1975a, 1975b]; Casey [1980]; Zimmer [1980]; Abdel-khalik and El-Sheshai [1980]). In these studies, the loan officers used displayed a high degree of accuracy, consistency, and consensus.

Abdel-khalik and El-Sheshai's study is significant in attempting to separate the effects of data selection and data processing on the accuracy of judgments. Their results suggest that individuals are better at processing information than selecting which information to process. These results shed light on repeated findings that simple linear models often outperform human decision makers (Libby [1975a]; Wright [1979]; exceptions to this finding are reported by Libby [1976]; and Libby and Blashfield [1978]). The success of these models may simply be due to their ability to select independent variables from among an information set with the strongest statistical relationship with the dependent variables of interest. (Ashton [1982] suggests that these discrepancies may reflect the motivations of decision makers.) It has also been found that composites of peoples' judgments often outperform all but the most successful individuals (Libby [1975a]; Wright [1979]), presumably because the composite choice of cues is superior to most individual choices.

In the studies discussed in the last few paragraphs, the focus of the research undertaken was on the inputs and outputs of decision processes, and how subjects actually use information was either inferred or ignored. Several studies, using process tracing methodologies (Newell and Simon [1972]), have attempted to make these processes the focus of investigation. Bowman [1984], for example, compared the decision process of "expert" (CPAs or university faculty) and "novice" (MBA students) analysts in a laboratory study. The most significant differences occurred during the reasoning process. Experts tended to develop a holistic view of "what's going on," while novices concentrated on the selection of particular facts (see also Abdel-khalik [1980]; Dillard [1984]). Another promising process-oriented approach is to examine subjects' abilities to learn from experience (Uecker [1978, 1980]; Gibbins [1984]; Waller and Felix [1984a, 1984b, 1984c]; Gibbins and Emby [1984]). This area is just developing and conclusive results are lacking.

Although these approaches may improve our understanding of how actual decisions are made, normative models provide a standard by which decisions may be evaluated and serve as a basis for the development of decision aids. The discovery of accurate linear and composite models of decision making, or at least cue choice, also suggests various "bootstrapping" techniques which could improve decision making. To date, the investigation of decision aids has been largely limited to management accounting (Lewis, Shields, and Young [1983]), computer-based accounting systems (Benbasat and Dexter [1979]; Cheverny and Dickson [1974]) and auditing (Chesley [1978]), but their potential in financial accounting is also worthy of investigation. Financial information may be viewed, in essence, as a decision aid for individuals concerned with the economic performance of the firm, yet the development of this "decision aid" is at a relatively low level of sophistication.

The significance of variations from formal decision-making models among subjects is moot. In some cases heuristics can prove to be efficient solutions to problems (Thorngate [1981]; Einhorn and Hogarth [1981]) and, on the observation plane, we are frequently able to revise our actions on an ongoing basis such that decisions are reached as a series of approximations rather than making a final decision at a particular point in time (Hogarth [1981]). In addition, the research on departures of decision making from normative models has focused on the individual decision maker and ignores the context in which decisions are made. Einhorn and Hogarth [1981] and Hogarth [1981] have argued that the context of decision making may affect the nature of decision processes. Demski [1980], meanwhile, suggests that the comparative advantage of accounting researchers lies in studying the nexus between institutional arrangements and decision making. This area has, however, received little attention from behavioral researchers. A promising approach is the experimental economics of Smith [1982] and Plott [1982], which has been applied in an accounting context by DeJong, Forsythe and Uecker [1985], DeJong, Forsythe, Lundholme and Uecker [1985], and Plott and Sunder [1982, 1984]. This work has demonstrated that the outcome of individual decision processes varies with the institutional context in which decision making occurs.

The significance on the observation plane of institutional influences on decision making cannot really be assessed at this point. The social organization of information analysis has not been subject to empirical investigation. For example, the degree of dependence of individual investors on brokerage houses for analyses and the internal organization of the analysis function in brokerage houses may be significant factors affecting the distribution and performance of the analysis role. These aspects of the observation plane have yet to be reflected on the theory plane.

USE

Financial accounting is traditionally regarded as providing information relevant for investment decision making and the stewardship of resources. In recent years, however, financial information has been implicated in a surprising array of social and economic processes, while the actual utility of accounting information in some of its traditional roles has been subject to question. The traditional functions claimed for financial accounting information may be best regarded as normative statements rather than empirical descriptions of the use of that information, and attention has turned to consideration of the roles which accounting information actually plays in organizations and society (Burchell *et al.* [1980]).

The role of financial accounting information in investment decision making was given precedence in the Financial Accounting Standards Board Conceptual Framework [1978]. Surveys of users, however, provide mixed results. For example, Epstein [1975] reported that financial statements are not a primary source of information for investment decision making and the SEC's Advisory Committee on Corporate Disclosure [1977] reported that analysts relied on informal sources of information, whereas Most and Chang [1979] reported the opposite. In experimental work using bankers and loan officers as subjects, a similar lack of consensus emerges (Kennedy [1978]; Libby [1975a, 1975b, 1979a, 1979b]; Estes and Reimer [1977]; Eyes and Tabb [1978]; Stanga and Benjamin [1978]; Abdel-khalik and El-Sheshai [1980]; Casey [1980b]; Zimmer [1980]; Schepanski [1983]; Campbell [1984]; Abdel-khalik, Graul, and Newton [1986]). While overall it is clear that these subjects do use financial statements in their credit decisions, they respond to very few dimensions of those data and are not very good at selecting the best cues for their particular tasks.

The ambivalent reaction of individuals to financial statement information for investment and credit decision making is consistent with market-based research which indicates that most of the content of formal releases of financial information is incorporated into security prices well before the release date (e.g., Ball and Brown [1968]; Foster, Jenkins, and Vickrey [1986]). Although this result may be limited to large stable firms about which there are many alternative sources of information, at the very least financial accounting information must be regarded as only one aspect of a competitive market for corporate financial information, and by no means the most timely of sources.

The stewardship role of financial information dominated academic work prior to 1945 and has experienced a rebirth with the development of agency theory models and an expansion of the number of parties seen as legitimate stakeholders in the firm (Butterworth, Gibbins, and King [1982]). Whereas the investment role of accounting information relies on that information's ability to predict uncertain future events (and there is no logical reason why historic cost financial information should have this property), the stewardship or contracting role of financial information requires only that this information should serve as an a priori means of agreeing on risk and profit-sharing rules and an ex post means of settling up. Leftwich [1981], for example, demonstrated that the measurement rules in corporate lending agreements were negotiated as part of the contract. These rules varied systematically from GAAP in ways which would prevent management from transferring wealth from bondholders to shareholders. Work investigating the development of government contracting is also providing useful insights into the contracting roles of accounting (Loft [1986]). DeJong, Forsythe, and Uecker [1985] have developed experimental methods for exploring the effect of various contracting rules on managerial behavior.

These uses of accounting information focus on the narrow relationship between the suppliers, or potential suppliers, and the users of capital. Financial information, however, also attracts the attention of other stakeholders in the firm, notably labor and the state. Labor, particularly as represented by trade unions, may be interested in financial statements as an input to the development of bargaining strategies. Owen and Lloyd [1985] provide a summary of literature which indicates that there is great variation in the use of financial information by union representatives. They provide a tentative analytic typology of actors and institutional contexts as a basis for exploring these variations.

The focus of much of the research on the use of financial information in labor relations has been to determine the "optimum" level of disclosure to achieve consensus on the distribution of profit between labor and capital (Foley and Maunders [1977]; Palmer [1977]; Craft [1981]; Pope and Peel [1981]). The optimum level of disclosure in these articles is that which provides the greatest net benefit to the firm (i.e., owners). Ogden and Bougen [1985] suggest a radical perspective on the disclosure of financial information to unions. They argue that decision making in organizations is not economically rational; therefore, the use of models which assume such processes is invalid. They also suggest that a major use of financial information is to distract attention from nonquantifiable areas which are of greater concern to management, such as control over the labor process. Amernic [1985, 1986] and Foley and Maunders [1977] have each used Walton and McKersie's [1965] behavioral model of bargaining to explore the process of using financial information in labor relations. This is the most promising direction in this area.

The role of financial information in the relationship between organizations and the state has not received extensive investigation. It is clear that much of the initial impetus for the development of accounting systems was the demands by the state for information for taxation, the regulation of specific industries (primarily utilities and financial institutions), the administration of bankruptcies and securities markets, and microeconomic planning (Littleton [1933]; Singer [1943]; Chatfield [1977]). A number of authors suggest that firms respond to these demands ritualistically, without any concern for the actual usefulness of the information they provide. The production of information is simply regarded as maintaining a myth to ensure the legitimacy of the firm (Coppock [1977]; Douglas [1977]; Gambling [1977]; Meyer [1979]; Wildavsky [1976]). Another stream of research regards accounting as a mechanism of state control and attempts to explore the political implications of state-generated demands for financial information (Lowe and Tinker [1977]; Tinker [1980]; Tinker *et al.* [1982]). This is a growing area of research, particularly among accountants in those countries where the intervention of the state in economic activity and/or accounting practice is significant.

A continuing dilemma in research on the use of accounting information is that the focus has been on individual decision makers but often the issues which attract attention are concerned with reactions at a more aggregate level such as the market, firm, or profession (cf. Gibbins and Newton [1986]). Aggregate behavior is unlikely to have properties deducible from separately observed individual actions (Milgram and Toch [1968]; Beaver [1972]; Schelling [1978]). Further, the processes by which individual actions or values are aggregated into market or social behavior have been subject to only rudimentary analytic or behavioral analysis as yet (e.g., Schelling [1978]; Demski [1980]; Plott and Sunder [1981]). Many of the behavioral issues, such as functional fixation or conservatism, noted above, apparently disappear at an aggregate level of behavior. The precise mechanisms by which this occurs have not received the attention which they deserve.

DISCUSSION

In this chapter we have adopted a role theory framework to organize a review of the behavioral literature concerned with the production and use of financial information (we have on occasion commented on ties between this literature and those approaching the same issues from different perspectives). Within this framework, we have suggested that these processes may be thought of as a series of interdependent, institutionally embedded roles. The performance of role behaviors is regarded as the outcome of a complex interaction of contextual factors, communicated role expectations, role tasks, and individual variation. Analytically, we have divided the field into three areas—disclosure, analysis, and use—and have examined the current state of knowledge in each area.

Our attempt to provide a framework within which to systematically review this research should not divert attention from the general paucity of results and the lack of a critical mass of research activity. The research reviewed is fragmentary, drawing on a wide variety of sociological and psychological theories but rarely exploring these theories systematically. In addition, much research is conducted without explicit reference to theory, making it difficult to evaluate research or integrate the results of separate studies. This should not, however, be interpreted as a criticism of the diverse perspectives which have emerged to consider the issues in this field of research. On the contrary, the growing diversity of research perspectives evident in recent years is testimony to the richness of the phenomena and to the development of accounting scholarship. More than anything else, this observation is simply recognition that behavioral accounting research, and arguably all accounting research, is in its infancy and that much more effort is necessary to continue its development.

Although there is a lack of consensus on the appropriate approach to issues, there is greater consensus on which issues need to be addressed. In the disclosure area, the central empirical issue has been the determinants of accounting policy choice. The research has attempted to explore (or infer) the motivations of management and the external forces acting on the firm. The disclosure practices of the firm are seen as a shifting equilibrium of these forces. A question which has received little attention is whether disclosure is an individual or group phenomenon. Derivatively, we may ask how the disclosure process emerges. If disclosure is an individual phenomenon, then cognitive studies of the decision to disclose (or not disclose), similar to research on the analysis process, may help to uncover the factors which are most significant in management's decisions. If the decision to disclose is a group phenomenon, then field studies of the social processes within the firm that result in disclosure decisions would be fruitful.

In the analysis area, the key issue has been the cognitive structure of analysis. Research has attempted to document the way in which information is selected and processed. One outcome is recognition of consistent deviations from normative models of decision making (biases and heuristics) and the exploration of decision models which depart from traditional notions of rationality. Along with this result have been attempts to identify the mechanisms which have evolved to overcome or control bounded rationality. These studies are more highly developed at a cognitive than at an organizational level of analysis. Williamson's *Markets and Hierarchies* [1975] framework provides an entrance to the latter level of analysis but this has yet to be exploited in the financial accounting literature. An aspect of the observation plane which has not been addressed, however, is the significance of these biases and the mechanisms which have evolved to overcome them. In examining the latter issue, there is a need to overcome traditional boundaries between psychology and sociology, that is, to find ways of integrating multiple levels of analysis within the same study.

The momentum in behavioral research which we have reviewed currently lies in the exploration of the use of financial information. The shift in focus from investment decision making to the stewardship role of information, and the broadening of the range of stakeholders considered has resulted in a rich, if embryonic, literature. Studies of the use of accounting information in contracting, labor relations, and interactions with the state are beginning to capture some of the complexity of the observation plane as the economists' model of atomistic competition gives way to political economy models. This area of research has been enriched by the simultaneous use of a variety of research methods. For example, experimental methods have been used to examine organizational and market-level phenomena, and a resurgence of field studies is providing new insight into the use of financial information in a variety of contexts.

A noticeable trend in the research we reviewed is the movement toward the development of comparative institutional analyses. This may be a reflection of the development of contingency theories in management accounting, or a part of the more general trend in the social sciences to abandon the search for grand theories and universal truths in favor of conditional truths and "theories of the mid-range." In each of the areas reviewed we have highlighted attempts to develop analytic typologies which provide a starting point for the exploration of various phenomena. These typologies, of course, are not final. The dimensions across which phenomena vary will be refined as future work develops but such work must be undertaken if research is to provide useful insights into accounting phenomena and if a cumulative research tradition is to develop.

We began by outlining the epistemological assumptions which we brought to this review. Throughout, we have used the "two-plane" concept to indicate areas on the observation plane which were not captured in the theory plane. We also indicated that the key evaluative concept was "utility" rather than correspondence: What has the theory plane contributed to our ability to operate within the financial accounting environment?

The most obvious contributions have been the use of some results of the exploration of the analysis role in training programs and the creation of decision aids in areas where judgment appears prone to systematic error. The work on the disclosure role may eventually find its way into the design of accounting regulation, although such an effect is not currently evident (Gibbins and Brennan [1982]; Gibbins and Newton [1986]). The work on the use of financial information, particularly that undertaken with "emancipatory" goals, is being aired in legislative circles, for example, the National Coal Board Study in England (Berry *et al.* [1986]), but, again, with little current effect. Overall, academic research has yet to attain the degree of utility which may be expected of a professional discipline. Much of the research being undertaken, however, must be considered "basic" or exploratory and as the field develops this evaluation may change. We have provided a critical analysis which, along with others undertaken in this book, may serve to encourage the development of the field in ways which contribute to a richer understanding of accounting and a realistic assessment of challenges which remain to be met in the development of the field.

BIBLIOGRAPHY

Abdel-khalik, A. R., "Three Generations of Research on Quarterly Reports: Some Thoughts on the Research Process" in *Perspectives on Research*, University of Wisconsin (May 1980) pp. 60-103.

Abdel-khalik, A. R. and K. M. El-Sheshai, "Information Choice and Utilization in an Experiment on Default Prediction", *Journal of Accounting Research*, (Autumn 1980), pp. 325-342.

Abdel-khalik, A. R., P. R. Graul, and J. D. Newton, "Reporting Uncertainty and Assessment of Risk: Replication and Extension in a Canadian Setting", *Journal of Accounting Research*, (Autumn 1986), pp. 372-382.

American Accounting Association, "Report of the Committee on Theory Construction and Verification", *The Accounting Review*, (Supplement 1971), pp. 51 -80.

American Accounting Association, Committee on Human Information Processing, "Report of the Committee on Human Information Processing", Mimeographed. Sarasota, Fla.: American Accounting Association, (1977).

American Institute of C.P.A.'s Technical Services Division, "An Opinion Survey on Price-Level Adjustment of Depreciation", *Journal of Accountancy*, (April 1958), pp. 36-42.

Amernic, J. H., "The Roles of Accounting in Collective Bargaining", *Accounting, Organizations and Society*, (1985), pp. 227-253.

Amernic, J. H., "Towards a Theory of the Roles of Accounting in Collective Bargaining", Unpublished paper, University of Toronto, (1986).

Ashton, R. H., "The Predictive-Ability Criterion and User Prediction Models", *The Accounting Review* (October 1974), pp. 719-732.

Ashton, R. H., "Cognitive Changes Induced by Accounting Changes: Experimental Evidence on the Functional Fixation Hypothesis", *Journal of Accounting Research*, (Supplement 1976), pp. 1-17.

Ashton, R. H., *Human Information Processing in Accounting*, Studies in Accounting Research No. 17, American Accounting Association, Sarasota, FL. (1982).

Backer, M., *Financial Reporting for Security Investment and Credit Decisions*, New York: National Association of Accountants, (1970).

Backer, M., *Current Value Accounting*, New York: Financial Executives Research Foundation, (November 1973).

Ball, R. and P. Brown, "An Empirical Evaluation of Accounting Income Numbers", *Journal of Accounting Research* (Autumn 1968), pp. 159-178.

Barnea, A., J. Ronen, and S. Sadan, "Classifactory Smoothing of Income with Extraordinary Items", *The Accounting Review* (January 1976), pp. 110-122.

Beaver, W. H., "The Behavior of Security Prices and Its Implications for Accounting Research (Methods)", In "Report of the Committee on Research Methodology in Accounting." *The Accounting Review*, (Supplement 1972), pp. 407-437.

Benbasat, I. and A. S. Dexter, "Value and Events Approaches to Accounting: An Experimental Evaluation", *The Accounting Review*, (October 1979), pp. 735-749.

Berry, A. T., T. Capps, D. Cooper, P. Ferguson, T. Hopper, and E. A. Lowe, "Management Control in an Area of the NCB: Rationales for Accounting Practices in a Public Enterprise", *Accounting, Organizations and Society*, (1986), pp. 3-28.

Birnberg, J. and N. Wilner, "Methodological Problems in Functional Fixation Research: Criticism and Suggestions", *Accounting, Organizations and Society*, (1986), pp. 71-80.

Bowman, M. J., "Expert vs. Novice Decision Making in Accounting: A Summary", *Accounting, Organizations and Society*, (1984), pp. 325-327.

Bradish, R. D., "Corporate Reporting and the Financial Analyst", *The Accounting Review*, (October 1965), pp. 757-766.

Brennan, W. J., ed. *The Internationalization of the Accounting Profession*, Toronto, The Canadian Institute of Chartered Accountants, (1979).

Brenner, V. C., "Financial Statement Users' Views of the Desireability of Reporting Current Cost Information", *Journal of Accounting Research*, (Autumn 1970), pp. 159-166.

Burchell, S., C. Clubb, A. Hopwood, J. Hughes, and J. Nahapiet, "The Roles of Accounting in Organizations and Society", *Accounting, Organizations and Society*, (1980), pp. 5-27.

Butterworth, J. E., M. Gibbins, and R. King, "The Structure of Accounting Theory: Some Basic Conceptual and Methodological Issues", In *Research to Support Standard Setting in Financial Accounting: A Canadian Perspective*, Proceedings of the 1981 Clarkson Gordon Foundation Research Symposium, (ed) B. Sanjoy and J. A. Milburn, (1982).

Campbell, J. E., "An Application of Protocol Analysis to The 'Little GAAP' Controversy", *Accounting, Organizations and Society*, (1984), pp. 329-342.

Casey, C. J., "Variation in Accounting Information Load: The Effect on Loan Officers' Predictions of Bankruptcy", *The Accounting Review*, (January 1980), pp. 36-49.

Casey, C. J., "The Usefulness of Accounting Ratios for Subjects' Predictions of Corporate Failure: Replications and Extensions", *Journal of Accounting Research*, (Autumn 1980b), pp. 603-613.

Casey, C. J., and M. J. Sandretto, "Internal Uses of Accounting for Inflation", *Harvard Business Review*, (November/December 1981), pp. 149-156.

Cerf, A. R., "Corporate Reporting and Investment Decisions", Berkely, CA Institute of Business and Economic Research, (1961).

Chatfield, M., *The History of Accounting Thought*, Krieger, (1977).

Chesley, G. R., "Subjective Probability Elicitation Techniques: A Performance Comparison", *Journal of Accounting Research*, (Autumn 1978), pp. 225-241.

Cheverny, N. L. and G. W. Dickson, "An Experimental Evaluation of Information Overload in a Production Environment", *Management Science*, (June 1974), pp. 1335-1344.

Comiskey, E. E. and R. E. V. Groves, "The Adoption and Diffusion of an Accounting Innovation", *Accounting and Business Research*, (Winter 1971), pp. 67-75.

Copeland, R., "Income Smoothing", *Journal of Accounting Research*, (Supplement 1968), pp. 101-116.

Copeland, R. and R. LiCastro, "A Note on Income Smoothing", *The Accounting Review*, (July 1968), pp. 540-545.

Copeland, R. and J. K. Shank, "LIFO and the Diffusion of Innovation", *Journal of Accounting Research*, (Supplement 1971), pp. 196-230.

Coppock, R., "Life Among the Environmentalists", *Accounting, Organizations and Society*, (1977), pp. 125-130.

Craft, J. A., "Information Disclosure and the Role of the Accountant in Collective Bargaining", *Accounting, Organizations and Society*, (1981), pp. 97-107.

Dejong, R., R. Forsythe, R. J. Lundholme, and W. Uecker, "A Laboratory Investigation of the Moral Hazard Problem in an Agency Relationship", *Journal of Accounting Research*, (Spring 1985), pp. 81-123.

Dejong, R., and W. Uecker, "The Methodology of Laboratory Markets and its Implications for Agency Research in Accounting and Auditing", *Journal of Accounting Research*, (Autumn 1985), pp. 753-793.

Demski, J. S., "The General Impossibility of Normative Accounting Standards", *The Accounting Review* (October 1973), pp. 718-723.

Demski, J. S., "The Value of Financial Accounting", Research Paper, Graduate School of Business, Stanford University, (January 1980).

Dillard, J. F., "Cognitive Science and Decision Making Research in Accounting", *Accounting, Organizations and Society*, (1984), pp. 343-354.

Dopuch, N. and D. F. Drake, "The Effect of Alternative Accounting Rules for Nonsubsidiary Investments", *Journal of Accounting Research*, (Supplement 1966), pp. 192-219.

Dopuch, N. and S. Sunder, "FASB's Statements on Objectives and Elements of Financial Accounting: A Review", *The Accounting Review*, (January 1980), pp. 1-21.

Douglas, M., "Accounting and Anthropology", Unpublished opening address to the Social Science Research Council Conference on Accounting Research, Oxford, (1977).

Driver, M. J., and T. J. Mock, "Human Information Processing, Decision Style Theory and Accounting Information Systems", *The Accounting Review*, (July 1975), pp. 490-508.

Dyckman, T. R., M. Gibbins, and R. J. Swieringa, "Experimental and Survey Research in Financial Accounting: A Review and Evaluation", in *The Impact of Accounting Research on Practice and Disclosure*, (ed) A. Rashad Abdel-khalik and Thomas F. Keller, Duke University Press, (1978), pp. 48-105.

Ecton, W. W., "Communication Through Accounting—Bankers' Views", *Journal of Accountancy* (August 1969), pp. 79-81.

Eger, C., and J. Dickhaut, "An Examination of the Conservative Information Processing Bias in an Accounting Framework", *Journal of Accounting Research*, (Autumn 1982), pp. 711-723.

Einhorn, H. J., and R. M. Hogarth, "Behavioural Decision Theory: Processes of Judgment and Choice", *Journal of Accounting Research*, (Spring 1981), pp. 1-41 .

Epstein, M. J., *The Usefulness of Annual Reports to Corporate Shareholders*, Bureau of Business and Economic Research, California State University, (1975).

Estes, R. W., "An Assessment of the Usefulness of Current Cost and Price-Level Information by Financial Statement Users", *Journal of Accounting Research*, (Autumn 1968), pp. 200-207.

Estes, R. W. and M. Reimer, "A Study of the Effect of Qualified Auditors' Opinions on Bankers' Lending Decisions", *Accounting and Business Review*, (Autumn 1977), pp. 250-259.

Eyes, A. D., and J. B. Tabb, "Bank Managers' Use of Financial Statements", *The Accountants' Journal*, (April 1978), pp. 81-85.

Financial Accounting Standards Board, "Objectives of Financial Reporting by Business Enterprises", Statement of Financial Accounting Concepts No. 1, Stamford, CN, FASB, (1978).

Financial Accounting Standards Board, "Accounting for the Translation of Foreign Currency Transactions and Foreign Currency Financial Statements", Statement of Financial Accounting Standards No. 8, Stamford, CN, FASB, (October 1975).

Firth, M., "Consensus Views and Judgment Models in Materiality Decisions", *Accounting, Organizations and Society*, (1979), pp. 283-295.

Firth, M., "Perceptions of Auditor Independence and Official Ethical Guidelines", *The Accounting Review*, (July 1980), pp. 451-466.

Foley, B. J. and K. T. Maunders, *Accounting Information and Collective Bargaining*, London: MacMillan, (1977).

Foster, T. W., D. R. Jenkins, and D. W. Vickrey, "The Incremental Information Content of the Annual Report", *Accounting and Business Review*, (Spring 1986), pp. 91-98.

Gagnon, J. M., "Purchase Versus Pooling Interest: the Search for a Predictor", *Journal of Accounting Research*, (Supplement 1967), pp. 187-204.

Gagnon, J. M., "The Purchase-Pooling Choice: Some Empirical Evidence", *Journal of Accounting Research*, (1971), pp. 52-72.

Gambling, T., "Magic, Accounting and Morale", *Accounting, Organizations and Society*, (1977), pp. 141-153.

Garner, D. E., "The Need for Price-Level and Replacement Value Data", *Journal of Accountancy*, (September 1972) pp. 94-98.

Gibbins, M., "Propositions about the Psychology of Professional Judgment in Public Accounting", *Journal of Accounting Research*, (Spring 1984), pp. 103-125.

Gibbins, M. and P. Brennan, "Behavioural Research and Accounting Standards", in *Usefulness to Investors and Creditors of Information Provided by Financial Reporting*, Griffin, P.A. (ed.), Stamford, CN, FASB, (1982).

Gibbins, M., and C. Emby, "Evidence on the Nature of Professional Judgement in Public Accounting", *Proceedings of the Sixth Illinois Auditing Research Symposium*, (November 1984), University of Illinois.

Gibbins, M. and J. D. Newton, "Behavioural Research, Reporting Standards and Information Usefulness", Chapter for revised edition of *Usefulness to Investors and Creditors of Information Provided by Financial Reporting: A Review of Empirical Research*, (ed) Griffin, P.A.

Gibbins, M. and F. M. Wolf, "Auditors' Subjective Decision Environment—the case of a normal external audit", *The Accounting Review*, (January 1982), pp. 105-124.

Gordon, M. J., "Postulates, Principles and Research in Accounting", *The Accounting Review*, (April 1964), pp. 251-263.

Gordon, M. J., B. N. Horowitz, and P. T. Meyers, "Accounting Measurements and Normal Growth of the Firm", in *Research in Accounting Measurement*, Jaedicke, R.K., Ijiri, Y. and Nielsen, O. (eds), American Accounting Association, (1966).

Gray, C. W., "Ingredients of Intuitive Regression", *Organizational Behaviour and Human Performance*, (February 1979), pp. 30-48.

Gray, S. J., "The Impact of International Accounting Differences from a Security-Analysis Perspective: Some European Evidence", *Journal of Accounting Research*, (Spring 1980), pp. 64-76.

Gul, F. A., "The Joint and Moderating Role of Personality and Cognitive Style on Decision Making", *The Accounting Review*, (April 1984), pp. 264-277.

Hanna, J. R., "An Application and Evaluation of Selected Alternative Accounting Income Models", *The International Journal of Accounting Education and Research*, (Fall 1972), pp. 135-167.

Hanna, J. R., *Accounting Income Models: An Application and Evaluation*, Special Study No. 8., The Society of Industrial Accountants, (1974).

Harrison, G. L. and J. L. McKinnan, "Culture and Accounting Change: A New Perspective on Corporate Reporting Regulation and Accounting Policy Formulation", *Accounting, Organizations and Society*, (1986), pp. 233-252.

Hofstedt, T. R. and G. D. Hughes, "An Experimental Study of the Judgement Element in Disclosure Decisions", *The Accounting Review*, (April 1977), pp. 379-395.

Hogarth, R. M., "Process Tracing in Clinical Judgement", *Behavioural Science*, (September 1981), pp. 298-313.

Horngren, C. T., "Security Analysts and the Price Level", *The Accounting Review*, (October 1955), pp. 575-581.

Horngren, C. T., "The Funds Statement and Its Use by Analysts", *Journal of Accountancy*, (January 1956), pp. 55-59.

Horngren, C. T., "Disclosure: 1957", *The Accounting Review*, (October 1957), pp. 598-604.

Horngren, C. T., "The Marketing of Accounting Standards", *Journal of Accountancy*, (October 1973), pp. 61-66.

Johnson, H. T. and Kaplan, R., *The Rise and Fall of Management Accounting*, Harvard University Press, (1986).

Johnson, O., "An Events Theory of Accounting", *The Accounting Review*, (October 1982), pp. 82-92.

Joyce, E. J. and G. C. Biddle, "Anchoring and Adjustment in Probabilistic Inference in Auditing", *Journal of Accounting Research*, (Spring 1981), pp. 120-145.

Kahneman, D. and A. Tversky, "Prospect Theory: An Analysis of Decision Under Risk", *Econometrica*, (March 1979), pp. 263-291.

Kennedy, H. A., "A Behavioural Study of the Usefulness of Four Financial Ratios", *Journal of Accounting Research*, (Autumn 1978), pp. 389-399.

Kinney, W. R. and W. C. Uecker, "Overcoming the Effects of the Anchoring and Adjustment Heuristic in Audit Judgements: An Experiment", Unpublished manuscript, University of lowa, (December 1979).

Koch, B. S., "Income Smoothing: An Experiment", *The Accounting Review*, (July 1981), pp. 574-586.

Leftwich, R., "Evidence on the Impact of Mandatory Accounting Changes on Corporate Loan Agreements", *Journal of Accounting and Economics*, (March 1981), pp. 3-36.

Lewis, B., M. D. Shields, and S. M. Young, "Evaluating Human Judgements and Decision Aids", *Journal of Accounting Research*, (Spring 1983), pp. 271-285.

Libby, R., "Accounting and the Prediction of Failure: Some Behavioural Evidence", *Journal of Accounting Research*, (Spring 1975a), pp. 150-161.

Libby, R., "The Use of Stimulated Decision Makers in Information Evaluation", *The Accounting Review*, (July 1975b), pp. 475-489.

Libby, R., "Man versus Model of Man: Some Conflicting Evidence", *Organizational Behaviour and Human Peformance*, (July 1976), pp. 1-12.

Libby, R., "Discussion of Cognitive Changes Induced By Accounting Changes: Experimental Evidence on the Functional Fixation Hypothesis", In *Studies on Human Information Processing in Accounting*, (Supplement to *Journal of Accounting Research* 1976b), pp. 18-24.

Libby, R., "Bankers' and Auditors' Perceptions of the Message Communicated by the Audit Report", *Journal of Accounting Research*, (Spring 1979a), pp. 99-122.

Libby, R., "The Impact of Uncertainty Reporting on the Loan Decision", *Journal of Accounting Research*, (Supplement 1979b), pp. 35-57.
Libby, R., *Accounting and Human Information Processing: Theory and Applications*, Prentice-Hall Contemporary Topics in Accounting Series, (1981).
Libby, R., "Comments on Weick", *The Accounting Review*, (April 1983), pp. 370-374.
Libby, R. and R. K. Blashfield, "Performance of a Compositive as a Function of the Number of Judges", *Organizational Behaviour and Human Performance*, (April 1978), pp. 121-129.
Libby, R. and B. L. Lewis, "Human Information Processing Research in Accounting: The State of the Art in 1982", *Accounting, Organizations and Society*, (1982), pp. 231-285.
Littleton, A. C., *Accounting Education to 1900*, American Institute Publishing Co., (1933).
Loft, A., "Towards a Critical Understanding of Accounting: The Case of Cost Accounting in the U.K., 1914-25", *Accounting, Organizations and Society*, (1986), pp. 137-169.
Lowe, E. A. and A. M. Tinker, "Siting the Accounting Problematic: Towards an Intellectual Emancipation of Accounting", *Journal of Business, Finance and Accounting*, (Autumn 1977), pp. 263-276.
Lusk, E. J., "A Test of Differential Performance Peaking for Disembedding Task", *Journal of Accounting Research*, (Spring 1979), pp. 286-294.
March, J. G. and H. A. Simon, *Organizations*, John Wiley, (1958).
Marchant, G. A., "Data Fixity: Some Further Empirical Evidence", Unpublished Honours Thesis, University of New South Wales, (1979).
Mattessich, R., *Accounting and Analytical Methods*, Richard D. Irwin, (1964).
McDonald, D. L., "A Test Application of the Feasibility of Market Based Measures in Accounting", *Journal of Accounting Research*, (Spring 1968), pp. 38-49.
McGhee, W., M. D. Shields and J. G. Birnberg, "The Effects of Personality on a Subject's Information Processing", *The Accounting Review*, (July 1978), pp. 681-697.
Meyer, J., "Environmental and Internal Origins of Symbolic Structure in Organizations", Paper presented at the Seminar on Organizations as Ideological Systems, Stockholm, (1979).
Meyer, J., "Social Environments and Organizational Accounting", *Accounting, Organizations and Society*, (1986), pp. 345-356.
Milgram, S. and H. Toch, "Collective Behavior: Crowds and Social Movements", In *Handbook of Social Psychology*, 2nd ed. *Group Psychology and Phenomena of Interaction*, Lindzey, G. and Aronson, E. (eds), Addison-Wesley, (1968), pp. 507-510.
Moonitz, M., *Obtaining Agreement on Standards in the Accounting Profession*, American Accounting Association, (1974).
Moriarity, S. and F. H. Barron, "A Judgement-Based Definition of Materiality", *Journal of Accounting Research*, (Supplement 1979), pp. 114-135.
Most, K. S. and L. S. Chang, "How Useful Are Annual Reports to Investors?", *Journal of Accountancy*, (September 1979), pp. 111-113.
Newell, A. and H. A. Simon, *Human Problem Solving*, Prentice-Hall, (1972).
Nisbett, R. E. and T. D. Wilson, "Telling More Than We Can Know: Verbal Reports on Mental Processes", *Psychological Review*, (May 1977), pp. 231-259.
Ogden, S. and P. Bougen, "A Radical Perspective on the Disclosure of Accounting Information to Trade Unions", *Accounting, Organizations and Society*, (1985), pp. 211-224.
Opinion Research Corporation, *Public Accounting in Transition*. Arthur Andersen and Company, (1974).

Owen, D. L. and A. J. Lloyd, "The Use of Financial Information by Trade Union Negotiators in Plant Level Collective Bargaining", *Accounting, Organizations and Society*, (1985), pp. 329-352.

Palmer, J. R., *The Use of Accounting Information in Labor Negotiations*, National Association of Accountants, (1977).

Pattillo, J. W., *The Concept of Materiality in Financial Reporting*, Financial Executives Research Foundation, (1976).

Piaker, P. M. and J. Dalberth, "Acceptance of Changes Among Accountants: An Examination of Attitudes Toward Current Controversies", *The CPA Journal*, (February 1973), pp. 132-138.

Plott, C., "Industrial Organization Theory and Experimental Economics", *Joumal of Economic Literature*, (December 1982).

Plott, C. and S. Sunder, "Efficiency of Experimental Security Markets with Insider Information: An Application of Rational Expectations Models", Social Science working paper, 331, revised., California Institute of Technology, (January 1981).

Plott, S. and S. Sunder, "Efficiency of Experimental Securities Markets with Inside Information: An Application of Rational-Expectations Models", *Journal of Political Economy*, 1982.

Plott, S. and S. Sunder, "Rational Expectations and the Aggregation of Diverse Information in Laboratory Security Markets", Working Paper, University of Minnesota, (1984).

Pope, P. F. and D. A. Peel, "Information Disclosure to Employees and Rational Expectations", *Journal of Business, Finance and Accounting*, (1981), pp. 139-146.

Prakash, P. and A. Rappaport, "Information Inductance and Its Significance for Accounting." *Accounting, Organizations and Society*, (1977), pp. 29-38.

Pratt, J., "The Effects of Personality on a Subject's Information Processing: A Comment", *The Accounting Review*, (July 1980), pp. 501-506.

Rakes, G. K. and W. S. Shenkir, "User Responses to APB Opinion No. 19", *Journal of Accountancy*, (September 1972), pp. 91-94.

Ritts, B. A., "A Study of the Impact of APB Opinions on Practicing CPAs", *Journal of Accounting Research*, (Spring 1974), pp. 93-111.

Rommetveit, R., *Social Norms and Roles*, University of Minnesota Press, (1955).

Ronen, J. and S. Sadan, *Smoothing Income Numbers: Objectives, Means and Implications*, Addison-Wesley, (1981).

Roper, E., *A Report on What Information People Want About Policies and Financial Conditions of Corporations*, Controllers' Institute Foundation, (1948).

Rosen, L. S., *Current Value Accounting and Price-Level Restatements*, Canadian Institute of Chartered Accountants, (1972).

Sanders, T. H., *Company Annual Reports to Stockholders, Employees and the Public*, Andover Press, (1948).

Savich, R. S., "The Use of Accounting Information in Decision Making", *The Accounting Review*, (July 1977), pp. 642-652.

Schelling, T. C., *Micromotives and Macrobehavior*, Norton and Company Inc., (1978).

Schepanski, A., "Tests of Theories on Information Processing Behavior in Credit Judgement", *The Accounting Review*, (July 1983), pp. 581-599.

Schultz, J. J. Jr. and S. G. Gustavson, "Actuaries' Perceptions of Variables Affecting the Independent Auditors' Legal Liability", *The Accounting Review*, (July 1978), pp. 626-641.

Schwarzbach, H. R. and E. P. Swanson, "The Use of Replacement Cost Accounting Information for Decision Making during Inflationary Times", *Journal of Contemporary Business*, (August 1981), pp. 65-76.

Scott, G. M. and P. Troberg, *Eighty-eight International Accounting Problems in Rank Order of Importance: A DELPHI Evaluation*, American Accounting Association, (1980).
Securities and Exchange Commission, *Report of the SEC Advisory Committee on Corporate Disclosure*, U.S. Government Printing Office, (1977).
Shafer, G., "Two Theories of Probability", Technical Report No. 1. National Science Foundation Grant MCS78-01887., The University of Kansas, (October 1978).
Shank, J. K. and R. M. Copeland, "Corporate Personality Theory and Changes in Accounting Methods—an Empirical Test", *The Accounting Review*, (July 1973), pp. 494-501.
Shank, J. K., J. F. Dillard, and R. J. Murdock, "FASB No. 8 and the Decision-Makers", *Financial Executive*, (February 1980), pp. 18-23.
Simon, H. A., "Rational Decision Making in Business Organizations, *The American Economic Review*, (September 1979), pp. 493-513.
Singer, H. W., *Standardized Accounting in Germany*, National Institute for Economic and Social Research Occasional Paper V3, Cambridge University Press, (1943).
Smith, V., "Microeconomic Systems as an Experimental Science", *American Economic Review* (December 1982).
Sorter, G. and S. W. Becker, with the assistance of T. R. Archibald and W. Beaver, "Corporate Personality as Reflected in Accounting Decisions: Some Preliminary Findings", *Journal of Accounting Research*, (Autumn 1964), pp. 183-196.
Sorter, G., S. W. Becker, R. Archibald, and W. H. Beaver, "Accounting and Financial Measures as Indicators of Corporate Personality—Some Empirical Findings", In *Research in Accounting Measurement*, Jaedicke *et al.* (eds), American Accounting Association, (1966), pp. 200-210.
Stanga, K. G. and J. J. Benjamin, "Information Needs of Bankers", *Management Accounting*, (June 1978), pp. 17-21.
Sterling, R. R., "A Test of the Uniformity Hypothesis", *Abacus*, (September 1969), pp. 37-47.
Sterling, R. R. and R. Radosevich, "A Valuation Experiment", *Joumal of Accounting Research* (Spring 1969), pp. 90-95.
Sterling, R. R., J. O. Tollefson, and R. E. Flaherty, "Exchange Valuation: An Experimental Test", *The Accounting Review*, (October 1972), pp. 709-821.
Swieringa, R., T. R. Dyckman and R. E. Hosking, "Empirical Evidence about the Effects of an Accounting Change on Information Processing", In *Behavioural Experiments in Accounting II*, Burns, T. (ed)., The Ohio State University, (1979) pp. 225-259.
Thomas, A. P., "The Contingency Theory of Corporate Reporting: Some Empirical Evidence", *Accounting, Organizations and Society*, (1986), pp. 253-270.
Thorngate, R., "Efficient Decision Heuristics", *Behavioral Science*, (1981).
Thornton, D. B., "Non-Historic Cost Accounting Disclosures: Theory and Canadian Evidence," University of Toronto, (October 1984).
Tinker, A. M., "A Political Economy of Accounting", *Accounting, Organizations and Society*, (1980).
Tinker, A. M., B. D. Merino, and H. D. Neimark, "The Normative Origins of Positive Theories: Ideology and Accounting Thought", *Accounting, Organizations and Society*, (1982), pp. 167-200.
Uecker, W. C., "Behavioural Study of Information System Choice", *Journal of Accounting Research*, (Spring 1978), pp. 169-189.
Uecker, W. C., "The Effects of Knowledge of the User's Decision Model in Simplified Information Evaluation", *Journal of Accounting Research*, (Spring 1980), pp. 191-213.

Waller, W. S. and W. L. Felix Jr., "The Effects of Incomplete Outcome Feedback on Auditors' Self-Perceptions of Judgement Ability", *The Accounting Review*, (October 1984a), pp. 637-646.

Waller, W. S. and W. L. Felix Jr., "The Accuracy of Auditor's Inferences about Empirical Relationships between Audit-tax Variables Based on Observed Data", Unpublished manuscript, University of Arizona, (1984b).

Waller, W. S. and W. L. Felix Jr., "The Auditor and Learning from Experience: Some Conjectures", *Accounting, Organizations and Society*, (1984c), pp. 383-406.

Walton, R. E. and R. B. McKersie, *A Behavioural Theory of Labour Negotiations*, McGraw-Hill, (1965).

Watts, R. L. and J. L. Zimmerman, "Towards a Positive Theory of the Determination of Accounting Standards", *The Accounting Review*, (January 1978), pp. 112-134.

Watts, R. L. and J. L. Zimmerman, "The Demand for and the Supply of Accounting Theories: The Market for Excuses", *The Accounting Review*, (April 1979), pp. 273-305.

Watts, R. L. and J. L. Zimmerman, *Positive Accounting Theory*, Prentice-Hall, (1986).

Weick, K. E., "Stress in Accounting Systems", *The Accounting Review*, (April 1983), pp. 350-369.

Wildavsky, A., "Economy and Environment/Rationality and Ritual: A Review Essay", *Accounting, Organizations and Society*, (1976), pp. 117-129.

Williamson, O. E., *Markets and Hierarchies: Analysis and Antitrust Implications*, New York Free Press, (1975).

Wright, W. F., "Self-Insight into the Cognitive Processing of Financial Information", *Accounting, Organizations and Society*, (1977a), pp. 323-331.

Wright, W. F., "Properties of Judgement Models in a Financial Setting", *Organizational Behaviour and Human Performance*, (February 1979), pp. 73-85.

Zimmer, I., "A Lens Study of the Prediction of Corporate Failure by Bank Loan Officers", *Journal of Accounting Research*, (Autumn 1980), pp. 629-636.

Zmijewski, M. and R. Hagerman, "An Income Strategy Approach to the Positive Theory of Accounting Standard Setting/Choice", *Journal of Accounting and Economics*, (August 1981), pp. 129-149.

Part IV: Positive And Financial Accounting Research: Continuation Of Established Trends

Journal of Accounting Literature Vol. 5, (1986), pp. 1-33; reprinted with permission.

Stock Valuation Models and Accounting Information: A Review and Synthesis*

Rowland K. Atiase and Senyo Tse

*We gratefully acknowledge the helpful comments of Linda Bamber and two anonymous reviewers.

1. INTRODUCTION

The relationship between accounting data, particularly earnings information, and security price behaviour has received considerable attention in financial "market-based accounting research" (MBAR) since the seminal works of Ball and Brown [1968] and Beaver [1968]. However, most of the research has been concerned with the association between accounting data and security returns[1] (i.e., security price changes), while ignoring the more basic issue of security valuation by fundamental accounting variables. Such measures as the abnormal performance index (API), the cumulative absolute residual (CAR), and other return based indexes[2] have been used extensively to evaluate the security market's association with and reaction to various pieces and forms of accounting data. Furthermore, as Lev and Ohlson [1982] note, empirical evidence suggests that unexpected accounting information (on earnings in particular) is associated with unexpected returns, but the evidence also clearly shows that the explanatory power of the examined data with respect to the security return distribution is quite low. Thus there is good reason to consider alternative methods of relating accounting signals to security price characteristics in the financial markets. Besides, if the relevance of accounting information to investors is at issue, certainly the extent to which this information explains the values of securities, rather than the change it induces in these values, should be of major concern.

In expressing the importance and potential contribution of a stock valuation approach in accounting research, Lev and Ohlson [1982, p. 305] state:

> The issue of valuation by fundamental variables is obviously of considerable importance both from

> a policy point of view (what is the marginal contribution of accounting information in general, and specific data in particular, relative to other information sources, to determining capital values?) and from a strictly "practical" point of view (e.g., to what extent are accounting data useful in corporate valuation for mergers and acquisitions?). Why then has this issue been almost completely ignored in MBAR? Is it because the construction of empirical valuation models in uncertain and dynamic environments is much more complicated and risky (to the researcher) than simply registering a price reaction to an accounting announcement? Or does misinterpretation of the ECM hypothesis make valuation issues seem redundant, given the market's alleged ability to correctly (unbiasedly) price equities? Regardless of the reason, more research on asset valuation by fundamental variables is clearly called for.

Some recent studies have addressed accounting issues using the valuation approach. The purpose of this paper is to provide a critical review of security valuation models, their use and potential usefulness (as well as limitations) in MBAR.

Essentially, a valuation approach involves the study of the relationship between levels of stock prices and fundamental variables, primarily accounting data. This approach offers a potentially useful perspective that is different from (and complementary to) that provided by the standard returns analysis employed in MBAR. The key question is simply: To what degree are accounting data reflected in prices, or, can accounting data be used to explain prices at any time? The valuation approach may also enable the researcher to avoid certain practical pitfalls found in the implementation of the returns approach. For example, in most event studies that employ the latter approach, the determination of the exact timing of the event is of key importance. This is the situation studied by Brown and Warner [1980]. In a series of simulations, Brown and Warner show that failure to pinpoint the exact timing of an event can result in severe loss of statistical power when the returns analysis is used.

The issue of determining precisely when an event occurs is not as important under the valuation approach. In principle, information that affects prices would be expected to be reflected in prices up to the point where it is replaced by new or more relevant information. As a result, the identification of the exact event time (e.g., earnings or financial statement disclosure date) is not as crucial, so long as the prices examined are from a period that is clearly before or after the information is impounded in prices. Also, the researcher has a choice of several price observations on which to base the analysis of the effect of an event both in the pre-event and the post-event periods. A closely related issue pertains to events that span a relatively long period of time (e.g., accounting policy deliberations). The price reaction in any short sub-period may be minor or too small to detect (relative to all other factors that effect stock prices) using returns analysis. However, the cumulative effect over the entire period may be larger as a result of the cumulative price changes over time. The cumulative effect will be reflected in the level of stock prices and can be detected using a valuation approach. This rationale motivated Beaver and Landsman [1983] to employ a valuation approach (in addition to returns analysis) in their study of the information content of the Statement of Financial Accounting Standard (SFAS) No. 33.

The study of the economic consequence and/or effectiveness of new public disclosure rules is another research area in which valuation analysis may (in some instances) be preferable to returns analysis. For example, returns analysis cannot distinguish between the following types of information (1) information that is not pertinent to security valuation (i.e., useless information) and therefore will never be reflected in prices; and (2) information that is relevant for pricing securities but which has already been reflected in security prices. Returns analysis will typically yield a finding of no market reaction to the disclosure of both types of information, leading to the conclusion that neither type has information content. However, the two types of information have markedly different policy implications. If some accounting data are useless or irrelevant for valuing securities, then their required disclosure cannot be justified, at least on the basis of the pertinence of the data for pricing securities. However, some relevant accounting data may already be reflected in prices (e.g., through private information production and dissemination activities of some market agents). The policy issue pertaining to the required disclosure of this type of information then becomes the comparison of the social costs and benefits that will be associated with the (expected) changes in private and public information production and dissemination decisions resulting therefrom. Valuation analysis, on the other hand, can (potentially) distinguish between the above the types of information by investigating whether the data contribute to the valuation of securities, and therefore provide useful insights from a policy viewpoint.

The valuation approach also has limitations. Perhaps the most prominent problems in valuation analysis are: (1) the appropriate specification of the valuation model; (2) the measurement of independent variables; and (3) the temporal instability of the estimated coefficients. There are also good reasons to expect that valuation parameters may change over time due to changes in macroeconomic variables. These potential problems and attempts at their resolutions are discussed more fully in subsequent sections.

In addition, it is important to note that the valuation approach and returns analysis are not mutually exclusive. Indeed, valuation and value changes (returns) are complementary aspects of security price behaviour. From the purely theoretical viewpoint, if some data has information content, it must manifest itself in both security-price levels and changes (returns). In other words, a return relationship (i.e., with accounting data) is not possible unless there also exists a valuation relationship, and conversely. As an empirical issue, however, the validity of this point is largely dependent on the construction of good descriptive valuation models, the various problems associated with returns analysis, as well as the research question of interest. In general, we would expect each approach to provide complementary insights on the same issue. Thus, it is perhaps inappropriate to view either approach as being superior to the other in all circumstances. The complementary relationship between the returns and valuation approaches is well expressed by Lev and Ohlson [1982, pp. 309-10].

The outline of the rest of the paper is as follows. Section 2 presents valuation model development from a conceptual perspective. Major pieces of research on and using valuation models are reviewed in Section 3. Section 4 discusses some major unresolved methodological issues. Concluding remarks are made in Section 5.

2. VALUATION MODEL DEVELOPMENT

Virtually all valuation models rely on some notion of dividend discounting. One difference between approaches to valuation is in the derivation of the dividend stream. Another concerns the incorporation of risk in the analysis, for which two solutions have been adopted in the literature. The first approach adds a risk factor to the risk-free interest rate to obtain the company's discount rate. The second approach is to obtain certainty-equivalent dividend amounts by subtracting a risk adjustment from the amount of expected dividends. The discussion that follows does not preclude either of these solutions.

2.1 Approaches to Valuation

Conceptually, security valuation may be approached in one of three ways. First, the researcher could focus on a stream of exogenously determined (expected) dividends. The application of an appropriate discount rate to each dividend payment then yields a security price. While this approach is most closely related to the fundamental quantities in valuation, it is relatively impractical because of the difficulty of obtaining realistic predictions of dividends. However, the researcher can examine the implications of observed dividend streams for security values and discount rates. We refer to this approach as the pure discounting approach, and it is the starting point for the variance bound analysis of Shiller [1981a, 1981b], Grossman and Shiller [1981], and others.

A second approach to security valuation is to predict the stream of dividend payments on the basis of firm characteristics. This may be described as the structural form approach to valuation. Under this approach, firm characteristics take on meaning only to the extent that they provide (improved) predictions of future dividends. This is the informational perspective for accounting data discussed by Beaver [1981]. Having derived a projection of the data of primary interest—the dividend stream—the researcher can then study the relationship between the dividend stream, the appropriate discount rate(s), and security prices.

A simple structural form basis for valuation analysis therefore subsumes two distinct aspects of the security valuation process:

1. The prediction of future dividends as a function of firm descriptors and expected state descriptors. One is led to consider such variables as would affect aggregate payout levels as well as firm-specific payout levels through the variables' interaction with firm attributes.
2. The derivation of discount rates for the projected economic earnings stream. The key feature of this aspect of valuation is the risk-free rate of interest. Economy-wide expectations of the level of this variable may change over time. However, it is often assumed that there exists at any time a constant expected risk-free rate for all periods—that is, the term structure of interest rates is viewed as being flat. Since the discount rate reflects the cost of deferring consumption over time, other macroeconomic state descriptors may be expected to be of importance in the determination of the rate of interest.

Under the structural approach, the first step would be time series identification and estimation of the specified relationships. With X_t representing the set of all firm variables (including their history) at time t one would identify and estimate where

$$d_t = A(L)X_t + G_t$$

where

d_t = time t dividend

$A(L)$ = lag polynomial

G_t = vector of residuals.

The estimation would identify the appropriate lag structure and parameter values. (Transfer function modelling of the relationships may prove inordinately difficult for more than a few variables.) The final step is the application of a discount rate or rates to the projected dividend stream for the derivation of security prices.

The structural form approach demands that the researcher make several assumptions about the dividend stream and the discounting method. It is perhaps for this reason that this has not been a popular avenue for valuation research. However, with a few assumptions about the stochastic properties of the dividend generating process and discount rates, Garman and Ohlson [1980] showed how a linear mapping from firm variables to security prices is obtained. While the structural form approach may not be the easiest approach to valuation, the study of links between past and future dividends, earnings and other firm characteristics remains an area of fundamental importance to accounting. These issues are discussed in Beaver [1981] and Ohlson [1983]. Much remains to be done in this area.

The third approach to security valuation may be described as the pure reduced form approach. Under this approach the prediction of dividend streams and the application of discount rates are combined in a single step. This permits direct estimation of security prices based on firm characteristics, a formulation derived analytically in Garman and Ohlson [1980]. Models of this nature are often largely motivated by theoretical models based on the pure dividend discounting and related forms.

The derivation of a dividend stream is an important first step under the pure-discounting and the structural-form approaches discussed above. However, under the reduced-form approach, an attempt is made to find direct relationships between security values and firm characteristics without the intermediate steps of deriving a projected dividend stream to be discounted at some rate(s). Most valuation studies attempt to arrive at a reduced-form expression by analytical derivation from a dividend-discounting model. The major conceptual links are:

1. A link from all available information about the firm (present and past accounting and other data) to future accounting data. For example, a relationship between a series of historical earnings and next-period earnings.
2. A link between predicted accounting variables and future dividends. For example, the link between dividends and earnings in a particular year.

Although one can certainly posit a relationship between the set of available information and future dividends (for example, by assuming a growth rate for dividends), steps 1 and 2 above demonstrate the logic more clearly.

3. A link between predicted dividends and current prices. This is usually viewed as a discounting exercise at rates appropriate to the time value or money as well as the company's perceived riskiness.

Schematically the links are:

Comments on the links, particularly between prices, dividends, and earnings, can be found in

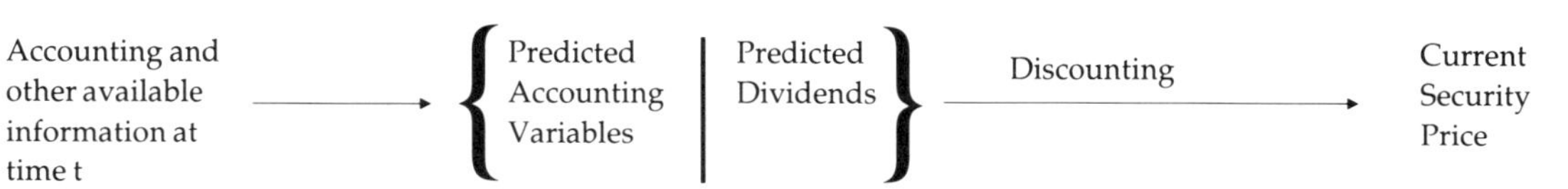

Beaver [1981] and in Ohlson [1983, p. 147].

2.2 Effects of Macroeconomic Variables

When valuation analysis is viewed as an attempt to relate current prices to future cash flows through historical data, valuation relationships would appear to be dependent on a wider set of variables than firm characteristics alone. Under the information perspective for accounting data, such data are viewed as providing a statistical link to the timing and amount of future cash flows, rather than as intrinsically meaningful data. However, a given set of historical financial accounting results may have different implications for future cash flows at different times. For example, under different economic conditions net income of one dollar may imply different firm prospects, depending on the following factors:

1. The level of activity of the economy—is the economy operating at a level close to capacity?
2. The economy's growth prospects—a correlate of firms' growth prospects at a broad level.

The above considerations suggest that a number of macroeconomic conditions may affect the implications of a given set of accounting data for prospective cash flows and hence for current security prices. These include the level of interest rates, which may affect the cost of operations as well as the level of investment. Other variables may be used to measure the economy's level of productivity and (perceived) growth prospects.

The implications of historical accounting numbers for prospective cash flows do not complete the picture. The final consideration in the derivation of prices is the attachment of dollar values (security prices) to prospective cash flows. Roughly speaking, such attachment of values may be seen as reflecting the price of intertemporal transfers of wealth. Although it is possible to enquire into the determinants of the price of postponing consumption (determinants of the marginal rate of time preference), we assume the price of intertemporal wealth transfers to be exogeneously determined. This price is given by the rate of interest. Therefore, to the extent that the rate of interest changes, the current values of prospective cash flows should also change. As a practical matter there does not exist a single rate of interest but rather several rates, depending on the period of wealth transfer, the level of risk, and other factors.

The relationship between accounting data and security prices may be pictured as follows:

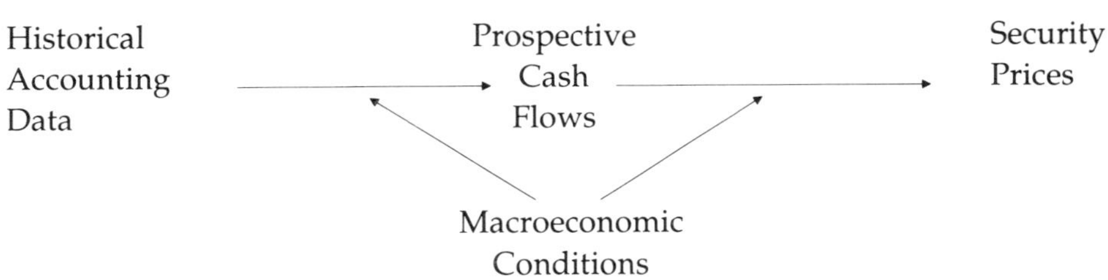

Macroeconomic conditions have a two-fold effect on security prices under this scenario. First, they affect the implications of given accounting data for future cash flows. In addition, macroeconomic factors—particularly the rate of interest—affect the monetary value attached to a given profile of prospective cash flows at any time.

The situation described above is clearly greatly simplified. The discussion assumes that macrocconomic data are exogeneous to the activities of firms—there is no feedback effect from firm activities to economy-wide conditions. Furthermore, there are in reality complex relationships between such variables as the rate of interest, companies' investment activities, consumption, and prospective cash flows to investors. Indeed, a realistic discussion of the problems alluded to would touch on virtually all area of economics. The use of the simplified discussion above is intended to suggest reasons for expecting changes in valuation relationships estimated at different times and, perforce, under different economic conditions. The discussion suggests that it may be useful to examine such variables as the rate of interest as a key to understanding changes in valuation relationships over time.

Work related to these issues has been done by Rosenberg and Marathe [1976] . Also, Aharony [1979] examined the effect of incorporating several macroeconomic variables in the valuation model. Recognition of the role of interest rates as determinants of the magnitudes of valuation model coefficients can be found in the literature dealing with the cost of capital. Several studies addressed the link directly by comparing estimated coefficients with those implied by the level of macroeconomic variables (e.g., Miller and Modigliani [1966], and Litzenberger and Rao [1971]).

2.3 Dividend Discounting-Based and Asset Pricing Models

It is instructive to examine the relationship between the dividend discounting-based models and other models of security pricing such as the Sharpe [1964], Lintner [1965], and Mossin [1966] Capital Asset Pricing Model (CAPM). The arbitrage pricing model of Beja [1971], Rubinstein [1976], and Garman [1978] is a convenient starting place for analysis. Essentially all pricing models, including the option pricing model of Black and Scholes [1974], can be derived using appropriate assumptions within the arbitrage model framework.

The basic arbitrage pricing relationship assumes the existence of a well-defined state space—for any given state, the payoff from each asset is known to all agents with certainty. The following assumptions are made:

1. Concordant expectations: Investors agree on which states of nature have positive probability of occurrence at cach time t, although not nccessarily on what the probabilities are.
2. No arbitrage opportunities exist. If for a given point in time we let:
   $s(t)$ = state of the world at time t,
   $\pi_i\,[s(t)]$ = investor i's subjective probability that state s will occur at time t,
   $z[s(t)]$ = current price of a unit of payment at time t contingent on state s(t) prevailing,
   $p_j\,(t)$ = conditional price of security j: $p(0)$ = current price,
   $d_j[s(t)]$ = conditional payoff on security j,

   then, the assumptions above imply that there exists a random variable $q_i(t)$ such that:

   $$P_j(0) = \sum_{t=1}^{\infty} [E[d_j(t)] + \mathrm{cov}(q_i(t), d_j(t) R_{Ft}] / R_{Ft}$$

   where
   $R_{Ft} = 1/\Sigma_s\, z[s(t)]$.

   R_{Ft}^{-1} is therefore the current price of a unit of payment for certain at time t, and
   $q_i(t) = \Sigma_t\, z[s(t)]/\pi_i s(t)]$.

The expression for current security price can therefore be viewed as the present value of the security's payoff stream adjusted by a risk factor determined by the relationship between the payoff stream and the probability-weighted random variable q_i.

2.3.1 Conditions For the Derivation of Pure Discounting Valuation Models

Models of valuation in which the risk adjustment to the payout stream (to obtain certainty equivalent dividend streams) plays a limited role can be derived from the basic arbitrage-free pricing relationships:[3]

$$P_j(0) = \sum_{t=1}^{\infty} [E[d_j(t)] + cov(q_i(t), d_j(t) R_{Ft}] / R_{Ft}$$

Strict dividend discounting requires that:

$$(cov\ (\Sigma\ \frac{z[s(t)]}{\pi[s(t)]}, d_n(t)) = 0)\ .$$

This condition is satisfied if:

1. $z[s(t)] = k\pi[s(t)]$, k a constant: the state-contingent price is proportional to the probability of state occurrance, and
   $\Sigma_s \pi[s(t)] = 1$, or
2. $q[s(t)]$ and $d_j[s(t)]$ are independent: the security payoff is unaffected by the prevailing state, or
3. $q[s(t)]$ and $d_j[s(t)]$ have a non-normal joint distribution and are uncorrelated but not independent.

Each of the above conditions essentially implies that expected payoffs can be discounted without prior risk adjustment for the stochastic relationship between expected payoffs and the state variable. If in addition the single-period risk-free rate of interest is constant, then we have:

$$R_{Ft} = r_1\ r_2\ r_3 \ldots r_t = R_1^t$$

where R, is the constant one-period (one plus) risk-free rate of interest, and r_i is the period i risk-free rate of interest (plus one). With any of the conditions (1) to (3) the constant interest condition yields:

$$P_j(0) = \sum_{t=1}^{\infty} [E[d_j(t)]] / R_1^t$$

Specific assumptions about expected dividends (for example, dividend growth) yield many of the pure dividend discounting models found in the literature.

2.3.2 A Simple Risk-Adjusted Model

The risk-adjusted discounted dividend model can be derived within the above framework. In particular, if the stochastic relationship between dividends and the q variable is

$$R_{Ft}\ cov(q(t)\ , d_j(t)) = k.d_j(t)$$

where k is a constant, then the valuation model becomes:

$$p_j = \sum_{t=1}^{\infty} \frac{E[d_j(t)](1+k)}{R_{Ft}}$$

By assuming a deterministic relationship for the stream of expected dividends, the valuation model can be expressed using a finite number of terms. If dividends are expected to grow at a rate of g each period and the single-period risk-free rate of interest is constant we obtain:

$$p_j = \frac{(1+k)\, E[d_j(1)]}{R_1} \sum_{t=1}^{\infty} [(1+g)/R_1]^{t-1}$$

$$= E[d_j(1)]\,(1+k)/(R_1-1-g)$$

$$= E[d_j(1)]\, h.$$

With these assumptions h represents the adjusted cost of capital for firm j, which is an alternative perspective to that of adjusted expected dividends discounted at the risk-free rate.

The conditions required for the derivation of the above expected dividend discounting valuation models are quite restrictive. The only risk adjustment permitted was one in which the level of risk depended on the size of the payout and the risk-free rate at any date. However, the formulation provides a simple illustration of valuation model derivation with a small set of intuitively appealing assumptions.

Other models such as the CAPM can be derived within the arbitrage pricing framework. However, the relationship between the dividend discounting models and the CAPM is perhaps best explored by examining the CAPM directly. In the presence of the risk-free asset this model is usually expressed as:

$$E(R_i) - R_f = \beta_i\, [E(R_m) - R_f]$$

where:

R_i = the return on security i,

R_m = the return on the market portfolio,

R_f = the return on a risk free asset, and

β_i = the systematic risk of security i.

In terms of current security price, the above single-period model becomes:

$$V_i = \frac{E(\tilde{D}) - \theta\, \mathrm{Cov}\,(\tilde{D}_i, \tilde{D}_m)}{r}$$

where

$$\theta = \frac{E(\tilde{D}_m) - r\, V_m}{\sigma m^2}$$

V_1 = Value of security i,

D_1 = Total payoff to security i at the end of period,

V_m and D_m = Value of the market portfolio and the total payoff to the market portfolio at the end of period respectively, and

σ_m^2 = the variance of the payoff to the market portfolio.

In this one period model, "dividends" represent the firm's economic earnings: equity distributions plus the change in security price. More importantly, the model is seen to be a discounting mechanism in which current price is obtained by discounting at the risk-free rate the total risk-adjusted proceeds one period from the present. The amount of risk adjustment depends on the covariation between the firm's expected payout and that for the economy as a whole. The valuation expression of the CAPM differs from the pure dividend discounting model in the use of a price change term instead of a stream of predicted dividends (or assumptions about dividend growth). The nature and extent of the required risk adjustment to the end-of-period cash payment is also more precisely expressed in the valuation CAPM. Moreover, as a discounting relationship, the CAPM is remarkably similar to the pure discounting models. The use of measures of earnings growth in the latter class of models is clearly an attempt to supplement information on expected next period income and/or dividends with information on how these are likely to behave beyond the next period. In the CAPM, the corresponding issue is the measure of prospects beyond the period using the change in the security's price during the period. These basic similarities were exploited by Litzenberger and Rao [1971] as discussed in section 3.1 below.

3. LITERATURE SURVEY

3.1 Finance and General

The earliest rigorous analysis of security valuation was based on the pure discounting approach and was developed by several authors, notably Williams [1938], Gordon and Shapiro [1956], Gordon [1962], Modigliani and Miller [1958, 1963, 1965], and Miller and Modigliani [1961, 1966]. The original models proposed assumed certainty and perfect capital markets. Under these conditions the main analytical problems involved the presence of growth or above-normal earnings opportunities arising from unique investment avenues available to the firm. This situation was studied by Gordon and Shapiro [1956] and Gordon [1962], who expressed the present value of the firm as:

$$p_0 = \int_0^{\infty} d_0 e^{gt} e^{-kt} dt = \frac{d_0}{k-g}$$

where:

p_0 = current security price

d_0 = current dividend

g = growth rate of dividends: $d_t = d_0 e^{gt}$>

k = rate of decline of the value of the dividend stream V

t = time.

By assuming a constant earnings retention rate b and an all-equity capital structure the Gordon valuation formula can be written as:

$$p_0 = \frac{(1-b)Y_0}{k-rb}$$

where

r = company's rate of return on assets

Y_0 = current net income.

The presence of growth opportunities was also studied by Modigliani and Miller (MM) [1958].

Since the above models assume certainty and perfect capital markets, the relevant information was largely restricted to the firm's normal level of earnings and the economy-wide discount rate. With admission of uncertainty and market imperfections, several other variables become potentially relevant to valuation. Prominent among these are dividend policy, riskiness of the firm's investment opportunities and earnings stream, and leverage. The papers by MM form perhaps the most comprehensive attempt to address the questions raised by uncertainty and market imperfection. In addition, the MM papers epitomize the move to the structural form approach from the pure dividend discounting approach. Among the key issues they addressed are leverage and dividend policy. Many of the earliest valuation model derivations can be viewed as being based on the structural form approach (e.g., MM [1958, 1963]). Even in those derivations where earnings take the place of dividends in the models (e.g., Miller and Modigliani [1961]), it is on the basis of the assumed relationship to the dividend stream.

MM [1958] assume that firms can be placed in homogeneous risk classes—groups of firms whose earnings are discounted at the same rate. Focusing first on the questions raised by uncertainty, they point out that with perfect capital marketg and no taxes leverage is of no effect in valuation, given the company's investment schedule. This was in contrast to the then-traditional view in rmance that asserted that for each firm a value-maximizing level of debt existed. The MM argument, summarized in proposition I of the 1958 paper, was founded on stockholders' ability to remove any differences in security values through profitable riskless arbitrage (using home-made leverage). MM show how the cost of equity capital—the required rate of return on common stock—can be derived using the company's debt-equity ratio. In later papers [MM, 1963, 1965] the authors modify their assumptions to allow:

1. different corporate and individual borrowing rates
2. lower corporate borrowing risk resulting from limited liability
3. the existence of borrowing-related corporate risks, in particular, bankruptcy, and the effects of leverage on project selection
4. the presence of transaction costs to arbitrageurs
5. corporate income taxes affecting net interest costs

With the above changes in the MM conditions the company's cost of capital is found to first decrease and then increase, suggesting that an optimal level of debt exists.

The role of the dividend payment pattern in valuation also generated much debate. Miller and Modigliani argued that if the company's risk class and proposed investment schedule do not change with the pattern of dividends, and if in addition there is no dividend tax effect, then the timing of dividends is irrelevant to valuation. Any differences in dividend payments are exactly reflected in price adjustments, and investors eliminate any other price differences between otherwise similar (along valuation-relevant characteristics) companies through arbitrage. As with the problem of leverage, the incorporation of more realistic assumptions complicates the analysis considerably. Some of the criticisms made in the literature were by Gordon [1962], among others. These include:

1. The dividend payout pattern may not be independent of the investment plans.
2. Differences in new investors' expectations may affect the substitutability of internal and external equity financing.
3. Investors may view future dividends as being more risky—a variant of the bird-in-hand argument.[4]

4. Transaction costs may reduce the number of options available to the firm and to investors.
5. Investors face different capital gain and dividend (current income) tax rates.

The above considerations resulted in ambiguous analytical results on the effects of leverage and dividends on valuation. Two more recent examples of debate on the effects of leverage on valuation can be offered. The first is the dividend clientele effect originally hypothesized by Miller and Modigliani [1961] and re-examined recently by Lewellen, Stanley, and Schlarbaum [1978]. The hypothesis suggests that groups of investors who face different tax regulations regarding the treatment of capital gains and the taxability of dividends will select securities with payment patterns suited to their peculiar positions. Firms, recognizing this, attempt to identify and attract dividend "clienteles". However, in equilibrium there is no marginal gain to changes in the dividend pattern. The effect of dividends is again zero at the margin, due in this case to firms' having removed potential gains.

The second example of debate on leverage and dividend policy effects is based on the signaling models introduced by Spence [1973,1974] and studied by Laub [1976], Bhattacharya [1979], Leland and Pyle [1977], Gonedes [1978], and Penman [1983]. With regard to leverage, Leland and Pyle suggest that the proportion of debt financing used by a company may convey management's estimation of the company's prospects to the market. In particular, with moral hazard problems increasing as equity funding (often shared by management) is reduced, management has the incentive to signal superior firm prospects by using higher levels of equity financing, thereby placing a greater level of risk on common equity. With regard to dividend payments, it has been noted by Penman [1983] that increases in dividend payment levels are generally associated with superior security price performance—specifically positive residual returns after the influence of the market is eliminated. As noted by Lintner [1956], firms' dividend payout ratios tend to remain stable over several years. It was therefore suggested that investors interpret changes in dividends as reflecting management expectations about future performance. Thus dividend payments are hypothesized to imply more than a mere intertemporal transfer device. The signaling perspective derives its importance from the fact that it emphasizes two major points:

1. The limitations of a priori analysis for explaining the factors affecting security valuation.
2. The influence of information asymmetry between management and shareholders on the roles of some discretionary variables.

The discounted present value-based reduced form approach valuation models outlined above are among the most extensively tested relationships in finance. We now summarize the tests performed and the main results obtained.

Major tests of valuation models include Miller and Modigliani [1966], Malkiel [1963], Benishay [1961], Gordon [1962], and Bower and Bower [1969, 1970]. The model was generally formulated with security price or the price earnings ratio as the dependent variable and with the debt level, expected net income, dividend payout, expected dividends, the level of assets, and the growth rates of assets or net income among the explanatory variables. In the Miller–Modigliani paper a two-stage least squares formulation was used, in which net income was itself hypothesized to depend on company tax rates, leverage, asset levels and growth, preferred stock, and dividends. This was done to remove measurement error in earnings. Two-stage least squares is a potentially important technique, particularly since it has implications for income measurement and time series behavior. In particular, the success of a two-stage approach would suggest that transitory components of earnings can be removed from net income figures. The importance of such a result extends beyond valuation model research, but the technique has not received much attention since.

The other valuation model estimation studies were generally of linear single-equation models of the form:

V = f(expected dividends, expected net income, assets, growth, leverage).

Examples of this approach are Friend and Puckett [1964] and Benishay [1961] . The papers by Bower and Bower [1969, 1970] illustrate an attempt to remove the effects of companies' accounting methods from pure economic influences on firm characteristics. They estimate a model based on the assumptions of constant earnings growth and dividend payout rates. A log linear relationship is hypothesized in which the logarithm of the price earnings ratio is dependent on (the logarithm of) the earnings growth rate, dividend payout ratio, security marketability, conformity with market price movements, price variability, and firm effects. All of the explanatory variables are straightforward except for 'firm effects'. This was designed to measure the discrepancy between predicted and observed price earnings ratios for earlier periods, predictions being based on the explanatory variables. "Firm effects" was found to be of considerable importance in explaining intercompany differences in price earnings ratios. The variable may not be as arbitrary as might appear at first. Beaver and Morse [1978] found great persistence in rankings of price earnings ratios over a 14-year period and were only able to explain this partially using differences in growth and risk (the security's market coefficient in the single-factor CAPM). Beaver and Morse concluded upon further analysis that differences in price earnings ratios that persist over three or more years are often a result of differences in accounting practice. A variable such as firm effects may therefore serve as a proxy for such differences. However, while this variable increases the models' explanatory power significantly, it contributes little to our understanding of the microeconomic determinants of security prices.

Several of the valuation model studies focused on fairly homogeneous groups of companies, usually with the objective of staying within a risk class (e.g., Miller and Modigliani [1966] and Malkiel [1970] studied public utilities). The researchers generally found high explanatory power—reported adjusted coefficients of determination of 0.7 and above are common—and high statistical significance for such variables as earnings, dividends, growth, and leverage. However, a number of difficulties are apparent from a perusal of the results reported, particularly:

1. The instability of parameter estimates over time
2. The consequent inability of the models to answer unambiguously such questions as the effects of leverage and other firm characteristics

The applicability of the MM valuation models was restricted by the requirement that firms in a sample belong to the same risk class. More important, the concept of risk was not precisely defined and incorporated. Perhaps the most cohesive modern attempt to specify a valuation model that explicitly incorporates differences in risk across firms thereby facilitating general estimation is the one by Litzenberger and Rao (LR) [1971]. LR combined the MM [1966] and the CAPM approaches by assuming that the company's earnings stream could be split up into a no-growth component and a component expected to grow at some company-specific rate over an economy-wide T-year horizon. The no-growth component is valued using the CAPM, while the growth component is valued using the MM model. LR express the market value of the company as:

$$P_i = \frac{E_i - b\rho_{im}\delta_{E_i}}{I} + [\frac{\Delta B_i(\pi_i - R_i)}{R_i(1+R_i)}]T$$

where

E_i = Expected (economic) earnings of firm i,

B_i = Book value of equity investment of firm i,

I = Risk-free rate of interest,

R_i = Required rate of return on equity investment of firm i,

P_i = Market value of firm i,

δ_{E_i} = Standard deviation of firm i's earnings,

π = Rate of return on new equity investment,

T = Period of abnormal growth,

b = Rate of return on market portfolio per unit of market return standard deviation,

ρ_{im} = Correlation coefficient of return on market with return on security i.

For estimation purposes LR normalize the valuation equation using net book values and compute estimates of E_i/B_i (a 3-year average of accounting rates of return), δ_{E_i} (an estimate of the standard deviation of the accounting rate of return, E_i/B_i), growth in book values (based on the average change over 7 years), and the required rate of return (computed from Moody's Utility index). The estimation was for the period 1960 to 1966.

The regression model therefore yielded estimates of $\frac{1}{I}$, $\frac{-b\rho_{im}}{I}$ and T.

3.2 Valuation Model Research in Accounting

The most fundamental modern accounting research into security valuation examined the determinants of prices and the relationship between prices and earnings. Beaver and Morse [1978] examined the behavior of price-earnings (PE) ratios over a 14-year period for 25 portfolios of firms ranked by PE ratios. The portfolios were formed at the beginning of the 14-year period. The authors found that the rankings by PE ratios were in part determined by transitory elements in reported earnings. These temporary elements appeared to have been perceived as such by the security markets. As a result, prices did not adjust proportionately to (extreme) earnings changes, which in turn led to extremely high or low PE ratios. Since the earnings levels were often a result of short-term influences, there was some reduction in the dispersion of the initial portfolios' PE ratios after formation. Much of the initial difference in magnitudes of median price-earnings ratios had disappeared 3 years after the portfolios were formed. In the year of formation the portfolio median PE ratios ranged from 5.8 for the lowest PE portfolio to 50.0 for the highest—a factor of 8.6. By the third year after formation the range was from 7.8 for the lowest PE portfolio to 13.8 for the highest PE portfolio—a factor of less than two. The magnitudes of the extreme portfolios' median PE ratios stood at 8.9 (highest PE portfolio) and 8.3 (lowest PE portfolio) 14 years after formation. Transitory influences did not account for all of the variation in price-earnings ratios, however. In spite of the trends in the magnitudes of the median PE ratios, the ranks of the medians showed considerable stability. There were significant levels of rank correlation (between ranks at formation and ranks for the same portfolios subsequent to formation) as many as 14 years after formation. Only some of the difference could be explained using earnings growth and risk (CAPM beta). The authors suggested that the remaining differences were in part a result of differences in accounting methods.

This view was supported by Beaver and Dukes [1972]. Their study showed that firms that used accelerated depreciation for reporting purposes tended to have higher price-earnings ratios than firms that used straight-line depreciation. Both groups of firms used accelerated depreciation for tax purposes. The difference in PE ratios did not appear to be a result of differences in risk and growth, since measures of these attributes were quite close for the two groups. It appeared that the difference in accounting methods was the reason for the difference—the two groups' PE ratios were almost identical once the earnings of the straight-line firms were adjusted to what they might have been had accelerated depreciation been used for reporting purposes by both groups of firms.

The research on PE ratios was important because it studied such influences on security prices as accounting methods. Although PE ratios *per se* are of interest to users of accounting information, more general valuation models permit the examination of a wider range of issues than PE ratios. An example of such studies is Dukes [1976], which studied, in part, the relationship between security prices and accounting policy for research and development (R & D) expenditures. Dukes studied 41 firms in the chemical, drug, and electronics industries to determine the influence of research and development expenditures on security prices. Dukes hypothesized that since such expenditures are required to be treated as expenses in the period incurred regardless of potential future benefits, earnings of companies with high levels of research and development expenditures would be related to security prices in a different way than earnings of other companies—a result of perceived future benefits from research expenditure. After estimating and using the research intensity of each industry in the valuation model, Dukes concluded that earnings appeared to be adjusted for companies' research intensity before being impounded in prices. Furthermore, the adjustment appeared to be industry-specific.

The above studies illustrate the possibility of using valuation models in examining accounting alternatives. The results suggest that companies' earnings numbers are not used naively. Adjustments appear to be made for income differences that result solely from accounting methods (for example, accelerated versus straight-line depreciation methods for reporting purposes). Also, research expenditures do not appear to be viewed as current-period expenses merely because they are reported as such. The studies suggest a potentially useful methodology for evaluating the effects of accounting methods using valuation models. By explicitly controlling for such influences on security values as growth and risk, the researcher may be able to isolate the effects of specific pieces of information on security prices. Many studies that have adopted this approach have, like Dukes [1976], been based on the Litzenberger-Rao model.

Perhaps the most robust result in valuation research is that the coefficient of earnings is generally of the expected (positive) sign and magnitude. Accordingly, it seems appropriate that much of the valuation-based research in accounting has examined the earnings variable. Of particular importance is the research on income components and their role in the determination of security prices. It seems logical that different components of a company's total income number should have different implications for security valuation, and the valuation approach has proved to be a useful vehicle for addressing this issue.

One of the first papers to examine the role of different components of income on security prices was Foster [1977]. The study evaluated three different definitions of income for property-liability insurance companies: underwriting earnings (U), the sum of underwriting and investments earnings (U + I), and the sum of underwriting and investment earnings and capital gains on equity securities (U + I + C). The Litzenberger-Rao valuation model was estimated for a sample of 22 firms in the years 1968 to 1972, with earnings defined as U, U + I, or U + I + C. These income measures were evaluated on the basis of the closeness of the estimated coefficients to their theoretical values as well as on the explanatory power of the model and coefficient statistical significance. Foster concluded that the U series of earnings was least associated with stock prices among the three series. While the choice between U + I and U + I + C was not as clear-cut, Foster concluded that U + I + C provided the best specification based on the criteria above.

Foster [1977] demonstrated the use of economic and statistical criteria to determine the composition of net income that is most consistent with observed security prices. An interesting question is whether the different components of insurance companies' earnings are assigned different weights in securily valuation. It seems likely that while more income would generally be strictly prererred to less regardless of the source, some types of income may be viewed as being more desirable. For example, certain types of income may be viewed as being transitory and others as permanent. However, this question is somewhat different from the one examined by Foster.

A paper by Bowen [1981] addresses the issue of income components and security valuation more directly. Bowen [1981] used a sample of some 107 electrical utilities in the period 1962 to 1975 to determine whether income from operations and the allowance for funds during construction (AFC: imputed interest included in income) have different implications for security pricing. Bowen used the LR model, modified to include separate earnings terms for operating income and AFC. Both year-by-year and pooled versions of the model were estimated. The models estimated were evaluated on both economic and statistical criteria. The author concluded that although the AFC earnings coefficient was statistically significant and had the predicted sign, AFC earnings were less valuable per dollar than operating earnings.

A third study that has examined the relationship between security prices and different definitions of earnings is Beaver and Landsman (BL) [1983], which compared historical cost-based and price-level-adjusted accounting data required under FAS statement 33. The study differs from Foster [1977] and Bowen [1981] in focusing on income computation rules rather than on various components of income. BL's main analysis was done using security returns, and the valuation approach was used to provide supplementary evidence. The BL model expressed security price as a function of earnings, risk (CAPM beta) and projected earnings and book value growth. Except for the risk variable, this is very much like the LR valuation model, although the BL model was not derived from the LR model. Since different methods of computing accounting data—including measures of book values—were being compared, sales was used as a deflating variable to reduce heteroscedasticity. The historical cost and FAS 33 data were compared on the basis of their explanatory power for security prices. Because the models were deflated for estimation, it was necessary to express their explanatory power in terms of average deviations of predicted from actual prices in order to compare the different measures of earnings. The results of the BL valuation analysis appeared to be anomalous, although they were consistent with the return-based results: price-adjusted data did not appear to improve the explanation of security prices once historical cost data were used.

One of the most important applications of valuation model research has been in the area of pensions. Pension reporting has attracted much attention recently, specific areas of concern being the influence of unfunded pension obligations on security values and the effects of specific funding policies and assumptions. This area of research is especially interesting because it examines the effects of unreported *de facto* liabilities: to what extent are these off-balance sheet items reflected in security prices?

Oldfield [1976] used the Modigliani-Miller model to examine whether unfunded vested benefits resulted in dollar-for-dollar reductions in security prices. The sample consisted of 166 COMPUSTAT firms whose beta estimates for the periods 1972-73 and 1973-74 fell within specified ranges for both periods. This choice was made in order to approximate stable homogeneous risk classes. The coefficient of the unfunded vested pension obligation variable was statistically significant and negative in the main regression. Although not significantly different from -1 (the theoretical value), the estimated coefficient was less than -1, leading the author to conclude that the reported value of unfunded obligations "is treated by the market as a fairly accurate but somewhat understated representation of the true pension obligation".

Feldstein and Seligman (FS) [1981] and Feldstein and Morck (FM) [1983] also examined the issue of pensions, but with particular emphasis on the relationship between pension practices and national savings. Briefly, since pension plans are a substitute for employees' savings, aggregate savings may be lower if pensions are not fully funded and this fact is not reflected in security prices. FS and FM posit that if unfunded obligations are reflected in prices investors will increase their savings to a level that would at least partially offset the short-fall from less-than-full funding of obligations.

FS and FM are based on Tobin's asset valuation equation:

$$V = qA$$

where

V = market value of assets

A = replacement cost of assets

q = function of firms ability to provide above-average earnings growth in preceding decade,

= f (accounting rate of return, earnings growth in preceding decade, research and development expenditure, risk).

By dividing the relationship by A and measuring risk using Merrill Lynch beta estimates and the market value of net debt, a linear valuation model was obtained in which pension liabilities appear as a term separate from other debt. FS also estimated a version of the model in which the replacement cost of net assets (A minus recorded liabilities), or common equity, is used in place of A. The estimation was based on samples of 117 and 193 firms in 1976 and 1977, respectively. The coefficients were generally significant and of the expected sign, except for the coefficient of beta. As in Oldfield [1976], the coefficient of the unfunded vested pension liability was estimated at below -1, although FS found their estimate to be statistically "compatible with a one-for-one substitution as well as a more substantial effect". The results also suggested that the unfunded vested pension liability (UVPL) is the relevant variable for security pricing, not unfunded past and prior service costs. The FS study is interesting because it uses replacement cost data, although the use of such variables as earnings, growth, and risk as the main determinants of security values was not different from other formulations. The paper, however, does not provide a comparison of historical costs and inflation-adjusted data. Such a comparison is provided by FM.

FM examine the effect of pension liabilities on security values as a test of market efficiency. The valuation model used was similar to the main model estimated by FS (independent variables are earnings, earnings growth, R & D, beta, leverage, and UVPL). The sample consisted of 132 firms in 1979. The model estimates with inflation-adjusted data were comparable to those in FS, particularly for UVPL. The lack of significance of leverage and the negative and significant beta coefficient in FM were two differences from the earlier study. The estimation using historical cost data yielded roughly similar results. However, the estimated coefficients were higher in absolute magnitude for historical cost data for all variables except R & D, which had a lower coefficient.

FM also examined the sensitivity of the model to differences in interest rate assumptions. Standard rates were used in computing pension liabilities in place of the six to nine per cent used by most companies.[5] The liabilities computed by using the average of the firms' discount rates yielded the highest explanatory power of the rates examined. In addition, the pension liability coefficient obtained under this specification was closest to the theotetical value. This suggested that the market uses a common (average) discount rate for pension liabilities.

Several aspects of the pension reporting issue were examined by Daley [1984] in a study using the Litzenberger-Rao valuation model. Based on the assumption that security prices incorporate future pension costs, the research enquires into which of three measures of pension costs is most closely related to security prices. The measures are unfunded prior service costs, pension expenses, and unfunded vested benefits. The study considers pension costs as a component of net income (pension expenses) in one estimation and as a liability (the capitalized amount of expense) in the remaining two. Noteworthy features of the estimation are the use of an instrumental variable regression (see Miller and Modigliani [1966]) to reduce the errors-in-variables problem for earnings and the use of price-adjusted data on assets. In addition, the author examines the effect on the estimation of the interest rate chosen by the company to compute pension obligations. The estimation was performed for samples of 117 firms in 1976 and 193 firms in 1977. The pension costs measures were evaluated using theoretical and statistical criteria.

Daley found coefficient estimates to be closest to theoretical levels when pension expense was used.[6] The effects of firms' interest rate assumptions were examined by allowing the coefficient of the pension cost variable to vary depending on which of ten interest rate groups a firm was classified in. The interest group coefficients were not statistically significant for any of the definitions of pension costs. This is consistent with the findings of Feldstein and Morck [1983], in which it was suggested that a common discount rate is imputed by the market.

Valuation model research in accounting has followed two main channels. The first of these evaluates the components of net income, attempting to determine if different sources of income have different implications for security price determination. While comprehensive definitions of income may be more relevant than restricted definitions (Foster [1977]; Bowen [1981]), the research suggests that not all sources of income are seen as equivalent (Bowen [1981]).

The second, closely related channel of valuation research has examined the role in valuation of off-balance sheet items. The most important application to date is to pensions, where the effects of unfunded benefits are often examined. However, Duke's [1976] study may also be viewed as an attempt to determine whether firms in different industries have different amounts of unrecorded R & D-related productive assets. Regardless of the method of analysis used, it seems clear that valuation models have improved our understanding of accounting phenomena. The approach is particularly useful in examining the role of finer information sets than net income alone, and it is a helpful adjunct to the analysis of changes in accounting data and returns in an area where changes in specific variables and components of income may be isolated easily.[7] However, the contributions of valuation research have been made in spite of a number of problems and criticisms, issues to which we now turn.

4. SOME UNRESOLVED ISSUES

Although some progress has been made in improving valuation model specification and statistical testing, some problems remain. This section examines some key problem areas.

Gonedes and Dopuch [1974] conducted an important review of empirical research in accounting and identified two main problem areas in valuation model research. The first is the lack of theory and the *ad hoc* nature of the models. There is still room for improvement in the theoretical foundations and empirical specification of valuation models. For example, although the models typically include a variable for expected growth, the empirical measures of growth used vary widely. To a large extent the problem of linking price-based models to observable firm attributes is not peculiar to valuation model research. As pointed out by Lev and Ohlson [1982], dividend discounting and other valuation models can, with appropriate assumptions, be derived from the basic no-arbitrage conditions of Beja [1971] and Rubinstein [1976]. Other return-based models such as the CAPM can also be derived from this framework (Rubinstein [1976]). What is needed is a refinement of the assumptions to derive empirical valuation models.

The second problem area pointed out by Gonedes and Dopuch [1974] concerns econometric issues. These include multicollinearity, heteroscedasticity, and serial correlation (i.e., the dependence in successive years' observations, and the effect on results based on such data). Other related issues pointed out by Gonedes and Dopuch are the cross-sectional dependence of error terms for firms in the same industry and the influence of public utility commissions' behavior when utility firms are studied. More recently, Christie [1984] examined some econometric issues in cross-sectional empirical research.

Some major unresolved issues in valuation model research are now discussed under the broad headings of model specification and model estimation.

4.1 Model Specification

Perhaps the most common criticism of valuation research is that the models used are *ad hoc*. Indeed, the above literature review listed several different approaches to model derivation used in recent research. The main models are summarized in Table 1.

Table 1
Summary of Some Major Research

	PRIMARY ISSUES	MODEL TYPE OR MAJOR VARIABLES	RISK MEASURE	MODEL DEFLATED BY	MAIN RESULTS
Dukes [1976]*	Differences in valuation model parameters related to research intensity.	LR-based	$\sigma(E)$	Security prices	Differences in estimated parameters of firms grouped by industry research intensity.
Foster [1977]*	Definitions of insurance company earnings most consistent with security prices.	LR	LR	Book value of firm assets	Comprehensive definitions of income found to be more closely related to security prices than less comprehensive definitions.
Bowen [1981]*	Differences in valuation model coefficients of components of income of electric utilities.	LR	LR	Book value of equity	Allowance for funds during construction component of total income is valued less than operating income component in security valuation model.
Beaver and Landsman [1983]	Comparison of historical cost and FAS 33-based accounting data.	Earnings, earnings growth, risk	Beta	Sales; book values of common equity	Consistent with results of returns analysis, historical cost data more closely related to security prices than price-adjusted data.
Oldfield [1976]	Role of unfunded vested pension liabilities in valuation.	MM	Firms grouped in risk classes based on beta	Book value of firm assets	Unfunded pension liabilities associated with reduced equity values, but liabilities may be understated.

Table 1 (cont'd)
Summary of Some Major Research

	PRIMARY ISSUES	MODEL TYPE OR MAJOR VARIABLES	RISK MEASURE	MODEL DEFLATED BY	MAIN RESULTS
Feldstein and Seligman [1981]	Pensions and national savings.	Earnings, earnings growth, research and development expenditure, pension liability	Beta, leverage	Replacement cost of total assets; net replacement cost of assets	Estimates consistent with Oldfield [1976]. Lack of full funding apparently does not lead to a reduction in national savings.
Feldstein and Morck [1983]	Evaluate effect of pension liabilities on prices.	Earnings, earnings growth, research and development expenditure, risk, pension liability.	Beta, leverage	Replacement cost of total assets	Consistent with Feldstein and Seligman [1981]. Price-adjusted data yield results comparable to those from historical cost data. Market apparently uses a common interest rate to discount pension obligations.
Daley [1984]*	Determine which measure(s) of pension costs most consitent with security prices.	Earnings (from instrumental variable estimation), asset growth, risk, pension costs.	LR	Book value of firm assets	Pension expense found to be more consistent with security prces than other measures of obligations. Coefficients of pension cost variable not dependent on interest rate company selects.

* LR model used. Earnings variable is defined as average accounting rate of return (of earnings on the deflating variable).

Risk variable is the standard deviation of rate of return in Bowen.
Daley measures risk as earnings standard deviation times the correlation between firm and market rates of return.

The most widely used model in recent research is the LR model. This model combines elements of two asset-pricing models—the capital asset-pricing model and the Modigliani-Miller valuation model. A summary of the literature suggests that most of the cross-sectional valuation models suggested give expression to a few basic ideas:

1. Security prices depend on the level and riskiness of future cash flows to stockholders.
2. (Market expectations of) future cash flows can be completely described by observed accounting earnings and measures of growth based on previous performance.
3. The riskiness of cash flows to investors can be estimated using such measures as the past variability of the earnings stream.
4. The pricing relationship can be approximated by a linear function.

However, the links from expected cash flows to firm variables have not been developed analytically. The specification of links from theoretical models to tractable empirical specifications remains an important problem. One early approach to specifying links between accounting information and cash flows is by Miller and Modigliani [1961]. The authors discuss several approaches to valuing the firm and obtain a specification in terms of earnings by considering in detail the relationship between the cost of capital, investment, dividends, and earnings. The paper attempts to obtain a theoretical relationship between accounting variables and security prices. A different approach was used by Litzenberger and Rao [1971], who use earnings in the CAPM to value (expected) current earnings and the Miller-Modigliani [1961] framework to value growth opportunities. However, in the one-period capital asset pricing model, earnings and net cash flows are equivalent. Thus, the use of the CAPM does not resolve the issue of the appropriateness of using accounting earnings in the model. Following Tobin [1961], other researchers have viewed earnings and other firm characteristics as determinants of the relationship between firms' book and market values (see, for example, Feldstein and Seligman [1981]). As observed above, the differences in the interpretation of firm variables are more apparent in the theoretical discussions than in the empirical formulations. However, a firm theoretical underpinning would make empirical specifications less *ad hoc*.

The formulations by Garman and Ohlson [1980] and Ohlson [1983] are based on arbitrage-free conditions and on the time series behavior of valuation-relevant firm data. These studies indicate a possible direction for future research.

4.2 Model Estimation

Model estimation and statistical inference in the presence of heteroscedasticity pose important practical problems in cross-sectional research. As is well known, the nonuniformity of error variances between companies leads to incorrect estimation of regression coefficient standard errors. The heteroscedasticity problem is usually addressed by deflating the regression equation by a firm-specific variable thought to be proportional to the true standard deviation of the error term for each firm. This procedure has been criticized on the grounds that it can lead to spurious correlation and that the statistical tests are misleading. A review of the econometrics literature suggests that some of the concern is misplaced.[8]

Since error variances are generally hypothesized to depend on firm size, typical deflating variables have been sales (Beaver and Landsman [1983]), assets (Miller and Modigliani [1966]), Daley [1984]) and the book value of common stocks (Litzenberger and Rao [1971]). An alternative is to deflate the equation by the market value of common stock—the original dependent variable—and use the earnings-price ratio as the new dependent variable. This approach was used by Miller and Modigliani [1966] and Litzenberger and Rao [1971]. Although model deflation is usually motivated as a solution to heteroscedasticity, an important benefit of deflation is to ensure that a few observations (large companies) do not exert an inordinate influence on model estimates. Such differences in scale may be avoided if the model is deflated by a size-related variable. Thus, the model may be deflated to achieve greater uniformity in the data. While the coefficient estimates from the deflated model are unbiased, there is the possibility that deflation will not eliminate heteroscedasticity and may lead to biased variance estimates. A solution to (and avenue for empirical investigation of) this problem is to use a variance estimator that is still valid in the presence of heteroscedasticity. Such an estimator is suggested by White [1980], who derives a variance-covariance matrix estimator that yields consistent estimates in the presence of heteroscedasticity.[9]

The estimator offers a solution to problems with inference caused by heteroscedasticity and also provides a means of evaluating the influence of deflation on extant results.

Changes in valuation model coefficients over time offer another fruitful area of research on valuation models. As discussed, security valuation is generally viewed as being dependent on a stream of dividend payments and a discount rate appropriate to the security's risk level. In valuation analysis, firm characteristics are viewed as indicators of the level and variability of future cash flows to stockholders. When the hypothetical links from firm characteristics to security prices are analyzed, it seems clear that in general the theoretical valuation model coefficients *should not* be constant over time, unless these links are incorporated into the model. This is because the firm's earnings level and dividend-paying ability depend on current and future economic conditions: a particular set of firm characteristics is likely to be perceived by investors as having different implications for future dividends if investors expect a depression than if the economy is expected to grow. Changes in expectations about economy-wide conditions therefore provide one reason for nonstationarity of theoretical and estimated valuation model characteristics.

The implications of various attributes and conditions for firm profits are only one side of the valuation picture. The demand for securities—the other aspect—is derived not only from the prospective payoffs from the securities but also from investors' evaluation of the desirability of risk and the deferment of consumption. Therefore, even where expected real profits are unchanged, the desirability of such profits, and hence their real current price, may change with investors' attitudes.

Some attacks on the credibility of results obtained from valuation models have been based on the assertion that since the variation in model coefficients over time is high relative to the coefficients' standard errors in any year the standard errors must be grossly understated. The above discussion suggests that the nonconstancy of valuation model coefficients over time ought to be the rule rather than the exception. As such, no inferences regarding the precision of any one year's estimated coefficients can be drawn from an analysis of changes in estimated coefficients over time. One ought to at least consider the influence of macroeconomic conditions on the coefficients before comparing estimated coefficients from different periods. With the exception of a few studies (see Aharony [1979] and Rosenberg and Marathe [1975, 1976]), this remains a relatively unexplored area.

One reason why there is variation in estimated coefficient may be that these coefficients are related to the level of the dependent variable. This relationship is not as obvious in returns analysis. Studies that use the returns approach typically focus on returns after the market effect has been eliminated (i.e., residual returns) and do not attempt to explain market returns. Indeed, the explanation of market returns is a complicated and unsettled issue. The issue of the nonconstant relationship between security prices and earnings levels is highlighted in several recent studies that examined the phenomenon of declining price-earnings ratios, the role of earnings levels and expctations, and the role of nominal and real interest rates in valuation. These studies include Fama [1981], Feldstein [1980a, 1980b], and Modigliani and Cohn [1979]. The analyses in these studies suggest that it would be misleading to view the relationship between price and earnings (as well as other firm variables) as an intertemporal constant. While valuation models appear to explain prices at a point in time fairly well, comparison across time periods is not straightforward.

The issue of temporal variation in the estimated valuation model coefficients remains an open one. Perhaps the most promising approach would be to examine global influences on firms which would be consistent with an almost monotonic decline in the ratio of security prices to firm accounting variable levels from the 1960s to the prescnt (see Modigliani and Cohn [1979]).

5. CONCLUSION

The discussion above suggests that the cross-sectional valuation approach to addressing accounting questions is a useful complement to returns-based analysis. The two approaches may be used for cross-validation, since, in principle, results obtained using one approach are generally obtainable under the other approach also. However, both approaches have advantages and disadvantages. As discussed in section 1, valuation analysis may be preferable for evaluating certain types of accounting information.

The discussion of valuation model development illustrates some features common to different cross-sectional valuation and return models. The no-arbitrage condition may be used as a common and very general starting point for deriving various models of security pricing, including the present value relationships used in cross-sectional valuation analysis. Because of the generality of the no-arbitrage models, specific assumptions are needed for obtaining empirical specifications. The analyses of Ohlson [1983] and Garman and Ohlson [1980] provide examples of this. Their research may be a fruitful approach to formalizing the valuation model and, more important, to specifying links from model variables to observable firm characteristics. Easton [1985] is a noteworthy exploration of the links between security prices and fundamental variables.

Much of the accounting research using valuation models has examined the effects on valuation of the components of income. This is an important and interesting issue to which the valuation approach appears to be particularly well suited. Another major branch of research using valuation models has examined the implications for security valuation of off-balance sheet items—specifically pension assets and liabilities. It would seem from these major areas of research that the valuation approach can contribute much to our understanding of the influence of various items on prices, and that studying such influences through price changes need not be the only approach.

In the survey of unresolved issues in valuation it was pointed out that much remains to be done on such issues as model specification and parameter variation over time. The survey of the modern econometric literature suggests that not all of the criticisms of cross-sectional valuation analysis are wellfounded. Econometric solutions to some of the problems with statistical inference that do exist were reviewed. Indeed, research on and using cross-sectional valuation models is a tractable and promising subject.

Endnotes

1. Major developments in finance, such as portfolio theory, the capital asset pricing model (CAPM), and the concept of informationally efficient capital markets (ECM) provided the primary impetus for these studies. See Lev and Ohlson [1982] for an elaboration on this point.
2. See e.g., Beaver [l968], Patel [1976], and Atiase [1985].
3. The restricted nature of the model does not eliminate the possibility that dividend expectations may depend on the projected state evolution. In addition, the discount rate may be affected by the prevailing and projected states.
4. The relevant arguments are summarized in Bhattacharya [1979].
5. The standard ratios were the Baa bond rate and the average of the companies' rates.
6. Coefficient estimates were found to be roughly consistent with those in Oldfield [1976] and Feldstein and Seligman [1981] .
7. The relationship between valuation and return-based models is illustrated by this concept of serial correlation. Assume a price-relevant event (which for simplicity is assumed not to affect systematic risk) is observed under continuous trading. Its effect on returns would be restricted to (periods which include) the time it takes for the information to be assimilated into prices. However, as long as the information remains relevant, prices should continue to reflect the data once assimilation has occured.
8. Criticisms in the accounting literature of the use of deflation in valuation research have usually relied on Kuh and Meyer (KM) [1955].

   Kuh and Meyer discuss the influence of deflation by a common variable on the level of correlation between variables of primary interest. The paper derived conditions for various types of influence deflation may have on correlation an issue pointed out by Pearson [1897]. In spite of the potential influence of deflation on correlation levels KM note (p. 407) that

   > if the error term increases as the square of the size factor . . . then deflation will yield the most efficient unbiased estimates when least-squares techniques are applied. While the proportionality in the error term may not hold exactly, in most economic cross-sections such a relationship would usually be a reasonable approximation. At the very worst deflation should usually be superior to arbitrarily assuming that a constant unitary weight is appropriate.

   The subject of deflation has been examined further since KM [1955].

   Belsley [1972] examined the problem of spurious correlation induced by deflation. The author considered both random and nonrandom deflators and different model forms. Belsley concludes (p. 926)

   > Deflation, for whatever reason it is undertaken, can introduce correlation between the dependent and independent variates. Fortunately, the significance of this correlation for the practicing econometrician is nil. Indeed, within the context of a linear model, correlation will typically exist between the undeflated variates from the outset. Deflation merely

changes this correlation but does not make it perfect and does not affect the properties of least-squares estimation . . . Least squares applied to the deflated variables still produce unbiased, minimum-variance estimators, provided the explanatory variable is independent of the resulting error term and *provided the relevant population parameter exists.* (Belsley's emphasis)

Although deflation usually proceeds on the assumption that the resulting coefficient estimates are unbiased and consistent this is not necessarily the case. This is emphasized by Casson [1973] who notes that the presence of error in the deflator may lead to inconsistency in the coeffcient estimators. Casson observes (p. 754) that the analysis of measurement error

applies not only to the case where there is an explicit deflator in the regression, but also to cases where a deflator should be used but is not. In other words, the conclusions apply whenever there is some hidden variable which influences all the measurements in a multiplicative fashion.

The author used consistent estimators of coefficients in a regression of annual investment on various firm variables to evaluate the effects of errors on inconsistency. The model was deflated by the book value of fixed assets and was estimated with a sample of 84 United Kingdom firms. Based on the analysis Casson concluded that there was little inconsistency in the estimated coefficients. The author notes (p. 758) that the analysis

indicates that the higher the R^2 of the fitted regression is, the smaller the inconsistency in the estimators tends to be. This suggests that, in practice, if an estimated regression is a good fit, then the inconsistency in the estimators will tend to be small. The fit of the regressions shown . . . is on the whole very poor, but the inconsistency is still small. These results suggest that the errors in the measurement of the deflator must be relatively large before the inconsistency in the regression estimators becomes important.

To summarize, in the presence of size-related heteroscedasticity, deflation is alw-ys preferable to estimation without deflation. Even if a perfect surrogate cannot be found for the variation in error variances the inconsistency induced by errors in the surrogate is not likely to be large. Casson's model coefficients of determination (R^2) ranged from .007 to .258 Valuation models usually have much higher R^2 levels (these range from .46 to .62 in Table 3 of Daky [1984] and the deflating variables used would not seem to have substantially greater error than the book value of fixed assets used in Casson [1973].

Furthermore Belsley [1972] points out that any induced correlation does not result in invalid

$$y_i = X_1\gamma + \varepsilon_i$$

$i = 1, \ldots, n$ observations

where

X_i = $1 \times k$ vector of variables for ith observation>

γ = $k \times 1$ vector of model coefficients>

ε_i = error term

X and ε are independent

inference in the regression context.

9. Briefly, assume a model

$$\hat{V} = n^{-1} \sum_{i=1}^{n} \hat{\varepsilon}_{in}^{2} x'_i x_i$$

White [1980] suggests ordinary least squares estimation of the equation and estimation of the heteroscedasticity-consistent matrix defined as

$\hat{\varepsilon}_{in}$ is the ordinary least squares estimate of the residual term.

White also derives a test for heteroscedasticity based on the above result and demonstrates an alternative method of computing the consistent variance estimator.

With the above matrix the researcher can evaluate linear hypotheses. For example. the restriction $R\gamma_0 = r$ where R is q X k and r is q X 1 can be tested using the fact that $n(\hat{R}\gamma_n - r)' [R(X^1X \mid n)' \hat{V}_n (X'X \mid n)' R']^{-1} (\hat{R}\gamma_n - r)$ is asymptotically distributed as a *chi*-square variable with q degrees of freedom.

REFERENCES

Aharony, J., "Time Effects in Empirical Stock Valuation Models," *The Review of Economics and Statistics* (August 1979), pp. 460-466.

Atiase, R. K., "Predisclosure Information, Firm Capitalization, and Security Price Behavior Around Earnings Announcements," *Journal of Accounting Research,* (Spring 1985), pp. 21-36.

Ball, R., and P. Brown, "An Empirical Evaluation of Accounting Income Numbers," *Journal of Accounting Research,* (Autumn 1968), pp. 159-177.

Beaver, W. "The Information Content of Annual Earnings Announcements," *Journal of Accounting Research,* (1968 Supplement), pp. 67-92.

Beaver, W., *Financial Reporting: An Accounting Revolution* (Englewood Cliffs: Prentice Hall), 1981.

Beaver, W., and R. Dukes, "Interperiod Tax Allocation, Earnings Expectations, and Behavior or Security Prices," *The Accounting Review,* (April 1983), pp. 320-332.

Beaver, W., and W. Landsman, *Incremental Information Content of FAS 33 Disclosures,* Research Report, FASB, Stamford, Conn, (1983).

Beaver, and D. Morse, "What Determines Price-Earnings Ratios?" *Financial Analysts' Journal,* (July–August 1978), pp. 65-76.

Beja, A., "The Structure or the Cost of Capital Under Uncertainty," *Review of Economic Studies* (July 1971), pp. 359-368.

Belsley, D., "Specification with Deflated Variables and Specious Spurious Correlation," *Econometrica,* (September 1972), pp. 923-927.

Benishay, H., "Variability in Earnings-Price Ratios of Corporate Equities," *American Economic Review,* (March 1961), pp. 81-94.

Bhattacharya, S. "Imperfect Information, Dividend Policy and the 'Bird in the Hand Fallacy'," *Bell Journal of Economics,* (Spring), pp. 259-270.

Black, F., and M. Scholes, "The Effect of Dividend Yield Policy on Common Stock Prices and Returns," *Journal of Financial Economics,* (May 1974), pp. 1-22.

Bowen, R, "Valuation or Earnings Components in the Electric Utility Industry," *The Accounting Review,* (January 1981), pp. 1-22.

Bower, D., and R. Bower, "Test of a Stock Valuation Model," *Journal of Finance,* (May 1970) pp. 483-492.

Bower, R., and D. Bower, "Risk and the Valuation of Common Stocks," *Journal of Political Economy*, (May-June 1969), pp. 349-362.

Brown, S., and J. Warner, "Measuring Security Price Performance", *Journal of Finance* (September 1980), pp. 205-258.

Christie, A., "On Cross-Sectional Analysis in Accounting Research", Working paper, University of Southern California, (1984).

Daley, L., "The Valuation of Reported Pension Measures for Firms Sponsoring Defined Benefit Plans", *The Accounting Review*, (April 1984), pp. 177-198.

Dukes, R., "An Investigation of the Effects of Expensing Research and Development Costs on Security Prices", *Proceedings of the Conference on Topical Research In Accounting*, (M. Schiff and G. Sorter (Eds.), New York University, (1974).

Easton, P., "Accounting Earnings and Security Valuation: Empirical Evidence of the Fundamental Links", *Journal of Accounting Research*, (Supplement 1985) pp. 54-77.

Fama, E., "Stock Returns, Real Activity, Inflation and Money", *American Economic Review*, (September 1981), pp. 545-565.

Feldstein, M., "Inflation, Tax Rules and the Stock Market", *Journal of Monetary Economics*, (1980a), pp. 309-331.

Feldstein, M., "Inflation and the Stock Market", *American Economic Review*, (December 1980b), pp. 839-847.

Feldstein, M., and R. Morck, "Pension Funds and the Value of Equities", *Financial Analysts' Journal* (September–October 1983), pp. 29-39.

Feldstein, M., and S. Seligman, "Pension Funding, Share Prices and National Savings", *Journal of Finance*, (September 1981), pp. 801-824.

Foster, G., "Valuation Parameters of Property-Liability Companies", *Journal of Finance*, (June 1977), pp. 823-836.

Friend, I., and M. Pucket, "Dividends and Stock Prices", *American Economic Review*, (September 1964), pp. 656-682.

Garman, M., "A Synthesis of the Pure Theory of Arbitrage", Working Paper, University of California, Berkeley, (1978).

Garman, M., and J. Ohlson, "Information and the Sequential Valuation of Assets in Arbitrage-Free Economics", *Journal of Accounting Research*, Vol. 18 (Autumn 1980), pp. 420-440.

Gonedes, N., "Corporate Signaling, External Accounting and Capital Market Equilibrium: Evidence on Dividends, Income, and Extraordinary Items", *Journal of Accounting Research*, (Spring 1978), pp. 26-79.

Gonedes, N., and N. Dopuch, "Capital Market Equilibrium, Information Production, and Selecting Accounting Techniques: Theoretical Framework and Review of Empirical Work", *Journal ofAccounting Research*, (Supplement 1974), pp. 48-129.

Gordon, M., (1962), *The Investment, Financing, and Valuation of the Corporation* (Homewood, Ill.: Richard D. Irwin).

Gordon, M., and E. Shapiro, "Capital Equipment Analysis: The Required Rate of Profit", *Management Science*, (October 1956), pp. 102-110.

Grossman, S., and R. Shiller, "The Determinants of the Variability of Stock Market Prices", *American Economic Review*, (May 1981), pp. 222-227.

Kuh, E., and J. Meyer, "Correlation and Regression Estimates when the Data are Ratios", *Econometrica*, (1955), pp. 400-416.

Laub, P., "On the Informational Content of Dividends", *Journal of Business*, (January 1976), pp. 73-80.

Leland, H.. and D. Pyle, "Informational Asymmetries, Financial Structure and Financial Intermediation", *Journal of Finance*, (May 1977), pp. 371-387.

Lev, B., and J. Ohlson, "Market-Based Empirical Research in Accounting: A Review, Interpretation, and Extension", *Journal of Accounting Research*, (Supplement 1982), pp. 249-322.

Lewellen, W., K. Stanley, and G. Schlarbaum (1978), "Some Direct Evidence on the Dividend Clientele Phenomenon", *Journal of Finance*, Vol. 33 (December).

Lintner, J., "Distribution of Income Among Dividends, Retained Earnings and Taxes", *American Economic Review*, (May 1956), pp. 97-113.

Lintner, J., "Security Prices, Risk, and Maximal Gains from Diversification", *Journal of Finance*, (December 1965) pp. 587-616.

Litzenberger, R., and C. Rao, "Estimates of the Marginal Rate of Time Preference and Average Risk Aversion of Investors in Electric Utility Shares", *Bell Journal of Economics and Management Science*, (Spring 1971), pp. 265-277.

Malkiel, B., "Equity Yields, Growth, and the Structure of Share Prices", *American Economic Review*, (December 1963), pp. 1004-1031.

Malkiel, B., "The Valuation of Equity Securities", *The Bell Journal of Economics and Management Science* (Spring 1980), pp. 143-160.

Miller, M., and F. Modigliani, "Dividend Policy, Growth and the Valuation of Shares", *Journal of Business*, (October 1961), pp. 411-433.

Miller, M., "Some Estimates of the Cost of Capital to the Electric Utility Industry 1954-1957", *American Economic Review*, (June 1966), pp. 333-391.

Modigliani, F. and R. Cohn, "Inflation, Rational Valuation and the Market", *Financial Analysts' Journal* (March-April 1979), pp. 24-44.

Modigliani, F., and M. Miller, "The Cost of Capital, Corporation Finance and the Theory of Investment", *American Economic Review*, (June 1958), pp. 261-297.

Modigliani, F., "Corporate Income Taxes and the Cost of Capital: A Correction", *American Economic Review*, (June, 1963), pp. 433-443.

Modigliani, F., "The Cost of Capital, Corporation Finance and the Theory of Investment: Reply", *American Economic Review*, (June 1965), pp. 524-527.

Mossin, J., "Equilibrium in a Capital Asset Market", *Econometrica* (October 1966) pp. 768-783.

Ohlson, J., "Price-Earnings Ratios and Earnings Capitalization under Uncertainty", *Journal of Accounting Research*, (Spring 1983), pp. 141-154.

Oldfield, G. S., "Financial Aspects of the Private Pension System", *Journal of Money, Credit and Banking*, (1976), pp. 48-54.

Patell, J. M., "Corporate Forecasts of Earnings per Share and Stock Price Behavior: Empirical Tests", *Journal of Accounting Research* (Autumn 1976), pp. 246-276.

Pearson, K., "On a Form of Spurious Correlation Which May Arise When Indices are used in the Measurement of Organs", *Proceedings of the Royal Society of London*, (1897).

Penman, S., "The Predictive Content of Earnings Forecasts and Dividends", *Journal of Finance* (September 1983), pp. 1181-1199.

Rosenberg, B., and V. Marathe, "The Prediction of Investment Risk: Systematic and Residual Risk", *Proceedings of the Seminar for Research in Security Prices*, University of Chicago, (1975).

Rosenberg, B., "Common Factors in Security Returns: Microeconomic Determinants and Macroeconomic Correlates," *Proceedings of the Seminar for Research in Security Prices*, University of Chicago, (1976).

Rubinstein, M., "The Valuation of Uncertain Streams and the Pricing of Options", *Bell Journal of Economics and Management Science*, (Autumn 1976), pp. 407-425.

Sharp, W., "Capital Asset Prices: A Theory of Market Equilibrium Under Conditions of Risk", *Journal of Finance*, (September 1964), pp. 425-442.

Shiller, R., "The Use of Volatility Measures in Assessing Market Efficiency", *Journal of Finance*, (May 1981a), pp. 291-304.

Shiller, R., "Do Stock Prices Move too Much to be Justified by Subsequent Changes in Dividends?", *American Economics Review*, (June 1981b).

Spence, A., "Job Market Signaling", *Quarterly Journal of Economics*, (August 1973), pp. 355-374.

Spence, A., "Competitive and Optimal Response to Signals: Analysis of Efficiency and Distribution", *Journal of Economic Theory*, (March 1974), pp. 296-332.

Tobin, J., "Money, Capital and Other Stores of Value", *American Economic Review*, (May 1961), pp. 26-37.

Tse, S., "Security Valuation, Accounting Information and the Usefulness of Segment Information", Ph.D. dissertation, University of California, Berkeley, (1983).

White, H., "A Heteroskedasticity-Consistent Matrix Estimator and a Direct Test for Heteroskedasticity", *Econometrica*, (May 1980), pp. 817-838.

Williams, J., *The Theory of Investment and Value* (Cambridge: Harvard University Press), (1938).

Contemporary Accounting Research Vol 6. No. 2–II, 1990, pp. 648—676, reprinted with permission.

A Synthesis of Security Valuation Theory and the Role of Dividends, Cash Flows, and Earnings*

James A. Ohlson

* The author has benefitted from comments of the participants of workshops at the University of Chicago and Washington University (St. Louis). Special thanks are due the reviewer of this paper, Jerry Feltham, and Trevor Harris, Russ Lundholm, Shashi Murthi, and Steve Ryan.

Introduction and Summary

Accounting research frequently views accounting data as relevant in security valuation. This information perspective motivates the empirical studies that investigate the relation between security prices and accounting variables. In spite of the considerable success of this research, much of it is confined because the hypotheses investigated do not relate to any theoretical constructs.

The absence of theory use in empirical research impinges on its future developments, and progress will probably require more sharply delineated hypotheses than typically has been the case. A number of recent papers—notably Beaver, Lambert, and Morse [1980]; Beaver, Lambert, and Ryan [1987]; Collins, Kothari, and Rayburn [1987]; Collins and Kothari [1988]; Daley [1984]; Easton [1985]; Easton and Zmijewski [1987]; Kormendi and Lipe [1987]; Lipe [1985]; and Ryan [1986]—recognize the limits to "brute empiricism", and they consider formal security valuation models prior to the empirical hypotheses. However, this research taken in its totality leaves a disjoint and ad hoc impression regarding the underlying theoretical constructs. Some papers embed the analysis in the Litzenberger and Rao [1971] valuation model, and the capital asset pricing model (CAPM), while others do not. Another source of confusion arises because the security valuation models make reference to at least three different capitalization (discounting) attributes: cash flows, earnings, and dividends. Moreover, the precise capitalization formula used to discount a given attribute is by no means standardized. The cited papers neither reconcile the variety of valuation models nor explain the extent to which they derive from different assumptions about the economy. Yet another problem stems from notions that complete markets somehow make a difference.

To clarify the issues raised by the lack of theoretical unity, this paper reviews and synthesizes the theory of security valuation for multiple-date settings with uncertainty. The key concepts presented constitute an integral, well-accepted, part of modern financial economics. I believe that only by extending these concepts to explicitly model the behavior of information variables can one expect to extract theoretically sound and rich implications concerning an information perspective on accounting.

The focal point of the discussion concerns the most complex aspect of security valuation, namely, intertemporal valuation consistency. A multiple-date setting requires that sequences of information realizations map into sequences of endogenous security prices, and yet the derived expected returns must reflect the underlying market risk. This instrinsically dynamic analysis cannot place ad hoc or tautological restrictions on the factors that determine security returns. Following the development of an appropriate model framework one can derive (1) valid capitalization (discounting) concepts as they relate to security price; (2) the relation between current security price and current information (such as earnings); (3) the relation between current security price and expectations of future information realizations; and (4) the relevance of, respectively, cash flows, dividends, and earnings in security valuation.

The major results can be summarized as follows.

1. The central theoretical insight derives from a powerful condition of no arbitrage (within perfect markets). This weak equilibrium requirement on the security prices leads to the existence of implicit (consumption) prices that ultimately determine the value of an uncertain dividend stream. Complete markets are redundant in this analysis, and, more generally, such an assumption provides no additional results.
2. As a corollary of point 1, only (anticipated) dividends can serve as a generically valid capitalization (present value) attribute of a security.
3. The theory results in a formula that determines security value as a function of expected dividends adjusted for their risk and discounted by the term-structure of risk-free rates. The notion of risk is general yet meaningfully identified. Models such as the CAPM occur only as special cases. The same can be said for the formula that capitalizes expected future dividends using compounded expected future security returns as discount factors.
4. The notion that one can capitalize some measure of anticipated cash flows (rather than dividends) holds only under extremely restrictive assumptions, and dividend policy irrelevance (i.e., conditions for "MM") is necessary but not sufficient. Moreover, the cash flow measures capitalized are in general ex-post unobservable.
5. Existing theory of "pure" earnings under uncertainty lacks consistency regarding its meaning and characteristics. Three distinct approaches can be identified, and two of these are arguably conceptually deficient. (1) Earnings used as a capitalization attribute i.e., the (discounted) present value of future (risk-adjusted) expected earnings leads to the same value as capitalized dividends. This valuation scheme applies in special cases, but the conditions required are stringent and seemingly devoid of economic content. These models do not make a clear economic distinction between earnings and dividends. (2) A more promising idea views pure earnings as an information variable that suffices to determine a security's payoff, price *plus* dividends. This earnings concept leaves the dividend policy unrestricted, and it does not directly depend on notions of earnings capitalization. (The two pure earnings concepts (1) and (2) are mutually exclusive in some settings.) (3) Earnings as an information variable that suffices to determine a security's value, price, *exclusive* of dividends. This concept is deficient because it contradicts basic notions of dividend policy

irrelevance, and the implications become unacceptable in the certainty case. In sum, only concept (2)—which is due to Ryan [1986]—satisfies properties that make good economic sense.

The paper develops the necessary theoretical constructs from scratch. The next section considers security valuation within a simple two-date economy. The analysis of this setting identifies the central concept of no arbitrage and the existence of implicit (consumption) prices. The third section extends the model to multiple dates, and it develops Rubinstein's [1976b] fundamental result of how to capitalize anticipated dividends.[1] The fourth section considers simplified versions of the dividend capitalization formula and the fifth section reviews linear Markovian models, showing how security prices depend on realizations of information variables. The examples presented illustrate the workings of intertemporal valuation consistency requirements. The sixth section analyzes the validity of cash flow (present value) capitalization. The subsequent section relies on the linear Markovian models to discuss the role of "pure" earnings concepts in valuation theory. The final section briefly remarks on the use of theory in empirical research.

Security valuation within a two-date economy

To develop the theoretical underpinnings for security valuation, a simple two-date economy provides a useful point of departure. An economy that ceases to exist after one period clearly eliminates the need to determine future prices, and each security's (dollar) payoff equals its terminal dividend payment. Multiperiod settings, on the other hand, require more complex analyses because a security's payoff equals the dividend plus the security price at the next trading date. The theory must determine prices for a sequence of dates rather than just one date, and this dynamic feature raises intertemporal equilibrium issues. Thus, to keep matters simple, this section considers valuation at one date whereas the next section extends the analysis to multiple dates.

For the two-date economy, assume that the uncertainty consists of a finite number of states, $s=1, \ldots, S$. Each security, $j, j = 1, \ldots, J$ pays a dividend of d_{js} in state s, and $d_j \equiv (d_{j1}, \ldots, d_{jS})$ defines the row vector of dividends across states for security j. The $J \times S$ matrix

$$D \equiv [\, d_{js} \,] \equiv \begin{bmatrix} d_1 \\ \cdot \\ \cdot \\ \cdot \\ d_J \end{bmatrix}$$

summarizes the dividends over securities (rows) and states (columns).

The analysis leaves D unrestricted, except that $d_J = (1, \ldots, 1)$. In other words, the investment opportunity set includes a risk-free security ($j = J$).

The current price of security j is denoted by P_j, so that in a two-date economy the return (one plus rate-of-return) on security j in state s is defined by $r_{js} \equiv d_{js}/P_j$. The price P_j values a claim on the dividend pattern d_j, and it excludes any dividend paid at the initial date. For $j = J$, P_J

equals the cost of a unit certain payoff; hence, $P_J^{-1} \equiv R_F$ is the risk-free return. Let $P \equiv (P_1, \ldots, P_J)$ denote the column vector of prices.

The most basic issue in the theory of valuation addresses the following question.

Q1: What is the relation between the vector P and the matrix D? That is, given some configuration of dividends across securities and states, can we say something about the price vector?

Because this question relies on few ingredients, more interesting results could possibly obtain if one also postulates the existence of probabilities (i.e., "beliefs") over the states. Let $\Pi_s > 0$, $\Sigma_S \Pi_s = 1$, $s = 1, \ldots, S$, denote the exogenous state probablitities. Given these probabilities, one poses a slightly different version of question Q1 by focusing on the collection of random variables $\{ \tilde{d}_j \}_j$.

Q2: Given some probability distribution for $\{ \tilde{d}_j \}_j$, what can be said about the price vector P?

Question Q2 does not deal directly with the concepts of risk and return, which are central in the modern theory of finance. This parametric perspective suggests that one should be able to determine a security's price in terms of three variables: (1) the expected payoff (i.e., $E[\tilde{d}_j]$), (2) the risk-free rate (R_F), and (3) a variable that relates to a security's risk. Hence, one can raise a third question.

Q3: If $P_j = f(R_F, E[\tilde{d}_j], risk_j)$, then what can be said about the function $f(.,.,.)$, and about the nature of security risk, i.e., "$risk_j$"?

The anaylsis next proceeds to answer questions Q1–Q3. The key economic concept used powerfully restricts the investment opportunities: P and D jointly must satisfy a *no arbitrage* (NA) condition. It goes almost without saying that an equilibrium cannot exist unless the economy excludes (pure) arbitrage opportunities. To develop the concept of NA, let the row vector $\lambda \equiv (\lambda_1, \ldots, \lambda_J)$ denote a portfolio with λ_j units of shares invested in security j. For $\lambda_j > 0$ the position is long, and $\lambda_j < 0$ represents a short position. Markets are assumed perfect, i.e., the model disregards transaction costs, including such real world phenomena as taxes and margin requirements for short positions. The cost of any portfolio λ therefore equals $\lambda \cdot P$. The payoff of a portfolio λ in state s equals $\Sigma_j \lambda_j d_{js}$; thus, to summarize the row payoff vector across states, write $\Sigma_j \lambda_j d_j$ or λD.

The definition of no arbitrage simply means that one cannot get "something for nothing." Formally, define NA as follows.

Definition (No arbitrage)

There exists no portfolio λ such that $\Sigma_j \lambda_j d_j \geq 0$, *all s*, $\Sigma_j \lambda_j d_j \leq 0$, and where at least one of the $S+1$ inequalities is strict.

It should be emphasized that NA makes no reference to probabilities; if NA applies for a vector $\Pi' > 0$, then it applies no less for any other vector $\Pi'' > 0$. NA is not a subjective matter given that the model unambiguously supplies the set of *possible* states.

The NA condition permits a direct link between P and D.

Lemma 1 (Steimke's Theorem; see Mangasarian [1969, p. 32]. There exists a positive vector $R \equiv (R_1, \ldots, R_s, \ldots, R_S) > 0$ such that

$$P_j = \sum_s d_{js} R_s, \quad \text{all } j,$$

if, and only if, NA holds.

Lemma 1 answers question Q1: given NA, one values a dividend pattern d_j by multiplying d_{js} with R_s and then adding up over the S states. More generally, the R vector values any portfolio's payoff pattern because the value of $\Sigma_j \lambda_j d_j$ equals

$$\sum_s \left(\sum_j \lambda_j d_{js}\right) \cdot R_s = \sum_j \lambda_j (d_j \cdot R) = \sum_j \lambda_j P_j.$$

The economics and finance literature generally refers to R as implicit (consumption) prices, state-contingent prices, or support prices. Thus, R_s is the implicit price of a claim to one unit of dividends (consumption) in states s. A unique R obtains if, and only if, markets are complete (i.e., the collection of vectors $\{d_j\}_j$ generates an S-dimensional space). (The result follows from basic linear algebra.) The potential nonuniqueness property of R introduces no problems. Moreover, the dichotomy between complete versus incomplete markets does not influence the substantive conclusions in the theory of valuation, a point which will become apparent later.

In contrast to any discussion of question Q1, to deal with questions Q2 and Q3 the probability vector Π comes into play. Its role is surprisingly modest, and the straightforward manipulations that follow may at first glance appear odd because these introduce Π through the "backdoor". The procedure and related analytical simplicity will highlight the essential equivalence between the "random variable perspective" on dividends and the apparently more primitive "mapping from states to payoffs perspective".

Define

$$Q_s \equiv R_F R_s / \Pi_s.$$

The random variable $\tilde{Q}$ satisfies $\tilde{Q} > 0$ with probability one. Further, $E[\tilde{Q}] = 1$ since $\Sigma R_s = \Sigma R_s d_{js} = P_j = R_F^{-1}$. (Recall that $d_j = (1, \ldots, 1)$). One can interpret Q_s as a state s consumption price normalized by the uncertainty of the state and the discount factor.

Using Lemma 1 it follows that

$$P_j = \sum_s d_{js} R_s = \sum_s d_{js} Q_s R_F^{-1} E[\tilde{d}_j \tilde{Q}],$$

and, since $\text{cov}[\tilde{d}_j, \tilde{Q}] = E[\tilde{d}_j \tilde{Q}] - E[\tilde{d}_j]E[\tilde{Q}] = E[\tilde{d}_j \tilde{Q}] - E[\tilde{d}_j]$,

$$P_j = R_F^{-1} \{E[\tilde{d}_j] + \text{cov}[\tilde{d}_j, \tilde{Q}]\}, \quad \text{all } j = 1, \ldots, J.$$

The last expression answers question Q2 in the following sense: Assuming NA, there always exists a random variable $\tilde{Q}, \tilde{Q} > 0$ and $E[\tilde{Q}] = 1$, such that $-\text{cov}[\tilde{d}_j, \tilde{Q}]$ naturally indicates a security's risk. The general valuation formula also partially answers Q3, because the formula bears on the structure of the function $P_j = f(R_F, E[\tilde{d}_j], \text{risk}_j)$. Even so, compared with Q1 and its answer, the above analysis merely replaces the valuation operator R with the random variable $\tilde{Q}$. In other words, given some R_F and Π, one infers Q_s from R_s, and conversely. And similar to R, $\tilde{Q}$ is unspecified aside from its existence and basic properties ($\tilde{Q} > 0$, $E[\tilde{Q}] = 1$).

Sharper insights regarding the determinants of value require that more be said about $\tilde{Q}$ (or R). The CAPM serves as a pertinent illustration. This equilibrium model specifies $f(R_F, E[\tilde{d}_j], \text{risk}_j)$ as

$$P_j = R_F^{-1}\{E[\tilde{d}_j] - K\,\text{cov}[\tilde{d}_j, \tilde{d}_m]\}, \quad \text{all } j,$$

where $K > 0$ is some constant independent of j, and $\tilde{d}_m \equiv \Sigma_j \tilde{d}_j$ denotes the aggregate dividend.[2] (Without loss of generality, assume unit supply for each security.) Hence to identify the CAPM within the more general framework, one puts $Q_s = K_1 + K_2 d_{ms}$, where $1 = K_1 + K_2 E[\tilde{d}_m]$ and $K_2 = -K < 0$. The CAPM is therefore based on assumpions that the uncertainty normalized consumption price, Q_s, is a linear function in the aggregate dividend, d_{ms}.

The CAPM yields a statement about Q because the model effectively assumes an economy in which a "representative individual" with quadratic utility determines the prices.[3] The idea of a representative individual permits generalization. Specifically, represent the preferences of this individual by

$$\rho U(c) + E\left[U\left(\sum_j \lambda_j \tilde{d}_j\right)\right],$$

where c denotes current consumption, $\Sigma_j \lambda_j \tilde{d}_j$ is future (uncertain) consumption given portfolio λ, $U(\cdot)$ denotes the utility function, and ρ is a patience parameter. As is standard in finance theory, $U(\cdot)$ is monotonically increasing and differentiable i.e., $\partial U(x)/\partial x \equiv u(x) > 0$.

Maximizing the preference function with respect to c, λ and simplifying the related optimality conditions one obtains[4]

$$P_j = E\left[\tilde{d}_j u\left(\sum_j \lambda_j \tilde{d}_j\right)\right] / \rho u(c), \quad j = 1, \ldots, J.$$

Further, since $P_j = E[u(\sum_j \lambda_j \tilde{d}_j)]/\rho u(c) = R_F^{-1}$ one derives that

$$P_j = R_F^{-1}\, E\left[\tilde{d}_j\left(\sum_j \lambda_j \tilde{d}_j\right)\right] / E\left[u\left(\sum_j \lambda_j \tilde{d}_j\right)\right].$$

Note next that aggregate supplies of shares equal the equilibrium holdings, $\lambda^* = (1, \ldots, 1)$. One thus obtains

$$P_j = R_F^{-1}\, E[\tilde{d}_j\{u(\tilde{d}_m)/E[u(\tilde{d}_m)]\}].$$

The last expression clearly resembles $P_j = R_F^{-1}\, E[\tilde{d}_j \tilde{Q}]$. More precisely, one can put

$$\tilde{Q} = u(\tilde{d}_m)/E[u(\tilde{d}_m)],$$

and it follows immediately that $\tilde{Q}$ satisfies its two basic properties: $\tilde{Q} > 0$, since $u(\cdot) > 0$, and $E[\tilde{Q}] = 1$. The variable $\tilde{Q}$ relates directly to the preferences of the representative individual and the payoff of the market portfolio.

CAPM, as usual, illustrates the concepts. Suppose that $U(x) = -\frac{1}{2}(\theta - x)^2$, so that $u(x) = \theta - x$, where θ denotes the representative individual's risk-aversion parameter. In this case, $u(\tilde{d}_m)/E[u(\tilde{d}_m)] = (\theta - \tilde{d}_m)/(\theta - E[\tilde{d}_m]) = K_1 + K_2\tilde{d}_m$ where $K_1 \equiv \theta/(\theta - E[\tilde{d}_m])$ and $-K_2 \equiv 1/(\theta - E[\tilde{d}_m])$.

Question Q3 has now been answered: The notion of security risk is logically captured by $-\text{cov}[\tilde{d}_j, u(\tilde{d}_m)/E[u(\tilde{d}_m)]]$.[5] The analysis therefore identifies risk as a concept the precise determination of which depends on the preferences and aggregate dividends in the economy. Although this concept of risk is easy to interpret, it does not suggest that one *must* identify $\tilde{Q}$ as $u(\tilde{d}_m)/E[u(\tilde{d}_m)]$. If markets are incomplete, one can find other Q that lead to the same measure of risk. But this possibility is of no economic signficance and one might as well put $\tilde{Q}$ equal to $u(\tilde{d}_m)/E[u(\tilde{d}_m)]$, which is necessary in the complete markets case. Alternatively, because the space spanned by the vectors $\{d_j\}_j$ is irrelevant in the derivations, an assumption of complete markets—including a complete set of Arrow-Debreu securities—entails no loss of generality.

Security valuation within a multiple-date economy

The simple two-date model generalizes to handle multiple dates with surprising ease. The flow of ideas and concepts—the use of NA in particular—parallels those of the previous section. The major new difficulty relates to the development of a framework that resolves uncertainty with the passage of time. Such model underpinnings are necessary because the resulting theory must determine the structure of security values at all dates and under all circumstances. As will be seen, information about securities takes on a concrete role in a multiple dates setting. This model enrichment occurs because the passage of time is conceptually and mathematically equivalent to changes in the environment as described by the available information.[6]

To generalize the two-date theory, let z_t denote the available information at date t. Thus, the economy's uncertainty is resolved by observing z_t. The information, or "environmental description", is generic, so that z_t in its most general form defines a set, i.e., an "event". A sequence of realizations $z_1, \ldots, z_t$ generates a history of the economy from its inception at date 1 through t. Without loss of generality, z_t can be defined as a subset of some z_τ when $t > \tau$. However, to maintain this subset relationship becomes notationally burdensome in parsimonious Markovian settings, and in such cases one usefully thinks of z_t as excluding those aspects of the environment that do not affect the valuation of securities.

Because the state description includes all relevant aspects of the environment, there exists j exogenous functions $d_{jt} = d_j(z_t)$ determining the dividends for each security j at date t given event z_t. Hence, one can view the dividends as either part of the event description, or equivalently as a function of the event description.

Functions $P_{jt} = P_j(z_t)$ determining the security prices must also exist because the security prices depend on the available information (event description). Unlike the dividends' functions, however, these price functions are endogenous and depend on all facets affecting the equilibrium. We will refer to $P_j(z_t)$ as the *valuation function* of security j.

The NA two-date analysis can now be applied without difficulty for a sequence of dates. A security's payoff given the event description z_t equals $P_j(z_t) + d_j(z_t)$. Ruling out arbitrage between two adjacent dates, t, $t+1$, Lemma 1 implies that

$$P_j(z_t) + \sum_{z_{t+1}} R(z_{t+1}\,;\, z_t)\,[P_j(z_{t+1}) + d_j(z_{t+1})\,],$$

for some positive implicit prices $R(z_{t+1}\,;\, z_t) + d_j(z_t)$, all z_{t+1}, z_t. The notation $\Sigma_{z_{t+1}}$ should be read as the sum over all conceivable z_{t+1} given z_t. Note that R depends on z_t as well as z_{t+1}, thereby conforming with the requirement that P_{jt} must be a function of z_t. Also,

$\Sigma_{z_{t+1}} R(z_{t+1}\,;z_t) = R_F\,(t+1\,;z_t)^{-1}$,
i.e., the sum defines the inverse of the risk-free rate over t, $t+1$ given z_t.

The valuation function appears on both sides in the last expression. By substituting recursively, one derives the cumbersome expression

$$P_j(z_t) = \sum_{z_{t+1}} R(z_{t+1}\,;z_t) \left\{ \sum_{z_{t+2}} R\,(z_{t+2}\,;z_{t+1})\,[P_j(z_{t+2}) + d_j(z_{t+2})\,] + d_j(z_{t+1}) \right\}$$

$$= \sum_{z_{t+1}} R(z_{t+1}\,;z_t)\,d_j(z_{t+1}) + \sum_{z_{t+2}} R\,(z_{t+2}\,;z_t)\,[P_j(z_{t+2}) + d_j(z_{t+2})\,]$$

where

$$R(z_{t+2}\,;z_t) \equiv \sum_{z_{t+1}} R\,(z_{t+2}\,;z_{t+1})\,R(z_{t+1}\,;z_t).$$

Continuing with this recursive substitution for $P_j(z_{t+2})$, $P_j(z_{t+3})$, ... implies more generally that

$$P_j(z_t) = \sum_{\tau=t+1}^{\infty} \sum_{z_\tau} R(z_\tau\,;z_t)\,d_j(z_\tau)\,, \qquad (1)$$

where

$$R\,(z_{t+\tau}\,;z_t) \equiv \sum_{z_{t+\tau-1}} R\,(z_{t+\tau}\,;z_{t+\tau-1})\,R(z_{t+\tau-1}\,;z_t).$$

The derivations clearly generalize the two-date model: depending on the current event description, the implicit prices $R\,(z_\tau\,;z_t)$, $\tau > t$, value any anticipated stream of dividends (consumption) over future dates and across conceivable event descriptions. For example, from the implicit prices one infers the term-structure of interest rates; $R_F\,(\tau\,;z_t)^{-1} \equiv \Sigma_{z_t} R(z_\tau\,;z_t)$ equals the cost of a certain (unconditional) unit payoff (consumption) at date τ given the current event description z_t.

From the development of the two-date model, it should be apparent how one deals with probabilities in the multiple-date setting. Let $\Pi(z_\tau \mid z_t) > 0$ denote the conditional probability of date τ event description z_τ given the current event description z_t, $\tau > t$. (The laws of probability apply in the usual fashion, and $\Pi(z_\tau \mid z_{t-1}) = \Sigma_{z_t} \Pi(z_\tau \mid z_t)\,\Pi(z_t \mid z_{t-1})$; recall that z_t is a subset of z_{t-1} or, more generally, provides a sufficient description of the environment at date t.)

Define

$$Q(z_\tau\,;z_t) \equiv R\,(z_\tau\,;z_t) \Big/ \left[\sum_{z_\tau} R\,(z_\tau\,;z_t) \right] \Pi(z_\tau \mid z_t)$$

$$= R\,(z_\tau\,;z_t) R_F\,(\tau\,;z_t) \,/\, \Pi(z_\tau \mid z_t)\,.$$

Given z_t and $\Pi(z_\tau \mid z_t)$, the above definition induces a conditional probability distribution for the random variables $\tilde{Q}_{t+1}\,(z_t)$, $\tilde{Q}_{t+2}\,(z_t)$, ..., $\tilde{Q}_\tau\,(z_t)$, ..., $\tau > t$, such that $\tilde{Q}_\tau\,(z_t) > 0$ with probability one for each z_t, and

$E[\tilde{Q}_\tau\,(z_t) \mid z_t] = 1$, all $\tau > t$, and z_t.

To simplify the notation, we suppress z_t in $Q_\tau\,(z_t)$ when the probability measure is conditioned on z_t; thus,

$E[\tilde{Q}_\tau(z_t) \mid z_t] = E[\tilde{Q}_\tau \mid z_t] \, (= 1)$.

Straightforward manipulations of expression (1)—which extend the two-date model in an obvious fashion—now yield the expression that determines the value of a security in terms of the probability distribution of future dividends given the current event description z_t:

$$P_j(z_t) = \sum_{\tau=t+1}^{\infty} R_F(\tau\,;z_t)^{-1}\left\{E[\tilde{d}_{j\tau} \mid z_t] + \text{cov}[\tilde{d}_{j\tau}, \tilde{Q}_\tau \mid z_t]\right\}.$$

The formula shows that one discounts the future expected dividends using the term-structure of risk-free rates only after first having deducted the risk-measures $\text{cov}[d_{jt+1}, -\tilde{Q}_{t+1} \mid z_t]$, $\text{cov}[d_{jt+2}, -\tilde{Q}_{t+2} \mid z_t]$, ... from the expected dividends as of related dates. Hence, in the *general* theory, the dividends capitalization formula deals with risk by adjustments in the numerators, and not in the denominators as is frequently done in the literature.

Next, suppose that the economy consists of a "representative" individual whose preferences are given by

$$U^t(c_t) + E[U^{t+1}(\tilde{c}_{t+1}) \mid z_t] + E[U^{t+2}(\tilde{c}_{t+2}) \mid z_t] + \ldots$$

where c_t denotes consumption at date t. In equilibrium the individual holds the market portfolio: $\Sigma_j d_j(z_t) = c_t = d_{mt} = d_m(z_t)$. From the first order optimality conditions and some routine manipulations it follows that one can always put

$$Q(z_\tau\,;z_t) = u^\tau(d_m(z_\tau)) \,/\, E[u^\tau(\tilde{d}_{mt}) \mid z_t],$$

where $u^t(\cdot) \equiv \partial U^t(c_t)/\partial c_t$.

In summary, the following proposition answers questions Q1, Q2, and Q3 in a multiple-date setting.

Proposition I (Rubinstein [1976b]): Consider an economy that excludes arbitrage (within perfect markets). Let z_t denote the event description, or available information, at date t.

1. Then there exist functions $R(z_\tau\,;z_t) > 0$, $\tau > t$, such that the value of each security j given the information z_t can be expressed as

$$P_j(z_t) = \sum_{\tau=t+1}^{\infty} \sum_{z_\tau} R(z_\tau\,;z_t)\, d_j(z_\tau).$$

2. Given the information evolution conditional probabilities $\Pi(z_\tau \mid z_t)$ there exist positive random variables $Q(z_\tau\,;z_t)$ satisfying $E[\tilde{Q}_\tau \mid z_t] = 1$, all $\tau > t$, such that

$$P_j(z_t) = \sum_{\tau=t+1}^{\infty} R_F(\tau\,;z_t)^{-1}\left\{E[\tilde{d}_{j\tau} \mid z_t] + cov[\tilde{d}_{j\tau}, \tilde{Q}_\tau \mid z_t]\right\},$$

where $R_F(\tau\,;z_t)$ denotes the risk-free rate over an $\tau - t$ date(s) interval.

3. Given the preferences

$$U^t(c_t) + \sum_{\tau=t+1}^{\infty} E[U^\tau(\tilde{c}_\tau) \mid z_t],$$

of a representative individual who determines the equilibrium prices one can put
$Q(z_\tau\,;z_t) = u^\tau(d_m(z_\tau))/E[u^\tau(\tilde{d}_{mt}) \mid z_t]$,
where $\partial U^t(c_t)/\partial c_t \equiv u^t(\cdot) > 0$, and $d_{mt} = d_m(z_t) = \Sigma_j d_j(z_t)$, denotes aggregate (random) dividends.

Possible simplifications of the dividends capitalization formula

In the literature one frequently encounters valuation formulae that use (compounded) expected returns as discount factors rather than the risk-free rates, and they leave out any risk adjustment in the numerator (e.g., Christie [1987]; Collins and Kothari [1988]). These approaches to valuation seem to be motivated by the idea that expected returns must reflect risk, and because the discounting by expected returns incorporates the risk factor, a numerator adjustment such as that in Proposition I, part 2, is unnecessary. Specifically, one may consider the relevance of the formula

$$P_j(z_t) = \sum_{\tau_2 = t+1}^{\infty} \left[\prod_{\tau_1=1}^{\tau_2 - t} E[\tilde{r}_{jt+\tau_1} \mid z_t] \right] E^{-1} [\tilde{d}_{j\tau_2} \mid z_t],$$

where $r_{jt} \equiv (P_j(z_t) + d_j(z_t))/P_j(z_{t-1})$ denotes the return on security j over the date interval from t-1 to t. However, this scheme is valid only under restrictive assumptions (see below), and it should not be accorded any theoretical standing. One can construct reasonable (albeit tedious) examples violating the above relationship.[7] (These examples also show that interchanging Π and E in the formula still leaves it invalid.)

To salvage the above approach to valuation, one generally needs to assume constant expected returns, i.e., $E[\tilde{r}_{jt+1} \mid z_t] = \mu_j$, independently of z_t for all t. Conversely, if the value of a security equals expected dividends discounted by some fixed parameter, the parameter equals the expected return.

Proposition II (Samuelson [1965]): The following two statements are equivalent:

A. $E[\tilde{r}_{jt+1} \mid z_t] = \mu_j$ independently of z_t for all t; and

B. $P_j(z_t) = \sum_{\tau=t+1}^{\infty} \mu_j^{t-\tau} E[\tilde{d}_{j\tau} \mid z_t].$

The hypothesis of z_t-independent expected returns is difficult to obtain in theoretical analyses unless one also restricts the term structure of interest rates to be "flat" and nonstochastic, i.e., $R_F(\tau; z_t) = R_F^{\tau-t}$ independently of z_t. In this case, $\mu_j - R_F = \text{cov}[\tilde{r}_{jt+1}, -\tilde{Q}_{t+1} \mid z_t] \equiv \sigma_j$ equals security risk. The result follows from the analysis in the previous section since

$$P_j(z_t) = R_F^{-1} \left\{ E[P_j(\tilde{z}_{t+1}) + d_j(\tilde{z}_{t+1}) \mid z_t] + \text{cov}[P_j(\tilde{z}_{t+1}) + d_j(\tilde{z}_{t+1}), \tilde{Q}_{t+1} \mid z_t] \right\}$$

which futher simplifies to

$$1 = R_F^{-1} \left\{ E[\tilde{r}_{jt+1} \mid z_t] + \text{cov}[\tilde{r}_{jt+1}, \tilde{Q}_{t+1} \mid z_t] \right\}$$

i.e., $\mu_j - R_F = \text{cov}[\tilde{r}_{jt+1}, -\tilde{Q}_{t+1} \mid z_t]$ as claimed. Hence, one now can express the value of a security as

$$P_j(z_t) = \sum_{\tau=t+1}^{\infty} (R_F + \sigma_j)^{-(\tau-t)} E[\tilde{d}_{j\tau} \mid z_t],$$

so that the discount factors incorporate risk.

In spite of the derivations' simplicity and economic appeal, we emphasize that they depend on constant (information-independent) expected returns. The more general approach captures risk by adjusting the expected dividends as opposed to the discount factors, and only this approach attains validity in all no-arbitrage economies. (See Bar-Yosef and Leland [1982], for further discussion of risk-adjusted discounting.)

Another limitation associated with the simplified dividends capitalization formula of Proposition II should be pointed out. The model treats the expected return (and risk) as an exogenous parameter, and thus an important question remains unanswered: What factors determine expected returns? In contrast, the general valuation theory implies an endogenous expected return. As some of the examples in the next section illustrate, the question raised permits systematic analysis, even if the expected return happens to be z_t-dependent.

The analysis of linear models

The general theory can be used to discuss several important aspects of an information perspective on accounting. To make these points as concrete as possible, this section reviews parsimonious models of valuation. All of these models result in linear, "closed form", valuation functions, which one derives without difficulty given appropriate linear modeling of the stochastic behavior of the information variables. The models' simplicity does not sacrifice any rigor because the valuation derives from Proposition I, part 2, or Proposition II. Thus, the examples also facilitate an understanding of the previously developed, relatively abstract concepts.

Each of the examples embodies three points that should be kept firmly in mind. First, because dividends constitute the relevant valuation attribute, the analysis derives a valuation function by modeling the stochastic behavior of dividends. Second, the valuation relevant information, z_t, relates to the information that predicts the present value of dividends, or, more precisely, the information that affects the quantities $E[\tilde{d}_{t+1} \mid z_t], E[\tilde{d}_{t+2} \mid z_t], \ldots$ and $\text{cov}[\tilde{d}_{t+1}, -\tilde{Q}_{t+1} \mid z_t]$, $\text{cov}[\tilde{d}_{t+2}, -\tilde{Q}_{t+2} \mid z_t], \ldots$. Third, the valuation function is endogenous, as is the (conditional) probability distribution of security returns. Thus, in the examples below, one *infers* the expected rate of return, which may, or may not, depend on the information. Of course, such an exercise becomes impossible if the example departs from Proposition II, because such cases assume an exogenous, information-independent, expected return. This simplification also eliminates any role for the risk-inducing measures $\text{cov}[\tilde{d}_{t+1}, -\tilde{Q}_{t+1} \mid z_t], \ldots$.

The examples are cast within a partial equilibrium framework. The term-structure of risk-free rates is flat and nonstochastic, and the distribution of the $\tilde{Q}_t, \tilde{Q}_{t+1}, \ldots$ variables as they relate to the information and dividends is exogenous. The partial equilibrium approach rules out and makes it unnecessary to consider how Q_t and the risk-free rate relate to (expected) aggregate dividends. Part 3 of Proposition I showed how the analysis extends to identify fully risk in terms of the preferences of a representative individual and aggregate dividends. In analyzing the relation between security price and information, the examples therefore usefully illustrate the absence of a need to postulate general equilibrium models such as the CAPM.[8] Even so, some readers may find it instructive and helpful to think of Q_t as (a linear function of) the market portfolio return; the examples that follow will retain their substantive content.

Example 1. (Adaptation of Miller and Rock [1985]) The setting has three dates: $t = 0, 1, 2$. Terminal dividends are paid at date two, and "intermediate dividends" are paid at date one.[9] Market values obtain as of the first two dates, zero and one. The stochastic evolution of dividends, and implicitly z_t, is as follows:

$\tilde{d}_1 = \theta_1 + \tilde{\varepsilon}_1,$

$\tilde{d}_2 = \theta_2 + \theta_3 d_1 + \tilde{\varepsilon}_2,$

where $E[\tilde{\varepsilon}_1 \mid z_0] = E[\tilde{\varepsilon}_2 \mid z_1] = 0$; θ_1, θ_2 and θ_3 are fixed and known parameters (θ_3 relates to the so-called "persistence factor"). Hence, z_0 is "no information", and $z_1 = \{d_1\}$. The variable ε_1 represents date one unexpected dividends. One can also equate z_1 to $\{d_1, \varepsilon_1\}$, but the scheme is redundant because knowing d_1 suffices to determine ε_1. The model implies that date one unexpected dividends affect the prediction of date two dividends:

$E[\tilde{d}_2 \mid \varepsilon_1] = \theta_2 + \theta_1\theta_3 + \theta_3\varepsilon_1.$

By assumption, the model disregards risk: $\text{cov}[\tilde{Q}_2, \tilde{d}_2 \mid z_1] = \text{cov}[\tilde{Q}_2, \tilde{d}_2 \mid z_0] = \text{cov}[\tilde{Q}_1, \tilde{d}_1 \mid z_0] = 0$. Applying Proposition I.2, the specification implies the following equilibrium values:

$P_0 = R_F^{-1}\,\theta_1 + R_F^{-2}(\theta_2 + \theta_3\,\theta_1)\,;$

$P_1 = P(d_1) = R_F^{-1}(\theta_2 + \theta_3\, d_1)\,.$

As an exercise, one easily verifies that $E[\tilde{r}_1 \mid z_0] = E[\tilde{r}_2 \mid z_1] = R_F$ for all z_1.

Example 2. (Rubinstein [1976b], and Ohlson [1979]) This Markovian model has an infinite number of dates. The information set is given by $z_t = \{d_t\}$, i.e., current dividends are sufficient to predict dividends at all future dates. Specifically,

$\tilde{d}_{t+1} = (\theta + \tilde{\varepsilon}_{t+1})\, d_t$

where $E[\varepsilon_{t+\tau} \mid z_t] = 0$, all $\tau > 0$ and z_t, and $\text{cov}[\tilde{\varepsilon}_{t+\tau}, -\tilde{Q}_{t+\tau} \mid z_t] = \sigma$ for all τ and z_t. In this model θ and σ are known parameters, and θ determines the expected growth in dividends since $E[\tilde{d}_{t+\tau} \mid d_t] = \theta^{\tau} d_t$. The greater θ and current dividends are, the greater the expectation of future dividends. Also, as will become apparent, σ determines the risk inherent in the anticipated dividend stream.

Similar to the previous example, there is no point in expressing z_t as $z_t = \{d_t, \varepsilon_t\}$ because ε_t can be inferred from d_t, d_{t-1}, and d_{t-1} is irrelevant in predicting dividends paid at dates $t+1$, $t+2, \ldots$

For $\varepsilon_t \equiv 0$ one obtains the familiar dividends growth model due to Williams [1938]. The example therefore generalizes this model by allowing uncertainty and risk.

Using Proposition I.2, a tedious but direct computation then shows that

$$P_t = P(d_t) = Bd_t, \tag{2}$$

where

$B = (\theta - \sigma)/(R_F - (\theta - \sigma)).$

The current price therefore equals a fixed multiple of current dividends, where the multiple discounts the growth adjusted for risk, i.e., $B = R_F^{-1}(\theta - \sigma) + R_F^{-2}(\theta - \sigma)^2 + \ldots$

An easier, but indirect, way to solve for the last expression (2) is as follows. From the third section we know that the NA condition and the definition of $Q(z_{t+1}; z_t)$ implies that in equilibrium

$$P(z_t) = R_F^{-1}\left\{E[P(\tilde{z}_{t+1}) + \tilde{d}_{t+1} \mid z_t] + \text{cov}[P(\tilde{z}_{t+1}) + \tilde{d}_{t+1}, \tilde{Q}_{t+1} \mid z_t]\right\}. \tag{3}$$

Hence, if one *conjectures* a linear solution $P(z_t) = P(d_t) = Bd_t$ for some yet to be determined constant B that depends on R_F, θ, σ, then

$$Bd_t = R_F^{-1}\left\{ (B\theta d_t + \theta d_t) - (B\sigma d_t + \sigma d_t) \right\}.$$

The d_t variables scale the RHS and LHS of the equation and they can be eliminated:

$$B = R_F^{-1}(B + 1)(\theta - \sigma).$$

Solving for B one obtains (2).

It is important to note that solving (3) is the same as solving for the expression in Proposition I.2 directly. Expression (3) meets the intertemporal valuation consistency requirements. Subsequent examples also exploit this solution technique.

Having solved for $P(d_t)$ one can derive the expected return:

$$E\,[(P(\tilde{d}_{t+1}) + \tilde{d}_{t+1})/P_t \mid z_t] = (B + 1)\theta d_t/Bd_t = (B + 1)\theta/B = R_F\,\theta/(\theta - \sigma).$$

Similarly, security risk is determined by

$$\text{cov}\,[\tilde{r}_{t+1}, -\tilde{Q}_{t+1} \mid z_t] = E\,[\tilde{r}_{t+1} \mid z_t] - R_F = R_F\,\sigma/(\theta - \sigma).$$

The model therefore leads to a z_t-independent expected return and risk. The latter quantities increase as σ increases, which makes economic sense.

Example 3. (Ohlson [1983]) As an elaboration of the previous example, consider the information dynamics

$$\tilde{x}_{t+1} = (\theta_1 + \tilde{\varepsilon}_{1t+1})\, x_t$$

$$\tilde{d}_{t+1} = (\theta_2 + \tilde{\varepsilon}_{2t+1})\, x_t$$

where $E\,[\tilde{\varepsilon}_{kt+\tau} \mid z_t] = 0,\ k = 1, 2,\ \tau > 0$, and $\text{cov}\,[\varepsilon_{kt+\tau}, -\tilde{Q}_{t+\tau} \mid z_t] = \sigma_k$ for all z_t. Thus, the primitive information variable x_t alone predicts future dividends, $z_t = \{ x_t \}$. For this dynamics one may think of x_t as a measure of earnings that suffices to determine price. The latter follows because x_t suffices to predict the future dividends. One then interprets θ_1 as the expected growth in earnings, and θ_2 as a pay-out factor relating next date expected dividends to current earnings.

Using the same scheme as in Example 2, one conjectures that the solution $P_t = P(x_t)$ is linear in x_t, i.e., $P(x_t) = Bx_t$ for some B. Inserting the conjectured solution into (3) implies that

$$Bx_t = R_F^{-1}\left\{ (B\theta_1 + \theta_2)\, x_t - (B\sigma_1 + \sigma_2)\, x_t \right\}$$

Eliminating x_t and solving for B yields

$$B = (\theta_2 - \sigma_2)/(R_F - (\theta_1 - \sigma_1)).$$

The solution thus shows that the value is a fixed multiple of earnings, and this multiple reflects the risk-adjusted growth in earnings scaled by the risk-adjusted pay-out factor.

The z_t-independent expected return equals

$$E\,[\tilde{r}_{t+1} \mid z_t] = (B\theta_1 + \theta_2)\, x_t/Bx_t = \theta_1 + \theta_2/B.$$

Again, note that the (conditional) distribution of returns derives from the information dynamics and the equilibrium valuation function. One shows without difficulty that $E\,[\tilde{r}_{t+1} \mid z_t] \geq R_F$ if $\sigma_1, \sigma_2 > 0$ (and $B_1, \theta_1, \theta_2, > 0$), and the equality holds if and only if $\sigma_1 = \sigma_2 = 0$. The risk in market returns therefore reflects the primary risk in the stream of dividends and earnings.

Example 4. (Garman and Ohlson [1980]) This model generalises both of the previous examples by retaining the linear information dynamics but expanding z_t to an n-dimensional vector. Let $z_t \equiv (x_{1t}, ..., x_{n-1t}, d_t)$ denote a column vector. Using matrix notation, the information dynamics is given by

$$\tilde{z}_{t+1} = [\theta_{ij} + \tilde{\varepsilon}_{ijt+1}]z_t,$$

where $E[\tilde{\varepsilon}_{ijt+\tau} \mid z_t] = 0$ and cov $E[\tilde{\varepsilon}_{ijt+\tau}, -\tilde{Q}_{t+\tau} \mid z_t] = \sigma_{ij}$. One interprets x_{jt} as one of n-1 potentially relevant information variables, out of which one (j=1, say) may represent an earnings measure.

The solution $P(z_t)$ is linear in z_t:

$$P(z_t) = Bz_t = \sum_{j=1}^{n-1} B_j x_{jt} + B_n d_t,$$

where $B = (B_1, \ldots, B_n)$ is a row vector. Using the same solution method as in previous examples, one can derive the solution for B:

$$B^t = R_F\, I_n - [\theta_{ij} - \sigma_{ij}]^{\,t}]^{-1} [\theta_{ij} - \sigma_{ij}]^t e_n\,,$$

where I_n is an $n \times n$ identity matrix, $e_n \equiv (0, 0, \ldots 0, 1)$ is an n-dimensional column-vector, and the superscript t denotes matrix (or vector) transposition. The expected rate of return is generally z_t-dependent because it equals the ratio of two functions that are linear in z_t. However, this expression becomes exceedingly elaborate for large n because one must invert a matrix of size n to solve for the B-vector.

The above result shows that linear information dynamics implies linear valuation functions. The model is as general as one reasonably can expect because the analysis of nonlinear dynamics is unlikely to be fruitful. There are no reasons suggesting that other kinds of models can be used to determine the value as a "closed form" function of a vector of information variables.

In contrast to previous examples, the information dynamics include cases in which current dividends affect future values of the information variables, i.e., $\partial E\,[\tilde{x}_{kt+1} \mid z_t]/\partial d_t \neq 0$. This feature of the model is of potential economic importance: descriptors of the firm, such as earnings, may naturally depend on past dividends.

Ohlson [1983] analyzes the case for n=2, that is,

$$\tilde{x}_{t+1} = (\theta_{11} + \tilde{\varepsilon}_{11t+1})\, x_t + (\theta_{12} + \tilde{\varepsilon}_{12t+1})\, d_{t>}$$

$$\tilde{d}_{t+1} = (\theta_{21} + \tilde{\varepsilon}_{21t+1})\, x_t + (\theta_{22} + \tilde{\varepsilon}_{22t+1})\, d_t\,,$$

and $P_t = P\,(x_t\,, d_t)$ is linear

$$P_t = B_1\, x_t + B_2\, d_t.$$

Let $\bar{\theta}_{ij} \equiv \theta_{ij} - \sigma_{ij}$; the solution for (B_1, B_2) equals

$$B_1 = \bar{\theta}_{21}\, R_F\, K^{-1}\,, \tag{4a}$$

$$B_2 = [(R_F - \bar{\theta}_{11})\, \bar{\theta}_{22} + \bar{\theta}_{21}\, \bar{\theta}_{12}]K^{-1}, \tag{4b}$$

and where $K \equiv (R_F - \bar{\theta}_{11})\,(R_F - \bar{\theta}_{22}) - \bar{\theta}_{21}\bar{\theta}_{12}$.

This model can be used to discuss the nature of concepts of "pure" earnings. The solution for (B_1, B_2), (4a) and (4b), is manageable, yet the model provides some richness in the ways current earnings and dividends can relate to future earnings and dividends. Specifically, standard accounting suggests that $\partial E\,[\tilde{x}_{t+1} \mid x_t, d_t\,]/\partial d_t < 0$ if one wants to interpret x_t as earnings, i.e., ceteris paribus, an increase in current dividends should penalize future expected earnings. (See the next section.)

Example 5. (Beaver, Lambert, Morse [1980], as extended by Ohlson [1989]) Using Proposition II, this model postulates an exogenous and z_t-independent expected return, μ:

$$P(z_t) = \mu^{-1} E\,[P(\tilde{z}_{t+1}) + \tilde{d}_{t+1} \mid z_t]\ .$$

The information dynamics is determined by

$$\tilde{x}_{t+1} = \theta_1\, x_t + \theta_2\, a_t + \tilde{a}_{t+1}$$

$$\tilde{d}_{t+1} = (\theta_3 + \tilde{\varepsilon}_{1t+1})\, x_t + (\theta_4 + \tilde{\varepsilon}_{2t+1})\, a_t + \tilde{\varepsilon}_{3t+1}\ ,$$

where $z_t = (x_t, a_t)$ and $E\,[\tilde{a}_{t+1} \mid z_t] = E\,[\tilde{\varepsilon}_{kt+1} + z_t] = 0,\ k = 1, 2, 3$ In this model d_t does not predict future dividends given (x_t, a_t); P_t is therefore independent of d_t. Beaver, Lambert, and Morse [1980] interpret x_t as "permanent" earnings and a_t as unexpected permanent earnings. Date t unexpected permanent earnings therefore affect the prediction of date t+1 permanent earnings. In a solution $P_t = B_1\, x_t + B_2\, a_t$, B_1 reflects the multiple associated with permanent earnings, and B_2 the multiple associated with unexpected permanent earnings.

Conjecturing a solution $P_t = B_1\, x_t + B_2\, a_t$ one obtains

$$B_1 x_t + B_2\, a_t = \mu^{-1}\{B_1\, (\theta_1\, x_t + \theta_2\, a_t) + (\theta_3\, x_t + \theta_4\, a_t)\}\ .$$

The equation must hold for all values of x_t and a_t. Hence,

$$B_1 = \mu^{-1}(B_1\, \theta_1 + \theta_3)\ ,$$

$$B_2 = \mu^{-1}(B_1\, \theta_2 + \theta_4)\ .$$

To solve for B_1 and B_2 in this system of equations obviously poses no problems.

In this example it follows that the multiples B_1 and B_2 generally derive from θ_3 and θ_4 as well as from θ_1 and θ_2. The earnings process, *by itself*, does not determine the equilibrium solution. (As Example 4, special cases of this model will illustrate concepts of "pure" earnings.)

Note that linear information dynamics combined with the assumption on returns in Proposition II yield a solution $P_t = Bz_t$ where

$$B^t = [\mu\, I_n - [\theta_{ij}]^t\,]^{-1}\, [\theta_{ij}]^t e_n\ ;$$

θ_{ij}, I_n and e_n are as defined in the previous example. The use of Proposition II rather than I implies that μ replaces R_F, and θ_{ij} replaces $\theta_{ij} - \sigma_{ij}$. Consistent with the discussion in the fourth section concerning Proposition II, the notion of risk in this example is ad hoc (and exogenous) since the analysis does not consider the σ_{ij} parameters, i.e., the risk inherent in the dividend stream itself.

The role of anticipated cash flows in valuation

The theory demonstrates clearly why future dividends across events and dates serve as the relevant valuation attributes: ultimately only payoffs count, and dividends alone can be consumed. The no arbitrage concept can be put to work given this payoff aspect of dividends, and one cannot replace dividends with cash flows, or earnings, as a capitalization attribute and thereby prove the existence of some (possibly alternative) set of implicit prices. As an empirical matter, cash flows or earnings might well take on an important function in the *prediction* of the present value of future dividends and thus in the valuation of securities. But this information function of cash flows or earnings does not automatically elevate any of the information variables to the status of a relevant attribute in a present-value calculation.

This simple point concerning prediction of information variables must be appreciated because intertemporal valuation consistency requires the prediction of all information variables that may affect values. The prediction of information variables merely reflects the recursive nature of predicting dividends further out in the future. Example 3 illustrates the process: the prediction of $x_{t+1}, x_{t+2}, \ldots$ at date t occurs because they relate directly to dividends at dates $t+2, t+3, \ldots$. Alternatively, intertemporal valuation consistency requires the prediction of x_{t+1} at date t because x_{t+1} (potentially) affects P_{t+1}, and to determine P_t we must predict P_{t+1} (and d_{t+1}), i .e., the analysis exploits expression (3).

To focus on dividends as the capitalization attribute is not only a matter of more or less esoteric theory. In the real world this role of dividends is seen at the time when a stock goes ex dividend. These events make a stock less valuable, and, on the average, the price declines approximate the dividends. This outcome is entirely consistent with the valuation theory developed. Of course, empirical research in finance and accounting recognizes the relevance of dividends at least implicitly by making an adjustment for dividends in the definition of the return on a security. Proposition II similarly illustrates the relevance of dividends as a valuation attribute. As a practical matter a stationary expected return may be quite reasonable, provided that one adjusts for dividends in the definition of returns. But this simple model then implies that the capitalized expected future dividends determine value.

In dealing with valuation issues, the accounting literature generally refers to cash flows—not to dividends—as the appropriate capitalization attribute. Although rarely (if ever) discussed in any detail, two closely related ideas seem to motivate this concept: (1) dividends must be paid out of cash flows, and (2) any reduction in current dividends leads to increased future dividends because the extra cash retained can be invested in bonds. Of course, Modigliani and Miller [1961] (MM) considered (2) in particular; they showed that, under certainty, all dividend policies are equally optimal. Rubinstein [1973, 1976a] generalizes this result for mean-variance (CAPM) and Arrow-Debreu (complete markets) settings.

The conditions that allow for an appropriate concept of cash flows as a capitalization (present value) attribute are, in fact, stringent, and dividend policy irrelevance is only necessary and not sufficient. An additional condition requires future investments (and borrowings) to have, ex ante, zero net present value, i.e., the investment—and borrowing—policy is irrelevant, and a value maximizing firm might as well cease making any new investments. It should further be explained that the (net) cash flows capitalized are those generated by existing assets (and debt); cash flows deriving from assets (investments) acquired (planned) in the future must be excluded. Thus, given new investments, investors and accounting researchers never get to observe the realizations of the (random) variables that were capitalized in the first place.

To formalize the above ideas, consider the sources of funds equals uses of funds identity:

$c_t + B_t \equiv d_t + I_t,$

where c_t = cash flows from operations, B_t = net borrowings, and I_t = net investments. Given date t, the generally uncertain cash flows at date τ, $\tau > t$, derive from two sources, namely from investments made at or prior to date t, $c^e_{\tau,t}$,, (read "e" as "from existing assets"), and from investments planned at future dates, $c^f_{\tau,t}$ (read f as "from assets acquired at future dates").

Hence, $c_\tau = c^e_{\tau,t} + c^f_{\tau,t}$, for all $t < \tau$, and the distributions of $\tilde{c}_\tau, \tilde{c}^e_{\tau,t}$, and $\tilde{c}^f_{\tau,t}$ depend on the information at the current date t (z_t).[10]

For ease of exposition, consider next a pure equity firm, that is, $B_t = 0$ for all t:

$$d_\tau = c^e_{\tau,t} + c^f_{\tau,t} - I_\tau , \tau > t.$$

Substituting the RHS into the valuation formula of Proposition I.2, one immediately concludes that

$$P(z_t) = \sum_{\tau=t+1} R_F(\tau; z_t)^{-1} \left\{ E[\tilde{c}^e_{\tau,t} \mid z_t] + \text{cov}[c^e_{\tau,t}, \tilde{Q}_\tau \mid z_t] \right\},$$

if and only if

$$\sum_{\tau=t+1} R_F(\tau; z_t)^{-1} \left\{ E[\tilde{c}^f_{\tau,t} - \tilde{I}_t \mid z_t] + \text{cov}[\tilde{c}^f_{\tau,t} - \tilde{I}_\tau, \tilde{Q}_\tau \mid z_t] \right\} = 0.$$

In other words, cash flows from existing assets can be used as a capitalization attribute if and only if the risk-adjusted net present value of future investments equals zero. The latter condition is obviously extremely stringent unless the firm gradually liquidates, and $I_\tau = c^f_{\tau,t} = 0$. And, of course, if future investments do occur, then it never makes sense to capitalize *total* future operating cash flows.

The above analysis by no means uncovers a flaw in the MM dividend policy irrelevance hypothesis because the latter result follows from weaker conditions. Given a z_t-dependent but otherwise fixed investment policy, possibly with positive net risk-adjusted present value, a change in the borrowing policy will generally change the pattern of future dividends. Such a policy change, however, would have no effect on the current price, P_t, provided the net present value of incremental borrowings equals zero. In other words, the irrelevance of dividend policy refers to incremental analysis, whereas the concept that the cash flows from existing assets and liabilities can serve as a capitalization attribute requires future investment/borrowing to be irrelevant in absolute terms.

One could perhaps argue that as a practical matter the assumptions necessary for discounting future cash flows (from existing assets) are at least approximately satisfied.[11] Nevertheless, this possibility is only of limited consolation because, as explained, one still deals with ex post unobservable variables. While ex ante cash flow capitalization may well be useful in capital budgeting, it does not follow that the concept is also central in the theory of valuation. Much of the accounting literature is, unfortunately, oblique regarding this point.

The role of earnings in valuation theory

What can be said about earnings in the theory of valuation? The broad answer is disappointing but unsurprising: very little. No published research has succeeded in integrating a model of accounting earnings with modern finance theory, and in this regard the absence of substantive insights is striking. To develop a theory of historical cost accounting and security valuation ought to be of extraordinary importance in accounting research. A natural departure for such research is the work by Paton and Littleton [1940], which so usefully—but informally—conceptualizes the structure of historical cost accounting and the measurement of earnings. Although their central doctrine of value surrendered equals value acquired obviously derives from notions of an equilibrium, this kind of reasoning has not found its way into "modern" research.

The literature often concerns itself, however, with "pure" earnings concepts, as is exemplified by the terminology *permanent earnings, ungarbled earnings, economic income, and earnings as a sufficient information variable.* The common thread of this research deals with the issue of how one generalizes the classical certainty analysis of earnings. The ideas and results are merely suggestive in the sense that these direct attention to the attributes that accounting earnings perhaps ought to satisfy under "ideal" but hypothetical circumstances. The formal analyses represent earnings as a primitive datum, and notably lacking in these models are substantive accounting ingredients such as "stocks and flows", "transactions", "property rights", and "contracts".

Keeping the above caveats in mind, I next review and discuss the models of pure earning concepts in terms of the general valuation theory (Propositions I and II). I use the examples in the fifth section to illustrate the various earnings concepts and how these relate to specific information dynamics assumptions. Each earnings concept places certain restrictions on earnings as it relates to dividends. The perspective invoked on "pure" earnings is therefore as an information variable with respect to future dividends. We avoid tautological or inconsistent concepts of pure earnings, which may occur if one relates P_t to (current or future) earnings *a priori* without consideration given to the information dynamics.

In the literature one can discern three distinct characterizations, or criteria, that a pure concept of earnings, "x_t" ought to satisfy:

(i) Earnings as a *capitalization attribute*; an appropriate present value calculation of future risk-adjusted expected earnings thus determines a security's value (P_t).

(ii) Earnings as a *sufficient information* variable that determines a security's *payoff*: $P_t + d_t = Bx_t$ (i.e.$P_t = Bx_t - d_t$).

(iii) Earnings as a *sufficient information* variable that determines a security's *value*: $P_t = Bx_t$.>

Analyses of case (i) can be found in Beaver, Lambert, and Morse [1980], in Ohlson's [1989] extension of that paper, and in Ohlson [1983]. These papers postulate linear information processes that include a primitive variable, x_t, and identify conditions such that a capitalization of (risk-adjusted) expected values of $x_{t+1}, x_{t+2}, \dots$, given z_t, results in P_t.

As a first illustration of case (i), Ohlson [1983] uses Example 4 with n=2, i.e., $z_t \equiv (x_t, d_t)$. For this setting, Ohlson proves that

$$P_t = [(\theta_{21} - \sigma_{21})/R_F] \sum_{t=\tau}^{\infty} R_F^{t-\tau} \left\{ E[\tilde{x}_\tau \mid z_t] + \text{cov}[\tilde{x}_\tau, \tilde{Q}_\tau \mid z_t] \right\},$$

if, and generally only if, $\theta_{22} = \sigma_{22} = 0$. The condition therefore restricts the dividend policy because current dividends cannot influence next period expected dividends. (Example 3 holds as a special case.) The motivation behind the analysis derives from earnings capitalization under certainty. Thus, $\theta_{21} - \sigma_{21}$ as it appears in the formula "corrects" the dividends capitalization formula for the payout coefficient of anticipated dividends (and their risk), and the summation runs from $\tau = t$ rather than $\tau = t+1$. These correcting procedures of the formula in Proposition I.2 are necessary under certainty as well. Evidently, at least for this model, "earnings capitalization" involves more than replacing d_t with x_t in the present value calculation.

As a second illustration of case (i), Ohlson [1989] considers Example 5 and shows that under appropriate parametric restrictions on the (x_t, a_t, d_t) process one obtains

$$P_t = \sum_{\tau = t+1}^{\infty} \rho^{t-\tau} E[\tilde{x}_\tau \mid z_t],$$

for some constant ρ. The discount factor ρ is implicitly assumed to reflect the risk in the earnings stream, just as Proposition II. But ρ does not generally equal μ (the expected security return). In fact, given the above model, it follows from Proposition II that $\rho P_t = E[\tilde{P}_{t+1} + \tilde{x}_{t+1} \mid z_t]$, and thus $\rho = \mu$ if, and only if, $E[\tilde{d}_\tau \mid z_t] = E[\tilde{x}_\tau \mid z_t]$. More generally, Ohlson [1989] shows that there exists a constant λ such that $\lambda E[\tilde{x}_{t+\tau} \mid z_t] = E[\tilde{d}_{t+\tau} \mid z_t]$, $\tau > 0$, and where one interprets λ as a payout factor. Similar to the previous example, the earnings capitalization formula is not fully identical to the underlying dividends capitalization formula, and the discounting depends on a payout factor that restricts dividends as it relates to earnings.[12]

Earnings as a sufficient determinant of the security's payoff, i.e., case (ii), has been considered by Ryan [1986]. Although Ryan does not require certainty, the certainty setting can be used to motivate the criterion. Pure earnings in this model are equal to (or are defined as) $x_{t+1} = (R_F - 1) P_t$. Further, because in equilibrium $P_t R_F = P_{t+1} + d_{t+1}$ it follows that $x_t = K_1 (P_t + d_t)$ where $K_1 = (R_F - 1)/R_F$. Hence, x_t and the security's payoff have a one-to-one relation. Alternatively, for this earnings concept the valuation function satisfies

$$P_t = B_1 x_t - d_t$$

where B_1 is a constant ($B_1 \equiv R_F/(R_F - 1)$). P_t therefore depends on d_t and *one* other primitive information variable, x_t.

Example 4 with n=2 usefully illustrates that the above valuation relation holds only for specific restrictions on the parameters of the (x_t, d_t) process. Specifically, given the general solution $P_t = B_1 x_t + B_2 d_t$ and the related expressions for B_1, B_2, (4a) and (4b), one shows easily that $B_2 = -1$ if and only if $\theta_{11} - \sigma_{11} = R_F$. The latter condition means that the next period risk-adjusted earnings growth rate equals R_F when current dividends are zero. It further follows that $B_1 = -R_F/(\theta_{12} - \sigma_{12})$. The last restriction implies that the parameters associated with the second predictive equation, $\tilde{d}_{t+1} = (\theta_{21} + \tilde{\varepsilon}_{21t+1}) x_t + (\theta_{22} + \tilde{\varepsilon}_{22t+1}) d_t$, can take on any values without affecting the equilibium value P_t. Alternatively, given $\theta_{11} - \sigma_{12} = R_F$ (or $B_2 = -1$) the valuation parameter B_1 depends only on the parameters that affect the prediction of next period earnings. The criterion (ii) for Example 4 with n=2 therefore leads to dividend policy irrelevance in valuation. Given $B_2 = -1$, it may also be noted that the restriction $B_1 = R_F/(R_F - 1)$ implies $\theta_{12} - \sigma_{12} = 1 - R_F$.

Cases (i) and (ii) may hold simultaneously. The previous example works if one combines it with $\theta_{22} = \sigma_{22} = 0$. On the other hand, Example 5 does not satisfy case (ii), and one may infer that the analyses in Beaver, Lambert, and Morse [1980] and Ryan [1986] are mutually exclusive.[13] (This implication follows immediately by the nature of dynamic valuation theory: d_t cannot affect P_t unless d_t also relates to the prediction of $d_{t+1}, d_{t+2}, \ldots$. A direct examination of the two predictive equations in Example 5 reveals that d_t is irrelevant as an information variable because d_t is absent in both equations' RHS).

Criterion (iii) has been proposed by Black [1980]. This concept of pure earnings is equivalent to an intertemporally constant price/earnings ratio. Clearly, such a relation holds if, and generally only if, x_t suffices to predict $d_{t+1}, d_{t+2}, \ldots$. The model in Example 3 illustrates this case: x_t alone predicts x_{t+1} and d_{t+1}, and, via recursive substitution, x_t suffices to predict $d_{t+2}, d_{t+3}, \ldots$ as well. The *P/E*-ratio equals $(\theta_2 - \sigma_2)/(R_F - (\theta_1 - \sigma_1))$, where the parameters θ_2 and σ_2 relate to the anticipated dividend payout, and θ_1, σ_1 determine the stochastic behavior (risk-adjusted growth) of the earnings process. The valuation setting has some empirical appeal because the risk-adjusted growth in earnings, $\theta_1 - \sigma_1$, enters logically into the valuation multiplier of x_t. The model to some extent distinguishes between dividends and ("pure") earnings because the payout ratio, d_t/x_t, is stochastic. Also, as noted, the expected return in excess of the risk-free rate has a simple expression: $E[\tilde{r}_{t+1} \mid x_t] - R_F = \sigma_1 + B^{-1}\sigma_2$ for all x_t, and where $B = P_t/x_t$ equals the multiplier. Hence, if $B^{-1}\sigma_2$ is small relative to σ_1 (which seems empirically reasonable), then the risk in the earnings process, $\text{cov}\,[(\tilde{x}_{t+1} - x_t)/x_t, -\tilde{Q}_{t+1} \mid z_t] = \sigma_1$ induces and approximates the risk in the security's return.

What do we make out of the above "pure" earnings concepts? Put briefly, both criteria (i) and (iii) embed severe theoretical problems, and I am inclined to view these problems as "fatal". Only criterion (ii) would seem satifactory, although certain limitations are present in this case as well. First, with respect to criterion (i), the notion of earnings as a capitalization attribute yields few, if any, sharp insights. The earnings capitalization formulae require adjustments depending on how dividends relate to earnings, and these adjustments do not flow from intuitive economic concepts. The analyses leave a "mechanical" impression because the theory becomes unworkable for complicated dividend policies. The payout constructs are too contrived, and to accommodate a richer set of models relating earnings to dividends seems, at best, difficult. It may further be noted that though criterion (i) (capitalization of earnings) can be combined with (ii) or (iii), the implications of the two latter criteria do not facilitate an understanding of why criterion (i) should be an economically meaningful restriction on pure earnings. Of course, none of these negative observations should be surprising because "x_t" describes the environment only in a predictive but otherwise primitive sense.

Second, concerning criterion (iii), we note that a constant P/E ratio violates basic MM precepts in an extreme sense: the price at date t does not depend on dividends paid at date t. Such a relation between current price and current dividends obviously makes little theoretical sense. From a somewhat different perspective, one should expect current dividends to affect future (expected) earnings, but this property is conspicuously absent in example 3. In a technical sense, these problems can be avoided if one assumes that "pure" earnings over the interval $t-1, t$ depend on dividends at date t. But to require such a property of pure earnings would seem to be exceedingly contrived (to say the least). The previously discussed appealing aspects of example 3 do not counter its more substantive theoretical problems.

Third, concerning (ii), this characterization of pure earnings satisifes basic MM concepts. A dollar of additional dividends reduces the market value by a dollar because $\partial P_t/\partial d_t = -1$ (and current dividends do not affect current earnings). As shown previously, this property of the valuation function mirrors the dividend *policy* irrelevance. Also note that current dividends affect *future* earnings, a relation that would seem to make economic sense. Another appealing aspect of (ii), which is emphasized by Ryan [1986], focuses on the fact that $B_1 = R_F/(R_F - 1)$ can be interpreted as a multiplier for current earnings. And if $d_t = x_t$ (i.e., the payout ratio is 100 percent), then one arrives at the proper perpetuity solution $P_t = x_t/(R_F - 1)$.

The discussion indicates that earnings as a sufficient determinant of pay-off (criterion (ii)) has none of the disadvantages of earnings as a sufficient determinant of price (criterion (iii)) because it aligns with basic and compelling MM precepts dealing with dividend policy irrelevance. On that basis alone, (ii) makes more theoretical sense than (iii). Similarly, (ii) does not rely on the contrived dividend policy assumptions necessary for earnings capitalization (criterion (i)). The latter concept seems unworkable if one allows for unrestricted dividend policies. (In any event, (ii) does not always rule out (i).) We are therefore inclined to conclude that Ryan's pure earnings characterization is the only theoretically viable concept out of the three proposed.

The major limitation with criterion (ii) relates to its "incompleteness." One may, for example, ask to what extent this concept relates to future cash flows (rather than dividends) as discussed in the sixth section. This issue of how current earnings/dividends reflect anticipated cash flows seems to be an unanswered question. Another problem relates to the dimensionless characterization of earnings. As a matter of accounting, one tends to think of earnings as a "flow" variable, but the analysis does not by itself allude to this property of earnings. The notion of flows then naturally leads to stock variables, thereby suggesting that a theory of earnings cannot exist without a theory of owners' equity (i.e., "net worth" or "book value"). The core of a more fully developed theory would then perhaps explain the logical relevance behind the equation that makes financial accounting cohesive: earnings minus the change in owners' equity equals (net) dividends (i.e., debits equal credits and the accounting model satisfies the clean surplus doctrine). But this approach toward accounting variables and valuation requires that owners' equity is put on a co-equal status with earnings, and one must question the adequacy of exclusive focus on "pure" earnings concepts.

Concluding remarks concerning the empirical literature

From the analysis one can infer the limitations of the theoretical constructs used in much of the empirical literature. In broad terms, all problems relate back to a non-recognition of the central fact in valuation theory: the price of a security is determined by the present value of its dividends, and every valuation function satisfies intertemporal consistency requirements to exclude arbitrage opportunities.

First, most papers generally finesse the linkage between the information variables studied and dividends. Only Easton [1985] and Easton and Zmijewski [1987] make an attempt to tackle this empirically complex issue. Others, such as Beaver, Lambert, and Morse [1980] and Kormendi and Lipe [1987], do not explore or identify an explicit role for dividends in valuation. Thus, in these cases the valuation models are best thought of as incomplete or underidentified. Ohlson [1989] discusses this point in some detail as it relates to Beaver, Lambert, and Morse [1980].

Second, to stipulate a role for unobservable valuation attributes—such as "ungarbled earnings" or "cash flows from existing assets"—in some ways introduces more problems than it solves. From the view point of theory, the scheme still necessitates a precise link to dividends; otherwise, such models become mere tautologies. And, in any event, to develop empirically testable propositions using this framework one must consider the difficult task of linking the "unobservable" variables to "observable" ones. (Without such a model the theoretical constructs superficially embellish the research.)

Third, it should be clear that the frequently applied Litzenberger and Rao [1971] model lacks both of the ingredients necessary to derive a theoretically valid valuation function. This CAPM-related model neither provides a linkage to dividends nor flows from a multiple-dates environment.[14] The latter means that any related valuation function typically does not satisfy the no arbitrage intertemporal consistency requirements around which valuation theory revolves. To be sure, this negative comment has to be put in perspective: Litzenberger and Rao published their paper in 1971, and they obviously did not have "access" to Rubinstein's seminal results, which were published five years later.

The above observations about theory use in empirical research should not be construed as a critique invalidating the studies. This paper merely synthesizes valuation theory in terms of modern finance economics and explicates how the various parts of the theory fit together. But such theoretical analyses do not predetermine the *questions* empirical researchers may wish to address. Theory is of limited relevance for most questions, and thus useful empirical studies can be conceived even when the concepts of what determine security value are unspecified or underidentified, or when the study maintains hypotheses that do not derive from more primitive assumptions. There is therefore nothing intrinsically wrong with *not* specifying an explicit link between the independent (accounting) variables and expectation of dividends or some other valuation attribute. Ball and Brown [1968], for example, rely on no such link. Given the question they raise, it would seem odd (to say the least) to suggest that their study suffers from deficiencies because no "linkage theory" embeds the empirical hypotheses.[15]

ENDNOTES

1. The material in the second and third sections is well known in finance theory (e.g., see Garman [1978], and Rubinstein [1976b].
2. The CAPM is normally expressed as $E[\tilde{r}_j] - R_F = \text{cov}[\tilde{r}_j, \tilde{r}_m] \times \hat{K}$ where $\tilde{r}_j \equiv \tilde{d}_j / P_j$ and $\hat{K} \equiv \{E[\tilde{r}_m] - R_F\} / \text{Var}[\tilde{r}_m]$. However, the above relation implies the one in the text if one defines K as $K \equiv \hat{K} / P_m$, where P_m = market values of all securities.
3. See Rubinstein [1974].
4. Specifically, the optimality conditions follow from

   $$\max_{c,\lambda} \rho U(c) + E\left[U\left(\sum_j \lambda_j \tilde{d}_j\right)\right]$$

   subject to the budget contraint

   $$c + \lambda \cdot P \leq \tilde{w},$$

   where $\tilde{w}$ is endowed wealth.
5. More generally, absent a representative individual, one can put $\tilde{Q} = u_i(\tilde{d}^i)/E[u_i(\tilde{d}^i)]$ where i refers to the ith individual: $-u_i$ is marginal utility and $\tilde{d}^i$ is the dividend from the equilibrium portfolio. Note that one can use *any* i, yet cov $[\tilde{d}_j, \tilde{Q}]$ does not depend on which i one picks. We further note that preferences of a representative individual always exist if one assumes that the economy achieves (full) Pareto efficiency. See Huang and Litzenberger [1988].
6. The modeling of multiple-dates uncertainty economies is due to Radner [1968].
7. An example showing that the valuation formula is false is available from the author upon request.
8. See Rubinstein [1976b] and Huang and Litzenberger [1988] for discussions of mutiperiod versions of the CAPM.

9. This example modifies the Miller and Rock [1985] model, which discounts "earnings" rather than dividends at date one. In my mind, their model cannot make sense given any reasonably prior ideas concerning the meaning of earnings.
   The point becomes obvious in case of certainty. The Miller and Rock model implies that $x_{t=2} = R_F P_{t=1}$ where R_F is the risk-free rate *plus* one (i.e., $x_{t=2} > P_{t=1}$). The result seems odd because under certainty next-period earnings and current price relate by $x_{t+1} = (R_F - 1)P_t$, all t. More generally, given that $x_{t+1} = (R_F - 1)P_t$ under certainty it is readily shown that the present value of future earnings calculation $\sum_{\tau=1}^{\infty} = R_F^{-\tau} x_{t+\tau}$ does not relate meaningfully to P_t. Of course, an exception to the latter occurs when $x_t = d_t$, but this would seem to be of only modest interest.

10. The z_t set remains primitive throughout this section. Specifically, it is not required that z_t include any of the cash flow or investment/borrowing variables.

11. The cash flow capitalization concept always works in the extreme case when one defines "existing assets" sufficiently broadly. That is, one may view "existing assets" as including all future opportunities that yield positive net present value. Thus "superior management abilities" can be viewed as an existing asset. This concept of cash flow capitalization turns into a virtual tautology, and under the circumstances it seems doubtful that the concept conveys any useful insights.

12. Of course, if the model requires μ (the expected market return) to equal ρ (the capitalization factor), then one must answer the awkward question: Why should we expect d_t to differ from x_t when $E[\tilde{d} - \tilde{x}_\tau | z_t] = 0$? This implication of proposition II applies in other contexts as well. Many papers (e.g., Collins and Kothari [1988]) capitalize "cash flows" using μ as a discount factor, and this valuation scheme makes no more sense. These papers seem unaware of the fact that $E[\tilde{d}_\tau - \tilde{x}_\tau | z_t] = 0$ where $\tilde{x}_\tau$ now denotes "cash flows", and they never address why one should not simply equate dividend and "cash flows". (Note that $\tilde{d}_\tau = c^e_{\tau,t} = c_\tau$ only if $I_\tau = B_\tau = 0$.)

13. Contrary to the requirements of criterion (ii) in the Beaver, Lambert, and Morse [1980] model P_t depends on two primitive variables (x_t, a_t) and P_t is independent of d_t.

14. The Litzberger and Rao [1971] model also includes a term that purportedly captures "growth opportunities". This term has no rigorous foundation under uncertainty.

15. Christie [1987] apparently disagrees. He concludes that "therefore, regardless of whether analysis is conducted in levels of returns, a model of future cash flows is *required*" (p. 233, emphasis added).

REFERENCES

Ball, R. and P. Brown, "An Empirical Evaluation of Accounting Income Numbers", *Journal of Accounting Research* [Autumn 1968] pp. 159–178.

Bar-Yosef, S. and H. Leland, "Risk Adjusted Discounting," Working paper, The Hebrew University [1982].

Beaver, W., R. Lambert, and D. Morse, "The Information Content of Security Prices", *Journal of Accounting and Economics* [March 1980] pp. 3–28.

Beaver, W., R. Lambert, and S. Ryan, "The Information Content of Security Prices: A Second Look", *Journal of Accounting and Economics* [July 1987] pp. 139–157.

Black, F., "The Magic in Earnings: Economic Earnings vs. Accounting Earnings", *Financial Analysts Journal* [November/December 1980] pp. 19–24.

Christie, A., "On Cross-Sectional Analysis in Accounting Research," *Journal of Accounting and Economics* [December 1987] pp. 231–258.

Collins, D., and S. P. Kothari, "A Theoretical and Empirical Analysis of the Relation between Earnings Innovations and Security Returns", Working paper, University of Iowa [1988].

Collins, D., and S. P. Kothari and J. Rayburn, "Firm Size and the Information Content of Prices with Respect to Earnings", *Journal of Accounting and Economics* [July 1987] pp. 111–138.

Daley, L. A., "The Valuation of Reported Pension Measures for Firms Sponsoring Defined Benefit Plans", *The Accounting Review* [April 1984] pp. 177–198.

Easton, P., "Accounting Earnings and Security Valuation, Empirical Evidence of the Fundamental Links", Supplement to *Journal of Accounting Research* [1985] pp. 54–77.

Easton, P. and M. Zmijewski, "Cross-Sectional Variation in the Stock Market Response to Accounting Earnings", Working paper, The University of Chicago [1987].

Garman, M., "A Synthesis of the Pure Theory of Arbitrage", Working paper, University of California, Berkeley [1978].

Garman, M. and J. A. Ohlson, "Information and the Sequential Valuation of Assets in Arbitrage-Free Economies", *Journal of Accounting Research* [Atumn 1980] pp. 420–440.

Huang, C.F. and Litzenberger, R., *Foundations of Financial Economics* [New York: North Holland, 1988].

Kormendi, R. and R. Lipe, "Earnings Innovation, Earnings Persistence, and Stock Returns", *Journal of Business* [July 1987] pp. 323–345.

Lipe, R., "The Information Contained in the Components of Earnings", Supplement to *Journal of Accounting Research* [1985] pp. 37–64.

Litzenberger, R. and C. H. Rao, "Estimates of the Marginal Rate of Time Preference and Average Risk Aversion of Investors in Utility Shares: 1960–66", *Bell Journal of Economics and Management Science* [Spring 1971] pp. 265–277.

Miller, M. and K. Rock, "Dividend Policy under Asymmetric Information", *The Journal of Finance* [September 1985] pp. 1031–1051.

Modigliani, F. and M. Miller, "Dividend Policy, Growth and the Valuation of Shares", *Journal of Business* [October 1961] pp. 411–433.

Mangasarian, O. L., *Nonlinear Programming* (New York: McGraw-Hill, 1969).

Ohlson, J. A., "Risk, Return, Security-Valuation and the Stochastic Behavior of Accounting Numbers", *Journal of Financial and Quantitative Analysis* [June 1979] pp. 317–336.

Ohlson, J. A., "Price Earnings Ratios and Earnings Capitalization Under Uncertainty", *Journal of Accounting Research* [Spring 1983] pp. 141–154.

Ohlson, J. A., "Ungarbled Earnings and Dividends: An Analysis and Extension of the Beaver, Lambert, and Morse Valuation Model", *Journal of Accounting and Economics* [July 1989] pp. 109–115.

Paton, W. A., and A. C. Littleton, *An Introduction to Corporate Accounting Standards* (Evanston, Ill.: American Accounting Association, 1940).

Radner, R., "Competitive Equilibrium under Uncertainty", *Econometrica* [January 1968] pp. 31–58.

Rubinstein, M., "A Mean Variance Synthesis of Corporate Financial Theory", *Journal of Finance* [September 1973] pp. 167–181.

Rubinstein, M., "An Aggregation Theory for Securities Markets", *Journal of Financial Economics* [September 1974] pp. 225–244.

Rubinstein, M., "The Irrelevancy of Dividend Policy in an Arrow Debreu Economy", *Journal of Finance* [September 1976a] pp. 1229–1230.
Rubinstein, M., "The Valuation of Uncertain Income Streams and the Pricing of Options", *Bell Journal of Economics* [Autumn 1976b] pp. 407–425.
Ryan, S., "Structural Models of the Price to Earnings Relation: Measurement Errors in Accounting Earnings", Working paper, Stanford University [1986].
Samuelson, P., "Proof that Property Anticipated Prices Fluctuate Randomly", *Industrial Management Review* [Spring 1965] pp. 41–49.
Williams, J. B., *The Theory of Investment Value* (Cambridge, Mass.: Harvard University Press, 1938).

Part V:
Income Measurement, The Ups And Downs Of Inflation Accounting, And Social Accountability

Contemporary Accounting Research, Vol. 3 No. 1 (Fall 1986) pp.1-34, reprinted with permission.

Current Cost Disclosers and Nondisclosers: Theory and Canadian Evidence*

Daniel B. Thornton

* CAR Editor's Note:
This is the first in a series of studies relating to the disclosure of nonhistoric cost financial statement data by Canadian corporations. John M. Jaskula, Deloitte Haskins & Sells Graduate Research Assistant for 1984, worked closely with the author in building the database. The support of Deloitte Haskins & Sells for the project generally, and the financial support for Mr. Jaskula's participation in particular, are very gratefully acknowledged. Of course the ideas and interpretations in the paper are solely the author's responsibility. The exposition has benefited from comments by Haim Falk, Howard Lyons, Alister Mason, George Benston, Rashad AbdelKhalik, Richard Mattessich, Bill Scott, Joshua Ronen, Tom Scott, Joel Amemic, Robert Crandall, Joan Conrod, Grace Lew, Duane Kennedy, an anonymous referee, and participants at Accounting Workshop Series at The University of Toronto, The University of Alberta, Concordia University, and Comell University. An early version of the paper was presented at the *Contemporary Accounting Research* conference at McMaster University in May, 1985 and the author is grateful to the discussants and the participants for their valuable comments.

Purpose of the study

In December, 1982, the Canadian Institute of Chartered Accountants (CICA) stated that, as of December, 1983 "supplementary information about the effects of changing prices should be disclosed by enterprises whose debt or equity securities are traded in a public market", provided that one or both of the following two conditions is (are) fulfilled:

1. Historic cost inventories plus gross fixed assets (henceforth, IGFA) total $50 million or more;
2. Historic cost total assets, net of depreciation, depletion and amortization (henceforth, TA) amount to $350 million or more (CICA *Handbook*, 4510.12).

The recommendation does not apply to banks, trust or insurance companies. It also does not apply to income producing real estate assets of any enterprise.[1]

Financial statements of Canadian enterprises that satisfied the CICA criteria for disclosure were reviewed. The number of firms that, according to the CICA, should have disclosed the data in their annual reports was 380, yet only 73 made either full or partial disclosure of supplementary, nonhistoric cost data. Why?

The question

Beaver and Demski [1979] show that generally, the choice of an income reporting method "cannot be resolved by applying fundamental measurement arguments" (p. 45). With imperfect or incomplete markets, no single number can be said to be the "true income" of an enterprise. Consequently, an accounting standard for income measurement or asset valuation may not contain intrinsic reasons for obeying it.

In this study, nonhistoric cost accounting methods are viewed as suggested ways of aggregating and conveying infornation to financial statement users cost effectively, not as ways of measuring income in any fundamental sense. It is assumed that the data will be disclosed by corporations only if the benefits of disclosure to them (broadly defined) exceed the costs of producing and disseminating the data (Benston [1984]).

Canada's inflation rate was abating when the pronouncement was issued.[2] That does not necessarily explain why so few Canadian companies disclosed the data because

1. The recommended disclosures involve accounting for the impact of changes in *relative* prices as well as the general price level. Nonhistoric cost measures may differ materially from historic cost numbers even under modest inflation (Edwards and Bell [1961]).
2. Inflation in the decade preceding 1983 was extraordinarily high. Its cumulative balance sheet effects were material, even if its incremental effects in 1983 were not.[3]

Rationale for using Canadian data

Much of the research aimed at inferring people's preferences for publicly reporting or not reporting nonhistoric cost measures has been carried out in the United States, where data have been available since the mid to late seventies.[4] In sharp contrast to Canada, compliance with the U.S. accounting standards has been virtually universal: large corporations must file supplementary, nonhistoric cost financial data in their 10K reports to the Securities and Exchange Commission, if they wish to sell securities to the public. Consequently, preferences for disclosing the supplementary data have been inferred only indirectly: e.g., from lobbying positions taken by firms for or against *proposed* standards (Watts and Zimmerman [1978]); from stock market reactions to standard setters' deliberations on inflation accounting (e.g., Noreen and Sepe [1981]); or from questionnaire surveys (Casey and Sandretto [1981]).

Canadian data offer very different research opportunities. Provincial securities commissions do not require the supplemental disclosures.[5] Furthermore, because the information is identified by the CICA as supplemental, it is not strictly a part of firms' financial statements, even though it is part of their annual reports. Canadian companies' legislation generally requires the CICA's historic cost accounting standards to be used in preparing *financial statements* (Thornton [1985]), but does not mention accounting disclosures that may be made in other parts of *annual reports.* Therefore, there is no legal compulsion for firms to disclose nonhistoric cost information. Finally, the data are not necessarily audited, and no audit qualification is issued if a firm chooses not to disclose them.

As mentioned above, only 19 percent of the firms that met the CICA criteria chose to make even partial disclosure of the data. Preferences may be inferred by comparing those firms that chose to disclose with those that did not. That appears to be a more direct and effective way of adducing preferences than examining lobbying behavior, interpreting stock market movements, or administering questionnaires.

It is important for standard setters to know the reasons behind users' preferences if they wish to increase the acceptability of the standards that they set. "... The [CICA] Committee believes that there are significant potential benefits to be derived by users of financial reports from the disclosure of information about the effects of changing prices" [CICA *Handbook s. 4510.11]*. If the benefits are significant, why didn't all firms disclose the information? Three possible reasons are advanced:

1. The premise is wrong: the benefits are not as significant as the Committee believed.
2. Costs of preparing and using the information are higher than the Committee predicted.
3. The institutional environment makes it more likely that some companies will disclose than others. In particular, public accounting firms are not indifferent to the kinds of disclosure made by their clients. Some appear to encourage their clients to disclose, while others do not.

The evidence in the present paper is consistent with the hypothesis that all three factors help to explain why firms disclosed the supplementary data.

Approach

Because the population of eligible disclosers rather than a random sample is examined, the findings of the study can be viewed as *describing* the firms that did and did not disclose. For that purpose, tests of statistical significance are not needed, because there is no sampling error. Standard setters may be interested in the results on that level. Statistical tests can, however, be regarded as tests of a theory or explanation advanced to substantiate a hypothesis (Morrison and Henkel [1970]). The question is whether *the theory* significantly improves one's ability to predict the characteristics of the disclosers and nondisclosers. The theory in the present paper is not well developed enough to rule out all competing theories, although it does raise the predicted odds of disclosure substantially from about 4:1 against to nearly 5:1 for disclosure.

The next part reviews pertinent previous work. The third section elaborates on the possible explanations mentioned above and advances five specific, testable hypotheses that bear on the research question. The data are described in the fourth part and the hypotheses testing is the subject of the fifth section. The sixth section partitions the population into various subgroups. Nonparametric statistical tests are applied. Generally, they substantiate the multivariate results in the fifth section. Except for regulated utilities, similar explanations for why firms disclosed the data apply to the subpopulations.

Thirty-five firms explained why they did not disclose the data recommended by the CICA. The reasons for nondisclosure are examined in the seventh part. The paper concludes with a discussion of the limitations and implications of the study.

Previous work

Political costs revisited

Watts and Zimmerman [1978] provide evidence consistent with a hypothesis that managers of firms, to avoid being regulated more strictly, tend to lobby for changes in GAAP that reduce (or that are likely to reduce) reported income. They argue that larger firms are more vulnerable to regulation than smaller ones, so have more to gain from lobbying. The authors found that, among firms whose reported net incomes would probably have been reduced by general price level accounting, larger firms were more likely than srnaller ones to lobby *for* GPL disclosures.

A weakness of this line of inquiry is that the theory is not well specified. As Butterworth and Falk [1983] point out, size could be a proxy for many things besides political costs:

> ... Watts and Zimmerman [1978] focus primarily on ... political costs whose economic origins are only vaguely conceptualized. Their work contains no economic theory which might help us to better understand and identify the crucial agency relationships, but does describe some of the consequences of those relationships as they are worked out in the political arena (p. 21).

Because Watts and Zimmerman were not able to develop their theory more fully, and because they did not establish the likelihood of regulation in the industries examined, care must be exercised in generalizing their results.[6] The Canadian data collected for the present study do, however, form an appropriate basis for testing the hypothesis that larger firms tend to make income decreasing disclosures, because the CICA rules do reduce net income below historic cost levels. Not one of the 73 disclosers had net income on a current cost basis greater than historic cost net income.

Of course, current cost disclosures encompass more than just net income. Firms are supposed to report shareholders' equity on a current cost basis as well. From that number, readers can compute an estimate of Tobin's Q ratio (Tobin and Brainard [1978]): the ratio of the market value of a firm's equity to its book value, where book value is measured using replacement costs in lieu of historic costs. It will be assumed, in the ensuing discussion, that the CICA rules allow readers to compute reasonable estimates of Q.

If Q exceeds 1, it appears that monopoly profits (rents) are available by entering the industry: in essence, a firm disclosing a Q of 1.10 is signaling: "If you invest $100 million in duplicating the firm's productive capacity, the firm will be worth $110 million (ignoring transaction costs)." That $10 million net present value is a quasi-rent. If there were no barriers, and if used equipment prices did not quickly impound the information, the disclosure would invite entry into the industry, which would compete away the rents. If Q is less than 1, there is evidently little incentive to enter the industry, and relatively little probability of private costly government regulation. In fact, corporations with $Q < 1$ might expect regulation to benefit them, if it were instituted.

As it happens, firms with larger net income reductions due to the application of section 4510 also tended to have lower Q ratios.[7] That is, the portfolio of numbers disclosed under CICA rules is such that the income reduction effect is reinforced by the Q-ratio effect: both could be attractive to firms subject to significant political costs.[8]

Questionnaire research

In 1982 (before section 4510 was introduced), Waterhouse [1984] conducted a survey of Canadian financial managers whose firms he expected to be affected by section 4510. He obtained 139 usable responses from 277 mailings. Four of his findings are relevant to the present study:

1. Little use in Canada compared with the U.S.:
   Only about 5 percent of Waterhouse's respondents said they used nonhistoric cost data internally.[9] In contrast, Casey and Sandretto [1981] found that about half of their U.S. respondents said they did. Though both studies are vulnerable to nonresponse bias, the difference in proportion of users is striking. It seems likely that the difference is due partly to the fact that by 1981, U.S. managers had already become inured to current cost data (whether they were useful or not), since the SEC or the FASB had required them since 1976.
2. Canadian SEC registrants' opinions same as nonregistrants':

Canadian SEC registrants, many of whom had to report the supplemental data in their 10Ks, did not find the data to be more useful than did nonregistrants.

If the benefits of developing and using current cost data internally exceeded the costs, one would expect internal uses to lead, not lag, public disclosure. The reverse was observed. Points 1 and 2, taken together, suggest the following hypothesis: once disclosure is mandatory the data *must* be collected, so data production costs are largely sunk. Then, the marginal benefits of using the data internally tend to exceed the negligible marginal costs—*even though* those marginal benefits are small.

If internal and external benefits from utilizing the information are correlated, this argument implies that Canadian SEC registrants will be more likely to follow the CICA recommendation than nonregistrants, since for them the costs of producing the information will be largely[10] sunk.

3. Industry preferences:
   Industrial products firms were more likely to see relevance in the data than other firms. That suggests there may be industry preferences for disclosing the data.
4. Regulation:
   Regulated firms tended to attach less relevance to the data than others. To some extent, that observation may be the converse of 3 above, since relatively few manufacturers are regulated in Canada. Invariably, the regulated firms surveyed by Waterhouse said that price regulation is based on historic cost data.

Hypotheses

It is hypothesized that disclosure of nonhistoric cost financial statement data is related to five factors:

1. Materiality of the disclosures: *ceteris paribus,* firms with more material differences between current and historic data will be more likely to disclose the supplemental information, since:
   a) disclosure of material, unrealized holding gains may substantiate the collateral value of a firm's assets, so credit worthiness may be enhanced.
   b) the data will be more useful to financial statement readers. These two motivations will be discussed more fully in a subsequent section. In general, firms with more material adjustments may have relatively more to gain compared with firms with less material adjustments.
2. SEC listing: there were 112 direct Canadian registrants with the SEC at December 31, 1982. Only 61 of them satisfied the CICA criteria for public disclosure in Canada. *Ceteris paribus,* the 61 SEC-listed firms will be more likely to disclose because their costs of producing the data are largely sunk and much of the information is known.
3. Auditor: *ceteris paribus,* firms whose auditors support the disclosures will be more likely than others to disclose the data.
4. Size: *ceteris paribus,* large firms will be more likely to disclose than smaller ones, because:
   — there may be economies of scale in collecting and disclosing the data
   — income reducing, low-Q disclosures may be more valuable in reducing the political costs of large firms than small ones,
   — large firms have a larger "nexus of contracts" (Jensen and Meckling [1976]) than small ones. For contracting, more information is generally better than less.
5. Industry: there may be industry preferences for disclosing price adjusted data. Each of the five factors is discussed more fully below.

Materiality

The proxy for materiality that was selected is the ratio of inventory plus gross fixed assets to total assets (IGFA/TA = "Materiality"). Both the numerator and the denominator are measured at historic, not current cost, because the objective is to develop a measure that can proxy not only for the materiality of restatements that were actually observed for the 73 disclosers, but also for the materiality of current cost restatements that *would have been* made by the 307 firms that disclosed only historic cost data.

Note that the numerator contains gross, not net fixed assets. Therefore, it should capture both (a) the relative importance of the two classes of assets subject to current cost restatement under CICA rules (i.e., inventory and fixed assets), and (b) the age of fixed assets: under conditions of inflation, the older the fixed assets (all else equal), the greater the discrepancy between historic and current costs, and the higher the ratio.

The proxy should, by construction, capture the materiality of restatements of assets. It should also be correlated with net income restatements, since holding gains on inventory and fixed assets make up a substantial amount of the difference between historic cost and nonhistoric cost net income.

A desirable property of a proxy for materiality is that it not be collinear with size, since size will be used as a proxy for other variables of interest. In fact, for the disclosing firms, IGFA/TA is significantly correlated with the percentage changes in both assets and net income caused by current cost restatements; and it *is not* significantly correlated with size, whether size be measured in terms of sales or assets.[11] It is assumed that those two properties would also hold for nondisclosers, if we could measure the restatements that they *would* have made if they had disclosed.

Why should firms with more material restatements be more likely to disclose? Two, complementary reasons may be advanced:

1. Section 4510 gives firms an opportunity to disclose, with the sanction of their auditors, credible estimates of unrealized holding gains, which may enhance their creditworthiness.
2. To some extent, accounting is said to be performed in a cooperative, ethical environment (Ijiri [1981]). All else equal, it is hypothesized that management will wish to disclose information if it is useful to readers of financial statements and not harmful to itself. To the extent that financial statement users are unable to estimate current cost data from historical cost data, current cost data may be more useful, the more they diverge from historical cost measures.

It is hypothesized that, *all else being equal,* materiality will tend to be associated with disclosure of the current cost information. Utilities, which customarily have high debt ratios, and to whom bond ratings are extremely important, may be especially prone to make the disclosures of unrealized holding gains.

SEC listing

As discussed above, if the total costs of developing and utilizing the data exceed the benefits, Canadian SEC registrants should be more likely to disclose publicly.

For registrants, many of the setup costs of developing the data are sunk, and only the marginal costs of disclosure are relevant. On January 13, 1984, Clarence Sampson, Chief Accountant of the SEC wrote to R.D. Thomas, CICA's Executive Director of Research:

> This letter responds to your request regarding the supplementary information on the effects of changing prices which Canadian registrants should include in filings with the Commission ... The staff believes that Canadian and other nondomestic registrants should include information on the effects of changing prices where standards are in effect in the respective countries of such registrants. Accordingly, since section 4510 was issued in December 1982, it appears that those Canadian registrants to which section 4510 is directly applicable (i.e., large publicly held enterprises which meet the threshold test of the Section) should include the specified information in SEC filings which include annual financial statements for 1983 ... (Copy of letter on file with the author)

Technically, not all Canadian SEC registrants who satisfied the threshold tests of section 4510 were required to file supplementary data with the SEC, because the threshold tests in the United States were substantially higher: IGFA 3 ≥ $125 million (compared with $50 million in Canada); and TA 3 ≥ $1 billion (compared with $350 million). However, Sampson's letter strongly encourages the provision of section 4510 data to the SEC by Canadian registrants that meet the *Canadian* size tests. This reinforces the expectation that Canadian SEC registrants will be more likely than nonregistrants to have incurred the setup costs of producing the data.

It is possible that the SEC listing status is a proxy for a legal requirement in the U.S., rather than a proxy for the relatively low marginal cost/marginal benefit ratio for Canadian disclosure.[12] To test for that possibility, SEC registrants that were supposed to disclose under section 4510 were subdivided into two groups: one containing firms that met the U.S. threshold test, and another containing smaller firms that met only the Canadian test. As the following contingency table shows, meeting the U.S. test did not guarantee disclosure in Canada:

TABLE 1

Disclosure firms in Canada meet U.S. test?		Yes	No	
Disclose in Canada?	Yes	32	2	34
	No	22	5	27
		54	7	61

Though Canadian disclosers almost always met the U.S. test, 40 percent of U.S. qualifiers did not disclose in Canada.[13] Meeting the U.S. test was an almost necessary but not sufficient condition for disclosure in Canada. Therefore, SEC listing is more than just a redundant proxy for size or U.S. legal requirements.

The hypothesis that SEC firms are more likely to disclose on costbenefit grounds can be examined only after controlling for other factors. For example, Canadian SEC firms tend to be larger than non-SEC Canadian firms. It is also hypothesized (later) that larger firms will be more likely to disclose than smaller ones. Therefore, size must be controlled for in testing the hypothesis.

The SEC firms that do not disclose in Canada may find that the benefits are not even worth the marginal costs of including the data (probably, already produced for the 10K) in their annual reports. At first glance, those costs appear to be small. The explicit ones consist of dissemination costs, such as printing extra pages in the annual report and coordinating with the auditor. Large corporations may experience economies of scale here.

However, there will also be implicit costs in modifying the disclosures to include features recommended by the CICA but not required by the SEC. One example of such a difference is the "financing adjustment" (CICA *Handbook* 4510.47). It seems likely that a nontrivial amount of managerial time is required to understand what the CICA means by that concept. Once managers have understood it, they must decide how to explain publicly what the numbers mean. That, too, requires managerial time and effort. If the elementary data are not useful for internal decision making, it seems particularly unlikely that managers will invest the time necessary to understand the additional, more complex requirements of section 4510, and to explain what they mean to extemal readers. It is more likely that large firms will be able to sacrifice the managerial talent required to do so than small ones.

Twenty-three of the 73 disclosers published nonhistoric cost data before section 4510 was issued. The early disclosers were evenly divided among SEC registrants and nonregistrants, as were the first-time 1983 disclosers:

TABLE 2

First-time versus early disclosure of nonhistoric cost data

		NON-SEC	SEC	TOTAL
Disclosed	1983 First time	27	23	50 68.5
	Pre-83	12	11	23 31.5
TOTAL		39 53.4	34 46.6	73 100

Chi-squared ≈ 0 (No relationship between row and column variables).

The issuance of section 4510 appears to have had a similar impact on SEC and non-SEC firms. This finding reinforces the expectation that the costs of disclosure are not completely sunk for SEC firms, though SEC firms should have a cost advantage over others.

Of course, data on SEC firms are available to Canadian investors at a fairly low explicit cost if they write away for 10K reports filed with the agency in Washington. Yet, only 56 percent (i.e., 34/61) of the Canadian SEC registrants satisfying the CICA criteria for disclosure showed price adjusted information in their annual reports. Why wouldn't *all* 61 SEC registrants make the public disclosures in Canada, given that they had probably already produced the data for that agency? Why would the nondisclosers put their readers to the trouble of writing away for the information? Even posing the question suggests that many managers do *not* believe that the information is useful to readers, or that it is not in their best interest to disclose the information in a public forum.

Disclosure in a firm's annual report normally implies endorsement of accounting procedures, whereas disclosure in a 10K report does not, necessarily: management can maintain that it disclosed the 10K data under duress. Consequently, even if people do get hold of price adjusted data from a 10K report, managers can assert that the data are "misleading, useless, inappropriate for this firm, etc.", and that therefore they should not be disclosed publicly. From this perspective, 10Ks are not perfect substitutes for annual reports.

Institutional environment

The importance of the institutional environment in which accounting decisions are made has been discussed by Thornton [1979]. In particular, it has been maintained that auditors may make a significant difference in the kinds of disclosures observed (Bryant and Thornton [1984]). For instance, some public accounting firms may have invested substantial resources in the current cost standard setting process. Those costs include partners' time in reading and commenting on exposure drafts, educating staff, serving on CICA standard setting committees, etc. After the pronouncement is promulgated, they may want to capitalize on those sunk costs, and to use the expertise they have acquired. [14] Auditors of the 380 firms affected by section 4510 are listed in Exhibit 1. "Big Nine" public accounting firms audited all but 33 of the 380 eligible corporations and virtually all the 73 disclosers. Even among the "Big Eight", chi-square analysis shows that the decision to disclose is significantly (0.00003 level) associated with auditing firm.

EXHIBIT 1

Auditors of disclosers and nondisclosers observed frequencies

Auditor	Number of clients disclosing	Number not disclosing	Total no. of clients
Arthur Anderson	4	10	14
Clarkson Gordon	23*	36	59
Coopers & Lybrand	6	31	27
Deloitte Haskins & Sells	2	19	21
Peat Marwick	4	37	41
Price Waterhouse	16*	57	73
Thorne Riddell	5	58	63
Touche Ross	12*	23	35
Other	1	32	33
Ernst & Whinney	0	4	4
TOTALS	73	307	380

Chi-square = 36.644 (9 degrees of freedom)**
Probability = 0.00003

* "Big Three" auditors who supported disclosure of nonhistoric cost data by clients.

** Since for four cells the expected frequencies are less than five and for one cell (Ernst & Whinney—nondisclosers) the expected frequency is less than one (see Siegel [1956] p. 110), the analysis was repeated by combining the "other" and Ernst & Whinney categories. This analysis resulted in a *Chi*-Square value of 36.623 (eight degrees of freedom).

Price Waterhouse (PW), Clarkson Gordon (CG) and Touche Ross (TR) made it clear that they were in a strong position to assist their clients in the disclosure of nonhistoric cost financial information. Others either were neutral or seemed to encourage their clients *not* to comply with section 4510.[15] The overall tendency of clients of those "Big Three" firms to disclose is evident from the following contingency table.

TABLE 3

Observed frequencies of firms disclosing and not disclosing the data

Auditor	Clients Disclosing	Not Disclosing	Total
CG, PW or TR	51	116	167
Others	22	191	213
Total	73	307	380

Chi-Square with continuity correction factor = 23.351
| Probability = 0.000001

Fisher exact probability: Lower tail = 1.0000
Upper tail = 0.000002

Whether the association will hold up when other factors (particularly, size and SEC-listing) are controlled for remains to be seen, however.

Size

As discussed earlier, it is hypothesized that, all else equal, large firms will be more likely to disclose than smaller ones, because of (a) possible political benefits, (b) scale economies in collecting and disseminating the price adjusted information, and (c) the possible benefits of extra information for contracting or demonstrating creditworthiness.

Regulated utilities may be important exceptions, for their rates are regulated on the basis of historic cost income. It might be argued that utilities, for political reasons, will also wish to show income reducing supplemental data, because they believe that there is a possibility that the new data will be used in the future in rate regulation, in lieu of historic cost. A new regulatory regime may, however, introduce changes in allowed rates of return, in addition to changes in the accounting rules used to measure those rates. There is no reason to expect that a utility would end up better-off or worse-off as a result.[16] Therefore, if size is a factor in disclosure for utilities, its basis is probably not the reduction of political costs.

Industry relevance

The CICA recommendations focus on the maintenance of operating capability of the enterprise (CICA *Handbook* 4510.06): income on a current cost basis excludes realized holding gains. Though other measures of income are also recommended in the section, income on a current cost basis generally must be computed and disclosed before the other measures. Maintenance of operating capability may be more relevant for some firms than for others. It can been argued that resource-based firms (mines, oil and gas drillers) *cannot* necessarily replace their operating capability, since the supply of resources is fixed. Thus it may be quite logical for them to run down a productive resource, paying high dividends and letting shareholders invest elsewhere at their opportunity costs of capital. If the resource is being depleted, there are probably more direct ways of communicating that information to security holders than by means of a hypothetical "replacement resource" that may not exist.

It can also be argued that, whereas resource firms *cannot*, some retailers and wholesalers *need not* replace their inventories to remain profitable. If input prices rise substantially, and if there is not a commensurate increase in selling prices, some firms can simply change the product lines they carry. This argument may apply to department stores and distributors that are not heavily specialized in a few product lines.

Manufacturers, on the other hand, cannot change product lines quickly if their production processes are capital intensive. Arguably, income on a current cost basis is relatively more important for such firms than for retailers and resource firms, since maintenance of operating capability is a real alternative, and the information shows readers what it would cost to maintain it.

It is hypothesized that *all else being equal,* firms in some industries will be more likely to disclose nonhistoric cost data than firms in others: manufacturers (based on relevance of maintaining operating capability) and utilities (based on the desire to disclose unrealized holding gains) are hypothesized to be more likely to disclose. Retailers, wholesalers and resource firms are hypothesized to be less likely to disclose.

Neither of the industry-relevance arguments is persuasive. Industry variables are included in the analysis however, to maintain linkages with previous work on accounting preferences (Watts and Zimmerman [1978], though ultimately they ignored industry differences; Waterhouse [1984]).

TABLE 4

The hypotheses and the ways proposed for testing them.

Summary of hypotheses regarding likelihood of disclosure

Variable	Hypothesis	Proxy Measure	Sign*
1. Materiality	– More likely if material	IGFA/TA	+
2. SEC	– Marginal cost < marginal benefit only if production cost sunk	SEC listing	+
3. Auditor	– Clients of Big Three more likely to disclose	Dummy for Clarkson Gordon Price Waterhouse, Touche Ross	+
4. Size	– Economies of scale re data	Sales,	+
	– Nexus of contracts	Total assets	+
	– Political costs		+
5. Industry	– Trade, resource	Dummy	–
	– Manufacture, utility	Dummy	+

* A positive sign means "more likely to disclose, negative "less likely".

Data

The population:

During the summer of 1984 all publicly available Canadian corporate financial statements were reviewed, to see if nonhistoric cost disclosures had been made. Sources consulted were as follows:

1. *InfoGlobe financial statement database (500 corporations):* This database was not on-line at that time, and even now does not allow access to nonhistoric cost numbers (except in text form, as part of footnotes to financial statements). Corporations are included in *InfoGlobe* on the basis of selection by sponsors, so that public accounting practitioners will be able to obtain texts of contemporary disclosures by typical firms. Many of the corporations on the database did not meet the threshold tests of section 4510.
2. *CanFil microfiche service:* This includes every corporation registered with the Ontario Securities Commission (Canada's largest provincial commission). Again, many did not meet the threshold tests.
3. *Metropolitan Toronto library.*
4. *University libraries:* The University of Toronto, McMaster, and Queen's Universities all subscribe to nonrandom samples of corporate financial statements. They were reviewed for firms that satisfied the CICA's criteria, and their disclosures were examined.
5. *CICA:* The list of firms whose statements had been reviewed was compared with another list compiled by the CICA analyst responsible for preparing the descriptive statistics in *Financial Reporting in Canada*. The 325 firms that are analyzed for that biannual publication are not drawn randomly, because its purpose is to illustrate prototypal disclosures, not necessarily to allow inferences about a particular population of Canadian firms. Figures on the two lists were compared, and in case of disagreement, the financial statements were reexamined to see which list was correct.

Altogether, 668 financial statements were seen. Of those, 380 met the criteria laid down in section 4510 for price adjusted disclosures. Disclosers and nondisclosers are broken down in Exhibit 2 along the lines suggested by the hypotheses in the previous section. Of the 288 firms that fell below the threshold tests, only one (Barbecon Limited) voluntarily disclosed price adjusted financial information. Of the 380 eligible firms, 73 made either full or partial disclosure recommended by section 4510. In fact, Barbecon Limited was the only firm that supplied complete, articulated current cost financial statements. Barbecon is not included in the analysis in the present paper, since it is clearly an atypical case.[17] Because section 4510 exempts income producing real estate assets and financial institutions from the disclosure requirements, financial statements of firms solely in those two industries were not examined.If a firm operated partially in the income producing real estate industry or was partially a financial institution, the historic cost carrying values of TA and IGFA were decreased by the amounts of assets used in those two industries before the size tests were made. However, if such firms qualified for disclosure on the basis of the adjusted asset totals, the amounts of the reductions were added back for measuring "size". The reason is that political costs and economies of scale probably relate to firms, not to segments of firms.

Four-digit SIC codes were obtained for all 668 firms.[18] Unavoidably, there are difficulties assigning every firm in the population unequivocally to one, primary SIC category. Many vertically integrated firms were evident, especially in the oil and gas industry. Thus, the industry classification is not a sharp one, and must be viewed as a first approximation only.

Data capture and statistical procedures

Data were collected by hand on a pretested data capture form, and were then recorded on the Ashton-Tate *dBase II* system. The *dBase* system was used to extract the 380 firms that met the disclosure criteria from the 668 examined. While there were no missing observations, there was one firm which did not disclose sales, having obtained an exemption from the Ontario Securities Commission. That is why there are only 379 observations in some analyses containing sales as a variable.

When the data file was complete, it was uploaded to the University of Toronto's *SPSSx* system for analysis.

EXHIBIT 2

Breakdown of disclosure patterns

Shows number of companies in each cell, with average sales in millions of dollars

	380 Total $820								
	307 No disclose $540				73 Disclose $2012				
	280 Non-SEC $518		27 SEC $767		39 Non-SEC $1376		34 SEC $2724		
	176 Not Big Three $495	104 Big Three $558	15 Not Big Three $579	12 Big Three $1001	14 Not Big Three $2201	25 Big Three $947	8 Not Big Three $1484	26 Big Three $3106	
Industry:									Totals
Resource									
No. of firms	41	24	5	6	2	3	4	7	92
Average sales	$214	$184	$41	$323	$60	$1050	$139	$752	
Manufacturer									
No. of firms	65	39	5	5	7	12	2	14	149
Average sales	$412	$513	$525	$1938	$2508	$1321	$3264	$2904	
Utility									
No. of firms	28	18	4	1	2	9	2	4	68
Average sales	$392	$1238	$1314	$386	$1348	$169	$2393	$6561	
Trade/service									
No. of firms	42	23	1	0	3	1	0	1	71
Average sales	$964	$458	$599	n/a	$2771	$3147	n/a	$8567	
	176	104	15	12	14	25	8	26	380

Overall hypothesis tests

Linear probability model

Choice of whether to disclose was regressed against the explanatory variables that were hypothesized to be significant in Table 4. This form of regression analysis is sometimes called the linear probability model (Pindyck and Rubinfeld [1981], ch. 10). The model has the form

$$Y = \alpha + \beta X + \varepsilon$$

Y takes the value 1 for a discloser and 0 for a nondiscloser. It is assumed that X (the independent variable or vector of independent variables) is fixed, that the expected value of the error term is zero, and that error terms are not correlated across firms. Let P be the probability of disclosure by a firm. Then P is also equal to the expected value of Y, because $E(Y)=P(1)+(1-P)(0)$. In other words, the model predicts the conditional probability of disclosure by a firm, given the variables on the right-hand side of the equation for that firm.

The model gives unbiased, consistent parameter estimates. Although one can interpret the marginal impact of the *X*s on the probability of disclosure, the residuals are by construction heteroscedastic; thus the procedure is inefficient. Furthermore, because the ε's are not normally distributed, t-tests are not strictly appropriate for judging the significance of the parameters. Finally, extreme values for X can give predicted probabilities of disclosure outside the range (0, 1), so predicted probabilities are biased, even though the parameter estimates are not. In such a regression, R^2 has upper limit substantially less than 1.[19]

TABLE 5

Linear probability model of factors influencing disclosure

Variable	Coefficient	Predicted sign	t (d.f. = 371)	Apparent significance
Size (log of sales)	.0622	+	4.697	0
SEC registrant (dummy)	.3651	+	7.182	0
Auditor (residual)	.1341	+	3.704	.00024
Industry dummies:				
Trade service	– .1202	–	1.982	.0482
Resource	– .0103	–	.172	not sig.
Manufacturer	– .0241	+	.477	not sig.
Regulated utilities	0	+	0	not sig.
Materiality	.0266	+	.443	not sig.
Constant	– .2703	?		

R squared = .244 (adjusted)

F-ratio = 18.5 (signifance level = 0, to 6 significant figures)

The auditor dummy was collinear with size and SEC listing. To capture the *marginal* impact of the auditor variable, it was first regressed against size, SEC, industry dummies and materiality. The residuals from that first stage regression were then used in the main regression summarized above.

Both the size and the SEC variables are significant at the level of a million to one or more, in the directions hypothesized. The auditor dummy (residual) is also very highly significant in the hypothesized direction. As mentioned above, t-tests that appear marginally significant can be misleading in the linear probability model; however, there can be little doubt that the size, SEC, and auditor effects are significant.

While the industry dummy for retailers, wholesalers and service firms appears to be significant at the .05 Ievel, and again in the expected direction, the t-value is too low to really maintain that the finding is significant. The lack of significance may be due to difficulty in defining industry, inappropriateness of using primary SIC to proxy for industry, or weakness in the argument for industry relevance. As will be seen later, utilities are significantly different from other corporations in several ways. That may be due to the comparative sharpness of the industry measure for those firms.

The materiality measure is insignificant in the overall model. As will be shown in later sections however, the materiality variable is significant in the regulated utility industry.

An interpretation of the findings is as follows:

1. *Ceteris paribus*, if a firm is SEC-listed, the predicted probability of disclosure is increased by about 37 percent.
2. *Ceteris paribus*, having a "Big Three" auditor increases the predicted disclosure probability by *at least* 13 percent. Recall that this variable's partial contribution to the probability of disclosure, reflected in size and SEC-listing, was already taken into account in the first-stage regression.
3. *Ceteris paribus*, being in retailing, wholesaling, service, or resource industries decreases a firm's probability of disclosure by 13 percent (i.e., .12 + .01, though there is substantial estimation error).
4. By letting S represent sales, one can see that $\delta P/\delta lnS = 0.06$. Hence, $\delta P/\delta S = (.06/S)$. The impact of an increase in S on the probability of disclosure is predicted to decrease as S increases. By setting S = \$820 million (average sales for the 380 firms), one can see that a \$100 million increase in sales increases the probability of disclosure by only 0.007 percent, ({.06/820} x 100). The size effect, though highly significant, is weak.

The procedure described above was repeated using the logarithm of assets as a proxy for size. Results were almost identical, except that the wholesale/retail dummy was not apparently significant at the 0.05 level.

Logit analysis

Once again, let P be the probability of disclosure by a firm. Logit analysis assumes that there is an unobservable measure, Z, of the propensity of a firm to disclose. Z is assumed to be a function of a vector of independent variables, X:

$$Z = \alpha + \beta X$$

Each firm is assumed to have a critical cut-off level of Z, Z*, such that Y = 0 (meaning "no disclosure") if Z < Z*, and Y = 1 (meaning "disclosure") if Z > Z*. Logit analysis assumes that Z* is logistically distributed[20] across firms in the population, i.e. that the probability of disclosing is based on the cumulative logistic probability function:

$$P = Pr(Z^* \leq Z) = \frac{1}{1 + exp\,(-Z)} = \frac{1}{1 + exp - (\alpha + \beta X)} \tag{1}$$

In particular, if firm i has a Z score equal to Z, then the conditional probability of that firm's disclosing is found by putting Z in equation (1).[21] Rearrangement of equation (1) gives

$$Z = LOG[P/(1-P)]$$

and the logit model becomes:

$$LOG\,(P/1 - P) = \alpha + \beta X + \varepsilon \tag{2}$$

giving an S-shaped curve as shown in Figure 1 when there is only one independent variable, X.

Figure 1

Cumulative Logistic Probability Distribution

(The vertical axis measures $P = Pr\,(\,Z^* \leq Z\,)$, the probability of disclosure, for various values of X on the horizontal axis.)

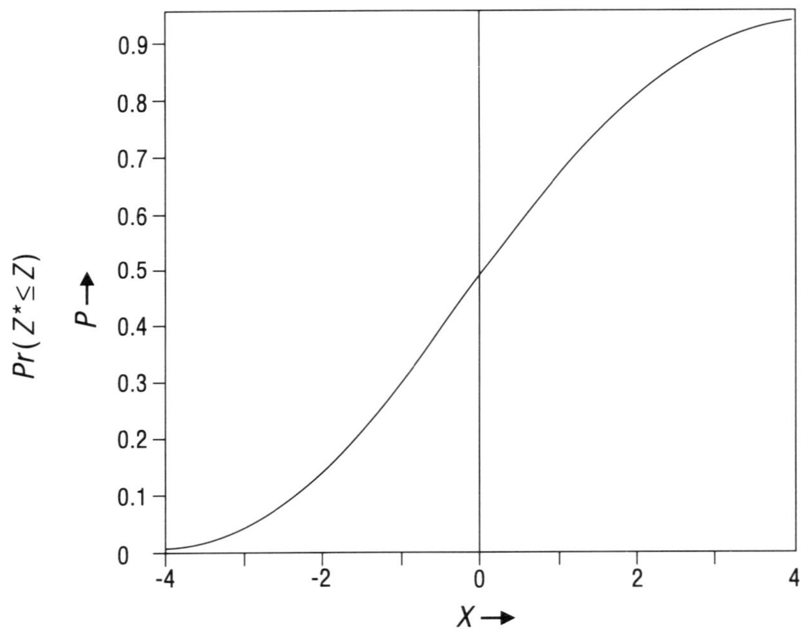

Though studies show (Pindyck and Rubinfeld [1981], ch. 10) that usually the signs, and often the relative magnitudes of logit models' coefficients are the same as those in linear probability models, there are several potential advantages of logit:

1. As a consequence of the assumed, S-shaped relationship between X and P, (see Figure 1) the marginal impact of a change in an independent variable is, by construction, assumed to be greatest when $P = 0.5$: i.e., where "fence sitters" (those with a 50:50 chance of disclosing) may be most sensitive to small δX. In fact, differentiating equation (2) with respect to X gives

   $$\delta P/\delta X = \beta[P(1-P)] \tag{3}$$

   which is a maximum when $P = 0.5$.

In contrast, the linear probability model (and multiple discriminant analysis) gives equal weight to outliers and fence sitters in computing the coefficients of the independent variables.

2. Because a maximum likelihood estimation procedure is used, parameter estimates are unbiased, consistent, and asymptotically efficient.
3. The significance of overall fit can be measured using a well-known, maximum likelihood *chi*-square distribution. Note that it is desirable to obtain an *insignificant chi*-square statistic, meaning that one *cannot* reject the hypothesis that the data are distributed according to the fitted logit model.

The best fitting logit model tested was as follows:

TABLE 6

Logit model and interpretation: dependent variable = log-odds of not disclosing

Parameter	(a) Coefficient	Q – Value (Q = 2 for .05 signif.)	(b = 2a) Two times coefficient	c = exp(b) Antilog	Reciprocal
Intercept	0.350	3.897	0.699	2.013	0.497
SEC listing	0.465	5.520	0.930	2.535	0.394
Auditor	0.269	3.479	0.537	1.711	0.584
Sales (high/low)	0.305	3.769	0.610	1.840	0.544
Materiality (")	0.0875	1.154	0.175	1.191	0.840

Goodness of fit statistics:

Likelihood ratio *chi*-square = 10.75 (10 degreees of freedom)
Probability = .464 (good fit)

Pearson *chi*-square = 11.32 (10 degrees of freedom)
Probability = .417

Measures of association:

Entropy[22] = .23
Concentration = .25

Analysis of dispersion:

Source of variation	Dispersion: Entropy	Dispersion: Concentration
Due to model	41.47	29.92
Due to residual	144.45	88.04
Total	185.92	117.95

Let *ND* stand for "probability of not disclosing" and *D* "probability of disclosing". (For technical reasons, it was convenient to utilize log $(1 - P)/P$ as the dependent variable rather than log $P(1 - P)$, interpreting the coefficients of the independent variables accordingly.) The regression-like model implied by *2-times* the maximum likelihood coefficients is log-odds. (See Norusis ([1985], p. 335) and Haberman [1978, 1982] for an explanation of why one must multiply the coefficients by *2* in the SPSSx version of logit.)

$LOG(ND/D) = \alpha + \beta(1)SEC + \beta(2)AUD + \beta(3)SALES + \beta(4)MAT$

Where:

α	=	intercept,	0.699
$\beta(1)$	=	SEC main effect,	0.930 when SEC = 0 (non-SEC)
			– 0.930 when SEC = 1 (SEC)
$\beta(2)$	=	auditor main effect	0.537 when AUD = 0 (not Big Three)
			– 0.537 when AUD = 1 (Big Three)
$\beta(3)$	=	Sales effect	0.610 when SALES = 0 (low sales)
			– 0.610 when SALES = 1 (high sales)
$\beta(4)$	=	Materiality effect	0.175 when MAT = 0 (low materiality)
			– 0.175 when MAT = 1 (high materiality)

Note that a negative coefficient means *LOG(ND/D) is reduced* by increases in the associated independent variable. That means *ND/D* is multiplied by a factor less than 1, which in turn means that the increases in the variable *increase* the odds of disclosing. All signs are in the hypothesized direction, and all coefficients except the one for materiality are statistically significant, as measured by the Q-value (Q > 2 is significant at the 0.05 level).

Materiality is measured by IGFA/TA. Firms are allocated to the low materiality group if IGFA/TA < 1 and the high group otherwise. Since sales in different industries are difficult to compare, it was deemed inappropriate to use sales as a continuous variable in the logit analysis. Instead, companies were allocated to the high sales group if total revenues in 1982 were greater than one billion dollars and to the low sales group otherwise.

To evaluate the model in terms of odds rather than log-odds, one can use an analogous, multiplicative model with antilogs of 2 times the coefficients:

$D/ND = a \times b\,(SEC) \times c\,(AUD) \times d\,(SALES) \times e\,(MAT)$

Where

a	=	0.497 the modeled overall tendency toward disclosure
b	=	2.535 for SEC firms
		0.394 for non-SEC firms
c	=	1.711 for firms audited by Big Three
		0.584 for firms not audited by Big Three
d	=	1.840 for firms in the high sales group
		0.544 for firms in the low sales group
e	=	1.191 for firms in the high materiality group
		0.840 for firms in the low materiality group

The odds of disclosing, given that the firm is SEC listed, has a "Big Three" auditor, high sales and high materiality, are expected to be 4.724 to 1. The odds can be decomposed as follows:

	0.497		overall
x	2.535	=	1.260 for SEC firms
x	1.711	=	2.156 for SEC firms with a Big Three auditor
x	1.840	=	3.966 for SEC, Big Three and sales > one billion dollars
x	1.191	=	4.724 for SEC, Big Three, high sales, IGFA/TA > 1

Interpretation:

1. Overall, the model predicts odds of 0.497 in favor of disclosure: i.e., there is about a 33 percent probability of disclosure. That is, $P/(1-P)$ is predicted to be 0.497, so $P = .497/1.497 = 0.332$.
2. The net SEC main effect on disclosure is 2.535. Other things equal, a SEC-listed firm is 2.535 times more likely to disclose than a non-SEC firm.
3. Similarly, a company audited by the "Big Three" is 1.711 times more likely to disclose, and
4. a large firm is 1.840 times as likely to disclose as a small one. (The cut-off between large and small was set at one billion dollars.)
5. Since materiality effect is 1.191, a company with a materiality ratio greater than 1 is 1.191 times more likely to disclose than a company with a ratio less than 1. The magnitude of the effect is relatively small, and there is substantial estimation error in the coefficient.

The predicted odds of disclosing can be computed for any combination of factors: for instance, the odds of disclosing for an SEC-listed firm with high sales are 0.497 x 2.535 x 1.840 = 2.318:

TABLE 7

Combinations of predicted odds of disclosure

	SEC	Big Three	High sales	High IGFA/TA
Main effects	1.260	0.850	0.914	0.592
SEC and...	1.260	2.156	2.318	1.500
Big Three and ...			1.565	1.013
High Sales and ...				1.089
SEC + Big Three and ...			3.966	2.570
SEC + Big Three + high sales and ...				4.724

Conclusions

Though industry variables were not significant contributors to the logit model's explanation of disclosure, all of the other variables had signs that were consistent with the hypotheses, and their signs were the same as the signs of coefficients in the linear probability model. The logit model fits the data extremely well, raising the conditional odds of disclosure from about 4 to 1 *against* (i.e., 307/73), to almost 5 to 1 *for* disclosure, given positive values on all four independent variables.

Descriptive statistics and tests on subpopulations

Disclosers vs. nondisclosers

As one might expect, after examining Exhibit 2, disclosers differ significantly from the population (at the 0.000001 level and below) on the following dimensions:

TABLE 8

Descriptive data for the population and disclosures

	Entire Population (380)	Disclosures (73)
Sales (mean – $millions)	820.0	2,012
Assets (at historic cost, $millions)	1.110	2,370
IGFA (at historic cost, $millions)	1.053	2,378
Percent that are SEC registrants	16.05	46.58

Significance levels were computed using the fact that, regardless of the skewness of the population, a random sample of 73 will have a normal sampling distribution of the mean. Since the population standard deviation, σ, is known, the standard error of the mean can be computed as $\sigma/\sqrt{73}$. Though 73 is a large enough sample for the central limit theorem to justify the procedure, the significance tests were repeated on the natural logarithms of sales, assets, and IGFA. Similar significance levels were obtained.

Industry and SEC effects

Exhibit 3 contains information on the subpopulations of non-SEC and SEC firms, broken down by primary industry. The *chi*-square analysis reveals that the decision to disclose in Canada is not independent of primary industry, as assessed by SIC codes. That may be due to a tendency to disclose on the part of regulated utilities that are not SEC-listed.

Exhibits 4 and 5 show that, among both the SEC and non-SEC subpopulations, size is an important explanatory variable. Nothing else shows up as a significant overall predictor of disclosure. In particular, materiality is insignificant. The significance of size for *both* groups is not surprising, since there is no reason to expect that SEC and non-SEC firms differ along the dimensions hypothesized in the third section.

Cutting the population along the primary industry dimension reveals an interesting difference between utilities and other firms. To ensure that significance levels did not depend on distributional assumptions, Wilcoxon rank-sum tests (or Mann-Whitney U-tests) for the discloser/non-discloser groups in each industry[23] were performed (see Table 9). They show that size is a significant predictor of disclosure among manufacturers and resource firms, but not among utilities. In contrast, materiality, as measured by IGFA/TA, is a significant predictor of disclosure for utilities, but not for the other two.

Without the SEC inducement to disclose, materiality also shows up, weakly (at the 0.06 level), as a predictor of disclosure in Exhibit 5. There is also a weak indication (0.08 level) in Exhibit 5 that, among non-SEC firms, disclosers contained a higher proportion of utilities than did the whole population of non-SEC firms.

EXHIBIT 3

Cross-tabulations of disclosure by industry: SEC and non-SEC firms

All firms

	Disclosers	Nondisclosers	Total	
Manufacturer	35	114	149	Corrected
Resource	16	76	92	*Chi*-square = 10.197
Utility	17	51	68	
Other	5	66	71	Probability = 0.0170
	73	307	380	

Non-SEC firms only

	Disclosers	Nondisclosers	Total	
Manufacturer	19	104	123	Corrected
Resource	5	65	70	*Chi*-square = 8.19
Utility	11	46	57	
Other	4	65	69	Probability = 0.0423
	73	280	319	

SEC-Listed firms

	Disclosers	Nondisclosers	Total	
Manufacturer	16	10	26	Corrected
Resource	11	11	22	*Chi*-square = 0.681
Utility	6	5	11	
Other	1	1	2	Probability = 0.8776
	34	27	61	

Non-SEC firms — grouped to highlight utilities

	Disclosers	Nondisclosers	Total	
Utility	11	46	57	Corrected
Other	28	234	262	*Chi*-square = 3.325
	39	280	319	Probability = 0.0072

TABLE 9

Wilcoxon rank-sum tests (Mann-Whitney U-tests)

Industry	Variable tested	Sum of ranks disclosures	Sum of ranks nondisclosures	Z Score	Significance level
Manufact.	Total Assets	3698	7477	– 4.805*	0.00000078
	Sales	3807.5	7367.5	– 5.295*	0.00000006
	IGFA/TA	2536	8639	– 0.399	0.345
Resource	Sales	956	3322	– 2.184*	0.0145
	IGFA/TA	438	3640	1.092	0.1374
Utilities	Total Assets	623	1723	– 0.517	0.3026
	Sales	635.5	1710.5	– 0.694	0.2438
	IGFA/TA	766	1580	– 2.542*	0.0055

* indicates significant difference between disclosures and nondisclosures

EXHIBIT 4

Analysis of disclosers among the 61 SEC firms*

	Population (61) Mean	$\sigma/\sqrt{34}$	Disclosers (34) Mean	t value	Signif. of test
Sales — $millions	1858	440	2723	1.9659	0.0288
— logarithm	6.308	0.3261	6.977	2.0515	0.0240
Assets — $millions	2529	627	3708	1.8804	0.0343
— logarithm	6.837	0.2614	7.403	2.1653	0.0187
IGFA — $millions	2564	693	3778	1.7518	0.0444
— logarithm	6.745	0.2705	7.271	1.9445	0.0301
Materiality — IGFA/TA	0.9451	0.04037	0.9112	– 0.8397	ns**
— logarithm	– 0.0899	0.04615	– 0.1313	– 0.8971	ns

Proportions of industries***:			fraction	
26 Manufacturers	0.4262	0.4706	16/34	ns
22 Resource	0.3607	0.3235	11/34	ns
11 Regulated	0.1803	0.1765	6/34	ns
2 other				
61				

* The hypothesis tested is that the 34 disclosers were drawn randomly from the population of SEC firms. The t value is computed by taking the difference between the mean for the population and the mean for the disclosing subpopulation, then dividing by the standard error of the mean ($\sigma/\sqrt{34}$) for a *random* sample of 34 drawn from the population. Even if the data are not normally distributed in the population, the t test is valid as long as the number in the *sample is* large enough. Since 34 may not be large enough. the test was repeated using logarithms, to see whether the significance levels were sensitive to distributional assumptions. A significant result means that one can reject the hypothesis that the 34 disclosers are a random sample of firms drawn from the population. The t values in the table are one-tailed, since the expectation is that disclosers are larger than nondisclosers.

** ns = not significant

*** The proportion of manufacturers in the population of SEC firms is $26/61 = 0.4262$; however, among the *disclosers* the proportion of manufacturers is $16/34 = 0.4706$. To see whether the latter fraction was significantly different from 0.4262, the null hypothesis was advanced that, among the disclosers, a firm had a 42.62% chance of being a manufacturer. The binomial distribution was generated for 34 trials, each with a 0.4262 chance of success, and the probability of getting 16 or more manufacturers among 34 randomly drawn firms was examined. The answer, in this case, was 0.242. Thus, the hypothesis that the disclosers have the same proportion of manufacturers as the whole population of SEC firms cannot be rejected. None of the tests turned out to be significant at the 0.10 level.

EXHIBIT 5

Analysis of disclosers among the 319 non-SEC firms*

	Population (319) Mean	$\sigma/\sqrt{319}$	Disclosers (39) Mean	t value*	Signif. of test
Sales — $millions	616	180	1341	4.0111	0.0001
— logarithm	5.454	0.2326	6.197	3.1943	0.0014
Assets — $millions	839	332	1203	1.0964	0.1398
— logarithm	5.772	0.2015	6.314	2.6898	0.0052
IGFA — $millions	763	313	1158	1.2620	0.1072
— logarithm	5.593	0.2203	6.309	3.2501	0.0012
Materiality — IGFA/TA	0.9475	0.05055	1.026	1.5529	0.0643
— logarithm	- 0.1792	0.12896	- 0.0052	1.3530	0.0919

Proportions of industries*

	Population	Disclosers	
123 Manufacturers	0.3856	0.4872	0.1271**
70 Resource	0.2194	0.1282	0.1146***
57 Regulated utilities	0.1787	0.2821	0.07544

* see Exhibit 4 for explanation

** i.e., there is a probability of 0.127 of getting 48.72 percent *or more* manufacturers in a random drawing of 39 firms from the population of 319 non-SEC firms.

*** i.e., there is a probability of 0.1146 getting 12.82 percent *or less* resource firms in a random drawing of 39 firms from the population of 319 non-SEC firms.

Conclusions

Both size and SEC effects are very robust with respect to measurement method (e.g., sales, TA, or IGFA as size proxy) and statistical technique. The materiality effect is not significant for the population as a whole, though it verges on significance in the subpopulation of non-SEC firms. It seems that, without the pressure from the SEC to produce price adjusted financial data, disclosure decisions tend (weakly) to be based on materiality.

EXHIBIT 6

Breakdown of explainers and disclosers

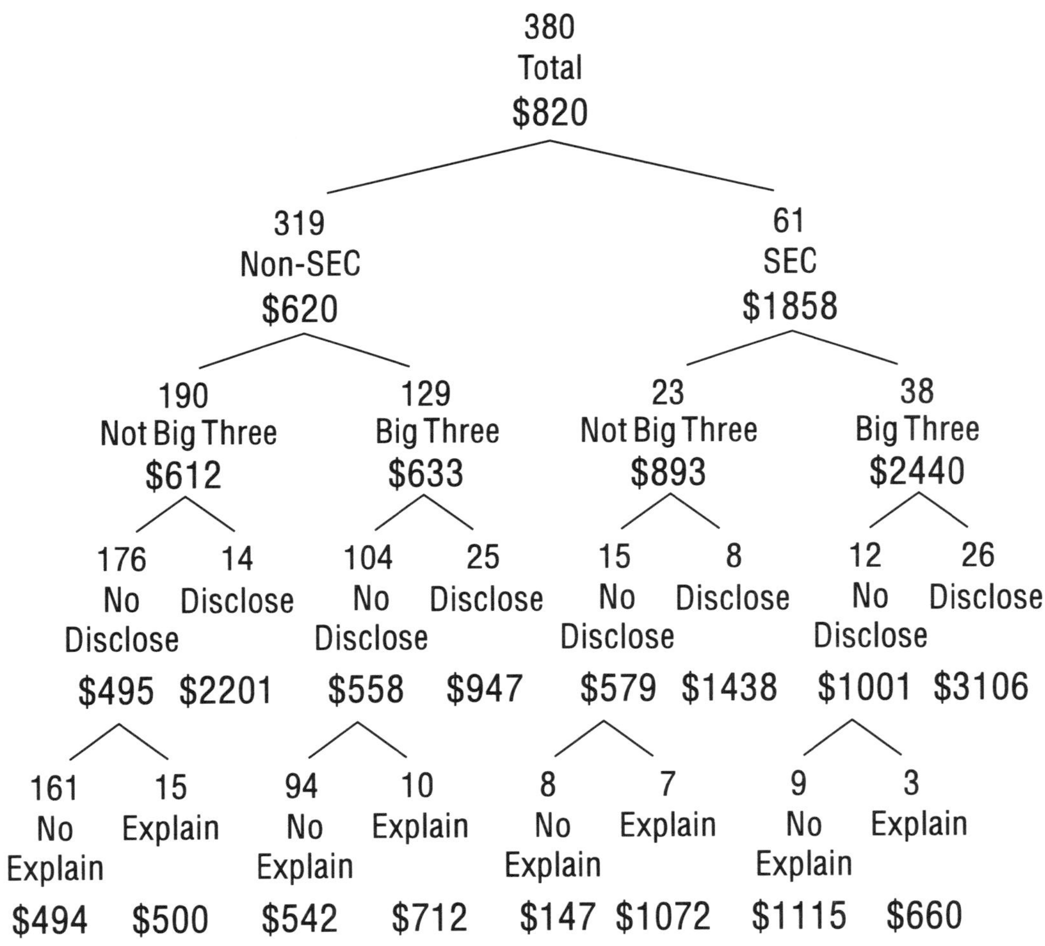

EXHIBIT 7

Profile of disclosers, explainers, and others

Analysis of variance

No. firms	Group	Means		
		Sales*	Net assets*	Materiality**
73	Disclose	2013	2370	0.972
35	Explain why not disclose	689	942	1.082
272	Neither of the above	521	794	0.923
380	F-ratios:	32.0	12.5	4.6
	Significance:	0	0.000005	0.01

* Millions of dollars
** Materiality = IGFA/TA

Industry distribution:

Industry	Observed frequencies			
	Disclosers	Explainers	Neither	Total
Resource	16	10	66	92
Manufacturing	35	13	101	149
Utilities	17	8	43	68
Trade/service	5	4	62	71
Totals	73	35	272	380

Chi-square = 13.4 (6 degrees of freedom; Probability = 0.037)

Correlation matrix — nondisclosers only:

	Log sales	Explain	Big Three	SEC	Materiality
Log sales	1.00000				
Explain (dummy)	0.07853	1.00000			
Big Three (dummy)	0.09649	– 0.00475	1.00000		
SEC (dummy)	0.02178	0.25048	0.04265	1.00000	
Materiality	– 0.06656	0.15981	– 0.04418	0.04593	1.00000

Critical value (1 tail, 0.05) = ± 0.09408

Critical value (2 tail, 0.05) = ± 0.011196

N = 307

Utilities are important exceptions to the rule that larger firms are more likely to disclose: for them, size *per se* had no discernible effect. Utilities are also exceptions to the rule that materiality does not matter. Greater materiality was significantly associated with the decision to disclose publicly in Canada. Moreover, among non-SEC firms, utilities were more likely to make the disclosures than firms in other industries. Possibly that is due to the utilities' desire to disclose unrealized holding gains on their inventories and fixed assets, hoping to improve their borrowing capability. However, that hypothesis warrants further investigation before definitive conclusions are drawn.

For nonutilities, whose political costs may depend on supplementary disclosures, size is significant and materiality insignificant. For utilities, whose political costs may depend more importantly on historic cost net income and assets, size is insignificant and materiality significant. This finding may be viewed as consistent with Watts and Zimmerman's contention that size is a proxy for political costs.

Reasons for nondisclosure

Thirty-five of the 307 nondisclosers (about 11 percent) provided reasons for not disclosing nonhistoric cost data in their annual reports. Exhibit 6 is a breakdown, by sales, of explainers and nonexplainers.

The reasons given are comparable to those found in Waterhouse's [1984] questionnaire survey.

Reasons given

The reasons given were allocated to six broad categories. Some judgment was required in a few cases to make the allocations.[24]

TABLE 10

Number of mentions made of reasons for nondisclosure, by industry group

	Resource	Manufact.	Utility	Other	Total
1. Misleading, not useful	6	10	5	1	22
2. Subjective, theoretical	4	2	1	1	8
3. Costly	1	3	1	2	7
4. Inappropriate for industry	1	2	2	2	7
5. Confusing to the reader, difficult to understand	0	3	2	1	6
Immaterial effect for this firm	0	1	0	2	3
Total no. of mentions*	12	21	11	9	53
Number of firms explaining	10	13	8	4	35

* Some of the 35 firms provided more than one reason; thus, the toal number of reasons exceed the number of firms

In addition, it should be noted that three firms in the table, whose primary industry was other than resource, mentioned that their reservations with regard to disclosing current cost information related primarily to their oil and gas divisions.

Interpreting the findings invites value judgments that are best left to readers. It may be of interest to note, however, that a very high proportion of explainers were manufacturers, to whom the notion of maintenance of productive capacity is allegedly relevant. The most common reason mentioned by those firms was that the CICA data would have been useless or misleading to readers of financial statements.

Explainers

Exhibit 7 profiles the disclosers, explainers, and nondiscloser/nonexplainers. The three groups differ significantly along the dimensions of size (whether measured by sales or net assets) and materiality. This is confirmed by simple correlation analysis.

To examine whether the simple correlations would stand up when other variables were controlled for, a linear probability model was utilized to predict the presence of an explanation for not disclosing (1 = explained; 0 = did not explain) as a function of size, materiality, and SEC existing.

TABLE 11

Linear probability model: explainers among the nondisclosers

Variable	Regression coefficient	t (d.f. = 303)	Significance
Size—log of toal assets*	.0291	2.048	.041
Materiality—IGFA/TA	.1648	2.973	.003
SEC listing—1 = yes; 0 = no	.2602	4.220	.00003

R squared (adjusted) = .0883

F-ratio = 10.89 (.0000008 significance level)

* Using log of sales resulted in a t-value of only 1.522 (apparently significant at the 0.13 level.) The t-value on materiality and SEC were 2.8 and 4.4 respectively

Compared with firms that neither disclosed nor explained why they did not, explainers were larger, tended to be SEC registrants, and had more material potential adjustments. Explainers were much smaller than disclosers, however.

Logit analysis was performed to corroborate the results in the lidear probability model. Results are listed in Table 12.

TABLE 12

Logit analysis explainers vs. nonexplainers (disclosers omitted)

Parameter	Coefficient	Q-value
Intercept	+ .6432	4.937
SEC listing	+ .4313	3.769
Sales	+ .1241	2.907
Materiality	+ .0937	0.9989
Big three auditor	− .0440	0.449
Significance of likelihood ratio *chi*-square = .003 (very poor fit)		

Results were the same under both analyses, except that the significance of materiality disappeared. Recall, however, that in the logit model materiality is a dummy (above and below 1), whereas in the linear probability model, as in the ANOVA, it is a continuous variable. Possibly, another cut-off would have produced more significant results for materiality in the logit model.

Conclusions

Though the reasons given may be of interest in motivating subsequent work, care must be exercised in interpreting them or generalizing to the population of nondisclosers. There may be significant self-selection biases. However, there is a definite pattern indicating that, among the firms that did give reasons for not disclosing, it was commonly implied that the costs of disclosing exceeded the benefits. The subpopulation of explainers differed significantly from nonexplainers and from disclosers in several ways. After the disclosers are removed from the population, the analysis implies that managers of firms felt compelled to explain why they did not disclose when the following conditions prevailed:

1. The firm was larger than average (though small compared with disclosers).
2. The firm was an SEC registrant.
3. If the firm had made the disclosures, it probably would have shown adjustments to historic cost data that were more material than those for the population as a whole: the average IGFA/TA was greater than the average in the whole population, and indeed even greater than the average for disclosers.

   Though no theory was advanced to explain these findings, *post hoc* they seem to indicate that if a firm is not huge, then the private benefits of producing and disclosing the data do not exceed the costs. All else equal, as size increases, eventually the benefits outweigh the costs. Possibly, the costs level out at some point and do not increase significantly with firm size. However, as the firm approaches a size at which it becomes subject to potential political costs, benefits of disclosing do increase, eventually exceeding the costs. When a firm is larger than average, though not nearly large enough to reap significant benefits by disclosing, and when it seems that it would have more material potential adjustments than other firms, were it to make the disclosures, excuses tend to be given for not disclosing.

Conclusions, limitations, and implications of the research

The findings support the hypothesis that Canadian firms disclosed nonhistoric cost accounting data on the basis of cost/benefit considerations, and that auditors played a role in influencing the disclosures. Utilities, arguably subject to different political pressures than other firms, were apparently influenced by the materiality of the disclosures. There was virtually no disclosure of the data by clients of auditing firms other than the "Big Eight".

Among the nondisclosers, firms that were larger than average, were SEC registrants, and apparently would have shown the most material current cost adjustments if they *had* disclosed, tended to give reasons for not disclosing.

The theories advanced to explain some of these findings, though plausible, are far from fully developed. Consequently, competing theories cannot be ruled out. The study must be viewed as primarily descriptive. It is hoped, though, that the findings will contribute to a better theoretical understanding of accounting preferences in future studies.

Implications

If the cost/benefit interpretation of the findings is accepted, then it is tempting to conclude that the CICA made a good decision in not *requiring* disclosure of section 4510 data in Canadian firms' financial statements. To have required disclosure apparently would have imposed net costs on the 307 firms that actually chose not to disclose.

Another interpretation of the findings is that in 1983, financial statement users and preparers did not yet appreciate the benefits of the proposed data, though they may, eventually. That would be consistent with Mattessich's [1984] view of accounting as an applied (conditionally normative) science: people don't like getting tetanus shots. Still, they *should* get them *if* they want to protect their health.

Preliminary indications are that this second interpretation may not be tenable. At the time of writing, about half of the 1984 annual reports of the 380 firms had been published. All of the 1984 disclosers had also disclosed in 1983. Not one 1983 discloser had failed to disclose in 1984. It seems very likely that the disclosure pattern will stabilize over time unless the CICA or the securities commissions take action to change it.

That leaves a disturbing question. Is it possible that something is wrong with the current section 4510, and that revamping it would increase its acceptability in the business community and its usefulness to financial statement users? Or would Canadian businesses continue to avoid disclosing current cost data in any form?

ENDNOTES

1. The disclosures were to be made in financial statements for the first fiscal year beginning in 1983. The size tests were to be applied at the beginning of the first fiscal year of disclosure. For a firm with a December year end, IGFA and TA would be measured as of January 1, 1983. If a company had income producing real estate assets, their historic costs would be deducted from TA and IGFA before applying the two tests.
2. The Conference Board of Canada [1984] reports that inflation in 1983 averaged about 6 percent, whereas 10-12 percent had been the norm during the period from 1980 to the end of 1982. As Canada's economy rebounded from a two year recession, corporate profits in 1983 (measured under historic cost principles) significantly increased over the average in recent years.

3. A concurrent study (Thornton [1980]) shows that often reported historic cost assets and the related depreciation charges are doubled when current cost measures are applied.

4. The Securities and Exchange Commission [1976] required large corporations to disclose certain elements of replacement cost information in 10K reports filed with the commission for fiscal periods beginning after December 25, 1976. The Financial Accounting Standards Board [1979], in FASB Statement #33 (supplemented by Statements #39, 40, 41, 46, 54, 69, and 70), later required public disclosure of similar information, along with general price level adjusted, historic cost data.

5. According to a press release by the Ontario Securities Commission (Canada's largest) dated November 18, 1983, "The Commission, although not actively involved, monitored the development of various methods of accounting for changing prices and in the process concluded that departing from the historical cost ... concept is a difficult step ... [T]he task is a matter of ... choosing from a number of significantly dissimilar methods ... Experience in other countries tends to caution against commitments to new, formal accounting methods, but to support disclosures regarding the impact of price changes as supplementary to financial statements. Accordingly, the Commission agrees with the CICA initiative but does not propose to take steps, at this time, which would mandate the implementation of the CICA recommendations by reporting issuers ... The Commission will monitor what it considers to be an important experiment designed to lead to improved reporting."

6. Other views of regulation may be equally relevant to the choice of accounting principles. Regulation can be a benefit as well as a threat to profitability (Stigler [1971, 1975]; Posner [1971]; Jordan [1972]).

7. There was enough information to compute Q-ratios for 55 of the 73 disclosers. For the 18 missing cases, generally common shares were not publicly traded (though bonds were) or the firm gave inadequate disclosure of shareholders' equity on a current cost basis. Since Q cannot be measured for nondisclosers, there *is* a possibility that the population of disclosers is not representative of the population of all eligible firms. Consequently, care should be exercised in drawing inferences beyond the 55 firms. The mean Q was 1.17. The high standard deviation, 1.62, was due largely to the contribution of two outliers: one firm with Q = .27 and another with Q = 8.94. Moreover, the frequency distribution of Q was not normal. Therefore, a nonparametric test was deemed appropriate. The Spearman rank-correlation coefficient between Q and the magnitude of the *reduction* of reported income is – 0.296, significant at the 0.015 level, suggesting that a larger reduction in income, by applying the CICA rules, *is* likely for firms with lower Q ratios.

8. Another interpretation of the finding is that firms with the larger "overstatements" of profits under historic cost accounting tended to have lower Q-ratios, and that the stock market had impounded the information efficiently. That intriguing observation forms the basis of a subsequent paper.

9. They said that nonhistoric cost accounting procedures were too subjective, too complex, and too costly to implement. They also indicated that there were other, superior ways to take the impact of changing prices into account for managerial decision making: e.g., revising standard costs more frequently, incorporating price change estimates into capital budgeting analyses.

10. There will be, however, costs in modifying the U.S. accounting numbers to meet the requirements of the CICA *Handbook*. Thus, the qualifier, "largely" seems appropriate. The costs are discussed later.
11. Correlation coefficients between the materiality proxy and size variables are as follows:

	IGFA/TA	LOG(IGFA/TA)
Sales	.00084	- .00650
Assets	.00161	- .02371
Log Sales	- .03645	- .00004
Log total assets	- .09491	- .11878

For 380 cases, critical values of the correlation coefficients, which would indicate significant association, are ± 0.08464 (one tail) and ± 0.10076 (two tail). It is concluded that the materiality proxy is not significantly collinear with size (except for log of total assets).

The correlation coefficient between IFGA/TA and the quantity, "(historic cost income minus income on a current cost basis)/sales" is 0.35146. Critical values for significance at the 0.05 level are 0.19551 (one tail) and 0.23172 (two tail). Therefore, the materiality proxy is significantly correlated with the reduction in income, as a percentage of sales, involved in restating historic cost net income to income on a current cost basis. Similar results were obtained in correlating the materiality proxy with the percentage increase in inventory plus fixed assets on a current cost basis compared with inventory plus fixed assets at historic cost.

12. The author is indebted to R. Abdel-Khalik for raising this issue, though it turned out not to be a problem.
13. Fisher's exact probability test was applied to the data in the contingency table. The probability of observing two or fewer firms in the upper right hand cell, under the hypothesis of no association between meeting the U.S. test and disclosure in Canada, is 13 percent.
14. Alternatively, it may be that auditors simply announce the kinds of disclosure they support, then corporations that wish to make those disclosures, (and to have them sanctioned by a public accounting firm), eventually become clients of those public accounting firms. Arguably, there are not enough cases where switching of auditors occurs to support that hypothesis, however.
15. This assertion is based on a review of literature circulated to clients, and of books and articles with which the "Big Three" and other public accounting firms in Exhibit I were associated. For instance, a type-set newsletter circulated to clients by Clarkson Gordon in December, 1982 read, in part, as follows:

> The issuance of the recommendations [in section 4510] follows nearly a decade of study and debate on how to overcome serious shortcomings in historical cost accounting during periods of significant price changes. The disclosures are intended not only to improve financial information for investment decision purposes, but also to permit better informed economic

decisions by govemment and an improved understanding by the public of corporate earnings. This newsletter

- provides an overview of the recommendations
- highlights certain key underlying concepts ...
- discusses the benefits of providing the information, and
- suggests some implementation considerations (p. 1).

... We suggest that clients who have not already done so may benefit from having us perform a brief evaluation of their circumstances to help them assess their best approach to implementing the Recommendations (p. 6).

In contrast, a newsletter from Deloitte Haskins & Sells (not a "Big Three" auditor) stressed that the disclosures were not mandatory, and "not essential for fair presentation."

16. On the other hand, subtle reductions in historic cost accounting numbers may be privately beneficial to a utility, since it may not be worthwhile for a regulator to reexamine the allowed rates each time a minor accounting change is made by a regulatee.

17. Barbecon's Vice-President, Finance had written several articles for *CAmagazine* extolling the virtues of nonhistoric cost data.

18. The sources consulted were Dun & Bradstreet's *Canadian Business* (1984 version) and the Canadian *Compustat* tapes. The tapes contained only about half of the 380 eligible firms. In cases of disagreement as to the primary SIC codes between those two independent publications, the financial statements of the firms were scrutinized, and segmented data examined if available, in order to break the tie.

19. In fact, if the probability of disclosure is uniformly distributed across a given interval, the upper limit on R^2 is 1/3 (Pindyck and Rubinfeld [1981], ch. 10).

20. The cumulative logistic probability function very closely resembles the t distribution with seven degrees of freedom (Hanushek and Jackson [1977], p. 189).

21. Note: P is the probability that $Z^* \leq Z$, i.e., it is the probability that Z exceeds the cut-off level. Consequently, P is the conditional probability that the firm *will* disclose, given its Z score.

22. The entropy statistic is analogous to Theil's [1970] entropy measure, while the concentration statistic is analogous to Goodman and Kruskal's tau-b (Haberman [1978]; Nie *et al* [1983], Ch. 29). Both measure the strength of association between the dependent variable and the predictor-variable set.

23. There were insufficient observations in the retail/service/other group to perform meaningful statistical tests.

24. The full text of reasons is available from the author upon request.

REFERENCES

Beaver, W. H. and J. S. Demski, "The Nature of Income Measurement," *Accounting Review* (January 1979) pp. 38-46.

Benston, G. J., "On the Value and Limitations of Financial Accounting," *Contemporary Accounting Research* (Fall 1984) pp. 47-57.

Bryant, M. J. and D. B. Thornton, "Public Choice of Corporate Accounting Standards," in: Mattessich, R.V. (ed. and cont.), *Modern Accounting Research: History, Survey and Guide*

(Canadian Certified General Accountants Research Foundation: Vancouver, B.C. 1984) pp. 151-163.

Butterworth, J. E. and H. Falk, "The Methodological Implications of a Contractual Theory of Accounting," *Workshop on Accounting and Methodology* (European Institute for Advanced Studies in Management 1983).

Canadian Institute of Chartered Accountants, CICA *Handbook* (Canadian Institute of Chartered Accountants: Toronto, Canada 1983).

Casey, C. J. and M. J. Sandretto, "Internal Uses of Accounting for Inflation, " *Harvard Business Review* (November-December 1981) pp. 149-152.

Conference Board of Canada, *The Canadian Economy—First Annual Report* (Saturday Night Publishing Company: Toronto, Canada 1984).

Edwards, E. O. and P. W. Bell, *The Theory and Measurement of Business Income* (University of California Press: Berkeley, California 1961).

FASB, *Financial Reporting and Changing Prices* (Financial Accounting Standards Board: Statement of Financial Accounting Standards No. 33: Stamford, Conn. 1979).

Haberman, S. J., *Analysis of Qualitative Data*, Vol.1 (Academic Press: New York: 1978).

Haberman, S. J., "Analysis of Dispersion of Multinomial Processes," *Journal of the American Statistical Association* 77 (1982) pp. 568-580.

Hanushek, E. A. and J. E. Jackson, *Statistical Methods for Social Scientists* (Academic Press: New York 1977).

Ijiri, Y., *Historical Cost Accounting and Its Rationality* (Canadian Certified General Accountants Research Foundation: Vancouver, B.C. 1981).

Jensen, M. C. and W. H. Meckling, "Theory of the Firm: Managerial Behavior, Agency Costs and Ownership Structure," *Journal of Financial Economics* 3 (1976) pp. 305-360.

Jordan, W. A., "Producer Protection, Prior Market Structure and the Effect of Government Regulation," *Journal of Law and Economics* (April 1972) pp. 151-176.

Mattessich, R. V., "The Scientific Approach to Accounting," in: Mattessich, R.V. (ed. and cont.) *Modern Accounting Research: History, Survey and Guide* (Canadian Certified General Accountants Research Foundation: Vancouver, B.C. 1984) pp. 1-20.

Morrison, D. E. and R. E. Henkel, *The Significance Test Controversy* (Aldine Publishing Company: Chicago, Illinois 1970).

Nie, N. H., C. H. Hull, J. G. Jenkins, K. Steinbrenner, and D. H. Bent, (1983) *Statistical Package for the Social Sciences (SPSS)*, (McGraw-Hill Book Company, New York: 1983).

Norusis, M. J. *SPSSx Advanced Statistics Guide* (McGraw-Hill Book Company: New York 1985).

Noreen, E. and J. Sepe, "Market Reactions to Accounting Policy Deliberations: The Inflation Accounting Case," *The Accounting Review* (April 1981) pp. 253-269.

Pindyck, R. S. and D. L. Rubinfeld, *Econometric Models and Economic Forecasts* (McGraw-Hill Book Company: New York 1981).

Posner, R. A., "Taxation by Regulation." *Bell Journal of Economics* (Spring 1971) pp. 22-50.

Securities and Exchange Commission, *Accounting Series Release No. 190* (1976).

Siegel, S., *Nonparametric Statistics for the Behavioral Sciences*, (McGraw-Hill, New York, 1956).

Stigler, G. J., "The Theory of Economic Regulation," *Bell Journal of Economics* (Spring 1971) pp. 3-21.

Stigler, G. J., The Citizen and the State (University of Chicago Press: Chicago 1975).

Theil, H., "On the Estimation of Relationships Involving Qualitative Variables." *American Journal of Sociology* 76 (1970) pp. 103-154.

Thornton, D. B., "Information and Institutions in the Capital Market," *Accounting, Organizations and Society* (September 1979) pp. 211-234.

Thornton, D. B., "Accounting Principles in Bond Covenants: Policy Perspectives and Canadian Evidence," *Canadian Journal of Administrative Sciences* (June 1985) pp. 139-160.

Thornton, D. B., "Inflation Accounting and the Canadian Corporate Tax Base: Evidence for 1983," forthcoming *Canadian Journal of Administrative Sciences* 1986.

Tobin, J. and W. Brainard, "Asset Markets and the Cost of Capital," Ch. 11 in: B. Balassa (ed.) *Economic Progress, Private Values, and Public Policy* (North-Holland Publishing Company: Amsterdam 1978) pp. 235-262.

Waterhouse, J. H., "Managerial Reporting of Non-Historical Cost Accounting Data," *Research Paper Series* (Canadian CGA Research Foundation: Vancouver, B.C. 1984).

Watts, R. L. and J. L. Zimmerman, "Towards a Positive Theory of the Determination of Accounting Standards," *The Accounting Review* (January 1978) pp. 112-134.

Part VI:
Agency–Contract Theory

Accounting, Organizations and Society, Vol. 15, No. 4, (1990), pp. 341-371; reprinted with permission.

Agency Research in Managerial Accounting: A Second Look*

Stanley Baiman

*This paper was originally prepared for the 1988 Management Accounting Research Conference sponsored by the School of Accountancy, University of New South Wales. I would like to thank Harry Evans, Nandu Nagarajan, Mark Wolfson and two anonymous referees for very helpful comments.

The aim of this paper is to survey the recent agency literature, emphasizing its implications for managerial accounting research.[1] The purpose of this survey is different from that of an earlier one written by the author (Baiman [1982]). The objective of that earlier survey was to provide a first introduction to one particular branch of the agency literature, the principal–agent model, and to explore its potential implications for managerial accounting. Other branches of the agency literature were excluded, not because they were thought to be less important, but to make the paper less confusing. While the present paper also concentrates on the principal–agent model, one of its objectives is to emphasize the connection between the different branches of the literature and to demonstrate how insights from the other branches of the literature can enrich the questions addressed in the principal–agent literature. A second purpose of the paper is to discuss the extent to which the promise of future managerial accounting implications mentioned in the earlier survey has been achieved.

The paper is arranged as follows. The second section briefly describes and compares three branches of the literature. They are: the principal–agent literature, the transaction cost economics literature, and the Rochester literature based on the work of Jensen & Meckling [1976].[2] The third section discusses some recent empirical tests of implications of the agency model. Because most agency research in managerial accounting has been based on the principal–agent branch of the literature, the rest of the paper surveys recent theoretical papers in that branch. The fourth section discusses recent papers in that branch which have responded to some of the criticisms of the principal–agent literature mentioned in the second section and, in particular, to those insights and criticisms offered by the transaction cost economics branch.

The fifth section discusses some recent principal–agent papers which explicitly model managerial accounting issues. The last section suggests ways in which principal–agent research might enhance its impact on the managerial accounting literature.

An agency relationship exists when one or more individuals (called principals) hire others (called agents) in order to delegate responsibilities to them. The rights and responsibilities of the principals and agents are specified in their mutually agreed-upon employment relationship. Within the term employment relationship I include the chosen: compensation arrangement, information systems, allocation of duties, and allocation of ownership rights.

In all agency models, individuals are assumed to be motivated solely by self-interest. An agency problem arises if the cooperative (or first-best) behaviour, which maximizes the firm's welfare, is not consistent with each individual's self-interest. This occurs if the employment relationships are such that, given that everyone else is acting cooperatively, one or more individuals could make themselves better off by deviating from their cooperative behaviour. Of course, if one or more individuals are expected to deviate from their cooperative behaviour, others may find it in their best interest to deviate. The end result is that when cooperative behaviour is not consistent with self-interested behaviour (i.e., it is not self-enforcing), the group suffers a loss of efficiency and all individuals are potentially made worse off.

All three branches of the literature provide similar frameworks for analyzing the interaction of self-interested individuals within an economic context; understanding the determinants and causes of the loss of efficiency created by the divergence between cooperative and self-interested behaviour (i.e., the loss from agency problems); and analyzing and understanding the implications of different control processes (e.g., budgeting systems, employment contracts, monitoring systems etc.) for mitigating the efficiency loss from agency problems. The three branches of the agency literature, however, differ primarily in two ways. First, they emphasize different sources of the divergence between cooperative and self-interested behaviour. Second, they emphasize different aspects of a common research agenda. This common research agenda includes: (a) careful modelling of the underlying economic context giving rise to the agency problems; (b) derivation of optimal employment relationships and understanding how the employment relationships mitigate the underlying agency problems; (c) comparing the results to observed practice as a check on the initial modelling and analysis. The similarities and differences in the three different agency branches will be discussed next.

COMPARISON OF MODELS

The principal–agent model

The first agency branch to be discussed is the principal–agent model. It typically takes the organization of the firm, including the allocation of tasks and ownership rights, as given and concentrates on the choice of the *ex ante* employment contract and information systems.

Assumptions.[3] In the principal–agent model, individuals are assumed to be rational and to have unlimited computational ability. Further, they can anticipate and assess the probability of all possible future contingencies. Any contingencies which are jointly observable can be costlessly used as arguments in contracts (i.e., are *ex post* verifiable).[4] The contracts are assumed to be costlessly and accurately enforced by the courts. As a result, the contracts studied are comprehensive and complete in the sense that for each verifiable event, they specify the actions to be taken by the contracting parties. Further, it is usually assumed that the courts will enforce a previously agreed upon contract even if, at some subsequent time, all the contracting parties would prefer to renegotiate the contract. Hence, there is no need for contracts to be self-enforcing.

In the principal–agent model, each individual's actions are endogenously derived, based on his well-specified preferences and beliefs. Further, each individual expects every other individual to act solely on the basis of his own preferences and beliefs.

Common to all principal–agent models is an information asymmetry assumption. The agent is assumed to have private information to which the principal cannot costlessly gain access. This private information may be with respect to the agent's action choice and/or state information. Finally, it is usually assumed that the agent is work-averse and risk-averse.[5]

What prevents the cooperative solution from being achieved. It is information asymmetry together with the agent's work-aversion and risk-aversion which typically prohibits the cooperative solution from being achieved by self-interested behaviour. That is, information asymmetry and agent work-aversion and risk-aversion prevent the simultaneous achievement of the cooperative allocation of risk and the cooperative level of production. For example, efficient risk-sharing would require that a risk-neutral principal bear all of the risk associated with production by paying the risk-averse agent a fixed wage. However, a fixed wage gives the work-averse agent no incentive to work. Efficient production would have the principal sell the firm to the agent for a fixed fee. But that would inefficiently impose all of the production risk on the risk-averse agent. Therefore, a trade-off between efficient risk sharing and efficient production must be made. In particular, the principal finds it optimal to impose more than the cooperative level of risk on the agent in order to improve the latter's motivation to produce.[6]

Focus. In the agency research agenda discussed in the introduction, the principal-agent branch has emphasized the first two steps more than the third. The literature has focused on the formal analysis of an explicit, internally consistent model of the underlying economic environment in order to understand how the design of the employment relationship affects the efficiency loss from agency problems. This then allows the researcher to derive the optimal employment relationship for the specified environment.

Managerial accounting research based on the principal–agent model has specialized this focus to study the role played by, and hence the demand for, managerial accounting procedures and processes within the firm. Examples of such procedures and processes studied include: monitoring systems, budgeting systems, variance investigation systems, cost allocation systems, and transfer pricing systems. This research has studied the effect of these and other managerial accounting processes on the interaction of individuals within the firm. Particular interest has been paid to conditions under which these systems are valuable in mitigating the firm's underlying agency problems and how the information which they produce should be incorporated into the employment contracts in order to accomplish this reduction in agency problems.

Contribution. A major contribution of the principal–agent model to managerial accounting research has been in its providing a coherent and useful framework within which we can view managerial accounting procedures and pose managerial accounting questions.[7] For example, based on the principal–agent model, one would expect to find a managerial accounting procedure only in contexts in which individuals would benefit from its use—by mitigating motivational problems within firms made up of self-interested individuals.

While this is a simple idea, it was often overlooked in previous managerial accounting research. Such research often lacked both any explicitly stated role for managerial accounting procedures (i.e., as the most efficient way of mitigating motivational problems) and the prerequisite for its use (i.e., the existence of a nontrivial motivational problem to overcome). For example, previous research into the role of transfer pricing and cost allocation studied these procedures within models in which there were no underlying motivational problems and in which the cooperative solution could be achieved without the managerial accounting procedures of interest.[8] Hence while the transfer pricing and cost allocation rules derived from these earlier studies are simple and straight-forward, their relevance is open to question. For what can one learn about specific managerial accounting procedures from models in which there is no *endogenous* demand for such procedures, i.e., in which their use does not make the players better off (and in some cases actually makes them worse off) relative to using some other procedure?

The principal–agent model's emphasis on internal consistency, rational players and optimal solutions forces the researcher to study the use of managerial accounting procedures within the context of models in which there is an underlying inefficiency for which the use of those procedures may be an optimal solution.[9] It is this new appreciation for the role of managerial accounting procedures and a more subtle understanding of the demand for and effect of managerial accounting policies and procedures which the principal–agent model has brought.[10]

Criticisms. A number of criticisms can be made of the principal–agent model. I will list them here and later discuss recent papers which address some of these and other criticisms.

The first set of criticisms deal with the realism of some of the assumptions underlying the principal–agent model. First, the computational requirements of the principal–agent formulation, the assumption that courts can costlessly and accurately enforce all contracts and the assumption that the courts will enforce contracts even when all of the parties subsequently wish to recontract are all unrealistic.

The second set of criticisms deal with the simplicity of the models analyzed. Because of the principal–agent model's emphasis on internal consistency and optimal solutions (and the computational requirements that they impose on the researcher) principal–agent research has been restricted to highly stylized, simplified models. For example, most principal–agent models take a restricted view of the environment in which the firm operates. The analysis of the interaction between the optimal contract and the labour and product markets is often ignored in modelling the agency problem. Related to this, the principal–agent model typically ignores the effect of the capital markets by assuming a single owner rather than a group of owners and debt-holders. In addition, an inherent characteristic of firms is that they are organized as hierarchies.[11] However, there has been little modelling of hierarchies in the principal–agent literature.[12] Finally, the principal–agent model has often been criticized as too narrow because it, apparently, leaves no room for trust and fairness, which are also claimed to affect behaviour.

A third set of criticisms deals with the results of the principal-agent model. While we often observe the use of simple and robust contract forms[13] (i.e., contracts forms which are not sensitive to the underlying parameters of the problem), as a result of the principal–agent model's emphasis on internal consistency, rationality and the optimality of contracts, we typically end up deriving complicated contracts whose forms are very sensitive to the model assumptions.[14]

As a consequence, some claim that the results of principal–agent research gives us little insight into the form and shape of observed contracts (see, for example, Baker *et al.* [1988]).

The criticisms with respect to model simplicity and solution complexity deserve some comment at this point. There are two responses which can be made to them. First, they are major criticisms if one views the role of the principal–agent research as providing managerial accounting algorithms which can be immediately applied in practice. These criticisms are less compelling if we view the principal–agent model as a framework for analyzing issues and highlighting problems which arise and must be considered in applying managerial accounting procedures to real-world situations.[15] Second, the observed contracts against which we compare the optimal principal–agent contracts are usually only the *explicit* or formula-based parts of actual employment relationships. At all levels of the firm there is often a great deal of discretion involved in determining the actual compensation received, especially when one considers job promotion, job assignment, and the allocation of bonuses and perquisites. The differences in complexity and sensitivity between principal–agent contracts and observed contracts may be much less when one factors in the discretionary aspects of actual contracts.[16]

This appeal to the discretionary aspects of observed employment relationships raises another criticism of principal–agent research. As noted, the decision as to who to promote and how to allocate bonuses and perquisites are, in practice, often left to the discretion of supervisors rather than completely specified in an employment contract. But principal–agent research has primarily focused on the design of explicit contracts, devoting little study to the possible role of discretion in rewarding agents.[17]

A final criticism is of the empirical content of the literature rather than of the model formulation. There has been relatively little direct empirical testing of principal–agent model results.

The transaction cost economics model [18]

Before we begin this section, it should be noted that the transaction cost economics approach has not, as yet, had a significant effect on the direction of managerial accounting research. Articles have advocated its use for understanding the evolution of managerial accounting procedures (Johnson [1983]) and as a conceptual overview of the managerial accounting process (Spicer & Ballew [1983]; Swieringa & Waterhouse [1982]). However, apparently no one has taken up this latter suggestion. Therefore, the transaction cost economics model is reviewed here, not because it has already been applied to managerial accounting issues, but because it has the potential to enrich our understanding of the role of the managerial accounting process.[19]

Assumptions. Like the principal–agent model, transaction cost economies assumes that all individuals act in their own self-interest (this is referred to as opportunistic behaviour). However, unlike the principal–agent model, transaction cost economics assumes that individuals do not have unlimited computational ability. Rather, while all individuals act to maximize their expected utility, their success in doing so is restricted by both their limited capacity to acquire and process information (as a result of bounded rationality) and the out of pocket cost of decision-making and contracting. Further, unlike the principal–agent branch, transaction cost economics assumes that the courts are imperfect enforcers of contracts.

As a result of bounded rationality, one cannot foresee all possible future contingencies and hence cannot incorporate these unforeseen contingencies into the *ex ante* employment contract. Further, as a result of contracting costs and the imperfect nature of their enforcement by the courts, one may choose to not incorporate into contracts some *foreseeable* contingencies, even ones that are *ex post* verifiable. Therefore, unlike the principal–agent model, contracts are assumed to be incomplete. That is, it is assumed that there exist events in the future for which the contract does not stipulate the appropriate actions for the contracting parties. Because of opportunism, when an uncontracted for contingency does arise, each party will try to exploit it (i.e., act opportunistically) to the extent that market conditions allow. Therefore, when an uncontracted-for event arises, cooperative and self-interested behaviour may diverge.

Notice that the use of incomplete contracts results in a potential loss of efficiency relative to the use of complete contracts. The reason is that contracting parties are never worse off, and are often strictly better off, by contractually precommitting to how they will act if specified events occur in the future. At worst, one can always precommit to act in the same way as one would act without such an earlier contractual precommitment, i.e., precommit to act opportunistically. By definition, complete contracts allow the parties to precommit to behaviour for a larger set of outcomes. For, if there exists events which cannot be foreseen or are not specified in a contract, one cannot credibly precommit to how one will act when those events arise.

What prevents the cooperative solution from being achieved. Thus it is bounded rationality, costly contracting and imperfect enforcement of contracts, and the implication of incomplete contracts, which potentially prevent the cooperative solution from being attained by self-interested behaviour. Notice that unlike the principal–agent model, the cooperative solution may not be achievable even in the absence of work-aversion, risk-aversion or limited liability on the part of the agent.

Focus. The focus of the transaction cost economics literature differs in a number of ways from that of the principal–agent literature. First, the idea motivating transaction cost research is that transactions are organized[20] so as to minimize transactions costs, where that term includes out of pocket costs (such as computational costs and the cost of writing and enforcing contracts) and the opportunity costs of inefficient contracts. Second, principal–agent research tends to focus on the contractual relationships between individuals within a firm, while transaction cost economics research tends to focus on the contractual relationships between firms.[21] Third, with respect to the research agenda mentioned in the introduction, relative to principal–agent research, transaction cost economics places less emphasis on the formal modelling of the underlying economic environment and on deriving optimal solutions. It places more emphasis on the empirical testing of hypothesized explanations for observed organizational relationships.[22] Fourth, because of the diminished role for court enforcement of contracts, transaction cost economics focuses more on the design of self-enforcing employment relations rather than on those enforced by the courts. Finally, because transaction cost economics allows for incomplete contracts (and hence for signals which are jointly observed by the contracting parties but not incorporated into those contracts), it naturally gives rise to the study of contracts which allow for discretionary compensation.

The procedures which the firm puts in place to limit the opportunistic behaviour that results from incomplete contracts are called governance procedures.[23] In essence, governance procedures set the rules of the *renegotiation game* which must be played when a contingency which is not covered by the *ex ante* contract arises. Factors such as market competition also act to discipline the opportunistic behaviour which arises when uncontracted for events occur. Transaction cost economics is especially interested in situations in which the role of competition as a disciplining device is reduced. One such situation occurs in the presence of asset specificity. This condition arises when the value of an asset within an ongoing relationship exceeds the value of the asset outside of the relationship; that is, there are quasi-rents to be gained by continuing the asset-specific relationship. Examples of asset specificities include: human capital or learning by doing; site or locational specificity such as that arising between adjacent coal mine and coal burning utility; and the use of special purpose physical capital in order to minimize the out of pocket cost of production.

Once the parties to a transaction have invested in relationship-specific assets, the parties are no longer completely protected by the market from the opportunistic behaviour of the other party, because the market no longer provides perfect substitutes for the other party. Hence, asset specificity worsens the problem associated with incomplete contracts because in these situations the extent of opportunistic behaviour which will be tolerated before ending the relationship and devoting the asset to its next best use is much greater. Thus the potential for investing in relationship-specific assets creates an increased demand for governance procedures which will mitigate the effect of opportunistic behaviour when uncontracted for events occur. A major focus of transaction cost economics is the study of how the design or organizational relationships, including governance procedures, affects the investment in relationship-specific assets, given incomplete contracting.

Contribution. With incomplete contracts, the division of surplus when uncontracted for events arise depends on the players' relative bargaining positions. One's relative bargaining position may depend on any previous investment in relationship-specific assets and the way in which the transaction is organized, including the agreed upon governance procedures. Therefore, a prior investment can influence both the total amount of amount of surplus to be bargained over and the players' relative bargaining positions when an uncontracted for contingency arises.[24] To the extent that the latter concern influences the previous investment decision, there is an investment distortion. Because the way in which the transaction is organized may also affect the players' relative bargaining positions, it may also indirectly affect one's *ex ante* investment decision.

The main insight provided by the transaction cost economics literature, therefore, is that governance matters. That is, incomplete contracts give rise to *ex post* opportunistic behaviour which distorts *ex ante* investment decisions in relationship-specific assets. Changes in the ownership of the asset and in governance procedures affect outcomes because they change the *ex post* bargaining positions of the contracting parties, which in turn affect the *ex ante* investment. Notice that the insight that governance matters depends crucially on there being uncontracted for contingencies and hence *ex poste* bargaining. This only arises when incomplete contracts are used. In the principal–agent model the manner in which a transaction is organized does not matter because contracts are assumed to be complete and hence there is no *ex poste* bargaining.

As we noted earlier, transaction cost economics has not yet been applied to specific managerial accounting issues. Transaction cost economics has, however, made a significant contribution to the industrial organization literature. It has provided an alternative explanation for the diverse ways in which firms organize their relationships. In particular, prior to transaction cost economics, the major explanation offered for non-standard relationships between firms was that they were attempts to build up or exploit monopoly power. Transaction cost econimics analysis has shown that some of these relationships can be explained as attempts to minimize transaction costs.

Criticisms. A number of criticisims of the transaction cost economics model have been made. Most of the criticisms deal with the imprecise specification of the model and the context being analysed. First, the sort and size of out of pocket contracting costs, while often used to motivate the incompleteness of contracts, are imprecise.[25] Further, it is never made explicit why the form of contract incompleteness assumed is the optimal response for those contracting costs. Second, the notion of bounded rationality, although often motivating the use of incomplete contracts, is not well-defined. This gives rise to several questions. At what point do these bounds prevent individuals from doing better? How do they cope with their bounds? And again, why does bounded rationality give rise to the form of contract incompleteness assumed? Further, if it is bounded rationality which is giving rise to contract incompleteness, how does one *ex ante* evaluate and choose between different governance procedures when their reason for being is that one cannot assess the probability or even forsee the contingencies for which the governance procedures will be used? Note that this criticism does not arise when the reason for incompleteness contracts is out of pocket cost of including contingencies in contracts.

Another model specification problem is that the equilibrium concept that gives rise to the particular organizational design adopted by the firm is often unstated and the context in which the issue is being addressed is not fully specified. As a result, the theoretical analysis done in transaction cost economics tends to be less formal and rigorous than in principal–agent research.[26] Finally, although transaction cost economics problems are usually posed within a multiperiod setting, the literature has not fully explored the role of reputation as a substitute for governance procedures.

The Rochester Model

The last branch of the agency literature to be discussed is that based on the work of Jensen & Meckling [1976], including the positive theory of accounting (Watts & Zimmerman [1986]). This literature shares many of the assumptions and the methods of analysis of the transaction cost economics model.

*Assumptions.*The Rochester model is similar to the transaction cost economics model in that both emphasize transaction costs and opportunistic behaviour. However, in the Rochester model the external labour and capital markets, which are assumed to be efficient and to accurately anticipate the incentives of management, play a much more central role than in the other branches. Thus the Rochester model addresses one of the criticisms made of the principal–agent model. This literature also assumes that observed employment and financial contracts are optimal, given transaction costs. The positive theory model is based not only on this agency model of the firm, but also on an economic theory of government regulation which views the political process as a competition among self-interested individuals for wealth transfers.

What prevents the cooperative solution from being achieved. Like transaction cost economics, the presence of transaction costs implies the use of incomplete contracts, which together with opportunistic behaviour potentially prevents the cooperative solution from being attained by self-interested behaviour.

Focus. Both the Rochester and the principal–agent branches of the literature share the objective of understanding how agency problems arise and how they can be mitigated by contractual, and more generally, organizational design. The focus and emphasis of the two branches differ however. In contrast to principal–agent research but like transaction cost research, the Rochester branch works with less formal and less explicit models and analyses and emphasizes the empirical testing of results. In particular, it studies the incentives faced by the contracting parties given observed contracts and what factors might have given rise to the observed contracts. It does so by studying the effect that (changes in) employment and financing contracts have on the behaviour of management (e.g., their financing and investment decisions) and on the stock price of the firm. The positive theory specializes the focus to management's choice of its financial accounting reporting procedures. Notice that the Rochester branch de-emphasizes the formal derivation of optimal contracts because, as noted above it *assumes* that observed contracts are optimal given transaction costs.

Contribution. All of the agency models assume that management acts in its own best interests and hence responds to the economic incentives embodied in its employment contract. One contribution of the Rochester model and the positive theory was in their early applications of the agency framwork to issues of management control and the choice of financial accounting policy. In particular, the positive theory expanded the role for financial accounting information in an efficient market to include a contracting role, and thereby enriched the explanation for the choice of different financial accounting procedures. A second, and continuing, contribution of the Rochester literature is in empirically testing this agency model of the firm and in identifying empirical regularities regarding management's behaviour and the form of executive compensation contracts.

Criticisms.[27] As with transaction cost economics, the concepts of equilibrium and efficiency as well as the size and source of transaction costs, while very important to the analysis, are not well-specified. Further, in the Rochester literature, careful modelling of the underlying context and deriving optimal contracts are de-emphasized because observed contracts are *assumed* to be efficient, given (usually unstated and unmeasured) transaction costs. But as a result, it then becomes difficult to explain what the motivation for the choice of those observed managerial contracts is (incentive, signalling, screening, tax, etc.) or why contracts differ across different firms and across time within firms.[28] For example, while Healy [1985] is an excellent study which documents the association between income manipulation and the form of compensation plans, it offers no convincing explanation as to why shareholders find it in their best interest to induce this behaviour. Without such an explanation it becomes problematic as to whether we are interpreting the observed phenomena correctly.

When attempts to explain observed phenomena are made, the lack of modelling often results in an appeal to unmodelled transaction costs and political costs. But this reduces the persuasiveness of the arguments. This is especially true in the positive theory's reliance on political costs to explain management's choice of financial accounting procedures. For example, Watts & Zimmerman [1986, p. 247] state, "To avoid congressional and regulatory agency attention with its consequent costs (and reduction in management compensation), the manager prefers the deferral method since it usually reduces the level and variance of reported earnings." But the deferral method can be converted to the flow-through method at almost no cognitive cost. So what is the transaction cost which prohibits this conversion and induces this choice of accounting technique?

EMPIRICAL TESTS OF THE AGENCY PARADIGM

All of the agency models discussed so far share a common view of the interaction between owners, managers and employment contracts: (1) managers act to maximize their expected utility and hence their behaviour can be influenced by the design of their employment contracts; and (2) owners and managers collectively bear the cost of any agency problems, hence they have an incentive to design contracts which efficiently mitigate any underlying agency problems. The first point implies that we should see managerial behaviour respond to (changes in) the design of compensation plans in predictable ways. The second point implies that in the presence of underlying agency problems we should see the adoption of plans which attempt to mitigate those problems.

Most accounting related empirical agency research are studies of financial accounting issues rather than managerial accounting issues and are based on the positive theory of accounting model. Further, these studies have been the subject of several prior surveys (see Holthausen & Leftwich [1983]; Kelly [1983]; Lambert & Larcker [1985]; Watts & Zimmerman [1986]). Therefore, in this section I will limit my discussion to papers which provide tests of the above two implications of the agency model.

Evidence on the behaviour of management

Most of the literature has been concerned with testing the proposition that managerial decisions are affected by managerial compensation plans. Empirical tests generally support the assertion that capital investment decisions (Larcker [1983]), merger and acquisition decisions (Lewellen *et al.* [1985]; Tehranian *et al.* [1987]; Walking & Long [1984]) and financial accounting procedure choices (Healy [1985]) are associated with managerial compensation plans.

However, these tests are indirect and do not establish causality. For example, Larcker [1983] demonstrates an association between the adoption of long-term performance plans and changes in corporate capital investments. It is possible that the adoption of the long-term plans increased the planning horizon of management which then led them to increase their long-term investments. However, as Larcker notes, it is also possible that management had already decided to increase capital investment and the adoption of the long-term plans was a way of signalling this to the market and of allowing management to benefit from this decision. This raises the issue of whether observed compensation plans are adopted to overcome agency problems or for other reasons, such as taxes and signalling.

Evidence on the design of contracts to overcome agency problems

Murphy [1986] and Lewellen *et al.* [1987] attempt to deal with this identification problem. Murphy analyses how compensation plans would differ depending upon whether the problem to overcome is one of incentives versus one of learning the agent's type. From the different models, he derives different implications for the variance of executive pay and for the relationship between pay and performance over time and compares them with actual pay-experience profiles for executives. While the hypotheses are not mutually exclusive, the data seem more supportive of the learning model than the shirking model.

Lewellen *et al.* [1987] examines whether executive pay packages can be explained as attempts to reduce agency costs resulting from management having a shorter decision horizon than owners. If this were the case, then one would expect to see the components of executive pay (such as cash versus stock based compensation) systematically differ across firms depending upon how severe the horizon problem is in those firms. Lewellen *et al.* [1987] hypothesizes that the severity of the horizon problem is associated with certain observable firm–specific variables and tests the association of these variables with the components of senior executive pay. The components of the executive pay packages are found to vary in the predicted manner, thus supporting the argument that these compensation plans are designed to overcome agency problems.

Wolfson [1985] studies contracts in the oil and gas limited partnership market in which there is both substantial moral hazard with respect to the general partner's decision to complete the drilling of a well and potentially important tax implications to contract design. Wolfson identifies four different types of contracts between general and limited partners which make different trade-offs between the tax and incentive effects. He then derives hypotheses about the types of contracts one would find in different kinds of drilling, where the moral hazard problems would be of different severity. The data support the hypotheses. Wolfson also derives a hypothesis about the pricing of reputation for oil and gas general partners. The data support the hypothesis that a general partner's past performance (reputation) is impounded in the offering price of his new partnerships. In summary, Wolfson's results are consistent with both reputation and explicit incentives being used to control moral hazard problems in oil and gas limited partnerships. Further, Wolfson [1985] is notable for directly incorporating both the tax and incentive aspects of contracts.

Other studies have tested formally derived results from the principal–agent model in which the underlying agency problem arises because of moral hazard on the part of the agent. Results from principal-agent models indicate that when the outputs of agents are subject to correlated shocks, relative performance evaluation contracts are optimal (see Baiman & Demski [1980]; Holmstrom [1982b]). Antle & Smith [1986] empirically tests this result and finds weak support. Banker & Datar [1989] demonstrates that for a large class of production functions, the relative amount of weight which the performance evaluation measure should place on different signals, is related to the sensitivity of those signals to the agents action and the precision of those signals given the agent's action. Lambert & Larcker [1987] tests this result using security market returns and accounting returns as the signals of performance. The results are weak but consistent.

The Wolfson [1985], Murphy [1986] and Lewellen *et al.* [1987] studies discussed above try to provide a more direct test of the assertion that *observed* compensation contracts are chosen to mitigate specific agency problems. In particular, the latter two papers attempt to differentiate between different demands for executive compensation and to empirically test for them. However two recent papers call into question whether the data which can be observed by an outside researcher is sufficient to discriminate between several of the competing demands for executive compensation contracts. If one takes the Murphy [1986] model but assumes that the agent already knows his own type, then Hagerty and Siegel [1988] show that, in a single period world, a contract written to overcome a moral hazard problem (in which the agent's private information is about his action) is observationally indistinguishable from that written to overcome an adverse selection problem (in which the agent's private information is about the state realization). In a similar vein, Amershi & Butterworth [1988] shows that the optimal contract between a principal and agent which is designed to overcome moral hazard in an environment with homogeneous beliefs is empirically indistinguishable from the optimal pure risk sharing contract between a principal and an agent who have heterogeneous beliefs[29] but no problem of moral hazard.

The Hagerty & Siegel [1988] and Amershi & Butterworth [1988] results obviously call into question the ability of empirical research to test the results of agency analysis and to distinguish between the different demands for observed executive compensation contracts. These papers indicate that observing the form of the contract alone, without any additional information, may not enable the observer to infer the economic environment which gave rise to the contract. That is, in these situations, the researcher would have to already know what the reason for the contract was before he or she could empirically test whether the observed contract efficiently fulfilled its purpose.

One way to know whether observed contracts are chosen to efficiently address specific agency problems is to actually create the environment in which the contract is being chosen. This is the approach used in experimental economics. Berg *et al.* [1985a] sets up an experimental laboratory market made up of subjects acting as principals and agents. Each agent is asked to choose some unobserved action from which he derives disutility. Each principal is asked to choose an employment contract for an agent, from a previously specified set of feasible contracts. Berg *et al.* [1985a] finds that the principals and the agents both act consistent with principal–agent results. Thus, this experiment provides direct evidence that agents act opportunistically but respond to their compensation plans, and that principals are aware of this and choose employment contracts which efficiently mitigate this agency problem.

Most management accounting textbooks emphasize the use of Responsibility Accounting and the Controllability Principle as the basis for designing managerial accounting reporting and performance evaluation systems. However, Holmstrom [1979, 1982b] demonstrates the central importance of the Informativeness Condition as the basis for determining which signals should form the basis of principal–agent contracts.[30] In general, the Controllability Principle and the Informativeness Condition are not the same and can lead to different information system choices. Therefore, one test of the principal–agent model would be to see which of these two rules has more descriptive validity. Berg [1988] conducts a laboratory experiment to test which principle is the better predictor for the signals on which subjects choose to base their contracts. The results indicate that while at first the subjects' choice behaviour is consistent with the Controllability Principle and not with the Informativeness Condition, over time their choice behaviour tends to converge to that predicted by the Informativeness Condition. Thus, after an initial period, the subjects behave in a way which is consistent with principal–agent results.[31]

In conclusion, empirical research based on data from naturally occurring situations has been successful in detecting a number of empirical regularities which are consistent with the agency framework, but less so in testing specific principal–agent results. However, the results have to be interpreted in light of the limitations of empirical research in this area which have already been discussed. In addition, there are other inherent problems with research in this area. First, at best, an outside observer can typically observe only the explicit parts of contracts. However, there is undoubtedly a great deal of discretion involved with the actual implementation of most contracts. The use of discretion in compensation reduces what an observer can infer by looking only at written contracts. Further, the empirical studies cited are not based on examining managerial contracts but rather are based on estimates of compensation paid. But looking at just the payments ignores the provisions for the events that did not occur and hence ignores potentially important features of the contracts.[32] Another problem is that contracts in agency models are based on a specific set of signals, and it may be difficult to correctly specify and measure these crucial variables given that the researcher is limited to externally available data. Instead, the researcher is forced to assume that included in the available data set are surrogates for the signals used in the agency model and in the implementation of the actual contracts.[33]

Thus empirical research based on data from naturally occurring situations has a number of formidable obstacles to overcome in testing implications of the agency model.[34] The experimental markets approach can address many of these issues because of the tighter experimental control which it can exercise. However, there is obviously a reduction in the richness of the context which can be analyzed in an experimental laboratory market. Finally, empirical and experimental research cannot explain why we observe the observed empirical regularities; only the theoretical literature can do that. I therefore turn next to a discussion of recent theoretical results.

RECENT DEVELOPMENTS IN THE PRINCIPAL–AGENT PARADIGM

The papers to be discussed in the rest of the survey can be classified into two groups. The first group extends the principal–agent model to address some of the criticisms discussed earlier and to incorporate some of the features of the transaction cost economics model. While these papers do not directly deal with managerial accounting issues, they are nonetheless usefully discussed here for two reasons. First, some of these papers suggest potentially interesting uses and implications of management accounting procedures which are not brought out by previous principal–agent models. Second, others provide additional understanding of the principal–agent model by addressing some of the criticisms of the model which were mentioned earlier. Whether the ideas in these papers lead to a better understanding of the managerial accounting process must await future research which applies them to managerial accounting issues. By mentioning them here, I hope to encourage such future research. These papers are discussed in this section. The second group of recent principal–agent papers, which more directly address management accounting issues, is discussed in the fifth section.

Court enforcement and contract incompleteness.

Two major differences between the principal–agent and transaction cost economics paradigms are the extent to which contracts are assumed to be complete and courts are assumed to be efficient in enforcing contracts. One of the encouraging recent developments has been the response of principal–agent theorists to some of the objections and insights of transaction cost economics related to these differences. The next three subsections survey some of these principal–agent papers.[35]

Contract enforcement by courts. Recall that the principal–agent model assumes that courts can costlessly and accurately enforce all contracts. What happens to the form of the optimal principal–agent contract and the optimal agent action choice when we continue to allow for complete contracts but assume that the courts do not prevent the contracting parties from renegotiating their contract at a later date? Further, what is the cost incurred when renegotiation is allowed?

Fudenberg & Tirole [1988] examines these issues in the typical principal–agent problem in which the agent derives disutility from his action choice. However, unlike in the usual agency model, the principal and agent are allowed to renegotiate the contract once, after the action choice but before the outcome occurs. Because the contracts are still complete, any contract which the principal and agent could agree to at the time of renegotiation could be agreed to before renegotiation. Therefore, there is no loss of generality in restricting attention to renegotiation-proof contracts. Fudenberg & Tirole [1988] first shows that the only agent action strategies which can be induced in this environment are (1) the one in which the agent chooses the *minimum* effort and (2) randomized strategies. It further establishes that for a large class of problems the cost of implementing any given supportable agent-effort strategy is the same with and without court enforcement of the contract. In these cases, dropping court enforcement of contracts does not change the way that (or the cost at which) given agent strategies are induced. It only changes which strategies can be induced.

Contract incompleteness and renegotiation. Principal–agent research has also recently begun to analyze the effect of contract incompleteness on the design of contractual relationships. These models assume that the incompleteness arises, not because of bounded rationality, but because some states of the world or output, while jointly observable, are not verifiable to outsiders and hence cannot be contracted on (for example Green & Laffont [1988a, 1988b]; Hart & Moore [1987]; Riordan [1987]).

With incomplete contracts, the demand for renegotiation arises for different reasons than it did in the Fudenberg & Tirole [1988] model. Renegotiation occurs in Fudenberg & Tirole [1988] because, even with complete contracts, after the agent has chosen his action but before any new information occurs (such as the outcome realization), risk sharing can be improved by changing the contract.[36] Renegotiation occurs with incomplete contracts when, subsequent to the original contract agreement, an event occurs which was not specified in the original contract and for which no action or reward has been agreed upon. Renegotiation is valuable at that point if it improves how the individuals would otherwise respond to the uncontracted for event.

Hart & Moore [1987] and Green & Laffont [1988a] address the basic issue of interest in transaction cost economics, the effect of incomplete contracts on the *ex ante* investment in relationship-specific assets, but in a more formal way than has been done in the transaction cost economics literature. With incomplete contracts, it is no longer true, as in Fudenburg & Tirole [1988], that without loss of generality we can restrict ourselves to renegotiation-proof contracts. It may be optimal to allow for renegotiation to occur when uncontracted for contingencies arise. Hart & Moore [1987] and Green & Laffont [1988a] demonstrate conditions under which the design of the *ex ante* contract can affect this *ex post* renegotiation game and can mitigate the *ex ante* investment inefficiency arising from the incompleteness of the contract.

The incorporation of incomplete contracting within a principal–agent model raises an interesting managerial accounting issue. It seems reasonable that the earlier choice of managerial accounting procedures could affect the renegotiation game that takes place when uncontracted for contingencies arise. For example, one's leverage in renegotiation may depend on what information is common knowledge or more generally on the distribution of information among the negotiating parties. This distribution of information can obviously be affected by the earlier choice of managerial accounting procedures (i.e., the design of the variance analysis procedures, monitoring system and budgeting system). Therefore, admitting the possibility of incomplete contracts and allowing for renegotiation as a way of dealing with contract incompleteness introduces a new strategic element in the choice of managerial accounting procedures that has been ignored in principal–agent models to-date.

Such strategic considerations about the distribution of information may provide a partial explanation for why, in multi-division firms in which the divisions' performances are stochastically related, we often observe a division manager's performance evaluated on the basis of his own division's profit, and possibly corporate profits, rather than, as predicted by the principal–agent model (Baiman & Demski [1980]; Holmstrom [1982b]), on the full vector of divisional profits. In these cases, it may be that corporate headquarters anticipates the possibility of having to renegotiate agreements with divisional managers (about budgets, resource allocation, compensation, transfer prices, etc.) and decides that its bargaining position would be improved by denying each division manager direct access to information about the performance of the other divisions. This would allow corporate headquarters to selectively reveal this information during any renegotiation. The cost of doing so, however, is that a division manager's performance evaluation and compensation cannot be based on information, such as the performance of the other divisions, to which he does not have access. The improvement in corporate headquarter's strategic bargaining position accomplished by reducing each division manager's direct knowledge about the performance of the other divisions, may more than compensate for the reduction in motivational and risk-sharing benefits from basing divisional performance evaluation on own-divisional profit rather than on the vector of divisional profits.

Contract incompleteness and reputation. Because most principal–agent research has assumed complete contracting, reputation,[37] with its potential for disciplining behaviour in a multi-period setting, has been largely ignored.[38] As a result, principal–agent research has often been criticized for not paying attention to the effect of one's action choice on one's reputation for trust and fairness. Allowing for jointly observable but unverifiable information and incorporating incomplete contracts in a multiperiod setting allows concerns for trust and fairness and more generally reputation to endogenously arise. It is interesting that, as noted earlier, transaction cost economics, which is based on incomplete contracting, has also not extensively exploited the potential disciplining role of reputation as a substitute for or complement to formal governance structures.

Transactions between "reputable" individuals can be more efficiently accomplished than between those without such reputations by reducing the cost of collecting information as well as the cost of writing contracts and by increasing the set of supportable actions. Note, however that building up and maintaining a reputation is efficient only if it allows one to engage in future transactions which earn an above average rate of return.[39] For otherwise, the cost associated with losing one's reputation would not be sufficient to dissuade a reputable party from acting opportunistically. In the case of a firm in which a supervisor has discretion over how to reward an agent when uncontracted for contingencies arise, the supervisor will act "fairly" if doing so increases his future opportunities to earn excess returns. In an interesting and far-ranging paper, Kreps [1984] summarizes this literature and advances the view that firms are essentially reputation bearers and that corporate culture is a vehicle for establishing and maintaining that reputation.

Introducing incomplete contracts and reputational considerations has a number of potentially interesting managerial accounting implications. All principal–agent based managerial accounting research has taken a complete contracting perspective. As a result, this research has viewed managerial accounting procedures as producing inputs solely for use in explicit incentive contracts rather than for use in a reputation generating process. Thus this research has ignored an observed use for managerial accounting information and the implications which this use may have for the design of managerial accounting procedures. The design of explicit incentive contracts and managerial accounting procedures in a world of incomplete contracts in which discretion arises and reputational considerations come into play may be quite different from those which we have derived so far, based on a world of complete contracts.

The above analysis raises additional questions. When would agency costs be mitigated by giving the supervisor (or principal) the right to exercise discretion in the performance evaluation and compensation of the agent? What are the industry, competitive, informational and production function characteristics which influence the decision as to how much discretion to allow the supervisor? Are the characteristics of the managerial accounting system different for firms which allow different amounts of discretion to supervisors? What are the different characteristics of the information on which explicit contracts are based and on which discretion is based? All of these are interesting issues for which both theoretical and empirical research are required.

So notice that this recent theoretical work dealing with incomplete contracts, renegotiation and reputation, while not addressing managerial accounting issues, does have potential implications for managerial accounting research. In particular, it suggests demands for managerial accounting procedures and implications that have previously been overlooked in the literature.

The complexity of contracts

One of the major criticisms of the principal–agent model is that the contracts derived are seemingly more complicated and more sensitive to the underlying technical parameters than those observed in practice.[40] This, of course, raises the issue of the descriptive validity of the model. A number of recent principal–agent papers have attempted to address this complexity issue.

Linear contracts. Linear incentive schemes are both simple and observed. Holmstrom & Milgrom [1987] shows that, by *enriching* the strategies available to the agent, but without imposing any cost of complexity or cost of contract design, one can construct models in which compensation schemes which are linear in time aggregated accounts are optimal. Paradoxically, a very complex model is needed to produce the optimality of this simple linear scheme.

Menus of linear contracts have also been shown to be optimal in some models in which the agent has private state information at the time that the employment contract is negotiated (Laffont & Tirole [1986]; Melumad & Reichelstein [1989]). However, Rogerson [1987] shows that the class of problems for which linear contracts are optimal is probably not large. Further, what the above papers find is the optimality of a menu of linear contracts where there are an infinite number of entries in the menu (one for every state realization). That is, while each entry of the contract is simple, the number of entries make the menu of contracts quite complicated.

Multiperiod contracts. Work by Lambert [1983] and Rogerson [1985] show that in repeated agency contexts, long term contracts have memory and hence may be quite different from (and much more complicated than) a sequence of already complicated one period contracts. However, Fudenberg *et al.* [1987] shows that the gains from long term contracting in the Lambert and Rogerson models are primarily due to the restrictions on the agent's ability to borrow and save. The multi-period nature of these contracts is used to substitute for the self-insurance that would be available to agents if they were allowed access to the capital markets.

In particular, Fudenberg *et al.* [1987] shows that if (a) principal and agent preferences over future contracts are common knowledge (for example there is no private state information); (b) the utility possibility frontier generated by the set of incentive efficient contracts is downward sloping; and (c) the employee is able to borrow and save at the same rate as the principal, then long term contracts will be no better than a sequence of one-period contracts. Thus, in multiperiod settings satisfying these situations, the complexity of optimal contracts is no greater than the complexity of single period contracts.

The use of cardinal vs ordinal measures of performance. The above papers look at conditions under which optimal contracts take a simple form. Obviously one reason for simple contract forms is that there is a cognitive and information processing cost to contract complexity. One approach to deriving simpler contract forms which are presumably more consistent with observed contract, is to incorporate a contract design cost within the agency model. Unfortunately, the form of that cost is not well-understood. Another approach to simplifying principal–agent contracts is to *exogenously restrict* the form of the contract or how information is used within the contract. An example of the latter is the use of ordinal (relative ranking) measures of performance rather than cardinal (absolute) measures. Such schemes, called tournaments, are used, for example, in rewarding salespeople based on their relative, rather than absolute performance.

Tournaments have been the subject of much work (see Mookherjee [1988] for a summary of this literature). One of the problems with tournaments is that the agents have a strong and obvious incentive to collude against the principal but no incentive to help each other, even if their absolute performance could thus be improved. However, an advantage of tournaments is that they provide the principal with less of an opportunity to not honour the contracts when verification is difficult. This is because the total amount of compensation paid out in a tournament, unlike in other compensation schemes, does not vary in the performance of the individuals. Hence checking that the principals complied with the contract should be easier in tournaments than in other types of incentive schemes.

One commonly observed example of tournaments promotion-based incentives where an individual's compensation depends solely upon his position in the hierarchy. The only direct influence which measured performance has on compensation is through its effect on job promotion. In fact, Baker *et al.* [1988] claims that promotion-based incentives are more prevalent than performance-based incentives at lower levels of the firm. An unresolved issue is why incentive compensation systems which seemingly use only a subset of the available data, like tournaments and promotion-based incentives, are so prevalent.[41]

The strategic aspects of contract choice

Most principal–agent research has ignored the indirect effect which the choice of the agents compensation plan can have on the other participants operating in the product, capital and labour markets. This is because they assume that the firm is playing a game against nature, or is operating in a market when it is so small that its actions have no effect on the actions of its competitors. However, Fershtman & Judd [1984, 1986], Fershtman *et al.* [1987] and Sklivas [1987] study the agent contracting problem in a situation in which a small number of agent-managed firms compete in the same output market. They derive two interesting and related implications of agent-managed firms competing in the same product markets rather than playing games against nature. First, they demonstrate that the optimal agent contracts derived under these two different assumptions are different. Second, as a result of the differences in these contracts, they show that the agent (or firm) behaviour which is induced in these two situations is significantly different. These results arise because once you allow for competition among firms, the choice of agent incentive contracts takes on strategic implications which are ignored in principal–agent models in which the firm plays a game against nature. The strategic implications of agent contracts can be illustrated for the following scenario.

First, assume a market in which two separately owned firms operate. Next, assume that each owner delegates his firms operations to a different agent; each owner precommits to his agent's compensation contract; and each agent knows the other agent's compensation contract. Now each agent's compensation depends upon his performance, which depends upon his compensation contract, his action choice and the action taken by the other agent, which is affected by the latter's compensation contract. Therefore, each owner's choice of compensation contract affects not only his agent's actions but also *the actions of the other firm's agent*. This is the strategic aspect of contract design. That is, each owner designs his agent's contract to not only manipulate his agent's incentives but also to manipulate the *other firm's agent's* incentives. The latter consideration in designing compensation contracts is, of course, absent in models in which the firm is playing a game against nature. Therefore, one would expect that the employment contracts in the two situations are quite different.

In summary, factoring in the strategic effects of contract design forces the principal to adopt contracts and induce agent behaviour which may be quite different from those in which this strategic effect is ignored. One might expect managerial accounting systems (which are designed, in part, to support the employment contracts) to also be sensitive to the extent of competition in the product markets. It would be interesting to derive such a theoretical relationship and then test it cross-sectionally for a sample of industries. The insight provided by Fershtman & Judd [1984, 1986], Fershtman *et al.* [1987], and Sklivas [1987] must also cause us to reassess some past empirical tests of principal–agent results. For example, the tests conducted by Antle & Smith [1986] and Lambert & Larcker [1987], which were discussed earlier, were with respect to results derived from models which assumed that the firm competed against nature. But the tests were conducted on data from agent-managed companies which competed against other agent-managed companies.

Partial equilibrium labour market

As mentioned above, most of the principal–agent literature ignores the strategic effects that contract choice can have on the product, capital and labour markets. In the same way, most of the literature has ignored the effect that the labour market can have on the design of the employment contract and on the underlying agency problem itself.

Fama [1980] asserts that the agency problems of management are mitigated by the effect of reputation on one's market wage. He goes so far as to state that a concern for reputation *alone* will take care of any deviant incentives; there is no need for explicit incentives. Holmstrom [1982a] formalizes Fama's model and finds that while reputational considerations may mitigate agency problems, they are, in general, not strong enough to eliminate them. Holmstrom's results are consistent with the empirical results of Wolfson [1985] vhich were cited earlier.

In fact, Holmstrom & Ricart-Costa [1986] shows that the operation of the labour market may actually serve as the *source* of agency problems rather than as a way of mitigating them. Assume that an agent is risk-averse but work-neutral and must pick an investment project which will generate outcomes over a period of time. Further, assume that the agent has an ability type which is unknown both to himself and to the labour market. If the agent could precommit to lifetime employment with the firm (or equivalently, if the labour market could be ignored), then the cooperative solution could be achieved by paying the work-neutral agent a constant wage. However, without such precommitment, the labour market will use the outcomes of the investment chosen by the agent as signals about the agent's type and will revise his market wage accordingly. As a result, the agent will choose an investment that maximizes his human capital returns while the principal wants the agent to maximize the financial value of the firm. It is the operation of the labour market which has created the agency problem.

Introducing the labour markets into the principal–agent model also has implications for the design of managerial accounting procedures. It is often observed that agents are evaluated on the basis of information which is coarser than that potentially available to the firm. The use of promotion-based incentives discussed earlier is one example of this. Another example is one in which individuals are evaluated and compensated depending upon whether they are rated to be in the, say, top third, middle third or bottom third of their peer group. If managers have a finer partitioning than this, why would the firm not use this finer partitioning to evaluate its workers? One reason is suggested by the Holmstrom & Ricart-Costa [1986] model. By basing an agent's evaluation on finer information, the firm can improve the agent's motivation. However, by basing the agent's evaluation on finer information, the firm is allowing the market to use that performance evaluation to better revise the agent's opportunity wage. To the extent to which this increases the agent's opportunity wage, the firm must increase the amount paid for the agent's services now and in the future.[42] Thus the firm may design its performance evaluation information system (including budgets, variance analysis procedures, cost allocation methods) in order to trade-off its incentive effects with its future wage effects. This reasoning is also consistent with the use of promotion-based vs performance-based incentives. Thus, as before, expanding the principal–agent model to include the effects of markets can raise additional implications for the choice of managerial accounting performance evaluation systems and offer possible explanations for the use of observed managerial accounting performance evaluation systems.

RECENT THEORETICAL PAPERS WITH MANAGERIAL ACCOUNTING IMPLICATIONS

In this section I discuss some of the recent principal–agent papers which model more directly managerial accounting issues.

The value of monitoring

Much of the managerial accounting related principal–agent research has dealt with the value of monitoring. A number of recent papers have extended this area and have given us additional insight into the optimal design of monitoring systems. For example, most of the value-of-monitoring literature has assumed a fixed monitoring technology whose quality is exogenously given. However, recently Kumar [1989b] and Suh & Kim [1989] allow the quality of the monitoring system to be a decision variable.

Kumar [1988b] studies an agency model of the firm in which the principal invests in a production process under the control of a manager. The manager is privately informed as to the firm's capital productivity. The agent can report to the principal on the productivity realization and can divert some of the principal's investment from production to personal (non-pecuniary) consumption. The principal can imperfectly monitor the amount of investment which has been diverted. The principal must decide on both how much to invest in the firm's production process and how much to invest in the monitoring system. Kumar [1989b] finds that the principal will invest more in monitoring and base the agent's compensation more heavily on the monitoring signal when the agent communicates a low productivity state. When the agent reports a high productivity state, the principal will invest less in monitoring and base the agent's compensation more on the observed output. The reason is that with low productivity, and compensation based solely on output, the agent sacrifices less pecuniary compensation by diverting the resources to nonpecuniary consumption. To avoid this diversion of resources the principal must give the agent a larger share of the output. Hence motivation through incentive schemes based on output alone is costly in low productivity states. This creates a demand for monitoring. For high productivity states, a smaller share of output as compensation can increase the agent's preference for the productive investment. Hence the value of monitoring is less for high productivity states. Further, with monitoring the principal incurs a lower investment distortion in providing the agent incentives for truthful revelation, i.e., monitoring and capital rationing become substitutes in terms of inducing truthful revelation.

Suh & Kim [1989] also analyses the monitoring problem and allows for costly conditional monitoring but in a slightly different context. They start with a standard principal–agent model in which the investment in production is fixed, there is a moral hazard problem with respect to the agent's action choice, but the agent does not possess superior state information. As in Kumar [1989b], Suh & Kim [1989] allows the principal to invest in a monitoring technology. However, Suh & Kim [1989] allows the principal to precommit to a monitoring investment policy which is conditional on the observed outcome. Suh & Kim [1989] finds conditions under which the optimal investment policy is decreasing in the observed outcome. That is, the lower the outcome, the more money is spent on monitoring the agent's action and the more accurate the monitoring. Hence monitoring is being used as a penalty rather than as a reward.

In the monitoring literature, the usual assumption has been that either the principal is able to monitor the agent's private state information (e.g., Gale & Hellwigt [1985]; Townsend [1979]) or the agent's private action information (e.g., Baiman & Demski [1980]; Dyet [1986]). In a model in which the agent has both private state information and action information Kumar [1989a] allows the principal to choose between what is to be monitored. In his model, the monitoring decision is contingent on both the outcome realization and the communicated state realization. Assuming that the cost of monitoring either the state or the action is fixed and the same, he shows first that, regardless of whether the state or the action is monitored, the monitoring will be low tailed with respect to the outcome realization. Second, with respect to the agent's state realization report, actions will be monitored when the agent communicates that he is in a high productivity state and the state will be monitored when the agent communicates that he is in a low productivity state. The reason is that high efficiency types have an incentive to announce low efficiency and then take low effort. This is mitigated by monitoring the state when low efficiency is announced. Conversely, with high announced efficiency, it is important to check that the agent has taken the proper action.

An interesting question related to monitoring, is whether the gross returns to monitoring are always concave, as they are assumed for other inputs, or whether they can be convex.[43] Singh [1985] and Baiman *et al.* [1988] show that for models of moral hazard and joint moral hazard/adverse selection, respectively, there can be convexities in the value of monitoring information.

As noted earlier, one of the basic findings of principal–agent research is that, as a result of agency problems, often the best that the principal can do is to distort production, risk sharing and wealth allocation from first best. For example, when an agent has private state information, it may not be efficient for the principal to design a contract which eliminates all of the rents which the agent earns on his private information or one which induces the agent to implement the same production rule as he would if his private information were publicly available. Baiman *et al.* [1988] studies how improvements in a monitoring system's ability to detect lying by a privately informed agent affect the size of the production distortion and the rents earned by the agent on his private information. One might suspect that the principal would always use an improvement in the ability of the monitor to detect lying by the agent about his private information to capture some of the agent's rents, thereby reducing them. However, Baiman *et al.* [1988] finds that as the ability of the monitor to detect the agent's private information improves, the optimal solution is sometimes to *increase* the agent's rents to his private information. The reason is that, sometimes, by increasing the agent's rents as the monitoring system improves, the principal is able to reduce the production distortion by an even greater amount.

Finally, Riordan [1987] addresses the value of monitoring in a two-period principal–agent model in which the contracts are constrained to be incomplete by the assumption that the principal cannot precommit to a two-period contract. He finds that the principal is not always better off by monitoring in the first period, even if the monitoring is costless. The reason is because the principal cannot precommit to how he will use the information in the second period. The agent anticipates that the principal will use the information opportunistically in the second period, and this negatively affects the agent's first period action.

The Riordan [1987] analysis is potentially interesting for two reasons. First, it again raises the point that the role and value of managerial accounting may be subtly different with incomplete contracts than it is with complete contracts, which is the way in which we are used to addressing the issue. In particular, it points out the connection between the use and value of monitoring and the contract length. It would be an interesting empirical study to see if differences in the observed use of monitoring systems are related to differences in observed contract length. Second, it emphasizes that agents are not the only ones whose behaviour is subject to opportunism. Principals, when given the chance will also act opportunistically. However, almost all principal–agent research has assumed that any choices made by principals are verifiable, can be contracted on, and hence are not subject to moral hazard.

Income manipulation

A stylized fact that has been around for a long time is that managers tend to smooth, or more generally manipulate, reported income. Healy [1985] provides evidence that management's choice of financial reporting method appears to be influenced by its compensation contract. This result raises two issues. Given that a principal (or superior) has decided to delegate the choice of the outcome reporting method to an agent (or subordinate), why would the former find it in his best interest to design a compensation package which induces this kind of manipulative behaviour by the latter? Second, why would it be in the principal's best interest to delegate the choice of the outcome reporting method to the agent? The first issue is addressed in this section while the second is addressed in the next section.

Lambert [1984] and Ramakrishnan [1988] deal with real income smoothing, which involves the choice of production decisions which result in smooth income. But the issue in accounting is the smoothing of reported income numbers. This, of course, involves a situation in which the agent is privately informed of the true outcome realization and misreports it to the principal.

If the explanation is based on the agent having private information, then the Revelation Principle and a focal point argument could be used to argue that one would tend not to see smoothing or manipulation of the *reported* income number by the agent. Instead, it is more likely that the principal would induce truth-telling from the agent and perform the smoothing himself.[44] However, for the Revelation Principle to work it is necessary that: (a) all individuals who receive messages from the privately informed agents can credibly commit to how they will use the messages; (b) the privately informed agents are physically able to communicate all of their information if they choose to do so; and (c) there are no restrictions on the form of the contracts. If one or more of these necessary conditions does not hold, then the Revelation Principle does not hold and it may no longer be true that the desired equilibrium can be achieved by truth-inducing contracts. In this case, it may be optimal for the principal to induce the agent to misreport the outcome. Therefore, one way to rationalize income smoothing, or more generally income manipulation, based on the agent having private information, is to look at a situation in which the Revelation Principle does not hold.

This is the approach adopted by Baiman *et al.* [1987], Dye [1988] and Penno [1986].[45] The last two papers model a situation in which the Revelation Principle is not accessible because the dimensionality of the agent's message space is assumed to be smaller than the dimensionality of the agent's private information. In addition Dye [1988] also points out that in an overlapping generations model, the Revelation Principle would not hold because the present generation of principals cannot precommit to the next generation of principals as to how they will have the manager report. The Baiman *et al.* [1987] analysis is also based on an inability to precommit—but by the auditor. Baiman *et al.* [1987] models a situation in which the agent privately observes the true outcome, issues an outcome report to the principal and a work-averse auditor is hired to audit the report. The paper demonstrates that there exists no equilibrium in which the agent accurately and fully reports the true outcome, the auditor observes the agent's report prior to auditing and the auditor expends the effort required to audit the reported outcome. The reason is that if the auditor observes the reported outcome and knows that it is the truth, he has no incentive to work. He can just corroborate the report and avoid all effort. But then the agent would not report the truth. As a result, the principal must induce the agent to choose other than full and honest reporting in order to get the auditor to audit. That is, the principal must induce the agent to distort the outcome report in order to make it auditable.

Hence the principal–agent model provides several scenarios in which, given that the principal delegates the choice of the outcome reporting method to an agent, it is Pareto optimal for the principal to provide a compensation contract to the agent which induces the latter to misreport the results of the firm's operations. The question still remains as to why the principal would ever find it in his best interest to delegate the choice of the outcome reporting method to the agent. This issue is addressed in the next section.

Delegating the choice of monitoring systems

One reason why principals may find it in their best interest to delegate the choice of the firm's outcome reporting method to agents is that they find it too costly to do otherwise. However, this is not a very helpful explanation. Recent principal–agent analyses offer other, more substantive, explanations.

Demski *et al.* [1984] offers one explanation which is based on the agent having private information which the principal would find it valuable to have. The principal may delegate the choice of outcome reporting method to the agent if that choice by the agent is observed; the choice signals his private information; and there is no other way for the agent to credibly convey that private information.

This might be an explanation for those outcome reporting methods whose choices are observed by the principal (for example the choice of depreciation method or inventory accounting in financial reporting). However many choices, such as changes in estimates and expense vs capitalization decisions, are not observed by the principal. An explanation for the delegation of the choice of outcome reporting methods to the agent, which would deal with these unobserved choices, is offered in Baiman & Kumar [1989] and is based upon a principal–agent model with double moral hazard.

If the choice of the outcome reporting method is made at the end of the period and cannot be contracted on, as for example when it cannot be observed, then no matter who gets to choose it, it will be chosen opportunistically. That is, in deciding who should choose the outcome reporting method, the two alternatives are (1) the choice can be delegated to the agent with the knowledge that the agent will choose that method which maximizes his expected utility; (2) the choice can be made by the principal with the knowledge that the principal will choose that method which maximizes his expected utility. In either case, the knowledge by the agent that the outcome reporting method choice will be subsequently chosen opportunistically, will have a negative motivational effect on the agent's previous action choice, relative to the situation in which the outcome reporting method could be contracted on. The only issue then is whose choice of reporting method has less distortionary effects. Baiman & Kumar [1989] finds conditions under which there is less distortion, and hence both the principal and the agent are better off, when the outcome reporting is delegated to the agent, than when the outcome reporting is delegated to the principal.

Another possible explanation for the delegation of outcome reporting to management is offered by Penno [1988]. He analyses a situation in which there exist many ways of monitoring the agent's action, i.e., many different available monitoring systems. The agent costlessly observes the signals from each of these systems but it is costly for the principal to do so. The principal has two monitoring strategies from which to choose. First, the principal may choose, at the start of the period, to subsequently receive the signal from one of these available monitoring systems. Alternatively, the principal can allow the agent, who has access to the signals of all of the available monitoring systems, to pick the monitoring system whose signal he most prefers to show to the principal and be evaluated on. The second alternative captures the situation in which an individual within firms is evaluated on the basis of information which he self-reports. This second alternative can also be thought of as the principal delegating the choice of monitors to the agent. Penno [1988] then investigates the efficiency of delegating the choice of monitoring system to the agent who is being evaluated. He shows that for low levels of the organization, such delegation can be Pareto superior to the first alternative, achieving a near first-best (i.e., cooperative) solution, where the agent's contract is essentially a constant. This result is certainly consistent with how low level workers in firms are compensated.

The reason for the first-best result with delegation is that at low levels it is *assumed* that the monitors from which the agent can choose all produce independent and identically distributed signals; the number of monitors from which the agent can choose is large; and all monitors produce signals which are both *verifiable* and correlated with the agent's performance. Hence, whatever signal the agent presents, the principal knows that all the other realized signals were *less* favourable. Therefore, if the agent provides a low signal the principal has a high degree of confidence (increasing in the number of monitors from which the agent can choose) that the agent did not take the first-best action. In this case the principal can severely penalize the agent. Otherwise, the principal can pay the agent the first-best compensation. This will be enough to motivate the agent to take the first-best (i.e., cooperative) action.

At higher levels of the firm, it is assumed that the available information becomes more aggregated and that the number of monitors to choose from becomes smaller. Because the informational environment is thus assumed to be less rich at higher levels of the firm, it is necessary to impose more risk on the agent in order to properly motivate him. Again this compensation result is consistent with how higher level agents are compensated in firms. Further, Penno [1988] shows that even in the case in which the number of monitors to choose from is small (as at high levels of the firm), if the principal's choice is between precommiting to the choice of one monitor upon which to base the agent's compensation and allowing the agent to *ex post* choose one monitor from a set of monitors after having observed each of their signals, as long as the choice of the agent's monitor is observed and can be contracted on, it is optimal for the principal to delegate the choice of the monitoring to the agent. The reason for this result is essentially the same as before. The principal can't be worse off, because he can always make the agent choose the monitoring system which he (the principal) would have chosen. Further, the improvement comes from the fact that whichever monitor and signal the agent chooses, the principal, by observing the monitor choice knows that all the other monitors must have produced less favourable signals. This additional information can be used to reduce the risk imposed on the agent.

Thus Penno [1988] provides another answer to the issue raised in the previous section of why principals find it in their best interest to delegate the choice of monitors to the agents whose performance is being evaluated. What is particularly interesting about the Penno [1988] paper, in addition to the results, is that it hypothesizes different characteristics for the informational environment at different levels of the firm and studies how that affects the design of the agents' compensation plan. Of course, it is an empirical question whether the informational assumptions hold. However, the approach taken in this paper is a step in the right direction for generating testable hypotheses and for making the principal–agent model better reflect the organization of the firm.

Cost allocation

Probably the most often used and hardest to rationalize managerial accounting procedure is cost allocation. Baiman & Noel [1985] analyses a multiperiod agency model in which it is optimal to allocate a project's capacity costs to an agent over time even though these costs are completely noncontrollable by the agent. This result is consistent with, for example, the observed use of depreciation in performance evaluation measures. In their model the agent can take long run or short run actions which are unobservable to the principal. Further, the jointly observed present capacity cost contains information about future capacity costs which will be used by the principal to subsequently determine whether to continue operations or shut down. Given that the agent's actions can have multiperiod effects depending upon the principal's subsequent investment decision, the principal's subsequent decision becomes a productivity parameter to the agent. At the time of the agent's action choice, the best information available about the principal's subsequent investment decision is the prior capacity cost realization. It thus conveys information about the expected duration or expected productivity of the agent's current action choice. The principal wants the agent to adjust his decision based upon the anticipated subsequent investment decision, and to do this the principal bases the agent's compensation on the previous capacity cost realizations. Therefore the agent's compensation depends on the *previous* capacity cost realizations not because they are directly informative about *his past* actions but because they are informative about the *principal's future* actions.

One distinctive feature of cost allocation among units of a firm is that it sets up a zero-sum game with respect to those allocations among the units. That is, because it is historical cost which is being allocated, a dollar more allocated to one unit means a dollar less allocated to the other divisions. A natural question then arises as to why a firm would want to design a system which forces its units to play a zero-sum game, in accounting profits, among themselves. In a recent paper Rajan [1989] offers one reason. In a multi-agent firm, when one or more agents have private information, the Revelation Principle assures that there is no loss of generality in restricting the choice of contracts for the agents to be from the set of contracts which induces truth-telling. The problem with the Revelation Principle in multi-agent settings is that a set of compensation contracts which induces truth-telling as an equilibrium may induce other, non-truth telling, equilibria as well. Further, one of these non-truth telling or non-obedient equilibria may make the agents strictly better off and the principal strictly worse off than under the truth-telling equilibrium. Hence the principal would be interested in a way of eliminating these non-obedient equilibria. Rajan [1989] shows that by basing the agents' compensation on the allocation of historical cost, and basing the allocation on the agents' reports of their private information, thereby introducing a zero-sum aspect to their reports, these non-obedient equilibria can be eliminated with no loss of efficiency, leaving only the desired truth-telling equilibrium.

The distinction between performance measures and reward measures

Managerial accounting is used to acquire and process information for performance evaluation purposes. In turn these performance evaluation measures are then used as inputs to the reward function to determine the agent's compensation. As managerial accountants we are primarily interested in studying the performance evaluation function.

However, the principal–agent model only solves for the incentive function which is the composition of the performance evaluation function and the reward function. In general, there may be many different performance evaluation function/reward function pairs whose composition is the optimal incentive compensation function. Thus while the agency model views the firm at a more micro level than does traditional microeconomics, it is still not at a micro enough level to address the question of why we observe particular performance evaluation measures or why compensation is in practice a two stage process: performance evaluation and reward. A further question is why many observed performance evaluation measures are linear aggregations of data. Performance evaluation on the basis of total profit, revenue or cost are the foremost examples.

Banker & Datar [1989] addresses this issue in a principal–agent model with a risk-neutral principal in which two post-action signals are generated. They derive necessary and sufficient conditions for some (although not necessarily the same) linear aggregation of the two observed signals to be optimal for all agencies. Further, for a subclass of distributions for which some linear aggregation is optimal, they are able to interpret the relative weight placed on each of the two signals in terms of the sensitivity and the precision of the signals. Note that even though the performance measure is a linear aggregation of the signals, the optimal incentive contract may still be non-linear in the linear aggregate. This linear aggregation result is particularly interesting because the class of distribution for which it holds is quite large.

STRATEGIES FOR ENHANCING THE CONTRIBUTION OF THE AGENCY MODEL TO MANAGERIAL ACCOUNTING

Given my own specialized interest in the principal–agent model, this last section discusses how research based on that model can enhance its impact on managerial accounting. One of the recent developments whose future growth will enhance the impact of the principal–agent model is the integration of the transaction cost economics and principal–agent models. Trying to incorporate the ideas of incomplete contracts, transaction costs and even bounded rationality into the more formal principal–agent model with force researchers in both branches of the literature to define these concepts and analyze their sources more carefully. This should lead to better modelling of managerial accounting problems. For example, one type of transaction cost is information processing and communication cost. Accounting is concerned with how to aggregate information. Blackwell type results (Holmstrom [1979,1982b]), which tells us that nothing is lost by aggregating information into sufficient statistics, are of limited usefulness because accounting systems would seem to go well beyond such limlted aggregation. The obvious reason for this is the cost to process and communicate information. Unfortunately, agency theory has not been able, as yet, to incorporate information costs and complexity in its models.

However, the network mechanism literature (Marschak & Reichelstein [1987]) does attempt to do this. This literature examines organizations in which there is asymmetric information, but, by assumption, no motivational problems. The objective of the literature is to design communication systems which maximize the organization's efficiency, including the cost of communication. The cost of communication is usually measured in terms of the dimensionality of the messages between the organization's units. I would conjecture that issues of cost of communication are as important in understanding the form of observed managerial accounting procedures as are issues of motivation. Therefore, incorporating both this information cost perspective and the incentive perspective would get us closer to a more realistic model of managerial accounting.

Another way to enhance the impact of principal–agent research on managerial accounting is to better coordinate it with empirical research. First and foremost we need to exploit the data we already have and to collect more based upon what our results tell us are important variables. In the first case we can use some of the empirical regularities which have been found in the Rochester literature. As noted earlier, that literature has been quite successful in detecting empirical regularities with respect to management behaviour and executive compensation contracts but not in explaining why contracts of those forms are efficient. The principal–agent branch's insistence on careful modelling and internal consistency can help to derive economic explanations for these stylized facts. The results obtained based on these models can then be used to direct new empirical research. The income smoothing and delegation of accounting method choice topics discussed earlier represent a start in this direction.

Coordinating principal–agent and field-based research could result in benefits to both areas. First, applying the principal–agent paradigm to the research question underlying the field study would sharpen the focus of the field study. Second, using the results of field based studies could sharpen our principal–agent models. For example, while most people would agree that transaction costs probably do affect the design of managerial accounting procedures, the source and size of those costs are not well understood and documented. Field based research into the nature and size of these costs and the relationship between them and observed managerial accounting procedures would be of great help to agency theorists in trying to model transaction costs and integrate them into the principal–agent model. Further, agency research would also benefit from field-based research which studied the information characteristics of different production functions in different industries and at different levels of the firm so that comparative statics results from our theoretical models could be compared to the data. Work such as Penno's [1988] would benefit from such field-based research.

Another approach to empirical validation of the agency model is to concentrate less on deriving optimal compensation contracts and concentrate more on more easily observed aspects of the firm. First, as noted earlier, the derived compensation schemes are complicated and sensitive to the technical assumptions and, hence, not suitable for the kinds of comparative statics analysis which are useful for empirical analysis. Second, as noted earlier, most compensation packages tend to be subject to a great deal of discretion, especially when one factors in job promotion. Therefore, it is not likely that we will ever see an actual fully specified and operational compensation package against which to compare our theoretically derived compensation scheme. As a result, more fruitful research might be devoted to variables which are more easily observed and for which better data may be available. These would include investments and the design of accounting procedures such as variance investigation, budgeting, etc.[46]

The information to be collected which has been suggested so far has been from either publicly available sources or from field-based studies. Data from experimental economics laboratory studies based on the agency model can make a significant contribution to agency research in general and to managerial accounting specifically. I have already mentioned Berg *et al.* [1985a] and Berg [1988] as examples of recent laboratory work which tests implications of the principal-agent pardigm. In addition laboratory experiments are ideal for helping to establish which of the many competing equilibrium concepts are descriptively valid (see Berg *et al.* [1985b] for an example). In addition, one of the problems with analyzing multi-agent firms is that the number of equilibria usually increases with the number of agents. The problem of coordination then arises. Managerial accounting procedures might be chosen as a way of establishing different focal points. This idea could be tested in an experimental economics setting.

In conclusion, the agency model has given us a coherent framework with which to analyze managerial accounting issues. In the short period of time in which it has been used, it has generated a number of insights into the managerial accounting process. The recent progress in both empirical and theoretical agency research has been especially impressive and I believe that it will allow us to increase the positive impact that agency research will have on managerial accounting.

ENDNOTES

1. For other recent surveys of the agency and related literatures, see Holmstrom & Tirole [1987] and Hart & Holmstrom [1987]. The present survey is not meant to be comprehensive. For example, I have tried to keep the overlap with Baiman [1982] to a minimum. Further, I have chosen to review only a representative sample of the recent literature. In addition, this paper does not review the literature which has proposed and tested alternative behaviourial

models of the determinants of managerial behaviour. For an excellent review of this literature, see Kren & Liao [1988].

2. Although it might be considered an agency model, the stewardship literature in accounting will not be discussed. The major reason is that those recently interested in this area have tended to base their analysis on one of the three agency models mentioned. For example, Gjesdal [1981] uses a principal–agent model to analyze the stewardship problem.

3. See Baiman [1982] for a more complete discussion of the assumptions underlying the principal–agent model.

4. An event is jointly observable if it is observable to the contracting parties. An event is verifiable if it is observable not only to the contracting parties but also to a third party (such as a court) who is responsible for enforcing the contract. Thus all verifiable events are jointly observable but not all jointly observable events are verifiable. The distinction between observability and verifiability is important because only verifiable events can be contracted on. Until recently principal–agent models did not distinguish between observability and verifiability but, instead, assumed that any jointly observable event was verifiable and could be contracted on. Some implications of this distinction will be developed later when issues of reputation are discussed.

5. An alternative assumption is that the agent is risk-neutral, has private state information and that the labour market is such that the agent must be guaranteed his minimum expected utility for each possible realization of his private information. For example, the agent may have private information about the productivity of the principal's capital. If the labour market is such that the agent can leave the firm after he has learned the capital's productivity but the principal wants to employ the agent for each productivity realization, then the agent's employment contract must assure the agent his minimum expected utility for each capital productivity realization. This labour market condition is referred to as limited liability.

6. When the agent is risk-neutral, has private state information and the labour market assures him limited liability, the agent is in a position to misrepresent his private information, and thereby earn rents on that private information. Again, the cooperative solution cannot be achieved by self-interested behaviour. In this case the principal may find it in his best interest to distort production away from the cooperative level in order to reduce the rent which the agent can earn on his private information.

7. Principal–agent analysis has also begun to appear in managerial accounting texts. See, for example, Kaplan [1982] and Magee [1986].

8. See, for example, Hirshleifer [1956], Kaplan & Thompson [1971] and Hamlen *et al.* [1977]. As an example, Hirshleifer studied transfer pricing in a model in which the owner had perfect information. As a result, there was no need for the owner to influence divisional behaviour by designing a transfer price system. Instead, the owner could achieve the cooperative solution simply by ordering the divisions to transfer the appropriate quantities and designing a forcing contract which assured their compliance.

9. For analyses of transfer pricing and cost allocation using a principal–agent perspective, see, for example, Baiman & Noel [1985] Demski [1981], Harris *et al.* [1982] and Rajan [1989].

10. The papers discussed in the fourth and especially the fifth section illustrate the insight into the managerial accounting process provided by recent principal–agent research.

11. A firm is a hierarchy if it is composed of two or more agents where the principal communicates and contracts with a strict subset of agents, who in turn communicate and contract with a strict subset of agents, etc.
12. For a notable exception see Melumad *et al*. [1989].
13. For example, linear or piece rate contracts are observed in many situations. Constant wage contracts are even more widely observed.
14. Because the model views all potential contracting variables in terms of their statistical (i.e., informational) properties and optimal contracts use all the information available, optimal contracts are sensitive to the underlying distributional properties of the contract variables. Optimal contracts are also sensitive to the assumed preferences of the contracting parties.
15. This point was emphasized by Rick Antle in his Plenary Address to the 1988 American Accounting Association Annual Meeting.
16. Contract complexity and discretion are addressed later.
17. In order to study discretion, one needs to distinguish between verifiable information on which one can base contracts and observable but unverifiable information on which one can only base discretionary behaviour. See the later discussion of reputation (endnote 37) in which this point is further developed.
18. For a more complete description of this literature see Williamson [1975], Williamson [1986a] and Williamson [1986b].
19. Examples of such potential enrichment are presented in the fourth and fifth sections.
20. Decisions as to how to organize a transaction would include whether an intermediate product is produced internally or externally, as well as whether to sell one's products through one's own stores, franchisee owned stores or independently owned stores.
21. However, this difference is not as significant as it first appears. For example, although the principal and agent in principal–agent models are usually *interpreted* as having an employer-employee relationship, the model does not require this. In many situations the analysis would be the same if one interpreted their relationship to be that of an owner and an independent contractor. The problem is that *none* of the agency branches provides a useful definition of a firm or a useful way of locating the border between a firm and the market.
22. Recently, principal–agent researchers have started to address traditional topics within transaction cost economics but with more emphasis on modelling the underlying environment and on deriving optimal solutions. As a result, the distinction between principal–agent and some recent transaction cost economics research has become somewhat blurred. Some of these papers will be discussed in the fourth and fifth sections.
23. Examples would include a firm's cost accounting system as well as budgeting, transfer pricing and cost allocation rules.
24. For example, if a supplier invests in a general purpose machine rather than a special purpose machine he will reduce the amount of surplus bargained over between himself and the buyer, but he may improve his relative bargaining position with the buyer.
25. However, for an excellent example of work where the sources of transaction costs are well-specified and indirectly measured, see Scholes *et al*. [1989].
26. However, see endnote 22.

27. See Christenson [1983] for other criticisms of this literature.
28. See Raviv [1985] for a discussion of this point.
29. Heterogeneous beliefs exist when two individuals' beliefs differ even though they have the same information.
30. The informativeness condition states that one costless public post-decision information system is strictly Pareto superior to a second, *regardless of the preferences and beliefs of the principal and agents,* if and only if the signals of the first system convey more information about the actions chosen by the agents than do the signals of the second system. The idea of more information as used here is that implied by the concept of statistical sufficiency as defined in statistics and decision theory.
31. Evidence from laboratory experiments by Berg *et al*. [1988] also support principal–agent results with respect to the value of communication when the agent is privately informed.
32. An alternative approach adopted by Walsh & Stewart [1988a, 1988b] is an archival approach in which one firm's written compensation contracts over time are analyzed.
33. The Antle & Smith [1986] and Lambert & Larcker [1987] studies are subject to this problem.
34. Jensen [1983] discusses some other difficulties with conducting formal tests of hypotheses dealing with organizational and contractual forms.
35. While I label these as examples of principal–agent research, others may label them as examples of transaction cost economics research. This merely illustrates the point that parts of the two literatures are starting to overlap.
36. For example, the agent can be relieved of the risk imposed in him for motivational purposes, because he has already chosen his action.
37. Reputation has been used in two different ways in the literature. Both uses are based on observations by others of an individual's actions or the results of his actions. The first way in which reputation is used is with respect to other's beliefs as to whether an individual possesses an *inherent* characteristic or *type* over which he has no control, but which affects his payoff function or utility for payoffs. For example, an individual may have a reputation for being a tough competitor (one who enjoys winning independent of its monetary effects), a condition over which he has no control. For reputation in this sense to be of interest, an individual must have private information about his type, and his past behaviour must be useful to others in making inferences about his type. Much of this work is based on Kreps & Wilson [1982]. In this section, reputation is used in a second way. Here reputation has to do with others' beliefs, based upon an individual's history of actions, as to whether he will *choose to act* in a certain way in the future. How others believe he will act in the future influences how they will act in the future which influences his payoff from acting in that way vs some other way. To illustrate, assume that two people are playing an infinitely repeated Prisoners' Dilemma game with known payoffs. Assume that they would both be better off by acting cooperatively. Further, assume that individual B announces that he will play cooperatively as long as Individual A maintains a *reputation* for playing cooperatively. This reputation is built up and maintained by always being observed to have played cooperatively. B also announces that he will take the noncooperative action forever once A acquires a reputation for acting noncooperatively. A would acquire such a reputation by once being observed to have acted noncooperatively. Thus A's past behaviour established his *reputation*, and B bases

his action choices on A's reputation. Notice that reputation is based on A's *jointly observed* action. If a contract between the two individuals could be written on their *verifiable* action choices, then there would be no need for reputation; B's punishment strategy could be built directly into the contract Therefore, for reputations to be valuable in this second sense, the parties must *not* be able to write contracts on the information on which the reputation is being built (for example, A's behaviour may be jointly observable but not verifiable). Reputational uses of information and contractual uses of information differ in terms of the extent to which players can precommit to those uses. If an enforceable contract could be written based on the A's past actions (i.e., the contract was complete with respect to observations of A's actions), then B would be *obligated* to act noncooperatively forever if he once observed A acting noncooperatively. If observations of A's past behaviour could not be written into a contract but could be used as a basis for B's action choice (i.e., the contract was incomplete with respect to observations of A's actions), then B would implement the punishment strategy once he has observed A act noncooperatively *only if it was then in B's best interest* to do so. In this latter case, B's use of A's history of action choices is discretionary.

38. See Fama [1980] and Holmstrom & Ricart-Costa [1986] for exceptions. However, they use reputation in the first sense discussed in the previous endnote (i.e., the market's belief as to one's type) rather than in the second sense, which is how it is used in this section.

39. Recall Wolfson's [1985] evidence that a general partner's reputation is impounded in the offering price of his new oil and gas partnerships.

40. However recall the response to this criticism in the second section.

41. See the section labelled "Partial equilibrium labour markets" for one possible explanation.

42. In a related model, Harris & Holmstrom [1982] finds conditions under which the optimal compensation contract increases when the agent's outside opportunity wage goes up, but does not go do down when the agent's opportunity wage goes down. In this case, the cost of providing the labour market with information about the agent's performance becomes even greater.

43. The gross returns to monitoring are concave (convex) if improvements in the monitoring system increase the gross value to the agency at a decreasing (increasing) rate.

44. The Revelation Principle shows that, under certain conditions, any equilibrium in which the agent is induced to misreport can be achieved by one which induces the agent to report honestly. The intuition is that if the principal can precommit to garble the agent's message in exactly the same way as the agent finds it optimal to garble the signal realization in the non-truthtelling equilibrium, then the agent's best message strategy is to tell the truth. This does not mean that we would expect to observe only truth-telling equilibria when the Revelation Principle held. In such cases, all parties should be indifferent between a non-truth-inducing equilibrium and its Pareto equivalent truth-inducing equilibrium. However, one can then argue that the truth-telling equilibrium would be chosen because it is a natural focal point.

45. Again it must be emphasised that it is not necessary for the Revelation Principle to not hold in order to observe misreporting. Hence, focusing only on situations in which the Revelation Principle does not hold in order to explain misreporting may result in not looking at some interesting situations involving misreporting.

46. This point is also made in Holmstrom & Tirole [1987].

BIBLIOGRAPHY

Amershi, A. H. & J. E. Butterworth, "Explorations in the Theory of Single and Multiple Agent Agencies", in Amershi, A., Feltham, G. & Ziemba, W. (eds), *Economic Analysis of Information and Contracts* Norwell, MA: Kluwer Academic Press, 1988).

Antle, R. & A. Smith, "An Empirical Investigation of the Relative Performance Evaluation of Corporate Executives", *Journal of Accounting Research* (1986) pp. 1-39.

Baiman, S. & J. Demski, "Economically Optimal Performance Evaluation and Control Systems", *Journal of Accounting Research* (1980) pp. 184-220.

Baiman, S., "Agency Research in Managerial Accounting: A Survey", *Journal of Accounting Literature* (1982) pp. 154-213.

Baiman, S., J. Evans & J. Noel, "Optimal Contracts with a Utility-Maximizing Auditor", *Journal of Accounting Research* (1987) pp. 217-244.

Baiman, S. & P. Kumar, "The Delegation of Financial Reporting", Unpublished Working Paper, Graduate School of Industrial Administration, Carnegie Mellon University Working Paper (unpublished, 1989).

Baiman, S., J. May & A. Mukherji, "Optimal Employment Contracts and the Returns to Monitoring in a Principal–Agent Context", *Contemporary Accounting Research* (1990) pp. 761-799.

Baiman, S. & J. C. Noel, "Noncontrollable Costs and Responsibility Accounting", *Journal of Accounting Research* (1985) pp. 486-501.

Baker, G. P., M. C. Jensen & K. J. Murphy, "Compensation and Incentives: Practice vs. Theory", *The Journal of Finance* (1988) pp. 593-616.

Banker, R. & S. Datar, "Sensitivity, Precision and Linear Aggregation of Signals for Performance Evaluation", *Journal of Accounting Research* (1989) pp. 21-39.

Berg, J., "Informativeness and Value of Public Information: An Experimental Test", Washington University Working Paper (unpublished, 1988).

Berg, J., L. Daley, C. Kanodia & F. Gigler, "The Value of Communication in Agency Contracts: Theory and Experimental Evidence", Washington University Working Paper (unpublished, 1988).

Berg, J. E., L. A. Daley, J. W. Dickhaut & J. R. O'Brien, "Tests of Principal–Agent Theory in an Experimental Setting", Accounting Research Center, University of Minnesota Working Paper (unpublished, 1985).

Berg, J., J. Dickhaut & D. Senkow, "Signalling Equilibria in Experimental Markets: Rothschild and Stiglitz vs. Wilson and Riley", University of Minnesota Working Paper (unpublished, 1985b).

Christenson, C., "The Methodology of Positive Accounting", *The Accounting Review* (1983) pp. 1-22.

Demski, J. S., "Cost Allocation Games", in Moriarity, S. (ed.), *Proceedings of the University of Oklahoma Cost Allocation Conference on Cost Allocation* (Norman, OK: University of Oklahoma Press, 1981).

Demski, J. S., J. M. Patell & M. Wolfson, "Decentralized Choice of Monitoring Systems", *The Accounting Review* (1984) pp. 16-34.

Dye, R. A., "Optimal Monitoring Policies in Agencies", *The Rand Journal of Economics* (1986) pp. 339-350.

Dye, R. A., "Earnings Management in an Overlapping Generations Model", *Journal of Accounting Research* (1988) pp. 195-235.

Fama, E., "Agency Problems and the Theory of the Firm", *Journal of Political Economy* (1980) pp. 288-307.

Fershtman, C. & K. Judd, "Equilibrium Incentives in Oligopoly", J. L. Kellogg Graduate School of Management, Northwestern University Working Paper (unpublished, 1984).

Fershtman, C. & K. Judd, "Strategic Incentive in Manipulation in Rivalrous Agency", Institute for Mathematical Studies in the Social Sciences, Stanford University Working Paper (unpublished, 1986).

Fershtman, C., K. Judd & E. Kalai, "Cooperation Through Delegation", J. L. Kellogg Graduate School of Management, NorthWestern University Working Paper (unpublished, 1987).

Fudenberg, D., B. Holmstrom & P. Milgrom, "Short-Term Contracts and Long Term Agency Relationships", Massachusetts Institute of Technology Working Paper (unpublished, 1987).

Fudenberg, D. & J. Tirole, "Moral Hazard and Renegotiation in Agency Contracts, Department of Economics", Massachusetts Institute of Technology Working Paper (unpublished, 1988).

Gale, D. & M. Hellwig, "Incentive Compatible Debt Contracts: the One Period Problem", *Review of Economic Studies* (1985) pp. 647-64.

Gjesdal, F., "Accounting or Stewardship", *Journal of Accounting Research* (1981) pp. 208-231.

Green, J. & J. Laffont, "Contract Renegotiation and the Underinvestment Effect", Harvard University Working Paper (unpublished, 1988a).

Green, J. & J. Laffont, "Renegotiation and the Form of Efficient Contracts", Harvard University Working Paper (unpublished, 1988b).

Hagerty, K & D. Siegel, "On the Observational Equivalence of Managerial Contracts Under Conditions of Moral Hazard and Self-Selection", *Quarterly Journal of Economics* (1988) pp. 425-428.

Hamlen, S. S., W.A. Hamlen & J. T. Tschirhart, "The Use of Core Theory in Evaluating Joint Cost Allocation Schemes", *The Accounting Review* (1977) pp. 616-627.

Harris, M. & B. Holmstrom, "A Theory of Wage Dynamics", *Review of Economic Studies* (1982) pp. 315-333.

Harris, M., C. Kreibel & A. Raviv, "Asymmetric Information, Incentives, and Intra-firm Resource Allocation", *Management Science* (1982) pp. 604-620.

Hart, O. & B. Holmstrom, "The Theory of Contracts", in Bewley, T. (ed.), *Advances in Economic Theory, 5th World Congress* pp. 71-155 (Cambridge: Cambridge University Press, 1987).

Hart, O. & J. Moore, "Incomplete Contracts and Renegotiation", Massachusetts Institute of Technology Working Paper (unpublished, 1987).

Healy, P., "The Impact of Bonus Schemes on the Selection of Accounting Principles", *Journal of Accounting and Economics* (1985) pp. 81-108.

Hirshleifer, J., "On the Economics of Transfer Pricing", *Journal of Business* (1956) pp. 172-184.

Holmstrom, B., "Moral Hazards and Observability", *Bell Journal of Economics* (1979) pp. 7-91.

Holmstrom, B., "Managerial Incentive Problems—A Dynamic Perspective", *Essays in Economics and Management in Honor of Lars Wablbeck* (Helsinki: Swedish School of Economics, 1982a).

Holmstrom, B., "Moral Hazards in Teams", *Bell Journal of Economics* (1982b) pp. 324-340.

Holmstrom, B. & P. Milgrom, "Aggregation and Linearity in the Provision of Intertemporal Incentives", *Econometrica*, (1987) pp. 303-28.

Holmstrom, B. & J. Ricart-Costa, "Managerial Incentives and Capital Management", *Quarterly Journal of Economics* (1986) pp. 835-60.

Holmstrom, B. & J. Tirole, "The Theory of the Firm", in Schmalensee, R. & Willig, R. (eds), *Handbook of Industrial Organization* (New Haven, CT: Yale University Press, 1987).

Holthausen, R. W. & R. W. Leftwich, "The Economic Consequences of Accounting Choice: Implications of Costly Contracting and Monitoring", *Journal of Accounting and Economics* (1983) pp. 77-117.

Jensen, M., "Organization Theory and Methodology", *The Accounting Review* (1983) pp. 319-339.

Jensen, M. & W.H. Meckling, "Theory of the Firm: Managerial Behavior, Agency Costs and Ownership Structure", *Journal of Financial Economics* (1976) pp. 305-360.

Johnson, H. T., "The Search for Gain in Markets and Firms: A Review of the Historical Emergence of Management Accounting Systems", *Accounting, Organizations and Society* (1983) pp. 139-146.

Kaplan, R., *Advanced Management Accounting.* (Englewood Cliffs, NJ: Prentice-Hall, 1982).

Kaplan, R. & G. Thompson, "Overhead Allocation via Mathematical Programming Models", *The Accounting Review* (1971) pp. 352-364.

Kelly, L., "Positive Theory Research: A Review", *Journal of Accounting Literature* (1983) pp. 111-150.

Kren, L. & W. M. Liao, "The Role of Accounting Information in the Control of Organizations: A Review of the Evidence", *Journal of Accounting Literature* (1988) pp. 280-309.

Kreps, D., "Corporate Culture and Economic Theory, Graduate School of Business", Stanford University Working Paper (unpublished, 1984).

Kreps, D. M & R. Wilson, "Reputation and Imperfect Information", *Journal of Economic Theory* (1982) pp. 253-279.

Kumar, P., "The Generalized Principal–Agent Problem and Optimal Monitoring: A First Order Approach", Graduate School of Industrial Administration, Carnegie Mellon University Working Paper (unpublished, 1989a).

Kumar, P., "Monitoring, Incentives, and the Generalized Agency Problem", Graduate School of Industrial Administration, Carnegie Mellon University Working Paper (unpublished, 1989b).

Laffont, J. & J. Tirole, "Using Cost Observation to Regulate Firms", *Journal of Political Economy* (1986) pp. 614-41.

Lambert, R., "Long-Term Contracting and Moral Hazard", *Bell Journal of Economics* (1983) pp. 441-52.

Lambert, R., "Income Smoothing as Rational Economic Behavior", *The Accounting Review* (1984) pp. 60-618.

Lambert, R. & D. Larcker, "Executive Compensation, Corporate Decision-Making and Shareholder Wealth: A Review of the Evidence", *Midland Corporate Finance Journal* (1985) pp. 6-22.

Lambert, R. & D. Larcker, "An Analysis of the Use of Accounting and Market Measures of Performance in Executive Compensation Contracts", *Journal of Accounting Research* (1987) pp. 85-125.

Larcker, D., "The Association Between Performance Plan Adoption and Corporate Capital Investment", *Journal of Accounting and Economics* (1983) pp. 3-30.

Lewellen, W., C. Loderer & K. Martin, "Executive Compensation and Executive Incentive Problems: An Empirical Analysis", *Journal of Accounting and Economics* (1987) pp. 287-310.

Lewellen, W., C. Loderer & A. Rosenfeld, "Merger Decisions and Executive Stock Ownership in Acquiring Firms", *Journal of Accounting and Economics* (1985) pp. 209-232.

Magee, R. P., *Advanced Managerial Accounting*, (New York: Harper & Row, 1986).

Marschak, T. & S. Reichelstein, "Network Mechanisms, Informational Efficiency and Hierarchies", Graduate School of Business, Stanford University Working Paper (unpublished, 1987).

Melumad, N., D. Mookherjee & S. Reichelstein, "Hierarchical Decentralization of Incentive Contract", Graduate School of Business, Stanford University Working Paper (unpublished, 1989).

Melumad, N. & S. Reichelstein, "Value of Communication in Agencies", *Journal of Economic Theory* (1989) pp. 334-368.

Mookherjee, D., "Competition and Motivation an Organizational Perspective", Graduate School of Business, Stanford University, University of Chicago Working Paper (unpublished, 1988).

Murphy, K, "Incentives, Learning, and Compensation: A Theoretical and Empirical Investigation of Managerial Labor Contracts", *Rand Journal of Economics* (1986) pp. 59-76.

Penno, M., "Accrual Accounting and Income Smoothing in a Principal–Agent Setting", Graduate School of Business, University of Chicago Working Paper (unpublished, 1986).

Penno, M., "Hierarchical Levels and the Decentralized *Ex Post* Choice of Monitoring Systems", Graduate School of Business, University of Chicago Working Paper (unpublished, 1988).

Rajan, M., "Cost Allocation in Multi-Agent Setting", Graduate School of Industrial Administration, Carnegie Mellon University Working Paper (unpublished, 1989).

Ramakrishnan, R., "Income Smoothing and Income Acceleration as Rational Equilibrium Behavior", Graduate School of Business, Columbia University Working Paper (unpublished, 1988).

Raviv, A., "Management Compensation and the Managerial Labor Market: An Overview", *Journal of Accounting and Economics* (1985) pp. 239-247.

Riordan, M., "Hierarchical Control and Investment Incentives", Stanford University Working Paper (unpublished, 1987).

Rogerson, W., "Repeated Moral Hazard", *Econometrica* (1985) pp. 69-76.

Rogerson, W., "On the Optimality of Menus of Linear Contracts", Northwestern University Working Paper (unpublished, 1987).

Scholes, M. S., G. P. Wilson & M. A. Wolfson, "Tax Planning, Regulatory Capital Planning, and Financial Reporting Strategy for Commercial Banks", Graduate School of Business, Stanford University Working Paper (unpublished, 1989).

Singh, N., "Monitoring and Hierarchies: The Marginal Value of Information in a Principal–Agent Model", *Journal of Political Economy* (1985) June 1985.

Sklivas, S. D., "The Strategic Choice of Managerial Incentives", *Rand Journal of Economics* (1987) pp. 452-460.

Spicer, B. H. & V. Ballew, "Management Accounting Systems and the Economics of Internal Organizations", *Accounting, Organizations and Society* (1983) pp. 73-98.

Suh, Y. S. & S. K. Kim, "Conditional Monitoring Policy under Moral Hazard", University of California, Los Angeles Working Paper (unpublished, 1989).

Swieringa, R. J. & J. H. Waterhouse, "Organizational Views of Transfer Pricing", *Accounting, Organizations and Society* (1982) pp. 149-166.

Tehranian, H., N. Travlos & J. Waegelein, "Management Compensation Contracts and Merger-Induced Abnormal Return", *Journal of Accounting Research* (1987) pp. 51-76.

Townsend, R. M., "Optimal Contracts and Competitive Markets with Costly State Verification", *Journal of Economic Theory* (1979) pp. 265-293.

Walking, R. & M. Long, "Agency Theory, Managerial Welfare, and Takeover Bid Resistance", *Rand Journal of Economics* (1984) pp. 54-68.

Walsh, E. J. & R. E. Stewart, "Agency Theory and Management Accounting: A Historical Perspective", London School of Economics and Political Science Working Paper (unpublished, 1988a).

Walsh, E. J. & R. E. Stewart, "*Ex Ante* Compensation and Performance: A Historical Study", London School of Economics and Political Science Working Paper (unpublished, 1988b).

Watts, R. L. & J. L. Zimmerman, *Positive Accounting Theory*, (Englewood Cliffs, NJ: Prentice-Hall, 1986).

Williamson, O. E., "The Economic Institutions of Capitalism" (New York: Free Press, 1986a).

Williamson, O., *Markets and Hierarchies Analysis and Antitrust Implications*, (New York: Free Press, 1975)

Williamson, O., "Transaction Cost Economics", Yale University Working Paper (unpublished, 1986b).

Wolfson, M., "Empirical Evidence of Incentive Problems and Their Mitigation in Oil and Tax Shelter Programs", in Pratt, J. & Zeckhauser, R. (eds), *Principles and Agents: The Structure of Business* (Boston Harvard Business School Press, 1985) pp. 101-125.

Biographical Notes On Contributors

Biographical Notes on Contributors

Rowland K. Atiase is an Associate Professor of Accounting and Ernst & Young Faculty Fellow at the Graduate School of Business and College of Business Administration (CBA), University of Texas at Austin. Prior to joining the University of Texas at Austin, he was a faculty member at the University of Florida. He is a Ghanaian and received his B.Sc. (Hons.) from the School of Administration, University of Ghana, Legon; he received his M.B.A., M.A. (Economics), and Ph.D. degrees from the University of California, Berkeley. He is a C.P.A. and was with Ayew Agyeman Price Waterhouse & Co.

Dr. Atiase's teaching interests are financial and cost/managerial accounting, and he researches financial reporting and capital market theory. He is a three-time recipient of an outstanding teacher award and was nominated for the CBA Research Excellence Award for 1987-88, 1988-89, and 1989-90. He was also nominated for the AICPA Award for Notable Contribution to the Accounting Literature in 1989.

Dr. Atiase's publications include articles in the *Journal of Accounting Research, The Accounting Review, Contemporary Accounting Research, Journal of Accounting Literature,* and *Accounting Horizons.* His article, "Predisclosure Information, Firm Capitalization, and Security Price Behavior Around Earnings Announcements" (*Journal of Accounting Research,* Spring 1985) advanced the "firm size-related differential information hypothesis", popularly known as the "size effect".

Dr. Atiase has served on a number of committees of the A.A.A. He serves on the Editorial Advisory and Review Board of *The Accounting Review,* and he has acted as an Ad Hoc Reviewer for several academic and professional journals including the *Journal of Accounting Research, Contemporary Accounting Research,* and *The Journal of Accounting, Auditing, and Finance.*

Stanley Baiman is Professor of Accounting and Chairman of the Doctoral Programs Committee at Carnegie-Mellon University's Graduate School of Industrial Administration. He received his B.S. in 1968 from Ohio State University and a Ph.D. from Stanford University in 1974. He became an Assistant Professor at Carnegie-Mellon in 1974, where he remained until 1980. He then spent four years at the University of Pittsburgh, returning to Carnegie-Mellon in 1984 as a full professor.

Professor Baiman has served on the editorial boards of the *Journal of Accounting and Economics* (since 1981); the *Journal of Accounting Research* (since 1982); *Accounting, Organizations and Society* (since 1988); and *The Accounting Review* (1982-1985). He has been honored as a Distinguished Visiting Faculty at the 1989 AAA Doctoral Consortium; he was a Distinguished Speaker at the Conference on Information Economics, Agency Theory and Accounting at Odense University, Denmark in 1990, and he was a Distinguished Visiting Scholar at the UK Accounting Doctoral Consortium at Manchester University in December 1990.

His main area of research has been information economics and agency theory related topics, especially principal–agent relationships. He has published extensively over the past decade, in such journals as *The Accounting Review*, the *Journal of Accounting Research*, the *Journal of Finance*, *Management Science*, *Contemporary Accounting Research* and *Accounting, Organizations and Society*.

Michael Gibbins was born and raised in Prince George, B.C., and began his accounting career with Deloitte Haskins and Sells. He was the Assistant Director of Education, Canadian Institute of Chartered Accountants from 1967 to 1971. After earning his Ph.D. from Cornell University in 1976, Dr. Gibbins joined the Faculty of Commerce and Business Administration at the University of British Columbia. He came to the Faculty of Business at the University of Alberta in 1984 as a Professor of Accounting and the first Director of the Centre for the Advancement of Professional Accounting Education. In 1987, he was appointed to the Winspear Foundation Distinguished Chair in Professional Accounting. In 1988, he was awarded the FCA designation by the Alberta and British Columbia Institutes of Chartered Accountants.

Dr. Gibbins' major research interests are in professional judgment and decision making in accounting, auditing and related subjects, and in corporate financial disclosure. His works have been published in a variety of academic and professional journals including *The Accounting Review*, the *Journal of Accounting Research*, *Contemporary Accounting Research* and *CA Magazine*. He has a broad interest in accounting teaching and has published many articles on accounting education.

Dr. Gibbins has served on many local, provincial, national and international boards and committees, including presidency of the Canadian Academic Accounting Association, and membership on the Council of the American Accounting Association.

Robert S. Kaplan is the Arthur Lowes Dickinson Professor of Accounting at the Harvard Business School and a Professor of Industrial Administration at Carnegie-Mellon University. He served as Dean of the Graduate School of Industrial Administration at Carnegie-Mellon University from 1977 to 1983 where he has been on the faculty since 1968. He received a B.S. and M.S. in Electrical Engineering from M.I.T. and a Ph.D. in Operations Research from Cornell University. Author of more than 70 papers in accounting and management journals, Kaplan received the Outstanding Accounting Educator Award in 1988 from the American Accounting Association (AAA). He also received the AICPA Accounting Literature Award in 1971, the 1984 McKinsey Award for an outstanding paper in the Harvard Business Review, and the 1987

AICPA/AAA Notable Contributions to Accounting Literature Award for his paper "Measuring Manufacturing Performance".

His current research interests focus on developing new management accounting systems for the rapidly changing environment of manufacturing and service organizations. He co-authored with Robin Cooper, *The Design of Cost Management Systems: Text, Cases, and Readings* (Prentice-Hall, 1991); and with Anthony Atkinson, *Advanced Management Accounting, Second Edition* (PrenticeHall, 1989). His book with Tom Johnson, *Relevance Lost: The Rise and Fall of Management Accounting*, published by the Harvard Business School Press in early 1987, was the cover story in the January 1987 issue of *Management Accounting*. It received the AAA/DH&S Wildman Medal in 1988 as the accounting publication with the greatest potential for influencing practice, as well as the first Notable Contribution to Management Accounting Literature Award from the Management Accounting Section of the AAA. Other books published by HBS Press are *Accounting & Management: Field Study Perspectives*, (1987, co-edited with William J. Bruns, Jr.) and *Measures for Manufacturing Excellence*, (1990) on performance measurement in advanced manufacturing environments.

Dr. Kaplan served on the Board of Directors of the Pittsburgh Branch of the Federal Reserve Bank (1980-1985), as Vice President of the American Accounting Association from (19851987), on the Executive Committee of the CAMI Cost Management Research Project (1985-1989), on the Financial Accounting Standards Advisory Council (1986-1989), and on the Manufacturing Studies Board of the National Research Council, (1985-1990). Currently, Kaplan serves on the Board of the J.I. Kislak Organization in Miami, and the AACSB Accreditation Review Task Force.

Richard V. Mattessich was Arthur Andersen & Co. Alumni Professor of the University of British Columbia and has been emerited since 1988. He held academic Chairs at the Ruhr University Bochum (co-director of its Institute of Business and Management Research) and at the University of Technology of Vienna (where he founded and directed the Institute of Industrial Administration and Methodology); he was Professor and Department Head at Mt. Allison University and held a tenured Associate Professorship at the University of California in Berkeley (and was a founding member of its Center for Management Science). He was a Visiting Professor at the Free University of Berlin, the University of St. Gallen (Switzerland), the University of Canterbury in Christchurch (N.Z.), and the Management Academy in Graz, and has been guest lecturer at more than a dozen other universities.

He was born in Trieste but grew up in Vienna, where he acquired a degree in Engineering, a degree in Business Administration, and a Doctoral Degree in the Economic Sciences (1945). For ten years, he practised as an engineer, accountant, economist (as a research Fellow of the Austrian Institute of Economic Research), and internal auditor (Prudential Assurance Co. of England) and held the Chartered Accountant designation until recently. Dr. Mattessich is a Ford Foundation Fellow (U.S.A.), a Distinguished Erskine Fellow (N.Z.), a Killam Senior Fellow (U.B.C.), and has received grants and fellowships from the Canada Council, the Social Sciences and Humanities Research Council, and other institutions; in 1980, he was elected a regular member of one of the national academies of Italy. In 1984 he became a corresponding member of the Austrian Academy of Sciences. For five years, he served as an Editor of the Monograph and Reprint Series of the Faculty of Commerce and Business Administration at U.B.C. and is still an Associate Editor of the *Journal of Business Administration;* he is also a member of the Board of Editors of *Economia Aziendale*, the *Accounting Historians Journal* (U.S.A.), *Praxiology* (Polish Academy of Science), *Teuken-Revista de Investigation Contable* (Argentina), and the new journal

Accounting, Business and Financial History (U.K.), as well as a member of the International Editorial Advisory Board of "Philosophy and Methodology of the Social Sciences" of the *Theory and Decision Library.*

As an author, editor, and co-editor, Dr. Mattessich has over a dozen books bearing his name and over one hundred thirty scholarly articles (published in *The Accounting Review;* the *Journal of Accounting and Business Research* and its predecessor: *Accounting Research;* the *Journal of Accounting Research; Management Science;* the *Quarterly Review of Economics and Business; Abacus; Zeitschrift für betriebswirtschaftliche Forschung,* as well as other journals and books). In 1973, he received the AICPA Award for Notable Contributions to the Accounting Literature and in 1988 the CAAA Award for Best Paper. In 1991 Dr. Mattessich received the Haim Falk Award for Distinguished Contribution to Accounting Thought from the Canadian Academic Accounting Association. Furthermore, he served on several committees of the AAA and the CICA, as Secretary Treasurer of the International House at U.B.C., on the Council to the Executives of the Association of University Instructors of Business Administration (BRD), on the Board of Nominations of the "Accounting Hall of Fame", on the Social Sciences and Humanities Research Council of Canada's Consultative Group on Management and Administrative Studies, on the Board of Governors of the School of Chartered Accountancy (ICABC), and for six years on the Board of Directors of the Canadian CGA Research Foundation. On occasion of his emeritation, the editor of Viewpoints (Spring/Summer 1988; U.B.C.'s Faculty of Commerce and Business Administration's Alumni Journal) pointed out that "he pioneered modern analytical methods in accounting, particularly axiomatization, matrix algebra, model building and computer programming in his book *Accounting and Analytical Methods* (1964/77) as well as in preceding and subsequent articles.

In recognition of this work he was ranked among the 20 significant contributors to accounting theory in this century by J.R. Gaffikin and M.J. Aiken in *The Development of Accounting Theory.* Professor Mattessich was also honored in *History of Accounting at Berkeley* by Moonitz. He also pioneered financial spread sheet analysis and simulation, and did the basic research on which such best selling microcomputer programmes as Visi-Calc, Super-Calc, Lotus 1-2-3, etc. are based. His book, *Simulation of the Firm Through a Budget Computer Program* (1964) contains the following basic ideas, decades later revived in those microcomputer programmes: the use of matrices or spread sheets, the simulation of financial events, and most importantly, the support of individual figures by entire formulas behind each entry. He was inducted into two national academies (Italy and Austria) as a result of his book *Instrumental Reasoning and Systems Methodology* which pioneered a systems-theoretically based philosophy of applied science.

James A. Ohlson is George O. May Professor of Accounting at Columbia University, and he previously was L.H. Penney Professor of Accounting at the University of Califormia, Berkeley. He also received his Ph.D degree from Berkeley in 1972. Dr. Ohlson's major research interests concern the role of accounting data within financial markets. He serves on the editorial board of all major accounting journals, and his research appears on a regular basis in these journals.

Alan J. Richardson is associate professor, and Chair of the Research Program, at the School of Business, Queen's University. He received a Ph.D. in Management from Queen's University in 1985 and taught at the University of Alberta before returning to Queen's in 1987. His research interests include the history and sociology of the accounting profession, and the organizational processes underlying financial disclosure. Recent publications in these areas have appeared in

Accounting, Organizations and Society, Journal of Accounting Research, Contemporary Accounting Research, and the *Accounting Historian's Journal* among others.

Daniel B. Thornton joined the University of Calgary in 1989 as Chartered Accountants' Professor of Accounting, following appointments as Professor at Toronto and Queen's, and as Distinguished Visiting Professor at Concordia. His empirical research in financial accounting won the Canadian Academic Accounting Association's first *Award for Distinguished Contribution to Accounting Thought* in 1987. He has been Clarkson Gordon Scholar-in-Residence at Queen's, Visiting Scholar at McMaster, and invited participant at the 1990 Stanford Summer Tax Conference as well as the 1990 Price Waterhouse Centennial Symposium.

As a doctoral candidate, Thornton held a *Seagram's Business Faculty Award* in 1978-80. He has since taught accounting, finance and managerial economics at several universities, as well as at Ontario's Professional School of Accountancy, and he has supervised numerous doctoral dissertations. For his teaching he received the Canadian Academic Accounting Association's *Outstanding Educator Award* in 1989.

Thornton has served as editorial board member and book review editor for *Contemporary Accounting Research,* Editor of *CAmagazine's* education section, chairman of the CAAA Research Committee, and Vice-President of CMA. A Chartered Accountant, he has consulted with both professional organizations and business corporations, and has appeared as expert accounting witness for the Department of Justice, Taxation. His current research, teaching and consulting interests are in the areas of income taxation, financial accounting, and financial instruments.

Senyo Y. Tse is an assistant professor at the University of Texas at Austin, and previously held a similar position at the University of Florida. He is a C.P.A., and received his B.Sc. degree from the University of Ghana, his M.B.A. degree from Stanford University, and his Ph.D. from the University of California, Berkeley. Dr. Tse is on the editorial boards of *The Accounting Review* and the *Journal of Accounting Literature.* He has published papers in the *Journal of Accounting Research, The Accounting Review* and *Contemporary Accounting Research.*

Index of Names

INDEX OF NAMES

A

B

G

H